COUNTY

OF

TODD,

KENTUCKY.

HISTORICAL AND BIOGRAPHICAL.

EDITOR:

J. H. BATTLE, TODD COUNTY HISTORY.

ILLUSTRATED.

F. A. BATTEY PUBLISHING CO.,

CHICAGO AND LOUISVILLE.

1884.

New Material COPYRIGHT 1979
By: The Rev. Silas Emmett Lucas, Jr.

SOUTHERN HISTORICAL PRESS
% The Rev. S. Emmett Lucas, Jr.
P. O. Box 738
Easley, South Carolina   29640

ISBN-0-89308-162-0

Library of Congress Card Catalog No.:79-66903

PREFACE.

THIS volume goes forth to our patrons the result of months of arduous, unremitting and conscientious labor. None so well know as those who have been associated with us the almost insurmountable difficulties to be met with in the preparation of a work of this character. Since the inauguration of the enterprise a large force has been employed in gathering material. During this time most of the citizens of each county have been called upon to contribute from their recollections, carefully preserved letters, scraps of manuscript, printed fragments, memoranda, etc. Public records and semi-official documents have been searched, the newspaper files of both counties have been overhauled, and former citizens, now living out of the counties, have been corresponded with, for the verification of the information by a conference with many. In gathering from these numerous sources, both for the historical and biographical departments, the conflicting statements, the discrepancies and the fallible and incomplete nature of public documents were almost appalling to our historians and biographers, who were expected to weave therefrom with some degree of accuracy, in panoramic review, a record of events. Members of the same families disagree as to the spelling of the family name, contradict each other's statements as to the dates of birth, of settlement in the counties, nativity, and other matters of fact. In this entangled condition, we have given preference to the preponderance of authority, and while we acknowledge the existence of errors and our inability to furnish a *perfect* history, we claim to have come up to the standard of our promises, and given as accurate a work as the nature of the surroundings would permit. The facts incorporated in the biographical sketches have in most cases been secured from the persons whom they represent, hence the publishers disclaim any responsibility as to their general tenor. Whatever may be the verdict of those who do not and *will* not comprehend the difficulties to be met with, we feel assured that all just and thoughtful people will appreciate our efforts, and recognize the importance of the undertaking and the great public benefit that has been accomplished in preserving the valuable historical matters of the counties, and biographies of many of the citizens, that perhaps would otherwise have passed into oblivion. To those who have given us their support and encouragement we acknowledge our gratitude, and can assure them that as years go by the book will grow in value as a repository not only of pleasing reading matter, but of treasured information of the past that will become an enduring monument.

OCTOBER, 1884.   THE PUBLISHERS.

CONTENTS.

HISTORY OF TODD COUNTY.

HISTORY OF TODD COUNTY.

E. G. Sebree

HISTORY OF TODD COUNTY.

CHAPTER I.

THE EARLY HISTORY OF KENTUCKY—ORIGIN OF ITS SETTLEMENT—PIONEER PROGRESS—FIRST SURVEYS—EARLY POLITICAL ORGANIZATION—CONSTITUTIONAL HISTORY—MATERIAL DEVELOPMENT—COUNTY ORGANIZATIONS.

IN preparing an historical sketch of Todd County, Ky., the logical impulse is to go back of the arbitrary limits of this subject, and trace somewhat of the remoter causes to which this county owes its origin. Within the narrow scope of this political division there is little to suggest the thrilling exploits, the noble endurance and tender romance which so richly embellish the historic annals of the "dark and bloody ground." Whatever his localities the true Kentuckian cherishes these pioneer legends as a priceless legacy and his rightful inheritance, and thus the writer is irresistibly led back to that undiscovered country in which the passing years have gathered this magnificent display of prosperous communities. In Kentucky the wilderness has indeed blossomed as the rose; the dark and bloody ground become the famed home of beauty and bravery. Nowhere else have the predominant traits of the sons and daughters of the land reached more perfect fruition: nowhere else does fatherland receive the devotion of more loyal hearts or a loftier patriotism from its children. But how shall the great transformation be measured? More facile pens than ours have made the attempt in vain. Past generations have labored, and the present has enterd into their labors; others have sown, and the present reaps the harvest of their sowing; the bold founders of this Commonwealth, whose deeds are emblazoned on every page of the Nation's early history, live again in the career of their children. Where could the pen of a ready writer seek grander inspiration, or the worthy sons of noble sires find loftier motives than in the annals of this fair land?

Early Explorations.—Kentucky lies within the region granted by royal charter to the colony of Virginia. For a hundred years it remained unexplored, unnamed and unprovided for, save to be included in the outlying County of Virginia for judicial purposes. In 1776 it formed a part of the comprehensive County of Fincastle, Va., and on the 31st of December of this year it was erected into a separate county, under the Indian name signifying dark and bloody ground, which it still bears, though somewhat modified in spelling and pronunciation. The vast territory thus erected into a separate county contained at this time something less than two hundred white inhabitants. The natural beauty of the country and the rare advantages offered for settlement, however, had long been known. As early as 1735 John Salling, who was captured by the Indians, had penetrated this region with his captors, and escaping had spread the story of its beauty throughout the frontiers. Some fifteen years later Dr. Thomas Walker, with a small party of Virginians, entered what is now the State of Kentucky, at Cumberland Gap, and had pushed his explorations to the discovery of the Cumberland, Kentucky and Big Sandy Rivers. Subsequently Christopher Gist, agent of the Ohio Company, and Capt. Harry Gordon, a Government Engineer, at different times made explorations along the course of the Ohio River. The land of promise thus discovered and duly described was too difficult of access to attract practical attention save from the hardiest of those times. It was not until 1769, therefore, that the pioneers of that immigration which eventually possessed the land entered this famous hunting-ground. In this memorable year John Findlay, who had been here previously on a trading expedition, piloted a worthy band of hunters, composed of Daniel Boone, John Stewart, Joseph Holden, James Mooney and William Cool, to this region. This party had come from the Yadkin River in North Carolina, and made the journey to a spot on "Red River, the northernmost branch of the Kentucky," in thirty-eight days. The party continued hunting with the greatest success until December 22, when Boone and Stewart, rambling apart from the rest, were captured by a party of Indians. Escaping after seven days' captivity, they returned to their camp to find it destroyed and their companions gone. Undaunted, the two determined to remain, and were soon joined by Squire Boone and another adventurer. Shortly afterward Stewart was killed by the Indians, which so alarmed the remaining companion of the Boones that he returned home alone. The brothers were thus left alone in the boundless wilderness. On May 1, 1770, Squire Boone returned to North Carolina for a supply of horses, provisions and ammunition, leaving Daniel alone, without bread, salt or sugar, and without the companionship of even a horse or dog. In the latter part of the succeeding July Squire Boone returned with the supplies, and the two brothers remained until March, 1771, when they returned to their home in North Carolina. In 1770 a party of forty hunters, organized for a hunting and trapping expedition west of the Alleghany Mountains, started from southwestern Virginia. Nine of them, under the lead of Col. James Knox, reached the country south of the Kentucky River in the vicinity of Green River and the Lower Cumberland. Here they remained some two years, without crossing any trail of the Boones, creating alarm among their friends for their safety, and gaining the sobriquet of the " Long hunters." Kentucky thenceforth became the favorite resort for the more adventurous hunters of the older settlements, and many who subsequently became prominent in the pioneer annals of the new State were among the number.

Early Surveys and Settlements.—The first authorized survey made by an official surveyor in this Territory was in the northeast corner of the State, in what is now Lawrence and Greenup Counties. One plat covered the present site of the town of Louisa, and the other eleven miles from the mouth of the Big Sandy, on the river. These were made for John Fry, to whom the lands were conveyed by patents. The corners were marked with the initials " G. W.," and it is believed in the locality that the surveys were made by George Washington himself, although no documentary evidence can be found to sustain this belief. These surveys, however, were probably not induced by the reports of the hunters in the interior of this region, but in the following year the royal Governor of Virginia, Lord Dunmore, dispatched a party of surveyors down the Ohio River to select and survey lands in the newly opened country for himself. One party, under Capt. Thomas Bullitt, selected lands under his warrant along the river from the falls to Salt River, and up that river to Bullitt's Lick ; the other, under James McAfee, following up the Kentucky River, surveyed the flats about the present site of Frankfort. In August of 1773 Bullitt platted the village of Louisville, probably under the same authority, but the Revolution occurring soon afterward brought these schemes on the part of the representative of royalty to naught. In May of the following year Capt. James Harrod, with a considerable party, laid out Harrodsburg, and erected a number of cabins, constituting the first attempt to effect a permanent settlement in the new country. Soon after this, in the same year, Simon Kenton cultivated corn on the site of Maysville, but both points were abandoned the same year on account of the Indian hostilities. The savages noted the encroachments of the whites upon their hunting-grounds with alarm. Notwithstanding the fact that the Six Nations had assumed to dispose of all the territory south of the Ohio and west of the Tennessee Rivers to the English by the treaty made in 1768 at Fort Stanwix, the tribes in possession of the land refused to recognize the validity of such a treaty, and began to offer a vigorous opposition to the settlement of the whites. In this year Col. Henderson projected a scheme by which, in consideration of £10,000, he should acquire the territory between the Ohio, Kentucky and Cumberland Rivers as far east as the Cumberland Mountains. While this negotiation was proceeding between Henderson, representing a syndicate of North Carolinians, and a chief of the Cherokees, Daniel Boone had been employed to cut out a road from Cumberland Gap to the site of the projected capital of this new territory. His party consisting of thirty men was attacked by the Indians, principally of the Shawanese nation, and while the attack did not frustrate Boone's plans nor greatly hinder him it exhibited the short-sighted character of the scheme in which Henderson was engaged. Boone at once caused a fort to be erected on the south side of the Kentucky, and sent word to Henderson of the progress of the expedition. Having consummated the arrangements with the savages Col. Henderson brought a considerable colony to the new fort, raising the military force to sixty men. Encouraged by this acquisition to the pioneer strength, those who had abandoned Harrodsburg returned, and forts were soon erected at this point, and others at Georgetown, and near Stanford, called Logan's Fort. Henderson's scheme, while based upon a misconception of the temper of the whites as well as Indians, and in defiance of the proclamations of the Governors of Virginia and North Carolina, nevertheless did much to hurry forward and establish the early settlement of Kentucky. Henderson & Company at once opened a land office at Boonesboro, at which by December 1, 1775, some 560,000 acres of land were entered, deeds being issued by this company as "Proprietors of the Colony of Transylvania." A difficulty arose at the outset from the conflicting claims of the neighboring settlements established at Harrodsburg, Boiling Spring and at Logan's Fort. This was adjusted, and resulted in a call for a meeting of representatives chosen by the people of these settlements, who in pursuance to this call met at Boonesboro to agree upon a proprietary government. Eighteen representatives assembled and organized on the 23d of May, 1775. The session lasted some four days, which were devoted to the passage of nine acts: For establishing courts of judicature and practice; for regulating a militia; for the punishment of criminals; to prevent swearing and Sabbath-breaking; for writs of attachment; for ascertaining Clerks' and Sheriffs' fees; to preserve the range; for improving the breed of horses; for *preserving game ;* after which the body adjourned to meet in the following September. What might have been the outcome of this ambitious venture if the originators had been equal to the demands of the situation cannot well be determined. Some difficulty arose among the proprietors, which eventually wrecked the whole venture. Through this dissension the force at Boonesboro, which had reached eighty men, was reduced by June to fifty, and was steadily declining. In the meanwhile another difficulty presented itself. The terms offered to those first assisting in the venture were exceptionally liberal, but it appears that the proprietors, believing the project estab-lished beyond the fear of failure, began to show an eagerness' to reap the advantages of their bargain with the Indians, and placed what was con-sidered an exorbitant price upon the land, the cost of entry and survey-ing. This aroused the pioneers to a consideration of the grounds upon which the company based its claims, and resulted January 3, 1776, in a remonstrating petition to the Legislature of Virginia, signed by eighty-four men. Under the circumstances, with these remonstrants unpropiti-ated, there was no hope for the final success of the venture, and while the company exerted themselves to save the purchasers from loss, they seem to have been wholly unfitted to save the matter from total wreck. The Legislature did not act upon the matter until November 4, 1778, when it declared the company's purchase void on the ground that under the charter the Commonwealth alone had the right to purchase land of the savages, " but as the said Richard Henderson & Company have been at very great expense in making said purchase and in settling the said lands—by which this Commonwealth is likely to receive great advantage, by increasing its inhabitants and establishing a barrier against the Indians —it is just and reasonable to allow the said Richard Henderson & Com-pany a compensation for their trouble and expense." This compensation was a grant of 200,000 acres at the mouth of Green River in Kentucky, and a similar grant in North Carolina, in consideration of the company's claim in Tennessee. The result of the " Transylvania " project, while not to the serious disadvantage of any individual, was greatly to the ad-vantage of the pioneer settlements of central Kentucky.

Indian Demonstrations.—The savages had not been inattentive to the activity of the whites. They met the very first organized party with slaughter, and up to 1775 had succeeded in disheartening and driving out all who had effected a temporary settlement. The cluster of settlements near and including Boonesboro seems to have impressed the natives with the necessity of better preparations to resist the encroachments of the whites which were growing more formidable in their character. In 1777 the attacks of the Indians, which had hithorto been made with very little concert of action, began to evince evidence of some guiding influence, and were so well directed that all settlements were soon abandoned save those at Boonesboro, Harrodsburg and Logan's Fort, which, combined, could barely muster 102 men. Early in the following year, Boone, with thirty men, was at the lower Blue Licks engaged in making salt, when he was surprised by a war party of some 200 Indians on their way to at-tack Boonesboro. The whole party was captured, but not before they had succeeded in gaining by parley very favorable terms of capitulation. By these terms, which were faithfully observed by their captors, the whites were taken to Detroit and turned over to the English Command-ant. Boone; however, was reserved and taken by the Indians to Chilli-cothe, where his captors treated him with great kindness and permitted him to hunt with but little restraint upon his movements. While here he learned of an expedition forming for the attack of Boonesboro, and saw some 350 Indians assembled to take part in the movement. He deter-mined to make his escape and warn the settlements of•the danger, and was so fortunate as to effect it immediately. He made the journey of 160 miles in ten days, undergoing extraordinary privations and suffer-ings. His escape, however, had the effect to again defer the premeditated attack, and after putting the place in the best possible condition to resist the onslaught, the settlers waited for several weeks in vain expectation of the foe. Impatient of this delay, Boone and Kenton with some thirty men set out to destroy one of the Indian towns on Paint Creek. While on this ex-pedition and in the enemy's country, Boone learned that the Indian army directed against Boonesboro had passed him, and hastily turning about he conducted his band with all speed, marching night and day, back to their starting point. The returned pioneers reached Boonesboro just be-fore the appearance of the savages. The attacking force consisted of 500 Indians and Canadians under the command of Capt. Duquesne. Such an army had never before been seen in Kentucky, and the little garrison numbering barely fifty men, without hope of assistance from Harrods-burg or Logan's Fort, which were both strongly menaced, might well view the chances of successful resistance with despair. Every artifice which savage cunning could suggest or the skill of the white allies could render effective was employed, but in vain. For nine days the vigorous attack was resisted with steady fortitude, the keen marksmen of the fort inflicting a serious loss upon the unprotected assailants. On the tenth day the Indians withdrew, having lost thirty men killed, and many more wounded. The Kentuckians suffered a loss of two killed and four wounded, but the destruction of stock and improvements proved a very serious damage.

Clarke's Campaign.—It was evident that these attacks were inspired, and munitions supplied, by the British stationed at Kaskaskia and Vin-cennes. George Rogers Clarke, who had visited Kentucky in 1775, had taken in the situation from a military standpoint, and had conceived a plan by which the infant settlements of Kentucky might be freed from this additional source of danger. He communicated it to Gov. Henry of Virginia, and had no difficulty in impressing him with the advantages of its successful prosecution. But the colony was then in common with the other twelve engaged in the stirring scenes of the Revolution. This struggle demanded every resource of the Revolutionists, and however attractive the plan might appear, the means for its accomplishment was felt to be a serious addition to the already great burden imposed by tho war. The Governor gave his support to the plan, however, and by June, 1778, Major Clarke had reached the Falls of the Ohio with 153 men composed of the Virginia line and Kentucky scouts. Proceeding down the river in the latter part of this month he disembarked on the Illinois shore and marched thence through the wilderness to Kaskaskia, a distance of 120 miles. The expedition was a complete success; the English force, completely surprised, surrendered without a shot on July 4, and two days later Cahokia furnished another bloodless victory. While engaged in securing the fruits of his victory here, Clarke learned that preparations were going forward to launch another expedition against the Kentucky frontier from Vincennes. Learning also that the post at that season was greatly weakened by the dispersion of the English forces, he by agents secured the voluntary capitulation of the post, and leaving a garrison he completed the occupation of the territory, which was erected into a county under the direction of Col. John Todd. Clarke then retired to Louisville where a fort was erected and his command rendezvoused. In December of 1778, Gov. Hamilton, the English Commandant at Detroit, made a descent upon Vincennes and captured it. In the following February, Clarke with 170 men recaptured the post together with eighty-one prisoners and $50,000 worth of military stores. This victory decided the contest in this direction, and with Clarke at Louisville, no further danger was apprehended from the Illinois country.

But peace was not to be so cheaply gained. The Indian stronghold in northwestern Ohio was still accessible to the English, and the savages accurately forecasting the inevitable result of the advancing tide of immigration needed less incentive from without than ever before. Indian attacks were returned by counter invasions only to cease with the treaty of peace in 1782. In May, 1779, occurred the unfortunate expedition of Col. Bowman against Old Chillicothe; in October of the same year the savages avenged the attack by the surprise and slaughter of fifty out of a party of seventy men bringing military supplies down the Ohio River from Pittsburgh; June, 1780, Col. Byrd, of the English Army, with six pieces of artillery and 600 Indians and Canadians captured Ruddle's and Martin's Stations; in July Col. Clarke with two regiments of troops surprised and destroyed the Indian towns of Chillicothe, Piqua, and Laramie's store; in 1781 the Chickasaws and Choctaws attacked Fort Jefferson, in Ballard County, but were repulsed with terrible slaughter; in 1782, Indian hostilities were unusually early and active. In May, a party of twenty-five Wyandots invaded Kentucky and committed some shocking depredations in sight of Estill's Station some three miles southeast of Richmond in Madison County. Capt. Estill collected a force and pursued them, when ensued one of the most deadly encounters known to the annals of Indian warfare. It resulted in a drawn fight, but is generally known as Estill's defeat. There were a number of other minor collisions between the two antagonizing forces, but these, though fatal to more or less engaged, were only the pattering drops which precede the tempest. In August, an army of 500 Indian warriors, made up of contingents from all the northwestern tribes, rapidly and secretly traversed northern Kentucky, and appeared before Bryant's Station, near Lexington, as unexpectedly as if they had risen by the hand of a magician from the soil. The garrison was about to march to the succor of a neighboring station and throw open the gates of the stockade to march out when the Indians discovered themselves. Aid was summoned from Lexington, which fell into an ambuscade and sustained a considerable loss. The garrison, however, protected by their palisades suffered little, while inflicting a terrible punishment upon the savages, who made an attempt to force one of the gates. Fearful that the whole country would rise and fall upon them, the Indians hastily decamped on the following morning without having effected their object. Soon after their retreat, 160 men had assembled from the neighboring stations. Col. Boone headed a strong party from Boonesboro; Col. Trigg brought up a force from the neighborhood of Harrodsburg, and Col. John Todd commanded the militia around Lexington. Others who held rank in this flower of the frontier militia were Majors Harlan, McBride, McGary, Levi Todd; Captains Bulger and Gordon. Gen. Logan had collected a strong force in Lincoln County, and the force assembled, assured that he would soon join them, began to clamor to be led against the retreating savages. The officers, quite as eager, decided to bring the Indians to bay, and regardless of facts which should have urged them to the greatest caution, the force moved on without waiting for the forces under Gen. Logan. Boone, who was outranked by others, held a subordinate command, but impressed by the evidences of the Indians' desire for a fight counseled caution, which, however, the eagerness of the officers and troops failed to regard. The whites were caught in an ambuscade and cruelly repulsed with the loss of sixty men, among whom were Cols. Todd and Trigg. The repulse became a disorderly rout, each man finding his way back to Bryan's Station as best he could. In the following November Col. George Rogers Clarke led 1,000 riflemen into the heart of the Indian country. No resistance was offered. Their towns were reduced to ashes, their corn destroyed and the whole country laid waste. From this time forward Kentucky was free from Indian invasions, and only occasional depredations of minor importance kept alive the fear and hatred of the redskins.

Development of the Settlements.—The present State of Kentucky was visited by various parties at different times from 1747 to 1772. The first of these which gave promise of the return of the parties were those made in 1773 by surveyors sent out by Dunmore and others. An "improver's cabin," a square of small logs, but neither roofed nor inhabited, was erected this year in Bracken County, but there were none elsewhere in the country at this time. In May, 1774, Capt. James Harrod settled near Harrodsburg with thirty-one persons, and soon after Isaac Hite with ten men joined them. These men erected their cabins in various places in the immediate vicinity, and in the following year Harrod established another settlement at Boiling Spring, six miles south of Harrodsburg. These settlements were temporarily abandoned, but were resumed later in this year, when the Transylvania Company made its settlement at Boonesboro. These, with the settlement formed by Col. Benjamin Logan, in Lincoln County, formed the "Transylvania Colony," and the nucleus of the State's growth. A single cabin was built near the site of Maysville by Simon Kenton, and a similar improvement by Floyd near the site of Louisville in this year. Other similar outlying improvements were projected, but all were abandoned in the same year, save the colony settlements in the valley of the Kentucky River. In 1776 important permanent settlements were made at Georgetown, in Scott County, at Leestown near Frankfort, and in Washington County. In 1777 Ruddle's Station was established in Bourbon County, and at the Falls of the Ohio in 1778. In the following year were established Bryan's Station, and a settlement by Robert Patterson at Lexington, in Fayette County; Bowman's Station in Mercer County; Brashear's Station in Bullitt County; and Martin's Station in Bourbon County. Each one of these stations and settlements was a center from which deployed an extended line of immigration, which chiefly confined the improvements to this valley. In this year the Virginia Legislature passed the celebrated Kentucky Land Law with very liberal settlement and pre-emption features, but out of which have grown some of the most difficult and vexatious land questions that have ever consumed the time of a court, or the substance of a litigant. The radical and incurable defect of the law was the neglect of Virginia to provide for the general survey of the whole country at the expense of the Government, and its regular subdivision, as was subsequently done by the United States. The plan of division by ranges and meridian lines had not then been suggested, but the Transylvania Company had conceived the idea of surveying "by the four cardinal points, except where rivers or mountains make it too inconvenient," and so far as this work proceeded was superior to what followed. By the Virginia law each possessor of a warrant was allowed to locate the same where he pleased, and was required to survey it at his own cost; but his entry was required to be so exact that each subsequent locator might recognize the land already taken up. To make a good entry, therefore, required a precision and accuracy of description which the early surveyors were not competent to make. All vague entries were declared null and void, and countless unhappy, vexatious lawsuits occurred, in which scant justice was secured to any one. In the unskillful hands of hunters and pioneers of Kentucky, entries, surveys and patents were filed upon each other, crossing each other's lines in inextricable confusion, the full fruition of which was not reached until the country became thickly settled.

The immediate effect of the law was to cause a flood of immigration. The adventurous pioneer hunter was succeeded by the less generous-hearted hunter of land; in this pursuit they fearlessly braved the tomahawk of the Indian, and the rigid exactions of the forest. The surveyor's compass and chain were seen in the wilderness as frequently as the hunter's rifle, and during the years 1779–81 the absorbing object was to enter, survey and obtain a patent for the richest portions of the country. The year 1781 was distinguished by a very large immigration, and by prodigious activity in land speculation. The savages seemed to rightly appreciate the inevitable consequences of this activity on the part of the whites, and redoubled their efforts to successfully resist the wide-spreading encroachments. Every portion of the land was kept in alarm; Indian ambushes were constantly pouring death and injury upon men, women and children. Many lives were lost, but the settlements made great and daily advances in defiance of all obstacles. The rich lands of Kentucky were the prize of the first occupants, and thousands rushed to seize them. A noticeable feature of the earliest settlements was the great disparity in the number of the sexes. Callaway and Boone brought their families here in September of 1775, and the latter's wife and daughter were the first white females that stood upon the banks of the Kentucky. The wives and daughters of McGary, Hogan and Denton came about the same time, and were the first white women in Harrodsburg. In 1781 was a remarkable immigration of girls to Kentucky, and from that time onward few settlers came unattended by their families. In 1783 the Indians at first assumed a pacific attitude, and in the meantime the settlements made great advancement. Kenton, after a nine years' interval, reclaimed his settlement at Maysville, where he was subsequently joined by others, and the general course of immigration henceforth was by the Ohio River to Maysville and thence to the interior.

Political Development.—Kentucky had been erected into a county of that name in 1776. In the spring of 1783 it was made a judicial district, and a court of criminal as well as civil jurisdiction was established,

John Floyd, Samuel McDowell and George Muter being appointed Judges; John May, Clerk; and Walker Daniel, Prosecuting Attorney. The first session was held at Harrodsburg the same spring, Floyd and McDowell only being present, Muter not putting in an appearance until two years later. Seventeen cases were presented by the grand jury, nine for keeping tippling houses and eight for fornication, which probably illustrates the prevailing vices of the time. In the summer a log court house and jail, of hewed or sawed logs nine inches thick, were erected on the site of Danville, which subsequently became the seat of justice for the district. In the latter part of 1780 Kentucky County was divided into three counties—Jefferson, with John Floyd as Colonel; William Pope, Lieutenant-Colonel, and George May, Surveyor; Lincoln, with Benjamin Logan, Colonel; Stephen Trigg, Lieutenant-Colonel, and James Thompson, Surveyor; and Fayette, with John Todd, Colonel; Daniel Boone, Lieutenant-Colonel, and Col. Tom Marshall (father of the Chief Justice of the United States), Surveyor. In the summer of 1784 some Indian depredations were committed on the southern frontier, and the fear became general that a serious invasion was contemplated by the savages. Col. Logan, acting upon his information and belief, summoned a public assembly of the leading pioneers at Danville to consult on measures for the public safety. Upon examination of the laws then existing it was decided that no effectual expedition against the Indians could be legally carried into effect. There was absolutely no power known to the law capable of calling forth the resources of the country, however threatening the danger, and all legislation came from Richmond, separated from Kentucky by a long, tedious journey of many hundred miles over desert mountains and through interminable forests traversed by roving bands of hostile Indians. The situation was sufficiently serious to give rise to the feeling that the necessity for a nearer government was imperative. Under the circumstances, the calm, deliberative action of the Assembly is worthy of notice. Having no legal authority, this body published a recommendation that each militia company in the district should elect a delegate, who should repair to Danville on the 27th of December, 1784, and form a convention which should take into consideration the necessity of the situation. While there was no division of opinion as to the demands of the district, there was some as to the means to be employed in securing the necessary relief. The more judicious of the number assembled prevailed in council, and the convention, after setting forth the urgency of the case, recommended that a second convention be held in May, 1785, at Danville, to consider the advisability of a separation from Virginia. In the meantime this topic formed the great subject of discussion in primary assemblies. At the appointed time delegates, apportioned by counties, met at the seat of Justice and agreed upon five resolutions calling for a constitutional separation from Virginia, for a petition to the Legislature, an address to the people of Kentucky, and for another convention to which the action of this convention should be referred. A third convention assembled in the following August. In the meanwhile the situation became more alarming. Indian hostilities multiplied, and the people, thoroughly informed upon the subject, became exasperated, and demanded by numerous petitions that the only effectual remedy be applied without delay. Under such incitement the action of the new convention was speedy and direct. The petition to the Legislature was drawn up and placed in the hands of George Muter, Chief-Justice of the district, and Harry Innes, Attorney-General, to present to the Government at Richmond, while an address to the people of Kentucky, much less judicial in tone, was multiplied by ready pens and sent throughout the district. The Legislature received the petition with the best possible grace, acceded to the wishes of the petitioners, and by an act of January, 1786, required a fourth convention to be held at Danville in the following September which should determine whether it was the will of the district to become an independent State of the Confederacy. The convention which assembled under authority of this act found itself without a quorum in September, a majority of its delegates having joined an expedition under Gen. Clarke against the Indian towns in Ohio. It was therefore obliged to adjourn from time to time until the next January, 1787. But in the meantime, the minority present prepared a memorial to the Virginia Legislature informing it of the circumstances and suggesting some alterations in the provisions of the act under which the convention had assembled. This led to an entire revision of the act, by which it was required that a fifth convention be held in September, 1787, for the same purpose as proposed for the previous convention, and requiring a majority of two-thirds to effect a separation. The time at which the operation of Virginia laws should cease to operate was fixed on the 1st day of January, 1789, and the 4th of July, 1788, was fixed upon as the period before which Congress should consent to the admission of Kentucky to the Confederacy.

This delay when the matter had seemed so urgent before this, while due largely to circumstances out of the control of both negotiating parties, nevertheless created a bitter state of feeling in Kentucky, which was further aggravated by National questions affecting the interests of the people. The fifth convention, however, quietly assembled and endorsed the action of its predecessors by a unanimous vote. An address to Congress was adopted praying that Kentucky might be admitted to the Confederation of States. Unfortunately this petition came before Congress in the transition period of the Nation when the Union was being evolved from the old Confederation, and the limitation set by the act of Virginia expired before Congress considered the question of admission, which was finally referred to the new Government. The fifth convention had provided for another convention to assemble in the following year, by which it was hoped a Constitution could be formed and the machinery of Government at once put in motion. It met on the 28th of July, 1788, to learn that Congress had refused to act upon the petition for admission as a State. Anger and disappointment were strongly expressed in all quarters, and a proposition to form a Constitution without delay was strongly urged upon the convention. The net result of the convention's deliberations, however, was the adoption of a resolution calling for a seventh convention, to assemble in November of the same year, with general power to take the best steps for securing admission to the Union. The election of delegates to this convention developed a most exciting discussion, involving issues which threatened to seriously disturb the freshly laid foundations of the new Government. In November the seventh convention assembled and was at once launched upon the troubled sea of exciting debate. The disposition to seek separation and independence only through constitutional means was covertly but strongly assailed by a disposition to dispel the irritation and delay of repeated conventions by more radical measures. The convention was about equally divided in sentiment, though no one was ready to make a clear declaration of his intention. The friends of constitutional measures finally succeeded in passing a resolution addressed to the parent State, couched in temperate, respectful language, asking the good offices of Virginia in securing the admission of Kentucky into the Union. The convention then adjourned to meet again at a distant day. In the meantime the Legislature of Virginia, on receiving information of the action of Congress, passed a third act in relation to the separation of Kentucky, which required an eighth convention to meet in Danville in July, 1789, and giving this convention ample powers to provide for the formation of a State Government. The convention assembled under this act, and drew up a respectful remonstrance to certain of its provisions. This remonstrance was promptly acceded to and the obnoxious conditions repealed in an act which required the assembling of another convention in the following year. The ninth convention met in July, 1790, formally accepted the Virginia act of separation, memorialized Congress, asked Virginia's good offices in securing admission to the Union, and provided for the tenth convention to assemble in April, 1791, to form a State Constitution. On June 1, 1792, Kentucky became a State of the Union under the provisions of an act of Congress signed by the President February 4, 1791.

Organization of Minor Divisions.—During the period in which the public attention was concentrated upon the efforts to secure the independence of Kentucky as a State, the population and material prosperity of the district were rapidly increasing. In 1780 Louisville was chartered by the Legislature of Virginia ; in 1783 Col. Broadhead established the first store there and the second in Kentucky, and this was followed the next year by another store established by Col. Wilkinson, who soon made the village the leading business point in the district. At this time there were in the village more than 100 cabins, 63 finished houses, 37 partly done, and 22 raised. This illustrates the rapid progress going on, and was proportionally true of the whole district. Nelson County was formed in 1784. In 1785 the counties of Bourbon, Mercer and Madison were erected, and the towns of Harrodsburg and Shippingport chartered. In 1786 Frankfort, Stanford and Washington were chartered, the latter having 119 houses four years later. In 1787 the first paper in the State, the Kentucky *Gazette*, was established at Lexington, and the towns of Beallsburg, Charleston, Maysville, Danville and Warwick were chartered. In the next year Bardstown was chartered, Columbia laid out, and the counties of Mason and Woodford organized. From this time forward the development of the country was so rapid and varied that no abstract which space will allow would give any adequate illustration. As the population increased towns sprang up and counties multiplied, the organization of which gives a pretty clear outline of the general development. The order of this expansion is gathered from the following list taken from Collins' Historical Sketches. Acts for the erection of new counties were passed in the order, at the dates and out of other counties, as below :

	NEW COUNTIES.	FORMED FROM.	YEAR.
1.	Jefferson	Kentucky	1780
2.	Fayette	Kentucky	1780
3.	Lincoln	Kentucky	1780
4.	Nelson	Jefferson	1784
5.	Bourbon	Fayette	1785
6.	Mercer	Lincoln	1785
7.	Madison	Lincoln	1785
8.	Mason	Bourbon	1788
9.	Woodford	Fayette	1788
10.	Washington	Nelson	1792
11.	Scott	Woodford	1792
12.	Shelby	Jefferson	1792
13.	Logan	Lincoln	1792
14.	Clark	Fayette and Bourbon	1792
15.	Hardin	Nelson	1792
16.	Greene	Lincoln and Nelson	1792
17.	Harrison	Bourbon and Scott	1793
18.	Franklin	Woodford, Mercer and Shelby	1794
19.	Campbell	Harrison, Scott and Mason	1794

NEW COUNTIES.	FORMED FROM.	YEAR.

20. Bullitt...............Jefferson and Nelson...........................1796
21. Christian............Logan..1796
22. Montgomery.......Clark...1796
23. Bracken.............Mason and Campbell...........................1796
24. Warren..............Logan..1796
25. Garrard.............Mercer, Lincoln and Madison................1796
26. Fleming.............Mason...1798
27. Pulaski..............Lincoln and Greene............................1798
28. Pendleton...........Bracken and Campbell.........................1798
29. Livingston..........Christian..1798
30. Boone...............Campbell..1798
31. Henry...............Shelby...1798
32. Cumberland.......Greene..1798
33. Gallatin.............Franklin and Shelby............................1798
34. Muhlenburg.......Logan and Christian............................1798
35. Ohio.................Hardin...1798
36. Jessamine..........Fayette..1798
37. Barren..............Warren and Greene..............................1798
38. Henderson.........Christian..1798
39. Breckinridge......Hardin..1799
40. Floyd...............Fleming, Montgomery and Mason...........1799
41. Knox...............Lincoln...1799
42. Nicholas...........Bourbon and Mason.............................1799
43. Wayne.............Pulaski and Cumberland.......................1800
44. Adair...............Greene..1801
45. Greenup...........Mason...1803
46. Casey..............Lincoln...1806
47. Clay................Madison, Knox and Floyd.....................1806
48. Lewis..............Mason...1806
49. Hopkins...........Henderson...1806
50. Estill...............Madison and Clark..............................1808
51. Caldwell..........Livingston...1809
52. Rock Castle.......Lincoln, Pulaski, Madison and Knox......1810
53. Butler.............Logan and Ohio..................................1810
54. Grayson...........Hardin and Ohio.................................1810
55. Union.............Henderson...1811
56. Bath...............Montgomery.......................................1811
57. Allen..............Warren and Barren..............................1815
58. Daviess...........Ohio...1815
59. Whitley...........Knox..1818
60. Harlan............Floyd and Knox..................................1819
61. Hart...............Hardin and Greene..............................1819
62. Owen.............Scott, Franklin and Greene....................1819
63. Simpson..........Logan, Warren and Allen......................1819
64. Todd..............Logan and Christian............................1819
65. Monroe...........Barren and Cumberland........................1820
66. Trigg.............Christian and Caldwell.........................1820
67. Grant.............Pendleton..1820
68. Perry.............Clay and Ford....................................1820
69. Lawrence........Greenup and Floyd..............................1821
70. Pike..............Floyd...1821

NEW COUNTIES.	FORMED FROM.	YEAR.
71. Hickman	Caldwell and Livingston	1821
72. Calloway	Hickman	1822
73. Morgan	Floyd and Bath	1822
74. Oldham	Jefferson, Shelby and Henry	1823
75. Graves	Hickman	1823
76. Meade	Hardin and Breckinridge	1823
77. Spencer	Nelson, Shelby and Bullitt	1824
78. McCracken	Hickman	1824
79. Edmonson	Warren, Hart and Grayson	1825
80. Laurel	Rock Castle, Clay, Knox and Whitley	1825
81. Russell	Adair, Wayne and Cumberland	1825
82. Anderson	Franklin, Mercer and Washington	1827
83. Hancock	Breckinridge, Daviess and Ohio	1829
84. Marion	Washington	1834
85. Clinton	Wayne and Cumberland	1835
86. Trimble	Gallatin, Henry and Oldham	1836
87. Carroll	Gallatin	1838
88. Carter	Greenup and Lawrence	1838
89. Breathitt	Clay, Perry and Estill	1839
90. Kenton	Campbell	1840
91. Crittenden	Livingston	1842
92. Marshall	Calloway	1842
93. Ballard	Hickman and McCracken	1842
94. Boyle	Mercer and Lincoln	1842
95. Letcher	Perry and Harlan	1842
96. Owsley	Clay, Estill and Breathitt	1843
97. Johnson	Floyd, Lawrence and Morgan	1843
98. Larue	Hardin	1843
99. Fulton	Hickman	1845
100. Taylor	Greene	1848
101. Powell	Montgomery, Clark and Estill	1852
102. Lyon	Caldwell	1854
103. McLean	Daviess, Muhlenburg and Ohio	1854
104. Rowan	Fleming and Morgan	1856
105. Jackson	Estill, Owsley, Clay, Laurel, Rock Castle and Madison	1858
106. Metcalfe	Barren, Greene, Adair, Cumberland and Monroe	1860
107. Boyd	Greenup, Carter and Lawrence	1860
108. Magoffin	Morgan, Johnson and Floyd	1860
109. Webster	Hopkins, Henderson and Union	1860
110. Wolfe	Morgan, Breathitt, Owsley and Powell	1860
111. Robertson	Nicholas, Harrison, Bracken and Mason	1867
112. Bell	Harlan and Knox	1867
113. Menifee	Bath, Morgan, Powell, Montgomery and Wolfe	1869
114. Elliott	Morgan, Carter and Lawrence	1869
115. Lee	Owsley, Estill, Wolfe and Breathitt	1870
116. Martin	Pike, Johnson, Floyd and Lawrence	1870

CHAPTER II.

FORMATION AND ORGANIZATION OF TODD COUNTY—ACT OF THE LEGISLA-
TURE—ORIGIN OF THE NAME—TODD COUNTY GEOGRAPHY—ITS GEOL-
OGY—ITS NATURAL RESOURCES—ITS AGRICULTURE—STAPLE PROD-
UCTS—STOCK INTERESTS.

THERE seems to have been no settled system in accordance with which the various counties of Kentucky were formed. The absence of a public, systematic form of survey has made it necessary to depend largely upon natural objects for fixed points, and county outlines are irregular and uncouth, inclosing areas of widely differing extent. Thus Todd County, in order of time the sixty-fourth county formed, erected as early as 1819, is a little parallelogram, imperfect in outline, wedged between and formed from the larger and wealthier counties of Logan and Christian. By its origin and location doomed for all time to labor under disadvantages in the race for prominence and distinction, it is likely never to emerge from the rural obscurity in which its early history has placed it. Lincoln County, formed in 1780, included all this portion of southwestern Kentucky, and when Logan was formed in 1792, it included the western portion of Lincoln. In 1796 the outlying territory of Logan was divided into Warren and Christian County, and in 1819 Logan and Christian Counties were called upon to contribute to the erection of Todd. The moving cause of Todd's origin is not far to seek. The early form of concentrated government made the presence of a large number of its citizens at the seat of justice a necessity, and social traditions more potent than law made it a pleasure to a still larger number. The character of the country and the meager internal improvements, made these long pilgrimages a frequent source of irritation and ripened a vigorous and influential demand for " home government." It was in response to this demand that the State Legislature by an act approved December 30, 1819, erected Todd County.

Act of Legislature.—The text of the act is as follows:

SECTION 1. *Be it Enacted by the General Assembly of the Commonwealth of Kentucky,* That from and after the first day of April next, all that part of said counties of Logan and Christian, contained in the following boundary, to wit: Beginning on the Tennessee State line, at the present corner of the counties of Logan and Christian, on said State line; thence on a straight line to the Muhlenberg County line, two miles east of the present corner of said counties of Logan and Christian, on said Muhlenberg County line; then westwardly with said Muhlenberg County line, until a due south line will strike a point ten miles due east of the most eastwardly boundary of the town of Hopkinsville, and continue south to the said State line, and eastwardly with it to the place of beginning, shall be one distinct county, called and known by the name of Todd, in honor of the memory of Col. John Todd, who gallantly fell in the service of his country on the [19th] day of August, 1782, at the battle of the Blue Licks.

SEC. 2. The said county of Todd shall be entitled to thirteen Justices of the Peace, who shall be appointed and commissioned as in other cases, who shall meet at the dwelling house of James Kendall in said county, on the second Monday in May next, and after taking the necessary oaths of office, and qualifying their Sheriff agreeably to the Constitution of the United States, and of this State as required by law, they shall proceed to elect and qualify a Clerk, to whose permanent appointment it shall be necessary for a majority of all the Justices in commission for said county to concur ; but if such majority cannot be obtained in favor of any one, then said court shall appoint a Clerk *pro tempore.*

SEC. 3. The County Court for said county shall hold their first term on the second Monday in May next, and on the second Monday in each month thereafter, except the months in which the circuits for said county shall be holden ; and the Circuit Courts for said county shall commence on the fourth Monday in April, July and October in each year, and may, if necessary, continue six judicial days ; and said county shall form a part of the seventh judicial district.

SEC. 4. The Circuit and County Courts, and Justices of the Peace in Christian and Logan Counties, shall have jurisdiction over all matters instituted prior to the commencement of this act ; and it shall be lawful for all Sheriffs, Collectors and Constables, in said Christian and Logan Counties, to collect all fines and moneys, and to execute all writs, executions and other process, as the law directs, which were put into their hands previous to the commencement of this act, and shall account for and return the same as if this act had not passed.

SEC. 5. The County Court of said county of Todd shall appoint Commissioners of the Tax in said county for the year 1820, who shall perform the duties, and be governed by the laws regulating Commissioners of Tax in this State ; and the Clerk and other officers of said county, shall in the like manner perform their duties in relation thereto ; and said county court shall also, as soon as practicable, after the place for the permanent seat of justice for said county shall have been fixed upon by Commissioners, as hereinafter mentioned, proceed to cause the erection of all necessary public buildings thereupon, for said county of Todd, and may lay off and establish a town there, and do and perform every other matter in relation thereto, that county courts are by law authorized to do in this State.

SEC. 6. The place for the permanent seat of justice for said county of Todd shall be fixed upon by five Commissioners, to wit: Thomas Champion, of Caldwell County ; William Thompson and Dickson Given, of Livingston County ; and Benjamin Vance and Leander J. Sharp, of Warren County ; who shall meet at the house of James Kendall, in said county of Todd, on the second Monday in May next, and thence proceed to select and point out an eligible place for the permanent seat of justice for said county; and said Commissioners are hereby enjoined to pay a just regard to the most central, convenient and eligible site for that purpose, and make report thereof to the County Court of said county of Todd ; but should said Commissioners, or a majority of them, fail to meet on the day herein mentioned for that purpose, they are hereby authorized and requested still to meet at said place herein appointed, and proceed to perform all the duties herein required of them, as soon as practicable thereafter, a majority or any three of whom are hereby authorized to act and perform all the duties herein required, provided no more attend for that purpose ; and each of said Commissioners attending on the performance of their said duties herein mentioned, shall receive for their services $3 per day, while necessarily absent from home attending on said business, to be levied and paid out of the first county levy laid for said county.

SEC. 7. The Surveyors of the counties of Logan and Christian are authorized and required to meet at the beginning corner of said county of Todd, on the said State line, on the first day of April next; thence proceed to lay off, run and plainly mark all lines of the said county of Todd, which have not heretofore been run and marked, and return a report thereof to the County Court of Todd ; for which services said Surveyors shall receive $3 per day each while they are necessarily engaged therein, besides a reasonable allowance for the employment of chain carriers and markers, to be allowed and paid out of the first levy to be laid for said county.

Origin of Name.—Col. John Todd, whose honored name this county bears, was the eldest of three brothers, and a native of Pennsylvania. He was educated in Virginia, at his uncle's—the Rev. John Todd—and at maturity entered upon the study of the law, subsequently obtaining a license to practice. He left his uncle's residence, and settled in the town of Fincastle, Va., where he practiced law for several years; but Daniel Boone and others having explored Kentucky, Col. Todd, lured by the descriptions given him of the fertility of the country, about the year 1775 came first to Kentucky, where he found Col. Henderson and others at Boonesboro. He joined Henderson's party, obtained a pre-emption right, and located sundry tracts of land in the present county of Madison, in Col. Henderson's land office. He afterward returned to Virginia, and in the year 1786 again set out from Virginia with his friend, John May, and one or two others, for Kentucky. They proceeded some distance together on the journey, when for some cause Mr. May left his servant with Col. Todd to proceed on to their destination, and returned to Virginia. Col. Todd proceeded on to the place where Lexington now stands, and in its immediate vicinity improved two places—the one in his own name and the other in that of his friend, John May—for both of which he obtained certificates for settlement and pre-emption of 1,400 acres. These pre-emptions adjoin and lie in the immediate vicinity of the city of Lexington. It appears from depositions taken since his death, that he accompanied Gen. Clarke in his expedition against Kaskaskia and Vincennes, and was at the capture of those places. After the surrender of these posts it is supposed he returned to Kentucky, but it appears from letters written by Gen. Clarke that Col. Todd was appointed to succeed him in the command at Kaskaskia. Under an act of Virginia Legislature passed in 1777, by which that part of Virginia conquered by Clarke, and all other of her territory northwest of the Ohio River, was erected into the county of Illinois, of which Col. Todd was appointed Colonel-Commandant and County-Lieutenant, with all the civil powers of Governor. He was further authorized, by enlistment or volunteers, to raise a regiment for the defense of the frontier. He immediately entered upon the duties of his office, and was seldom absent from his Government up to the time of his death. The regiment was raised for one year's service, but was continued in duty until about 1779, when the State of Virginia raised four additional regiments—two for the eastern and two for the western part of Virginia. Col. Todd was appointed to the command of one of these. In the spring of 1780, Col. Todd was sent a delegate to the Legislature of Virginia, from the County of Kentucky. While attending on the Legislature he married Miss Hawkins, and returned subsequently to Kentucky, settling his wife in the fort at Lexington. He again visited Illinois, and was engaged continually in the administration of its Government and in military affairs, so that he was seldom with his family until the summer of 1782, when in the month of August the Indians besieged Bryan's Station in great force. The disastrous battle of the Blue Licks followed on the 19th of that month. Among the noble brave who fell, fighting to the last, was Col. John Todd, in the midst of usefulness and in the prime of life. His wife survived him, and an only child, a daughter, about twelve months old. This daughter was still living in 1847 (as wife of Robert Wickliffe, Sr.), and was then the oldest female native of Lexington.

Col. Todd was a man of fine personal appearance and talents, and an accomplished gentleman; was universally beloved, and died without a stain upon his character, and it is believed without even one enemy upon earth. From the year 1778 he might be considered as residing in Illinois until his marriage in 1780. Settling his wife at Lexington, he was obliged to make a long and dangerous trip to visit his family, and besides aiding in the councils held by Clarke, and accompanying him in one or more of his expeditions, it is believed he passed the journey from Lexington to Kaskaskia twice, and often four times each year. An anecdote illustrative of his character as related by his wife is to this effect: During the winter succeeding their marriage the provisions of the fort at Lexington became exhausted to such an extent that on her husband's return home with his colored man, George, one night, almost famished with hunger, she had been able to save for him a small piece of bread, about two inches square, and about a gill of milk, which she presented to him. He asked at once, if there was nothing for George; she answered, "not a mouthful." He called George, and handed him the bread and the milk, and went to bed supperless himself.

Geography.—The county thus organized and named is situated in the southern part of the State, on the Tennessee line, and in the eastern border of that section of Kentucky arbitrarily called the Southwest. It is bounded on the north by Muhlenburg County, east by Logan, south by Montgomery, in State of Tennessee, and west by Christian, and contains about 330 square miles. The county lies partly in the Green River Valley, and partly in that of the Cumberland River, and represents the characteristics of both valleys. The dividing line between these valleys passes in a northwesterly direction through Todd several miles above Elkton, throwing the northern portion into the " Green River Country," and the southern in the Cumberland Valley. Curiously enough, in this county, the characteristics of these valleys are transposed; the Green River portion is broken and underlaid by freestone, and lies within the mineral belt, while the lower part belongs to the cavernous limestone formation, and possesses those rich agricultural characteristics which have made the Green River Country famous as the great wheat producing area of the State. The Russellville and Hopkinsville road, passing northwesterly through Elkton, forms the general dividing line between these two sections. South from this the surface is a gently rolling expanse of arable country, with little timber and much lowland, which for the lack of good artificial drainage is much of the year under water. North of this road the surface begins immediately to show the gradual rise and broken character which in the farther limits of the county develops into almost impassable cliffs, rising abruptly to the height of 300 feet in places. The main stream of the county is the Elk Fork of Red River; this taking its origin in Nance Creek and Sampson's Branch, just north of Elkton, flows a southeasterly course to Allensville, flows thence in a more southerly direction, and crossing the Tennessee line forms the corner from which the lines of the county are projected. Three and five miles above the point where the Russellville and Hopkinsville road crosses the east line of Todd County, Double Lick Fork and Breathitt's Branch cross into Logan County to form the Whippoorwill, and drain that portion of the country between Elkton and the dividing ridge northeast of the county seat.

The central part of the southern division of Todd is drained by Spring Creek, and the western line is marked by the West Fork, which finds its source in Fairview District. These streams all empty into the Red River, which joins the Cumberland in Tennessee just west of where the projected line of Todd's western boundary would intersect it. The drainage of the northern portion of the county is into the Green River through the Pond River and Clifty Creek, affluents of the former. Rogers' Branch, Slim Jimmy, Horse and Cow Creeks and Blue Lick Creek are found in the northwest corner, and Pigeon Roost, East Clifty and the head waters of the Clifty diversify and drain the northeast corner. The course of the Clifty in Todd County is noted for the freestone cliffs which rise in almost magnificent grandeur at its margin. This line of cliffs, extending for miles unbroken by passable fissures, and clothed with the varied timber of this region, affords a succession of views which for natural picturesqueness is not excelled by any other locality in the State. The visitor is shown many places of natural interest, and others about which tradition or the vivid imagination of a later day has framed " legends strange to hear." The " Narrows " is a natural wagon trail— the only one by which the rocky barrier may be passed in many miles of its extent, which affords a good opportunity to gain some idea of it as an obstacle to travel. Sweating stones, almost as phenomenal as the sweating statue of old, are pointed out. These are vast masses of rock standing high up from the ground, in isolated positions, the surface of which is continually covered with a moisture so profuse as to drip to the ground in trickling streams. This seems to be the normal condition of these objects, and the " oldest inhabitant," who is everywhere noted for his close observation, is said never to have seen them in any other condition. This was suggested by the " guide " as typical of the mental state of one who should attempt to gain a livelihood by farming in this portion of the county, but for the fair fame of Todd this impertinent analogy should be scouted. The " Indian Ladder " is a luxuriant, wild grapevine which has thrown out its tendrils along the face of the cliff, and grasping one tree or shrub after another has drawn itself with cords of strength from one point to another until it has reached a dizzy height. It is said that it leads to and covers the entrance to a considerable cave which in the olden time afforded shelter to the discomfited savage or a safe outlook to the runner of the tribe. Neither the cave nor the Indian is to be seen from the comfortable footing below it, and the " evidence of things not seen," probably rests entirely upon the conscience and imagination of the person who kindly shows up the region to the visitor. Besides these, there are buzzard roosts and dens of fabled monsters (now happily extinct) whioh, to use the language of the auction bill, are " too numerous to mention."

The lowlands of Todd, while of more utility and, therefore, less romantic, are not entirely devoid of natural objects of peculiar interest. Of these Pilot Rock is perhaps the most striking. This is a vast mass of rock some 200 feet high, resting upon elevated ground and entirely isolated. Its summit is a level area of about half an acre in extent, covered with a small growth of timber and wild shrubbery, and is a pleasant resort, frequented by picnic parties from the neighboring country. It stands north of Fairview on the line between Christian and Todd Counties, the larger portion of the rock lying within the limits of the latter. Its elevated summit, which is gained without much difficulty, affords a fine view of the surrounding country for many miles, presenting a prospect beautiful and picturesque. In the leafless season and a favoring atmosphere, it is said Hopkinsville, twelve miles away, may be distinctly seen from its summit, and in pioneer days it was known far and wide as an infallible landmark, hence its name. The cavernous limestone shows here the characteristics to be found elsewhere. Sink-holes are frequently found, but none of such character as to render them objects of especial interest. The tunneling of the Elk Fork a few miles in its course below Elkton, is characteristic of the rock formation found here. At the point where the river sinks out of sight, it originally flowed around and at the foot of a mass of rock some fifty feet high. A fissure made in its rock bed some forty feet from the base of the cliff, gave the water opportunity to burrow an underground passage which, gradually enlarging, has afforded passage for an increasing volume of water. Save in a very low stage of water a part of the river finds passage by its old course; the rest, dropping through the fissure in the bed, passes for several hundred yards under the obstructing mass of rock. The contracted form of the opening causes the descending water to take the form and bustle of a whirlpool, but it evidently falls to no great depth as it emerges into the open country without the precipitation of a spring, with a smooth, gliding motion which is gained in the short passage.

Geological Speculations.—No geological survey has been made of Todd County, and the State work is of such a general nature as to forbid the gathering of anything approaching a particular review of the geological features of this county from its pages. A brief general review is all that can be attempted in the time and space assigned to this topic here. The geological formations of Kentucky, in common with those of the other Western States, generally belong to that great system which extends from the Alleghanies on the east across the Mississippi and to the Rocky Mountains on the west. Throughout this vast region the primary fossiliferous or silurian devonian, and carboniferous rocks prevail with some of the upper formations. These rocks all belong to the class which is termed sedimentary, and were generally deposited upon the bottom of the primeval ocean. Here the fossil remains of the inhabitants of this ocean were gradually covered by clay and sand or limestone and other layers of shells, until, under the heavy pressure of superincumbent strata and by slow and long-continued chemical action, they were converted into solid rocks, and now that the waters of this ocean have retired, are exposed to view as the lasting records of earth's remotest history. The strata over nearly the entire surface of the State lie nearly horizontal with few dislocations. They have generally a slight dip which, in the lower strata, seems to be usually in every direction from a point near Cincinnati on the Ohio River as a center, and at this point the lowest surface rocks of the State are exposed. The lowest exposed formation is the blue limestone, generally considered equivalent to the lower silurian strata of Murchison. The main surface exposure of this formation is found in a great curved triangular area, the southern apex of which terminates in Lincoln County, and from which only a narrow strip or axis, occasionally to be observed in the deep cuts of the valleys, can be traced through Casey, Russell and Cumberland Counties to the Cumberland River in Monroe County. The second formation is the gray or cliff limestone. The termini of this formation are found on the Ohio River, always overlaying the blue limestone, extending from Lewis and Mason Counties above to those of Trimble and Oldham below. From these points this formation appears as a belt, varying from twenty-two miles in width in Jefferson County to only a fraction of a mile where it enters Tennessee from Monroe County, running in a course more or less meandering from its true termini on the Ohio around the blue limestone. Its dip corresponds generally with that of this lower formation. This formation is known also as the cliff limestone, because the hardness and durability of some of its layers causes it to stand out in bold cliffs and to be the cause of the falls of water-courses. It is believed that its lower beds are equivalent with the upper silurian strata of Murchison and its upper layers with some portion of his devonian. The third formation is variously termed black lingula shale, black slate, devonian shale. This formation, resting immediately on the second formation, appears also on the Ohio River at two points: in Lewis County and at the base of the falls of that river in Jefferson County. From these two points, where the Ohio River Valley cuts through these strata as they pass to the north and west, this formation like that below it sweeps around the gray limestone in a meandering, irregular belt, varying in breadth from eight to ten miles in parts of Lewis, Bath, Estill and Madison Counties to that of a fraction of a mile in Casey, Russell, Cumberland and Monroe Counties. Like the second formation it passes into the State of Tennessee near the Turkey Neck Bend of the Cumberland River in two neighboring narrow zones lying on each side of the axis described under the head of the first formation, and its two zones, nearly parallel in their northeasterly course from the Tennessee line to the confines of Lincoln County, begin here to diverge, like those of the second formation, so as to surround and invest that lower formation. Its thickness at the falls of the Ohio is a little over 100 feet, but it varies greatly in this respect. This shale is quite bituminous, and petroleum has been found in this as well as in the formations above and below it. Some search has been made in it for coal but only with disappointment. No workable beds of this mineral have ever been found so low as this in the strata of the earth in America. The fourth formation is knob sandstone. This formation, which is generally characterized by the presence of those low hills called "knobs," is mainly composed of olive gray shales and grits or sandstones of the same tint. It is calculated to be 350 to 550 feet in thickness, and some of the knobs, as Sweet Lick Knob in Estill County, rise to 500 feet above the level of the streams. This formation also sweeps around the central and lower formations on the outside and above the black shale very much in the same course as described. This formation is exposed in a belt of about fourteen miles wide, extending from the foot of the falls of the Ohio to the mouth of the Salt River; thence it bears up the valley of that stream nearly south, with a slight easterly curve, to Muldraugh's Hill, dividing Taylor, Marion and Larue Counties, occupying part of Bullitt to the northeastern edge of Hardin, the western corner of Nelson and a large portion of Larue; thence it curves more to the southeast through the corners of Taylor, Casey and Adair Counties, to be continued in the form of low beds of dark earthy limestones and marly shales through Russell and Cumberland Counties to the Tennessee line. Beginning at its upper limits on the Ohio River in Lewis County its trace is found through the northeastern part of Fleming, the northern portion of Rowan, through Bath, Montgomery, Powell, Estill, Madison, Garrard, Boyle and Lincoln, in its southeastern sweep, to Casey County; again to pass, on the other side of the central axis, to the Cumberland River. The fifth formation, known as cavernous limestone, sub-carboniferous limestone or mountain limestone, is the exposure found in the southern portion of Todd. This formation is made up of alternating layers of white, gray, reddish, buff, and sometimes dark gray colored rocks, varying in quality from the most argillaceous claystone to the purest limestone. The latter predominates here, however, and contains numerous caverns, of which the Mammoth Cave in Edmonson County is an exaggerated specimen. These caverns are especially marked in Todd County only by the "sinks" found here and there in which the drainage water of the country sinks to form underground streams. Clear and copious springs mark the junction of this limestone with the underlying knobstone, and its lower strata contain in many places the dark, flinty pebbles which furnished the material for the arrowheads of the Indians. Some of its layers are so compact and close textured as to be fit for the lithographer, others are beautifully white with an oolitic structure. In it are found valuable beds of iron ore, some zinc and lead ores, and large veins of fluor-spar. This formation is geologically important as being the basis of the true coal measures, no workable beds of that material having ever been found below this formation in any part of the world. It surrounds the coal fields on all sides, and, like the other lower formations, is believed to extend continuously under them, appearing always in its relative position in the beds of streams or bottoms of valleys which are cut down deeply enough in the coal measures. The principal surface exposure is in the central portion of the State, the counties of Adair, Allen, Barren, Greene, Warren, Logan, Simpson and much of Hart, Edmonson, Todd, Trigg, Christian, Caldwell, Crittenden, Monroe, Butler, Grayson, Ohio, Taylor and Larue being based upon it. The sixth formation, the carboniferous or coal measures, is found in the northern part of Todd. The lower member of this formation, resting on the sub-carboniferous limestone, is usually what is called the conglomerate, millstone grit or pudding stone, which is generally composed of quartz pebbles, more or less coarse and rounded, cemented together with a silicious or ferruginous cement, but sometimes represented by fine sandstone or even shaly layers. Where the hard layers of this rock, the millstone grit, prevail the hills are steep, cliffs prominent and the soil but little productive. The *true coal series*, based upon this rock, are made up of alternating layers of sandstones, shales, conglomerates and limestones, contain various beds of coal, and nodules and layers of iron ore. Two considerable areas of this formation exist in the State which are termed the Eastern and Western Coal Fields. The Western Coal Field is an extension of the Illinois and Indiana coal field, and occupies the whole of Union, Henderson, Daviess and Hopkins, and large portions of Hancock, Ohio, Muhlenburg, Grayson, Todd and Butler Counties, an area of about 3,888 square miles. The seventh formation is composed of the quaternary deposits found in the extreme southwestern counties of the Jackson Purchase, situated between the Tennessee and Mississippi Rivers. These are loams, marls, clays, etc., which have probably been transported there by the action of water in recent geological time.

Economic Geology.—Todd County, it will be observed, is geologically placed very high. The rock exposures belong entirely to the fifth and sixth formations of the State section, which brings the county within the region of the Western Coal Field. It lies, however, on the margin of this area and no important outcrops of coal have been worked to any great extent. One or two mines have been opened and the product sold to local consumers, but with no great pecuniary profit. There is but little known of the deposits of this mineral in Todd, the State survey having accomplished but little more than to demonstrate what was generally known before, that there was coal here to some indefinite extent. An attempt was made in 1859 under the guidance of the State Geologist, Mr. D. D. Owen, to trace the margin of the Western Coal Field. The work of the season began on the Ohio River, at Stephensport, Breckinridge County, extending into Breckinridge, Grayson, Edmonson, Hart, Warren, Butler, Logan, Todd, Christian, Muhlenburg, Hopkins, Ohio and Hancock Counties. The greater part of the region traversed was the roughest country in western Kentucky. The margin of this coal field is surrounded by the millstone grit, sandstones and the intercalated beds of limestone and aluminous shales; usually dipping at a considerable angle. These formations worn into deep ravines by most of the water-courses produce a broken country, while the interval between the streams is usually filled with steep, rocky hills. This is the character of northern Todd, and it is probable that no mines will ever be discovered here which will prove of considerable commercial advantage. The geological party approached Todd by way of the Greenville road. Several patches or outliers of coal measures were seen on the hills between the northern branches of Muddy River and Clifty Creek, rarely over sixty or seventy feet thick above the fifth sandstone of the general section. Near the crossing of Clifty Creek the fifth sandstone is seen in heavy masses twenty-five or thirty feet thick. North of Clifty the coal measures are reached at the Dughill, half a mile southeast of the Rochester and Elkton road. From this point to the "Narrows" the road lies about 150 feet above the fifth sandstone; near the Narrows the road suddenly descends to the fifth sandstone, i. e., the margin of the coal measures. The fifth sandstone dips to both sides of the road from the ridge (Narrows), which is probably an anticlinal wave; the synclinals on either side being in the beds of Clifty Creek on the east, and eastern branches of Pond River on the west side of the ridge. South of the Narrows the fourth limestone and the fourth sandstone dip rapidly toward the northeast, and are raised a considerable distance above the horizontal position of the fifth sandstone at the Narrows. The narrow part of the ridge is about sixty yards wide, being in fact only a huge mass of the fifth sandstone, eighty feet thick, which is little else than a loose mass of quartz pebbles about the size of marbles, through which the water percolates. Being arrested by the clay shales at the base of the sandstone, it breaks out in bold springs on the east side of the ridge, which is doubtless the direction of the greatest dip of this locality. About one mile south of the Narrows the road has descended to the third sandstone, and the rocks are quite level or are dipping gently to the southwest, with the line of the branches to Pond River. The coal measures lying between the head of Pond River and Clifty are only a few feet thick—80 to 110— from one to two miles wide, deeply indented by the streams especially on the west or Pond River side of the ridge. From the point of intersection of the " Old Highland Lick " road with the Elkton and Greenville road the line of survey turned to the westward to Bennett's Mill, White Plains and on to Christian County. At this point of deflection, sandstone No. 3, formed the surface rock, and on descending the first hill limestone No. 2 was reached. Near the East Fork of Pond River the dip becomes quite rapid and brings down the mass of limestone No. 3 with its associated shale beds to the East Fork, in a few places covered by fallen masses of the pebbly part of the fifth sandstone.

Economic Stones.—The line dividing the exposures of the fifth and sixth formations, the cavernous limestone and the grit sandstone or freestone, is nearly coincident with the Russellville and Hopkinsville road. In the former are found several beds of limestone, differing much in thickness and quality, which commend themselves for building purposes. The best of these is that used by the company quarrying near Bowling Green. It is an oolitic, magnesian limestone, occurring in layers of excellent form for use, readily worked, and with rare qualities of endurance. A very similar stone is found in Todd, which was used in the foundation of the court house built in 1835, and on which the tool marks can be quite distinctly traced at this day. When first taken from the bed the stone is rather soft, so that it can be carved with some facility, but when it is long exposed it acquires a much greater hardness. It is, for a limestone, very resistant to heat, and is likely to wear better than any other stone in the Mississippi Valley. Add to this a rare beauty of color, a cream tint, and an endurance of this color, and all the desirable qualities of a building stone are well represented. This stone may be sought about one hundred and fifty feet below the top of the main carboniferous limestone. The lithographic limestones which are found at a lower point in the carboniferous limestone series, are as yet less determined in their value than the building stones. The conditions which determine the goodness of this quality of stone are so many, and must be met with such accuracy, that it is by no means certain that there is any material here to satisfy these conditions. The extensive series of beds which lead to the hope that the stone of this county may be suitable for this purpose, were formed under the same general conditions as prevailed in the basin when the most trusted lithographic stone, that of Solenhofen, are found ;—a sea bottom, whereon an unbroken mass of fine sediment of mingled lime and clay is accumulating, an entire absence of animals large enough for the naked eye to see—these seem to be the conditions under which a lithographic stone must be formed. Unfortunately most of this stone here shows from point to point small hard bits, which are probably the remains of some silicious sponge which lived in these waters of the ancient sea. These stones are doubtless useful for the making of the coarser sorts of engraving and the ordinary run of crayon work. They may also prove suitable for ordinary transfer work. None have been found as yet suitable for the highest grades of work.

Timber.—There is a wide difference in the timber growth found in the different parts of the State. No coniferous tree or bush, with the exception of the swamp cypress and a few small cedars, are to be found in western Kentucky, and in this section the hemlock seems to be generally confined to the coal measures. Magnolias are found in the precincts of the lawn, but they are exotics. Originally, southern Todd was known as a "barren," where the timber was kept down by frequent burnings, and in this connection it may be observed this county was thus deprived of much valuable timber that otherwise would be found in great abundance in the forests that have grown since the settlement of the whites. It seems to be undisputed, that certain timbers, especially white oaks, do not return again to forests from which they have once been driven by such an agency as fire. In the State report upon this subject Prof. Shaler remarks : "The formations best adapted to the growth of the chestnut are the conglomerate and Chester sandstones (mill grit). On soils from these formations chestnut is normally found in the greatest abundance, and growing to the greatest perfection. In passing from western to eastern Kentucky my attention was therefore attracted to the fact that when the Big Clifty (Chester) sandstone first appeared, which was in the neighborhood of Hopkinsville and on Pilot Knob, no chestnut appeared with it. Moreover, the white oak and liriodendron, away from the streams, seemed scrubby and scarce. Otherwise the forest was normal, and I searched in vain for any clue to the absence of these timbers. Mr. Irvine Kennedy, who has lived in this part of Kentucky for sixty-eight years, and who now (1879) resides near Elkton, informed me that my conjecture* was correct, and that he could remember when all these heavy forests were a uniform growth of young trees, with not an old tree standing, except on streams too large for fires to sweep through their swamps. I was afterward informed that some chestnut groves exist not far from Elkton, though I did not see a tree. It is possible that they stand in a piece of woods for some reason protected from the ravages of fire. After passing Hopkinsville we begin to leave the St. Louis limestone and approach the Chester sandstone, which already caps the highest hills. The introduction of red oak, forming the larger part of the forest growth, is a marked feature in passing onto the calcareous limestone and lower Chester from the St. Louis limestone. Scarlet oaks crown the hill-tops, and post oaks are found in depressions, or largely on the hill-sides below the Chester. The latter feature is local, however, as on a high hill about five miles from Hopkinsville post oaks extend up onto the Chester. The blackjack, however, is clustered around the hills just at the base of the Chester, and this I noticed to be generally true. Sugar maple, bartram oak, swamp chestnut oak, white elm and black ash are found in considerable quantities along the streams. For six or eight miles beyond Hopkinsville, toward

---

*Become extinct through agency of fires.

Fairview, the timbers change little in kind or quality from those just
noted, except that some red haw and winged elm are found. There is no
white oak, no sweet gum, no chestnut (that I could find) and no lariodien-
dron. On Pilot Rock, which is a lofty bluff of Big Clifty sandstone,
cedar and liriodendron are both met with; but this is very local, and even
here no chestnut is to be seen, so far as I could gather. Between Fairview and Elkton the timbers, as a whole, are not valuable; but in places
black ash, white elm, pig and shag hickory, and such timbers, are exceedingly fine. Especially is this true on West Fork of Red River, about one
and one-half miles from Fairview. On this stream are also found splendid white oak, swamp chestnut oak, red and pin oak, white and shag
hickory, black and blue ash, sweet gum, liriodendron, white elm, syca-
more, box-elder, sugar maple, white maple and red bud. All of these
timbers are very fine. It is a peculiar, though an easily explained fact
that in a large part of the country through here the timbers are better on
the hill-tops than on the lower grounds. The reason is that the hill-tops
are capped with Chester sandstone, the detritus of which forms a damp
soil, favorable for large trees, while the upper St. Louis limestone here is
not adapted to timber growth."

Toward Elkton scattering bartram oaks and cedars are found in addition to the usual red oak, shag, pig and white hickory, winged elm,
small black ash, scrub white oak (in spots), Spanish oak, black oak, post
oak, black gum, etc. Yellow wood is also found near Elkton, with some
honey locust, red bud and red (slippery) elm. Of course the swamp timbers have never been affected by fire; and on streams fine white oak, liriodendron, white and sugar maples, sweet gum, laurel oak, etc., flourish.
The upland and lowland timbers alternate, with no changes worthy of
note until Russellville is reached.

Agriculture.—Something more than the southern half of Todd County was originally included in what was known as the "barrens," so called,
not because the soil lacked fertility, but because of the former absence of
timber and the numerous "sinks" to be found. This area lies upon the
cavernous formation, and the soil is notably of very high quality, but is
easily restored when worn. The soil of the northern portion of the county rests upon the clifty sandstone and is of a less desirable quality.
There are occasional patches of the red clay subsoil, but these are rare,
the greater part being the white pipe clay or kindred soils of meager fertility and difficult to build up. Todd is pre-eminently an agricultural
county. Its numerous streams in the early history of its settlement gave
rise to a number of mills, but these have had a local significance only.
Of the large number that have had existence less than a dozen now survive, and of these only the mills at Elkton are an important feature in the

manufacturing interests of the county. The lack of shipping facilities and the scarcity of merchantable timber has retarded the development of manufactures, so that Todd is not only a purely agricultural district, but is likely to remain so for all time to come.

The first settlers sought an agricultural region where timber and water united to furnish the simple demands of pioneer existence. The "barrens," covered with considerable underbrush and with scarcely a tree, looked very unpromising to the pioneer accustomed to the heavy timber of Virginia and North Carolina, and were passed by, the first settlements being made in the timber along the Elk Fork and streams of the northern part of this region. The consequence was that the pioneers seized upon the poorest land in the county to begin upon, and only necessity drove them later to the occupation of that portion which is the garden spot of Todd. The pioneers brought with them the notions gained in their former homes, and bringing their slaves sought to make plantations here for the cultivation of the staples of the country from which they came. Tobacco was the chief crop on which reliance for revenue was placed, and this proved an admirable growth to subdue the soil, but the thin soil first attempted soon proved inadequate to the trying demands of repeated crops of this plant, and some twenty-five years later there were hundreds of acres " turned out " as worn-out land. The " barrens " were then taken up and cultivated in the same way with the same result. There was this difference in the two sections, however: no profitable means of restoring the thin soil could be devised, while the red sub-soil lands were readily and cheaply renewed by fallowing with clover. Farmers have not given the subject that careful investigation which its importance demands, and careless, uninstructed methods are still employed, as a rule, here as elsewhere in the south. There are evidences of improvement in this respect here, and it is probable that the improvement will continue until the cultivated area in Todd County will be largely increased.

The plan of the first farmers was to plant a crop of tobacco on the new soil and follow it with corn until the soil was completely exhausted, when the field was abandoned. Later years have taught the advantages of rotation in crops, and this is now the rule. Tobacco is still the first crop on new or sod land. Occasionally a second crop is taken from the same field, but generally, corn is the succeeding crop for one or more seasons, then occasionally oats, succeeded by wheat and then clover. Tobacco has been, until very recently, almost the only source of revenue to the farmer, and beyond the demands of his family support his farm and energies were devoted by the farmer to the cultivation of this crop. The variety is known as the Clarksville leaf, a thick, gummy, heavy variety which is principally marketed at that point and nearly the entire product exported to foreign lands. The style of cultivation is of the better sort. Care is taken in all its stages and the product comes to market in pretty good condition. It is an exacting crop on soil and labor, and the farmer has always a crop in hand from the time he begins its cultivation until he stops. Like all other crops, it affords remuneration of a varied sort. The careful, attentive planter gradually grows rich, while the careless class gradually joins the indigent class, a "good year" only delaying his inevitable progress. More than most of agricultural products, the success of its culture turns upon critical junctures, when a day's unfaithfulness will ruin or greatly damage a promising field. The changes wrought by " the war " in the character of farm labor, has increased the demand for care, and the frequent remark is now heard, that " tobacco growing don't pay." Todd County, however, is quite as much devoted to the " noxious weed " as ever before, and will probably continue to be, the farmers depending upon increased care and intelligence to cure the clearly defined evils now observed in handling it.

Corn is an important product of husbandry in the county. An increasing acreage is planted each year, the farmers having discovered that it is more profitable fed to stock than to negroes. Its yield is large, its cultivation not exacting on soil or labor, and its returns, when fed on the farm, are highly satisfactory. In recent years a mixed form of husbandry has gradually made its way into favor, and the growth of live stock is modifying agricultural traditions in every way. But little attention is paid to grass as a merchantable crop, but meadows of mixed timothy, blue or orchard grass and clover alone or mixed with the other varieties, are becoming more frequent. Clover, for renewing purposes, is very largely sown. The general practice is to turn under the growth unpastured or cropped in the fall, to lie fallow until planting time in the following spring. On soil thus fertilized tobacco is first planted, which is followed by wheat. The acreage devoted to this cereal has largely increased of late years, and some of the best farmers plant only enough tobacco to pay the farm hands, and look to this grain for their principal revenue. Every farmer raises some wheat, and the aggregate quantity raised in the county reaches a large figure.

Stock-raising to any noticeable extent dates from about 1863. Before this date but little had been attempted in the way of improving stock, save in horses. Kentucky has long been noted for its horses, and the record of breeding horses and jacks which were licensed in the county indicates an early interest here in this subject. Up to the year 1833 the following horses are named in the record: Sir Clayton, Silver Heels, Young Pilgrim, Wormwood, Diomede, Bolivar, Richard, Faulkner, Arrasaka, Corsican, Bachelor, Aratas, Uncas, Sir Charles, Pacotel, Sir Archer, Mike,

The American Beauty, Hamiltonian, Comet, Niter, Selim, American Eagle, Young Stump Dealer, etc. These names indicate the prominent strains that have been used to improve the common stock. The interest in this class of stock has been maintained by the circumstances and tastes of the people. Horses are selected here with reference to their qualifications for the saddle or harness. Among well-to-do people, horses are kept especially for the one use or the other. "All purpose" horses are only in demand among the class of owners who cannot afford the expense of maintaining animals for road purposes. The mystery of "fox-trot, side-pace and running walk," is eloquently explained by the Kentuckian horse-lover (and what man is not?) and enters largely into every horse sale. The average horse in the county is well-bred, but rather run down. There are many fine-spirited animals to be seen, held or sold at prices varying from $250 to $500, but these are in the minority. The heavy draft horse has been introduced of late years, but does not find much encouragement, as mules are almost entirely used in farm work. The latter animal is found in large numbers in the county, and meets a ready sale at good prices.

About 1845 Dr. Garrard brought to Todd County a fine short-horn bull, which he had purchased at a cost of some $500. This attempt to improve the cattle was not appreciated, and it is said the investment was a complete loss. About 1863 the subject of improvement of cattle was revived, and some of the best families of short-horns were brought in from the blue grass region. Since then the interest in this stock has considerably increased. Jersey cattle were introduced here in 1878, and quite a number of this breed of animals are found. Webb C. Garth, of District No. 5 (Trenton), and M. P. Bailey, District No. 4 (Elkton), are prominently identified with stock-raising, dealing principally in herd-book animals. Other classes of stock are receiving some attention also. Hogs are a considerable source of profit, and are shipped to market to an important extent. The Berkshire, Poland-China and Jersey Reds are all represented in the breeds. Coarse-wool sheep are found to a limited extent in the county. There are no large flocks, but almost every farmer has a few head, kept principally to furnish the table with mutton. Wool is becoming more of an object of late, and within a few years past the flocks have materially increased.

CHAPTER III.

TRACES OF THE EARLIEST INHABITANTS—INDIAN TRADITIONS—THE EARLY
SETTLEMENT—A KENTUCKY BARREN—THE START IN A NEW COUNTRY
—PIONEER INDUSTRIES—SOCIAL CHARACTERISTICS.

IT is an interesting suggestion of the archæologist, that this land, which
on the coming of the whites was too forbidding for the habitation of
the Indian, centuries before was the home of a race of beings possessing
some approach to civilization. The discovery of footprints upon his deserted island by Robinson Crusoe was not more startling than the discov-
eries of archæologists to the followers of Petarius and Usher, who place
the operations of creation and the whole evolution of civilization within
the narrow limits of a few centuries. But science has multiplied its evidence until there is no room to doubt that these ancient people were a
living reality in the indefinite past, and worked out their destinies where
the whites pioneered their way a hundred years ago. Time has swallowed
up their identity, and loosely characterized by the character of their remains, they are known only as Mound-Builders. Their footprints may
be traced " wherever the Mississippi and its tributaries flow, in the fertile
valleys of the West, and along the rich savannas of the Gulf, upon the
Ohio, the Kentucky, the Cumberland, the Licking; upon the streams of
the far South, and as far north as the Genessee and the head waters of the
Susquehanna, but rarely upon mountains or sterile tracts, and almost invariably upon the fertile margins of navigable streams. Within these
limits the population of that old American world corresponded almost
perfectly in its distribution with that of the new. These ancient citizens
enjoyed a wide range of communication. Antiquarian research has gathered from the same mound the mica of the Alleghenies, obsidian from
Mexico, native copper from the northern lakes, and shells from the southern Gulf." The mounds themselves are multitudinous in number, peculiar in structure, and varied in character. They are found scattered
throughout the State, aggregating a large number which has never been
estimated. The prevailing form of these structures is ellipsoidal or
cone-like, many of them are pyramidal and of striking dimensions; they
are always truncated, are sometimes terraced, and generally have graded
and spiral ascents to the summits. These remains are variously classified
according to the ingenuity of the writer, but all furnish abundant evidence

of their artificial origin. The simplest classification is that which divides these structures into altar and temple and burial mounds, with others that do not readily fall into a distinct class. The first of this classification are supposed to have been places of sacrifice; are found within or near an enclosure; are stratified, and contain altars of stone, or of burned clay. Temple mounds are high places for ceremonial worship, and show no stratification, no evidence of human burial, no remains of altars, and stand in isolated positions. "Mounds of sepulture" are generally found isolated, unstratified in construction, and containing human remains. Other mounds have so little to mark the use to which they were devoted, that they have fallen into a fanciful classification, as mounds of observation, signal mounds, habitation mounds, etc. The temple, or terraced mounds, are said to be more numerous in Kentucky than in the States north of the Ohio River. The striking resemblance which these temple mounds bear to the *teocallis* of Mexico, has suggested the purposes to which they were devoted, as well as the name by which they are known. Some remarkable works of this class have been found in the counties of Adair, Trigg, Montgomery, Hickman, McCracken, Whitley, Christian, Woodford, Greenup and Mason. There are numerous mounds in Todd County, but to which of these classes they should be assigned it is difficult to determine from the meager accounts to be gained of them. But one or two have been examined, and these with insufficient care. Skeletons of extraordinary size were found, the skulls of which were passed over the head of a large man, and rested easily upon his shoulders. They were certainly not the remains of Indians, and are probably properly referred to the ancient builders of these mounds. Other works in the county are referred to the military structures of this people. The defensive or military character of an ancient work, seems to be indicated by its commanding position, its general strategic advantages, its contiguity to water, its exterior ditch, and its peculiar situation with reference to other works. There seems to have been a complete system of these defenses, extending from the sources of the Allegheny and the Susquehanna to the Wabash, as if designed by a peaceful and prosperous population to afford permanent protection against savage aggressions from the north and east. It has been suggested, however, that a tide of emigration flowing from the south, received its final check upon this line—these defenses marking the limit. Whatever be the correct theory, it seems certain that these defenses were not constructed by a migratory or nomadic people. They are the work of a vast population, well organized and permanently established on an agricultural basis. Within the limits of Kentucky the remains of ancient fortifications are numerous, but principally located in the northern part of the State. What was the final fate of these people is very obscure.

HISTORY OF TODD COUNTY.

Indian traditions point to the suggestion that the enemy against whom the northern line of defenses were built, were the Aborigines. While these are vague and little trusted by scholars, there are so many independent partial confirmations, that this theory seems to be gaining ground of late. An old Delaware tradition says, that many centuries ago, the Lenni-Lenape, a powerful race which swept in a flood of migration from the far West, found a barrier to its onward progress in a mighty civilization which was intrenched in river valleys east of the Mississippi. The people who occupied these fortified seats are traditionally denominated the Allegeni. The two nations thus confronting each other on the banks of the Mississippi, measured the situation with a civilized eye, the Lenni-Lenape diplomatically parleying for the right of passage, and the subtle Allegeni hypocritically affecting to hear. As a result of these negotiations, the Lenni-Lenape were treacherously assailed in an attempted passage, and driven back though not utterly destroyed by their perfidious foe. According to this tradition there was a coincident migration of the warlike Iroquois from the far West on a higher line of latitude, and these people sought a passage of the same stream at another point. The Lenni-Lenape recovering from their repulse, formed a league with the Iroquois, and the united force declaring a war of extermination against the Allegeni, reduced their strongholds, desolated their lands, and drove them southward in disastrous retreat.

But this tradition of the Delawares does not stand alone. That the pre-historic inhabitants of Kentucky were at some indeterminate period overwhelmed by a tide of savage invasion from the north, is a point upon which Indian tradition is positive and explicit. It is related upon good authority that Col. James Moore, of Kentucky, was told by an old Indian, that the primitive inhabitants of this State had perished in a war of extermination waged against them by the Indians ; that the last great battle was fought at the falls of the Ohio, and that the Indians succeeded in driving the Aborigines into a small island below the rapids, "where the whole of them were cut to pieces." This the Indian said was an undoubted fact handed down by tradition, and that the Colonel would have proofs of it under his eyes as soon as the waters of the Ohio became low. When the waters of the river had fallen, an examination of Sandy Island was made, and " a multitude of human bones was discovered." There is a similar confirmation by the Chief Tobacco, in a conversation with Gen. Clarke. It is said that the Indian Chief Cornstalk told substantially the same story to Col. McKee. The Chief said that Ohio and Kentucky had once been settled by a white people who were familiar with arts of which the Indians knew nothing ; that these whites, after a series of bloody contests with the Indians, had been exterminated ; that the old burial places were the graves of an unknown people, and that the old forts had not been built by Indians, but had come down from " very long ago " people, who were of a white complexion, and skilled in the arts. In addition to this traditional testimony, various and striking traces of a deadly conflict have been found all along the Ohio border. " And doubtless," says Dr. Pickett —from whose article the matter of this topic is largely drawn—" the familiar appellation of ' the dark and bloody ground ' originated in the gloom and horror with which the Indian imagination naturally invested the traditional scenes and events of that strange and troubled period." It is not improbable that the bloodiest battles were fought on the navigable streams, and, judging from the nature of the fortifications in northern Kentucky, this State was the scene of some of the sternest conflicts. *Kentucke*, in the Indian language meaning " the river of blood," was a land of ill repute, and wherever a lodge fire blazed, " strange and unholy rumors " were busy with its name. Indians could not fully understand how white people could live in a country where such conflicts had filled the land with the ghosts of its slaughtered inhabitants.

The Indians.—The relation of the Indians to the Mound-Builders has not been satisfactorily determined by scientists. Indian traditions are so vague, and so utterly lacking in the prime essentials for a scientific basis, that few archæologists have taken them into the account. Some, however, have hazarded an hypothesis in accordance with the traditions mentioned above, while others (among whom the late Mr. Morrison, an account of whose researches in New Mexico have been published by the Smithsonian Institute), have taken the ground that the Indian is a degenerate descendant of these ancient people, and that the famed Montezuma, whose halls have furnished so rich a store of poetic illusion, was nothing but a dirty Indian in a mud hut. Whatever may be the truth in all this, the Indian still stands, by the great mass of evidence, an independent race, and the successor of the Mound-Builder, whose remains are found in this county as well as elsewhere in the State. Whether the traditions quoted sufficiently account for the fact or not, it remains unquestioned that the Indian did not choose to make his home in the " dark and bloody ground," and while the pioneers possessed the land only after a long and determined struggle, the early annals contain no record of the wigwam blaze or the council fires in this State. There are abundant evidences of their presence in Todd County, as there are of their predecessors, but the early settlement of the county seems to have been singularly free of those dangers and thrilling exploits so common in almost every settlement of Ohio at the same date. The nuclei of Kentucky's early settlement were at Boonesboro and Harrodsburg, and against these and their deploying stations the savages engaged in a bitter and determined struggle ; but these were maintained from the region north of the Ohio, and ceased to be especially alarming to local communities by the beginning of the present century. The rock formation exposed in this county furnished an abundance of the material from which the Indians formed their implements, and places are pointed out in Todd where the debris would seem to indicate that the savages at some time had engaged in the manufacture of arrowheads on a large scale here. Many of the finished products have been found, some of unique design, but neither tradition nor reminiscence furnishes material " to point a moral or adorn a tale." The earliest settlers of the county did construct a fort on Spring Creek west of Guthrie, but it was probably on the general principle " that an ounce of prevention is better than a pound of cure." Here women and children found security behind a strong stockade and bolted doors, while the men worked in the field with guns at their backs. There are no' traditions of Indian hostilities perpetrated here, and while this peaceful issue contributed to the comfort and success of the early settlers, it leaves the chronicler of those times no " hair-breadth 'scapes mid the imminent deadly breach " with which to embellish his pages.

The Pioneers.—The early immigration to the State of Kentucky, as has been noted, came to the blue grass region and upper Kentucky Valley. A few of the more adventurous spirits pushed out to the southwest in the upper valley of Green River, and of these were the founders of Davis Station in Christian County, and Justinian Cartwright, in Todd County, in 1792. It is to be regretted that the sketches of the Hon. Urban Kennedy, published in a county paper, have not been preserved intact. Through the care of W. P. Stephenson, a few fragments have been secured to which the following summary is principally indebted for its facts. At the time Davis' Station was established, the Indians were still actively engaged in a determined effort to repel the encroachments of the whites, and this settlement was disturbed, if not broken up, later in the year. Cartwright's seems to have escaped the general fate of outlying improvements, and the settlement of the county dates in an unbroken line from 1792. A trace ran from the Russellville settlement, established in 1780, to the cabin of Bat Woods, on the present site of Hopkinsville, and across this trace, about four and a half miles west of Elkton, Cartwright built his cabin. It was situated in the edge of some timber near a good spring, and was the only house in the territory since brought within the lines of Todd County. Here he fenced and cleared a small patch of ground and planted it to corn and Irish potatoes, which with the abundant game of the country placed him above danger of want. Cartwright was a native of Maryland, of Scotch-Irish descent, and was the first Surveyor of Christian County. He was small in stature, but well made, and no mean antagonist in any contest. He had three sons, one of whom was a lawyer in Princeton (Caldwell County) afterward. In 1801, Robert Adams bought Cartwright's place, and in 1809 sold out to the father of Urban Kennedy. During this interval of some eighteen years, considerable additions were made to the settlement of this region, but of which there is no record in the fragments at hand. Mr. Kennedy's father was an old Revolutionary soldier, who, when the war was over, went to Greenbrier County, Va., married and settled down to farming and hunting in the Virginia mountains. Soon afterward in company with some forty or fifty families he emigrated to Kentucky, under the direction of Gen. William Logan. " They had to come in large companies, with pack-horses for their plunder, women and children, for in that day there were no wagon-roads through the wilderness. The men of the company, say 100 or more, took it afoot, armed with rifles, tomahawks and butcher-knives, keeping up a continual and vigilant military discipline both night and day. A brother-in-law of Kennedy's, Simon McCaffrey, was killed while acting as forerunner for the company. The whole party stopped first at Crab Orchard, Ky." Logan, Kennedy, the McKinneys, Burtons, Shackelfords and others came on to where Stanford now is, but what was then Logan's Station. Two years later, Kennedy, the Shackelfords, McKinneys, Burtons and Dooleys came eight miles west of Logan's, and built a block-house on the Hanging Fork of Dick's River. Here the little community suffered the vicissitudes of a frontier community, losing several of their number at the hands of the savages. In 1809 Kennedy sold his place here and moved to what is now Todd County.

At this time this region was beginning to be sparsely settled. On the road from Russellville to Hopkinsville were found, three miles west of the first-named place, a Mr. Blakely; five miles further on was Simons' Springs; next George McLean; then Ephraim McLean, a Cumberland Presbyterian minister, and father of Finis E. McLean; next was Jesse Irvine, at the creek west of the site of Daysville; then James Millen. The next " was a ditched field of about ten acres, without any cabin, belonging to Thomas Garvin, extending from near the public square of Elkton easterly nearly to the creek, and there was a small cabin near the spot where Ridley's ' Rathburn House ' was burned, occupied by Mc-Intosh, a hunter, who was a tenant of Maj. John Gray, to hold possession, as Gray and Garvin were at law for the land where Elkton now stands." Passing westward some five miles the improvement of a German, Kershner, was found; then George Tillerman, and next the Davis improvement in what is now Fairview. At this place and in the same cabin the Hon. Jefferson Davis was born. The elder Davis was a noted man in the country, and kept tavern here. A small mischievous lad, who plied the stranger guest with curious questions, has since gained notoriety as the head of the Southern Confederacy during the years of 1861–65. The nearest house to where Elkton now stands was the residence of Hon. Andrew New, then a Member of Congress from this district. He wore knee breeches, and was an old Virginia gentleman of the aristocratic type. The next nearest were William Blackwood, William Millen and Gideon Thompson, a half mile south of Millen's. The only water-mill was John Carson's, and was the first one in Todd County. It had one pair of runners, and the flour was "bolted" by hand. It was jocularly said to be doing a brisk business, for when it got one grain smashed it immediately attacked another. There were settlements at this time along the Elk Fork as follows: The Millens, Cunninghams, Coulters, Grahams, Chestnuts, and after some years D. N. Russell moved into the neighborhood. The next mill below Carson's was Smith & Laughlin's on the Gallatin road; then southwest of this mill lay the "pondy woods," with considerable timber, where were settled Henry Gorin, Gabriel Rooch, Elliot Vaughter; the last two married sisters of Maj. John Gray. In this neighborhood also lived James Allen, the first Coroner of Todd, and general auctioneer for all this country. He was of Irish origin, and in crying the sales of his employers made shrewd use of the wit which is popularly supposed to inhere in the son of Erin. When the enthusiasm lagged, and bids were reluctantly made, he would cry out, "Fair sale, gentlemen! and a dthram to the next bidder!" He always prepared himself for this emergency, and began his sale equipped with a bottle in one hand and his cane in the other. On Spring Creek, where it crosses the Nashville road, John Moore settled, and Maj. Samuel Moore settled on the site of Trenton, where the road from Clarksville to Greenville then crossed. He had located a large body of land, which he sold to Louis Leavell. Near him was Robert Coleman, and about two miles down the West Fork from Coleman's was Davis Station, where all the settlers forted. There lived the Davis family, the Clarks, the Blues, and Brewer Reeves. Then west of Coleman's lived the Bollingers, Kenners, Finleys, Norths, etc. Then, following up the creek, were the Adamses, McFaddens, and John Campbell, the old surveyor of Christian County. Henry Carpenter was one of the very first pioneers of the county, and lived in this vicinity. "He was a full-blooded Dutchman, and it was said when he cut the first timber at that place he was on a log chopping, his rifle standing near by, and his pipe in his mouth. The Indians slipped up near him and fired at him, putting a bullet hole through his shirt. He dropped his ax, picked up his gun, and started for the Davis Fort, some miles distant, on a sharp run, reaching it in safety, with his pipe still lighted." He afterward built a block-house with double doors, and port holes through which

to defend himself against the savages should they attack. A half mile up
the branch William Wallace had settled, and planted a large orchard, the
first one in the county. He was of French extraction, raised a large
family of boys, and in 1822 sold to Thomas Bryan. This settlement was
made about 200 yards southeast of where Bell's Chapel now stands. A
half mile east of this was Peter Thompson, a Dane. Coming north from
this neighborhood were the improvements of Andrew and John Mann,
and further up the creek that of Davis. In 1810 Matthew Logan settled
on the east edge of Croghan's Grove, and the next, south of the Russellville
and Hopkinsville road, was that of Kennedy already mentioned. The settlements north of the Russellville and Hopkinsville road at this date (1809)
were probably very few, but the paper containing the article in which
Mr. Kennedy describes them is so mutilated as to render his record of no
avail to this work, and what information it is possible to glean at this
time will be found under the head of the respective districts of that part
of the county. Heretofore the immigration had drawn its strength from
the emigrants of Virginia, who had settled at the earlier stations in Kentucky. In 1811 a fresh impetus was given to emigration, and large numbers were attracted to this fertile region from the older States. The tide
now set in from North Carolina, coming by way of the Nashville and Gallatin roads, and at Moore's (Trenton) would take the Muhlenburg road.
" You would see all sorts of old wagons, carts, pack-horses, pack-cows and
oxen. Weary and worn out, the immigrants would call out, ' Well, can
you tell me how far it is yet to the Pond River Country ? ' " Thus they
passed through the very Eden of Kentucky to reach the rough, heavy
timbered region of Pond River.

A *Kentucky Barren.*—The name popularly applied to the region embraced within the limits of Barren, Warren, Simpson, Logan, and the
lower part of Todd, Christian and Trigg Counties, is very misleading to
the modern ear. To the pioneers of the early part of this century, impressed by the stern experiences of frontier life, it meant a land "where
every prospect pleases " the eye only to dupe the understanding. They
had been brought up in a timbered country, and had been educated to believe that it was necessary not only to their comfort but to their very existence. They had an exaggerated idea of the amount of timber needed
for dwellings and fuel, and seemed to believe that soil too poor to grow
it would scarcely grow anything else, while the exposed situation would
expose them to the burning sun of summer and the fierce blasts of winter. The region thus early passed by presented a beautiful picture of the
splendor and bounty of untrammeled nature. Unlike the great prairies
of the Northwest, there was great variety in the configuration of the surface. Beautiful springs of unfailing water gave rise to small rivulets,

which, uniting, formed branches of creeks, the banks of which were skirted by more or less extended groves. The more open places between streams had been kept clear by the fires kindled by the Indians so long as they were lords of the soil, but as their power waned hazel bushes made their appearance in great numbers, interspersed with sumac and timber saplings. There were long stretches where the sward, radiant with flowers and fruitful with a mass of wild strawberries, lay unbroken for miles. So prodigal was nature with these unappreciated bounties that the odors were wafted on the breeze for miles, while the cows came home at the milking hour with white legs stained a blood red by the berries crushed in their wanderings. Vast herds of deer bounded leisurely over the gently rolling meadows; great flocks of wild turkeys in their panoply of glittering green and blue plumage were met in every direction, and thousands of " barren hens " (similar to if not identical with the "prairie chicken ") and quail could be had for the taking. Nor was there any remarkable dearth of timber, as in some of the early prairies of the Northwest. The region from Little River (Hopkinsville) to the Whippoorwill (Russellville) was devoid of timber save along the margin of the streams. The trace which connected these two points led along the open ground, and but one grove was to be found near it. This was a noted landmark known as Croghan's Grove, on the west branch of the West Fork of Red River. It was a military survey of 2,600 acres, heavily timbered and untouched by the ax. It belonged to Maj. Croghan of the Virginia Line. It has since been demonstrated that it needed only that the obstacles to the growth of timber should be removed to secure an ample supply. This fact, however, the experience of the pioneers furnished no means of discovering. In his sketches, Mr. Kennedy relates that :

" In an early day his father had business at Clarksville, and concluded to come through to John Harray's, now (1875) John Holland's, who formerly had lived with him in Upper Kentucky. On his way through the barrens, he called at Maj. Moore's to get his breakfast and horse fed. In conversation, Mr. Kennedy spoke of settling in this country, when the Major offered to give him 200 acres of the choice barrens near Trenton, at *fifty cents* per acre, and offered him 200 acres for the horse he was riding, but Kennedy refused, saying he did not wish to starve or freeze for want of fire, or timber for building or fencing purposes, so he afterward came to where I now live and bought land at $4 per acre." The pioneers were undoubtedly less foolish than would seem at first glance to-day. More fencing was done than was absolutely necessary, and the kind in vogue, the old Virginia worm fence, was not the most economical kind, but some fencing was absolutely necessary, and in those days of limited cash and more limited markets, the purchase of timber was not to be seriously thought of.

The Start in a New Country.—The first settlements were made in the timber, and the first step toward the establishment of a home was to clear a patch for corn and potatoes and plant a crop. The timber thus removed furnished material for the cabin and fences, which were then constructed. The earliest settlers generally brought their families to some strong station, and then, equipped with an ax, rifle, frying-pan and a small stock of salt and meal, the father would set out on a prospecting tour to be gone, frequently, for several months. Before his return he often made the first necessary clearing and erected a temporary hut to receive his family. Later, as cabins were found more frequently in the country, the immigrant had no hesitation in breaking up his home in a distant State, and with his family and household goods on wagons or pack animals start out for a new home, influenced and guided solely by rumors and picked-up information on the road. Deciding upon a locality for his future home, he found no difficulty in securing temporary shelter for his family in some cabin already well filled by its owners, but which the simplicity of early manners and an unstinted hospitality rendered elastic enough to comfortably entertain the welcomed addition to the community. A new arrival of this nature was heralded with welcome for miles about and a neighborhood which scarcely knew limits hastened to lend its friendly offices in rearing a house. A day was appointed, and no invitation was needed to draw together a company of willing, capable hands. To assist in raising a cabin for a new family was a duty which the unwritten law of the community imperatively laid upon every able-bodied man, and to know of the occasion was a sufficient invitation. On gathering, one party was told off as choppers, whose business it was to fell the trees and cut logs of proper dimensions; a man and team brought these logs to the site of the proposed building; others assorted, "saddled" and otherwise prepared the logs to form the structure, which was finished on one day and occupied on the next. The desires of the pioneer family were few and its necessities still less, so that the first efforts of the farmer were generally directed to the securing of food and shelter for his family. To this end nature gave her kindly aid. The pioneer brought with him his team and cows, the latter very frequently bearing in a pack a share of the family effects. Hogs were brought in, or were easily purchased from other settlers, and these animals found food and shelter in the barrens and timber with scarcely any care from the farmer. With one crop secured, there was no real danger of hunger. A mill was early built on Elk Fork, where the corn was converted into meal, or the wheat, when raised, converted into a coarse kind of flour. "Hog and hominy" was the general fare, though game and wild fruits and honey added a delicacy to the frontier feast which is scarcely surpassed to-day. The early farmer looked to the appreciation in the value of his land for his first profit, and in the absence of a market had little incentive to raising larger crops than the comfort of his family demanded. Clearing was the main end of his activities, but this gave him plenty of leisure for hunting which was generally fully improved. The early Kentuckian was bred to the use of the rifle and the pleasures of the chase, and considerable time was devoted to this pursuit by all, though all kinds of game were at first so abundant and unscared that it robbed the pleasure of much of its zest. Mr. Kennedy relates that in May, 1810, he and an old black woman, Margot, were working in a corn-field when they were attracted by a plaintive bleating in the adjoining bushes. " I said ' I must see what it was,' " he writes, "but she remonstrated, saying it might be very dangerous, but if I *must* go she would accompany me. Armed with our weeding hoes, we cautiously advanced through the barren grass and weeds, and discovered a beautiful fawn. It saw me almost at the same moment, and in its half-starved condition it staggered with all its capable speed up to me. Margot alarmed, cried out in fear and ran, but I gathered it up in my arms and brought it to the field. We took it to the house, gave it milk and reared it for some time, but eventually killed it by overfeeding. Some two weeks after the death of my fawn, I was sent to mill with a sack of corn. As I was jogging along on an old horse we called Blennerhassett, I discovered the head and neck of a deer above the grass. I stopped old Blenner, and while looking at it, I saw it sink gradually down and hide in the grass and weeds. Keeping my eyes closely on the spot, I rode cautiously along thinking I might find another fawn. When within twenty yards of the spot, the deer dashed off, but I rode on, and under a small crab-apple bush I discovered not ten feet away, quite a young fawn crouched upon the ground and perfectly still. I stopped old Blenner, rose to my feet on the sack of meal and sprang at full length upon the little creature, seizing it firmly with both hands. Alarmed lest its cries would call its mother back to its defense, I seized it by the hind legs, placed it over the horse and scrambling on after it, took it home. We reared it to a fine deer which was the pride and delight of our home." Another incident of raising a fawn is so remarkable, and at the same time so well vouched for, that it is worth recording : Messrs. Kennedy and Mann went one day to the Clay Lick on the Greenville road, which was a famous resort for game, to shoot a deer. A fine doe was soon secured, but on Mann's cutting its throat to bleed the animal, he discovered she was with young. With his hunting knife he quickly released a living fawn which struggled and rolled upon the grass. Carefully wrapping it up it was conveyed to Mr. Mann's cabin, where his wife fed it and put it in a hamper of picked wool. About daylight the next morning it jumped out of the basket and ran over the house bleating until it was fed again. This animal was kept two years and became a fine buck, but was accidentally run down and killed by a neighbor's hound.

Early Hunting in Todd.*—" After our West Fork country became somewhat densely settled, and the game became rather scarce, we branched out to the north part of Todd on the head waters of Pond River and Clifty, to hunt. On the Greenville road there were no settlements from Sears' to Shuffield's near the Muhlenburg line. This part of Todd was then heavily timbered and interspersed with hills, and many deep bottoms between the yawning cliffs. There had been some small settlements and cabins in an earlier time, but were nearly all deserted at the time of which I write. The first camp hunt in 1827 was made by John Petree, James Snaden, John Willis, J. Walker and myself. Snaden had a small mule called 'Jeff,' and he was geared to a cart in which we stowed our provisions and started along the Greenville road; you would have been diverted to have seen us climb the hills. Jeff was a good mule, but he was overloaded, and when he couldn't make the hill, we would alight from our horses and push the cart to the top of the hill; we were all stout and hearty and enjoyed the sport of helping Jeff with his load.

" Well, we got as far as, now Bivinsville, or as it is called, Lickskillet. Near the spring, Howell Edwards had built a cabin which he afterward sold to John Bivin; this cabin was unoccupied, and we lodged in it and hunted three or four days. All of us were strangers to that region, and only knew what I had learned by surveying and locating the vacant lands in that wilderness. My old friend, Capt. William Hopper, came to us and told us about the stands and crossing of the game which we found to be plentiful. We killed seven deer and several wild turkeys, and returned home greatly elated with our success. We had a neighborhood clan of hunters, and we organized and went every fall, and spent some ten days, sometimes twice in the same fall. Hazel Petrie, James Snaden, Nat Burrus, Reuben Ellison, John Petree and myself were the main hands, and after a few years others would join our hunts, to wit: Joe and John Gordon and their sons, John A. Bailey, Allen and Thomas Bailey, James Claggett and Uncle Johnny Christian would cross the cliffs when he heard our horns and hounds, and stay with us while we stayed. We would load our wagons with corn and fodder, boiled ham, and fat middling, for broiling, plenty of bread, sugar and coffee, cheese, etc. We took a boy with us to cook and take care of our camp in our absence. We went further down the ridge than at first, to an old cabin called the Rainwater's Cabin, where James Greenfield now resides. Our nearest neighbors

---

*Urban Kennedy's sketches.

were James and Williamson Chappell, some two or three miles distant. We had a joyful, pleasant time of it; we would sleep with our feet to the fire, and we enjoyed good health ; our rustic manner of living added to our health and spirits, and we never got sick. If any of us left home a little puny or complaining, we always returned hale and hearty ; we generally stayed eight or ten days. When Sabbath came we kept it as at home : tied up our hounds and never fired a gun, but read our Bibles and rested from our hunts. All were religious, and all Methodists (of the first named party) except myself and Col. Burrus; he was a Campbellite, and said he gloried in the name, and I was a Cumberland. Sometimes at night, or on Sabbaths, we would join issue on religious subjects, but always in a good-humored, Christian spirit. We generally had a jug of good whisky, and would all partake in the morning, or when we came in weary at night, except old brother H. Petrie, ' who was always down on us for drinking drams.' I recollect one of his cuts he made at us as we were taking our morning dram ; turning to me, he said : ' Urban, how many drams like that would make you drunk ?' ' Well,' I answered, ' Hazel, I suppose about four would make me tight.' ' Well, now,' said he, ' you are now one-fourth drunk.' The argument was new, and I have often thought of it.

" We had a good high time of it ; killed about eighteen fine fat deer, and would roast and broil the fat ribs, melts and livers. Oh ! it was fine. We killed many fine, fat turkeys, dried their wings for fans, and salted the meat to take home to our wives and children, for wild turkey is greatly preferable to tame. Some of us were in favor of taking a still hunt in the morning, but Brothers Petrie, Snaden and Burrus were opposed to it. Well, one morning about daylight, John Petree, Reuben Ellison and myself took our guns and started for a still hunt. I had a good shot-gun, John Petree, a good rifle, R. Ellison carried two guns, one of which was a most excellent shot-gun, borrowed from Col. R. E. Glenn ; its name was Niggerlegs ; the other a large smooth bore that carried an ounce ball. All of our guns were single barreled, and had flint locks. We proceeded to slip cautiously along about 150 yards apart, all abreast. After having gone about a mile, John Petree killed a very fat doe, which we hung up near where Sam McGehee now lives, and then started back towards camp, Petree on the edge or bench of the cliffs, Reuben Ellison 150 yards from him, and I about the same distance outside, all moving on cautiously abreast. As I was passing through a small sumac thicket, I saw a remarkably large buck with ten points on each beam, come tilting right to meet me, and was within thirty yards of me. I threw my gun up and hallooed, ' Where are you going ?' He turned to my left, and at about the fourth jump I fired at his head and neck, thinking to down him right there, but when the gun fired he stopped still and stuck his head forward, but never looked round at me nôr moved a foot or tail. I then tried to load my gun, but was so excited I couldn't find my ammunition, and couldn't take my eyes off of the big buck. I forgot my comrades, but soon heard the bushes cracking. I looked round, and there came Ellison with his two guns. He said, ' Urban, what did you shoot at ?' I beckoned him to come to me, silently, and when he got close up to me, I pointed to the buck. He whispered, 'I'll throw him.' I squatted down and told him to shoot over me. He raised his ounce-ball ' Fritz,' and fired at his heart. I had nothing to do but watch the shot, and when Fritz went off I saw the bullet hole in his side, that looked like I could have put my fist through it, but he never shook his tail nor winked his eye, nor moved his ear. Reuben looked astonished, and said, ' Urban, what on yearth ? ' Said I, 'Reuben, give him Niggerlegs,' and so he put seventeen buckshot right through the same place, and yet he never moved or winked his eye. Reuben said again, ' That beats all on yearth.' Well, here came John Petree, asking, ' What have you been shooting at ?' We pointed to the buck, still standing. ' Well,' said John, 'I can throw him,' and stepping forward he took aim at his eye, and his priming having got damp, his rifle flashed, and at the same moment down came the buck. On examination I found I had shot a hole through his ear, and that several shots had struck his horns, and one had gone under the burr of his horn. The bullet had gone through his heart, and with all this he stood upright for some time. Science may explain it, but I cannot."

In addition to the food game, black bear, panthers, wild cats and wolves were quite numerous in the county. They were a great annoyance to the early farmers. Calves, pigs and sheep were destroyed, unless protected, and were only preserved by the greatest care. Unsparing war was made upon them from the first, and nothing of the kind, save wild cats and foxes have been seen here since about 1827.

The Cabin.—The log-cabin was the universal residence for years. But there are distinctions even in this simple class of structures, and the majority of those found here were of the better sort. While the larger number of the first settlers were not wealthy for even that day, there were some that were well-to-do, and there was manifested a disposition to secure all the comforts to be had at the cost of labor simply. The cabins therefore were as neat and comfortable as the rude carpentery and materials at hand would afford. The roof was made of clapboards; boards were supplied by splitting a piece of straight-grained timber with a froe. These were about four feet long, as wide as the timber would admit, and used indoors and elsewhere without further dressing. Puncheons, split trees of about eighteen inches diameter, and smoothed upon the upper surface with a broad-ax, supplied the floor. The furniture was generally made from the same material and fashioned with an ax. A split slab supported by four legs did duty as a table; three-legged stools took the place of chairs, while the bedstead was made to go upon one leg. At a proper distance from the side of the cabin, adjacent to a corner, a single fork was placed with the lower end in a hole in the floor and the upper end fastened to a joist. Resting on this fork, and projecting at right angles to each other, were two poles, the other end of which found support upon the logs of two sides of the building. Upon this support was placed the foundation of the bed, which was really a fixture of the house. Thoughtful housewives brought with them the cord and tick. The latter was filled with dry leaves until the first corn crop furnished a better substitute in the husks. A few pegs on which to hang the limited spare clothing, and a buck-horn on which to hang the rifle, completed the wood-work of a frontier home. The fire-place was a large affair, and the cabin was sometimes so arranged that a log could be dragged in by a mule and rolled into its capacious jaws as a back-log. The lower part was constructed of stone, and above this a chimney of " cat and clay " reached to the height of the ridge of the cabin. This was the average dwelling until the manufacture of brick and lumber made more convenient houses possible. There were a few cabins which were quite pretentious, and one of these had the first shingle roof in the county. It belonged to Adams, who sold out to Kennedy in 1809, and is thus described by the latter : "Adams was a thrifty, industrious man, and said to my father, ' I gad, I thought I would build the best and finest house in all this country!' It was constructed of large, hewed white oak logs, twenty-four feet long by eighteen feet wide, covered with black walnut shingles rounded at the butt end, and every one put on with walnut pegs, bored through shingles and lath with a brace and bit. It was a good roof, and lasted about thirty years. Then the lower and upper floors were laid with poplar planks sawed by hand with a whip-saw, nicely dressed, tongued and grooved, and put down with pegs. Three windows two feet square, with nice shutters but not a pane of glass, nor a nail in all the house save in the three doors. For these a few nails were made by a blacksmith, his brother, Andy Adams. The chimneys were of stone, the first in the country, and contained at least 150 wagon-loads of rock. The fire-places were six feet wide, with wooden mantel-pieces."

The frontier cabin was the scene of busy activity. House-keeping was crowded into the smallest possible space to give place to the spinning-wheel and loom. Every woman took pride in such useful accomplishments as were involved in the preparation of the crude material, the manufacture of the fabric, and the fashioning of the wearing apparel of the whole family. The dress of the settlers was generally of primitive simplicity. The hunting shirt was worn universally. This costume was peculiarly adapted to the pursuits and habits of the people, and has been connected with so many thrilling passages of war and wild adventure that the Kentucky hunting shirt is famous throughout the world. This was usually made of linsey, sometimes of coarse linen, and a few of dressed deer-skin. The bosom of the dress was fashioned to form a wallet, to hold a piece of bread, cakes, jerk, tow for wiping the barrel of the gun, and any other necessary for the hunter or warrior. The belt, which was always tied behind, answered several purposes besides that of holding the dress together. In cold weather the mittens and sometimes the bullet bag occupied the front part of it. To the right side was suspended the tomahawk, and to the left the scalping-knife in its leathern sheath. A pair of drawers, or breeches and leggins, were the dress of the thighs and legs, and a pair of moccasins answered for the feet. Hats were made of the native fur. The dress of the women consisted of linen and linsey-woolsey. An overshadowing sun bonnet of linen, neatly washed and ironed, and a check made of the heavier material furnished the dress. This, with a pair of heavy cowhide shoes, made the lady's outfit for the most showy occasion.

With the increase of settlements, about 1811, society began to show some efforts to supersede this primitive style, and calico and broadcloth began to be seen more frequently. In 1820 it was not unusual to see on court days or special occasions considerable of the old magnificence of dress, as there were quite a number in the county who possessed considerable wealth. As described by Mr. Kennedy, " the garb of the sages, the ministers and the representative community, particularly at church on high days, were first, a fine cloth or velvet coat, cut round-breasted, with long or swallow tail; large, gilt buttons on both sides, set from the collar to the waist; then a vest, if for winter of swan's down, if for summer, beautiful white marseilles, with small gilt buttons; then, what we call pants, were 'breeches,' made for winter of cloth or velvet or corduroy; nankeen or home-made flax for summer, reaching down from the waist to the knee, at which point a cloth band reaching around close below the knee, with a silver buckle on the outside of each knee; then a long stocking, of worsted for winter, and silk or home-knit fleece for summer, the knee-band buckled tight around the top instead of a garter; then a pair of shoes with silver buckles on the outside of the instep. A white and black stock with a silver buckle took the place of a cravat. The hat was black, of fur or mixture of lamb's wool and fur, with very large brim, and if worn by an officer or man of distinction the brim was cocked with a silver boss to fasten it to the owner. If not disposed to dress in the above style, they wore what we call pants, but were then called 'overalls.' If they wore boots, which was rare, they were long to the knee, with a scallop in the front top with a silk tassel hanging down some three inches; these were known as 'fair-tops,' a nice piece of very fair leather. I forgot to speak of the finishing touch. Nearly all that could sported a queue. The back hair was suffered to grow long; this they wrapped up like a pig-tail, bound round with blue or pink ribbon with a double bow-knot; and if the hair was not long enough, some false hair was nicely spliced to the stub, and I have seem them reach down to the waist. The ladies of the same grade of society were less elaborate. A few silk gowns, bombazet and ginghams—often homespun—with what was then called a 'spencer,' was the in-door dress. Their hats or bonnets were of straw or silk, moderately trimmed. The gown was not so long as to hide a pair of nice shoes and buckles, and fine silk or thread stockings."

Amusements.—The early sports were allied to useful occupations. Quiltings, wool-pickings and spinning-bees were made up by the women, when the afternoon was given to work and the night to games, the young men coming in to share the entertainment and escort the girls home. House-raisings, log-rollings and husking-bees were occasions when the men after a hard day's work would spend the evening with the young women invited in. As society developed, however, the times showed "smart signs of wickedness" in place of these earlier amusements. Horse racing, shooting matches, raffling and dancing came in to disturb the staid people of the community, and intoxicate the young and giddy. Dancing had formed a part of the amusements at social gatherings, but then the jig danced by a gentleman and lady, the four and eight-hand reel and the horn pipe had prevailed. But when the cotillion and waltz came upon the floor it brought out the strongest disapproval. In the fall and winter of 1811 Armstrong Bailey, Jesse Irvine and Farrow White, all from near the present site of Daysville, came in company with a dancing master, and made up a dancing school at John Harvey's. This dancing accomplishment took the fancy of the young people and soon became the gossip of the neighborhood. Several of the young church members were enticed by a desire to improve their steps, a circumstance which precipitated the storm of opposition that had been slowly gathering. Rev. Finis Ewing and Ephraim McLean as ministers, and Thomas Bryan and William Downey waited on Harvey and the dancing party, and begged them to desist. But Harvey and his guests laughed at the idea, and quoted the example of David and the Old Testament saints. The dancing proceeded, and it is said even church members would go and look on with evident pleasure. Things went merrily on for several weeks, when —— the earthquake came, and that put an end to the dancing.

Courtship and Marriage.—Attending church had other merits to the young gallants of long ago than vigorous preaching. It was quite the thing if a young man had the means to escort his lady to church on horse back. The less fortunate walked and then " went home " with his girl after services. On such occasions it was no uncommon thing after getting out of sight of the church for the young lady to remove her morocco slippers and fine stockings and walk home with her escort barefooted. If Kennedy is to be trusted " the general custom was to see your sweetheart at night, take your seat by her and embrace her in your arms, with many kisses, sometimes reciprocated ; take her on your lap, with your arms wound around each other in all innocence and virtue." In describing an instance, when with a friend he put this theory in practice, Kennedy relates the story as follows : " Well, Henry took his girl to one corner and I the other one in the remote opposite corner. We sat down as close as we could, and Henry laid off his fine beaver (which cost $12) carefully in the corner near the wall, and happened to set it very plumb in the skillet in which they had fried meat for supper. It was quite dark in the house, the little fire had gone out, so we enjoyed ourselves until the small hours of the night. I proposed that we leave, and Henry, seizing his hat by the brim, raised with it the skillet and all. The gravy, a half inch deep, had cooled enough to stick tight. He soon discovered the situation, and the poor girls were greatly mortified. They got a little stump of a tallow dip, and with a case knife we scraped it all we could. We were not in the habit of swearing, but Henry said he could not do the subject justice without some profanity."

The early settlers generally married young. There was no distinction of rank and but little of fortune ; a bachelor was a helpless body as a pioneer, and a family establishment cost little more than labor to provide. These early weddings were picturesque affairs, as described by one who witnessed many of them. " In the morning of the wedding-day the groom and his attendants assembled at the house of his father for the purpose of proceeding to the home of his bride, which it was desirable to reach by noon, the usual time of celebrating the nuptials, which ceremony must at all events take place before dinner. On approaching within a mile of the house two young men would single out to run for the bottle, which, well filled with whisky, was in waiting for the successful competitor at the end of the race. The more difficult the path the better, as obstacles afforded an opportunity for the greater display of intrepidity. Returning to the company the victor distributed the contents to the company. After the marriage ceremony the whole company proceeded to dinner, which consisted of beef, pork, fowls, game and vegetables. After dinner the dancing began, which continued until late at night or till morning. About

9 or 10 o'clock a deputation of ladies stole off the bride and put her to bed. This done, a deputation of young men in like manner led off the groom and placed him snugly by the side of his bride. The dance still continued, and if seats happened to be scarce every young man, when not engaged in the dance, was obliged to offer his lap as a seat for one of the girls, and the offer was sure to be accepted. In the midst of this hilarity the bride and groom were not forgotten. Pretty late in the night some one would remind the company that the new couple must be in need of some refreshments; 'Black Betty'—the name of the bottle containing whisky—was called for and sent up-stairs, but generally it went well attended. Sometimes as much of the substantial edibles of the dinner as would suffice for a half-dozen working men would be sent also, and the new couple were obliged to partake of both. The marriage over, the same company took a lively interest in seeing the newly-married pair well settled. A site was chosen on the property of one of the parents, and if not already built a cabin was put up, and when ready for occupation, the house-warming gave occasion for another merry-making, with dancing continued far into the night." But these pioneer scenes, with their simple-hearted actors, their homely joys, their trials and their achievements have passed away " as a tale that is told." The changes which have concurred to make the advancement of the present are not unmixed with evil, and the few who remain as connecting links between that day and this may well be pardoned the

" Sigh for the grace of a day that is dead."

CHAPTER IV.

POLITICAL DEVELOPMENT—LOCATION OF THE COUNTY SEAT—FIRST SESSION OF THE MAGISTERIAL COURT—DISTRICT LEGISLATION—PUBLIC BUILDINGS—CARE OF PAUPERS—EARLY COURTS AND BAR—CHARACTER OF EARLY PRACTICE—THE KNIGHT OF THE NINETEENTH CENTURY.

THE final act of State authority in forming and organizing Todd County was the location of the seat of justice. Several points, Newburg, Old Elkton and the present site were in competition for the location. The competition was not very active, and there was but little difference in the advantages offered. At Newburg, James Kendall had established a hotel, the " half way house" between Russellville and Hopkinsville, and proposed this location as the most central point eligible for the county seat. Old Elkton had the merit of a good start on the banks of the river, but the new site satisfactorily combined the advantages of the others and added the donation of John Gray. The result was inevitable, and on the second day of the first session of the County Court, the State Commissioners appointed for the purpose made the following report:

To THE HONORABLE THE COUNTY COURT OF TODD COUNTY:

We the undersigned Commissioners, appointed by an act of the General Assembly of the Commonwealth of Kentucky, entitled " An Act for the formation of the County of Todd, out of the Counties of Logan and Christian," approved 30th of December, 1819, beg leave to submit the following report: Having in pursuance of the aforesaid act met at the house of James Kendall, on the second Monday in May, 1820, and proceeded to the discharge of the duties assigned us—after a mature and deliberate examination of the different places proposed as sites for the administration of justice at and near the center of said county; we are unanimously of the opinion that the two acres of land laid off and known as a public square in John Gray's addition to the town of Elkton, in said county, is the most central and eligible and convenient place for the permanent seat of justice for said county. We are therefore of opinion that the permanent seat of justice be fixed on the aforesaid two acres of land which said Gray has this day obligated himself to convey to the court for the use of the county aforesaid, together with other lots for public purposes, which bond is herewith subjoined as part of this report. Given under our hands this 8th day of May, 1820.

DICKSON GIVEN.
THOMAS CHAMPION.
LEANDER I. SHARP.
WILLIAM THOMPSON.
BENJAMIN NANCE.

Gray's bond subjoined was as follows:

I, John Gray, hereby bind myself, my heirs, etc., to the Commissioners appointed by law to fix upon the place for the seat of justice for the County of Todd, and to the justices of the County Court of said county and their successors in office, to make a donation to said County Court for the benefit of said county and sole purpose of erecting the public county buildings thereupon, the public square containing at least two acres of land inclusive of streets and alleys thereupon exhibited, and contained and exhibited upon the within plan for a town circumjacent thereto, which square is on the main road from Russellville to Hopkinsville, on the top of the first eminence on said road west of Elkton, and is bounded as follows, to wit : beginning at the southwest corner of a large brick house lately built by said Gray, on the north side of the said road, and running thence north 1° east, 6 poles to a stake ; thence north 85° west, 18 poles to a stake ; thence south, 80° west, 16½ poles to a stake ; thence south 85° east, 21 poles to a stake ; thence north 1° east, binding on A. Edward's brick house, and crossed said road to the beginning : *Provided*, said Commissioners fix upon that as the most central, convenient and eligible place for a permanent seat of justice for said county ; and I also hereby bind myself as aforesaid to make a donation of two other lots in some suitable and convenient places, one for jail and stray pen to be erected upon, and the other for a public seminary of learning and a public meeting-house or church to be erected upon. Given under my hand and seal, this 8th day of May, 1820.

JOHN GRAY.

Accompanying this was a bond by John Gray and Robert T. Baylor, as follows :

This is to certify that we, John Gray and Robert T. Baylor, bind and oblige ourselves, our heirs etc., to the County Court of Todd County or to any other person who may be aggrieved thereby, in the penal sum of $2,000 to open or cause to be opened, in case the Commissioners should fix on Elkton as the permanent seat of justice for Todd County, a road or lane to run southwardly straight with the main cross street from what is known as the public square on the top of the first eminence above Elkton as wide as the said street is, through each of our farms; and I, Robert T. Baylor, hereby agree and bind myself to let a road pass through the balance of my land in same direction. Given under our hands and seals, this 9th day of May, 1820. The above all to be done between this and the 1st day of October next.

JOHN GRAY.
ROBERT T. BAYLOR.

On May 8, 1820, pursuant to the act of the General Assembly forming the county, James Glenn, Robert Coleman, Henry Gorin, Edward Shanklin, John Taylor, H. C. Ewing, John S. Anderson, William Hopper, John Mann, John Gray and Joseph C. Frazer, met at the house of James Kendall and organized the first magisterial court of Todd County. Anthony F. Reade presented the Governor's commission as Sheriff and was qualified, and James Allen as Coroner. There were two candidates for the position of Clerk, and a spirited contest ensued. Elisha B. Edwards was finally elected over Willis L. Reeves by a majority of one vote. Nathaniel Burns and James L. Glenn were then recommended to the Governor as competent surveyors, and the first day's session brought to an end. The report of the State Commissioners was laid before the court on the second day, and a sort of "omnibus bill" passed which provided for the complete equipment of the county. The record is as fol-

lows: The Commissioners appointed by the act of Assembly for the formation of Todd County to fix upon a proper or eligible site in said county to erect the seat of justice upon, appeared and delivered their report,
etc., which report was read and ordered to be recorded, in which report
were enclosed and referred two bonds, one of which given by John Gray,
and the other by John Gray and Robert T. Baylor, which were also read
and approved and ordered to be recorded. Sheriff objects that there is
no jail in the county. The Court proceeded to appoint Archibald Bristow, Roger Burns, Thomas Haddon, Elisha Edwards and Gideon Thompson, Commissioners, who, or any three of them, are hereby authorized,
empowered and requested to make out and exhibit a plan for a brick court
house, not exceeding 40 feet square and two stories high, upon such part
of the public square as fixed upon by the report of the Commissioners
appointed by law for that purpose as they may deem most suitable; and
that they proceed as soon as possible to conclude a contract with John
Gray for the brick work thereof, which he has proposed to obligate and
bind himself to complete in the present year, as a donation to said county;
and that they proceed also to let out to the lowest bidder the carpenter's
and joiner's work necessary in the progress of the brick-work and to
cover and close the same with all necessary doors, windows, etc., with a
square roof, planned and made suitable for a cupola hereafter to be erected, with a plain bench and bar, etc. Said Commissioners are also hereby
authorized and requested to proceed as soon as possible to let to the lowest bidder a jail of hewed logs, at least 15 feet square in the clear, with
double walls filled in between with flat rocks, the loft and floor of hewed
logs, to be built on a bed of rocks 18 inches thick, and the loft filled with
rocks, and clapboard roof, strong doors well locked and bolted, iron grate
windows, etc. Also a stray pen of posts and rails upon the lot they and
said Gray may designate as mentioned in his donation bond for that purpose; which said carpenter's and joiner's work of the court house, jail
and stray pen are to be paid for, one-half out of the first, and the balance
out of the second county levy to be laid for said county, unless the amount
necessary for the purpose, or part thereof, can be sooner raised by voluntary subscription, which said Commissioners are hereby requested to open
for that purpose, the first to be applied toward paying for the carpenter's
and joiner's work of the court house. The court then proceeded to lay
off four constable districts. The county had heretofore been divided into
one district, with a voting precinct at Cash's store, under the jurisdiction
of Christian County, and the eastern portion, belonging to Logan, forming a part of two districts of that county. At the first session of the
Todd County Court, therefore, this territory was entirely re-districted and
made four divisions, as follows: *First District*, beginning at the State line

at the corner of Todd and Logan Counties, thence with said Logan line northerly to the road leading from Russellville to Clarksville; thence with said road to the crossing of Elk Fork; thence westerly to Henry Mabens, Arch Coulter, John Stephenson and John D. Gorin's; thence to the Lebanon Academy and Robert Coleman's mill, leaving each of those persons and places in the Second District; thence with the Hopkinsville road to the Christian County line; thence with said line to the Tennessee State line and with that to the beginning. The *Second District*, beginning at the Logan and Todd County line where it crosses the Clarksville road from Russellville; thence with said line to the Russellville and Hopkinsville road; thence with said road to the Christian line; thence with said line to the corner of the First District; thence with the line thereof to the beginning. The *Third District*, beginning at the sign post near the brick house in Newburg, thence northerly with the road to John Gray's saw-mill on the Elk Fork; thence up said fork to John Young's; thence with the road to John Higgins' storehouse in Raysville; thence a straight line to Hopper's tan-yard; thence a straight line to William Weir's on the Muhlenburg line, leaving all said persons and places in the Fourth District; thence with the Muhlenburg line to the corner of Todd and Logan Counties; thence with the line between said counties to the Hopkinsville and Russellville road; thence with said road to the beginning. The *Fourth District*, beginning at the sign post near the brick house in Newburg, thence northerly with the line of the third district to the Muhlenburg County line; thence westerly with the line of Muhlenburg and Todd Counties to the corner of Todd and Christian Counties; thence southerly with the line of said counties to the Russellville and Hopkinsville road; thence with said road to the beginning.

William M. Terry was appointed Constable of the First District, John D. Gorin of the Second, Jephtha Hollingsworth of the Third, and John H. Shankle of the Fourth. In August, 1820, a *Fifth District* was formed, its boundaries beginning on the Highland Lick road, where the Logan County line crosses it; thence with said road to the Christian County line; thence with said county line to the Muhlenburg County line; thence with said line to the Logan County line; thence to the beginning. In August, 1823, the *Sixth District* was formed, but in 1845 it was changed with the following boundaries: Beginning on the road leading from Elkton to Hadensville at John Prewett's; thence with said road to Hadensville; thence with the Russellville and Clarksville road to the State line; thence with the State line to the line between Logan and Todd Counties; thence with the said Todd and Logan Counties line to where it crosses the road leading from Russellville to Clarksville; thence with said road to where it crosses the Elk Fork at or near H. Muir's; thence on a straight line to the beginning, so as to include Judge Prewett. The *Seventh District* was formed in 1853, but no record of it can be found. It was subsequently changed in outline, and now occupies a triangular space between Districts No. 1 and No. 2, with its voting precinct at Bivinsville. The *Eighth District* was formed in March, 1872. The record is as follows: "Upon petition of a large number of the good citizens, residents of the lower part of District No. 6, in Todd Co., Ky., it is ordered by the Court that an additional justice's district be and the same is hereby created out of District No. 6, to be known as District No. 8, and bounded as follows, to wit: Beginning at the Elk Fork of Red River, at the Kentucky and Tennessee line; thence up said Elk Fork of Red River to Duck Spring; thence to John Snaden's, including him; thence to R. L. and T. J. Smith; thence to the line of the Elkton District, at or near C. M. Lowry's, excluding him; thence with the line of the Elkton District to the Clarksville road, the east boundary line of Trenton District; thence with it to the beginning, and that Hadensville and Guthrie City be the voting places in the district hereby created." The Legislature of the winter 1883–84 passed a bill authorizing a re-districting of the county and the necessary survey. The provisions of this act it is proposed to carry out some time during the present year, when the number of districts will be cut down to seven. The "district" is a very indeterminate quantity in the history or business of the county. Under the second Constitution, framed in 1799, it was called a constable's district, and served generally to apportion the number of these officers. Magistrates were appointed by the Governor, the law requiring simply a "competent number." Under the Constitution of 1850 magistrates were elected from certain sections of the county, and since then these divisions of the county have been known as magisterial districts, the boundaries of which serve to define the jurisdiction of the single magistrate. They are in no way analogous to the townships of the North and Northwest, having no independent organization, and no political or social individuality. But few know where the division line is located, and indefinite as they were originally, they are rendered still more confusing by the ease with which they are varied to suit the convenience or whim of the individual. The County seat and the County Court are the centers of influence and of executive power, and the county revolves about it as the wheel about the hub: a centralized form of government which is utterly inconsistent with the spirit of Kentucky's famous resolutions of 1798.

Public Buildings.—The general description of the first court house is contained in the order of the County Court quoted on a preceding page. Maj. Gray undertook his part promptly, pushing it forward with great vigor. He made the brick on the public square, and completed it early in 1821. The finishing of the inside was delayed some time for lack of funds, and was not finally completed until September, 1822. The first story was devoted to the court, and the upper story to a large room which served the various purposes of jury room, Masonic lodge room, etc. The county officers kept their records where it was most convenient, the Clerk of the Court being allowed to "keep his office anywhere in the bounds of Elkton." In the latter part of 1822 it was ordered by the court that the building of a "brick clerk's office," on or near the southwest corner of the square, be let to the lowest bidder. The specifications required a building one story high, 20x40 feet in dimensions, with two chimneys, two doors, two windows in front and two in the back, a plank floor, and a door in the partition which divided the long room into two apartments. This building was accordingly erected on the site of E. Garth's store, and held all the county offices. With sundry repairs these buildings sufficed for the uses of the court and county until about 1835. The court house was inconvenient in many respects, a good many repairs were required, and the coviction that these difficulties could best be met by a new structure finally gained expression in an order of the court in November, 1834, providing for a new court house. By this order Finis E. McLean, John Bellamy, Hazel Petrie, Thompson M. Ewing and Willis L. Reeves were appointed Commissioners to contract, superintend and receive the new building. The present structure was the result. The old court house was torn down and the new structure erected upon its site. It was "built on honor." Each of the four sides was assigned to a workman of approved skill, and a premium offered to the one who should erect the best wall. All did well, as the walls now attest, but the builder of the west wall is said to have won the prize offered. As originally constructed the court room occupied the lower floor. The entrance was in the eastern side, which opened into a vestibule, from which the upper story was gained by means of the stairs still remaining, and the court room by a doorway leading directly west of the main entrance. Opposite the door on the west side of the room, in a niche, the back of which was formed by a large window, was situated the "bench," while immediately in front were the ordinary furniture and belongings of the "bar," divided from the auditorium by railing. On either side of the "bench," the corners were partitioned off to serve as petit jury rooms. The upper story was left in one large room for the use of the grand jury, the County Court, and public gatherings. In November, 1856, the Clerk's office building was ordered renewed. A new site was chosen, and the structure standing on the west side of the square, north of the Russellville and Hopkinsville road, was erected. It was not built, however, until 1860, and cost the county some $2,000. During the four years following, the vicissitudes of war bore heavily upon the court house. Soldiers were frequently quartered in it, and by 1865 it was in a rather dilapidated condition. It was declared unfit for the use of the court, which held its sessions in the Masonic lodge building. Some repairs were made, but in 1871, the subject of repairs again came up, and an agitation for a more economical use of the capacity of the building, as well as a more convenient location of the county offices, was begun. It was accordingly decided to thoroughly repair the court house, and unite the offices and court room in one building, if it could be done for the sum realized from the sale of the "Clerk's office." This was found to be practicable. The court room with its old arrangement intact was transferred to the upper story; a hall was extended through the lower story from east to west, and another entrance made at the west end, and a series of office rooms made on either side of the hall. A new cupola was placed upon the structure, and neat furniture placed in the rooms, the whole cost being met by the proceeds of the sale of the outside office building. The structure is now reasonably convenient and neat. It lacks, however, an important feature which must sooner or later be supplied, i. e., fire-proof vaults for the official records. The building stands upon a slight eminence in the center of the village and commands a fine view of the four roads leading out from the public square to the four cardinal points. Its outer walls, though built nearly fifty years ago, scarcely betray the age of ten years, and bid fair to last for many years to come. It has no architectural beauty, and is only saved from a rather " squatty " appearance by an abnormally developed cupola placed upon the roof. A fastidious taste might demand something more of adornment in the surroundings of this temple of justice. Soon after the present structure was erected a plain board fence inclosed a small plat of ground circumjacent to the building, which was then sown with blue grass. The fence gradually wore out, and the green sward, attracting such stock as ran loose in the streets, presented a scene that aptly suggested the idea that justice had turned to agricultural pursuits. In 1841 the " enclosure " was paved, fenced again, and a little later a row of black locusts was planted to ornament the margin. This fence has long since disappeared, but the brick pavement, with its broken stone curbing and the locusts, still remains. The latter, " topped," and their lacerated trunks covered with a tuft of foliage like an ill-fitting wig on a bald head, are more useful as hitching posts and for sign boards, than ornamental as shade trees. The future has better things in store in this direction. A row of fine maples has been set out, which in the next quarter century will draw about the decaying building the shielding mantle of their delightful shade.

The Jail.—There is little of romance connected with this class of buildings anywhere, and none in Todd County. The victims whom its rude strength has sequestered from society have been the most prosaic sort of criminals, and nothing remains to the chronicler of its history, save that it was and is not. The old log jail was located on "Trading Alley," and was secure as any of its more pretentious successors. It was built according to the plan set forth in the order made at the first session of the court, and was finished in November, 1820. A "stray pen" was built near it and completed at the same time. This jail served the public until 1827, when a brick structure was erected on the same lot, but in front of the old jail. This still remains, the connecting link between the irrecoverable past and the later result of country architecture. The first brick jail was erected at a cost of $1,000, and like its predecessor "payed its way to obscurity." In 1869 the present brick jail was erected at a cost of $11,000, in the southern part of town, the contractor being W. A. McReynolds. This building is reasonably secure, is provided with improved fixtures and has been broken by few prisoners. Under the present Constitution the jailor is elected, and is remunerated by fees paid for the board and care of prisoners—those imprisoned on a charge of felony by the State, and those imprisoned on a charge for misdemeanors by the county. At times these fees have reached a very large sum, but the present official's lines seem to have been laid in ways of peace, and the fees for last quarter were only *three dollars and sixty cents.*

The Poor-House.—During the earlier years of the settlement of Todd County there was little need for any public provision for the support of indigent persons. All were poor, but the poor lived in abundance. A good and comfortable support was to be had for the seeking, and no drones were allowed in that early hive of workers. When misfortune in the guise of accident or disease visited the pioneer, there was no lack of willing hands to plow out the corn or harvest the crops free of charge. With the development of the community, however, social ties became relaxed, and the necessity of an older community demanded some other arrangement for the care of the unfortunate. In November, 1829, the establishment of a poor-house was projected, and in 1830 a hundred and fifty acres were purchased of George Kirkman, on which was a log-house. This has since been "weather-boarded," and sundry cabins built near it for the use of the residents of the farm. In 1856 it was proposed to sell the farm, but only about forty acres were disposed of and the farm, consisting of 110 acres, is still owned by the county. The number thus supported by the county has not been large, the present number being almost entirely made up of indigent blacks. At first the poor were maintained by some family in the neighborhood, for which the County Court appropriated a reasonable compensation. This method is still continued to some extent, especially in the case of the whites of this class. The cost of maintaining the poor-house is adjusted yearly by a contract with the keeper, who receives a stipulated price per week for the board and care of each pauper in his care. For the farm he pays a certain rental agreed upon. The first year the keeper received $143.50; this year the keeper receives the use of the farm free.

Courts and Bar.—Under the Constitution of 1799, there were three inferior courts, the Circuit Court, the County Court and the single Magistrate. The first was the same as at present, though in the scarcity of lawyers, the fashion was to travel the circuit, the Judge leading and the bar following as escort. Hopkinsville, Elkton, Russellville and Greenville were the principal points to which the practice of the time led the leading lawyers of the Todd County bar. The County Court was the great local arbiter of county interests, and was composed of a " competent number" of justices appointed from the county at large, and commissioned by the Governor of the State for good behavior. It was provided by law, however, that the Justice of the Peace longest in commission became *ex ipso facto* the Sheriff at the first vacancy. The official term of this officer was two years, so that at the expiration of this period the Justice of the Peace was once more relegated to the position of a " sovereign." The membership of the court was maintained by further appointments, which, while it was not actually for the term of good behavior, would in the natural order of things continue, after the first appointees were exhausted, some twenty-five years. As a matter of fact very few of the magistrates served as Sheriff, preferring to " farm out the office," as the phrase went. There were always those who were willing to pay from $800 to $1,000 for the position of deputy and the business and emoluments of the office, and this arrangement was almost invariably effected. Under the Constitution of 1850, all offices of the court and county were made elective, and the office of County Judge established. The single magistrate has jurisdiction of civil cases up to the value of $100, from whom an appeal can be taken either to the County Judge's Court or to the Circuit Court, where the value involved is $25 or more. The County Court now consists of a Judge who possesses the powers and jurisdiction of the old County Court, save in the matter of laying the county levy and passing upon claims against it. These matters come before the Court of Claims, composed of the two magistrates in each district, who assemble once a year to dispatch the business. The court of the County Judge is practically in session on every day save Sundays, though certain kinds of business must be done on regularly appointed court days. This officer holds two courts, one monthly for the discharge of business where the county is a party interested in the issue; the other, the Court of Quarterly Sessions, where the trial of all causes between citizens are had. This court has jurisdiction in matters of probate, in civil actions not exceeding $200, and has when the Circuit Court is not in session jurisdiction in cases of misdemeanors.

Todd County was first placed in the Seventh Judicial District, the first Circuit Court being held in 1820. Judge Ben Shackelford presided, and R. P. Henry attended as Commonwealth's Attorney. At this court Willis L. Reeves produced his commission, and was sworn in Clerk of the Circuit Court. He was a man noted no less for his ability than for his piety, was a Ruling Elder in the Cumberland Presbyterian Church, and remained in office until succeeded by Ben T. Perkins, Sr., under the present Constitution. The first term of court was held in what is now the " Nick and Will House," and the following grand jury, composed of some of the leading men of the community, was impaneled: William C. Davis, foreman ; Archibald Bristow, William B. Scott, Samuel Alley, John Kirk, John Fletcher, William Harlan, Wiley B. Jones, John Craften, George Clay, Thomas Allender, Thomas G. Greenfield, William Geartin, Thomas Hadden, William Parham, Green Rayburn, Alexander Gilmore, Bernard Edwards, William Crutchfield and James Kendall. But three presentments were the result of their deliberations, one for " suffering unlawful gaming and keeping a disorderly house," and three for " tippling," against three persons, two of whom were " surveyors of the roads." Judge Shackelford presided until April, 1822, when Henry P. Broadnax came to the bench, and a Mr. Macey was Commonwealth's Attorney. Broadnax continued until 1831, when the Hon. Asher W. Graham succeeded him. The latter was a man of marked uprightness, of no great intellect, but delighted in justice, kindness and mercy. Of the first two judges, Shackelford was a man of great firmness, and was moved from an opinion once formed with great difficulty. Broadnax was of rather skeptical notions, a self-important and somewhat aristocratic man, and quite eccentric. He was a wealthy old bachelor, a great advocate of temperance, and never suffered a drunken man to get out of the court house without paying a penalty or going to jail. He was also an outspoken Whig of the old line, and violently opposed to the Democracy of Gen. Jackson.

Urban Kennedy relates a story of him to the effect that at a very advanced age he concluded to seek the consolations of religion. " He had two friends, Uncles Billy Harris and Alexander Chapman, Cumberland Presbyterian ministers, who were his religious oracles. Under their advice he attended a camp-meeting a few miles southeast of Russellville. He set about the work in hand in good earnest, and when the anxious mourners were called up he walked into the altar and knelt at a seat in the straw, engaging in prayer. After the exercises had progressed awhile quite a young lad came into the light and was loud with happy shouting. The boy's attention was attracted to Judge Broadnax, and throwing himself down by the Judge began, with a tender hug, to instruct him in a noisy tirade. This was too much for the dignity of the man, and partially raising himself up he seized the boy by the arm with a shake and asked him if he had got religion. 'Yes, thank God, I know I have,' replied the boy. 'Then just get away from me and let me get it too,' said the Judge, as he released him with another shake. Immediately an Elder came who knelt down by the aged penitent and sought to instruct him. The Judge knew him, and raising up again asked the Elder if he did not carry on a distillery. The Elder replied that he did, whereupon the Judge gave him a shove, saying, that no man who manufactures that damnable stuff which is killing thousands, both in soul and body, should talk to him on a religious subject of so much moment as the present crisis. The Elder left, and the Judge called his two friends, Chapman and Harris, and asked them to go with him to the grove, saying that he could not get religion in such a state of confusion. So away they went by themselves. Kneeling down the ministers instructed their friend and prayed for him in alternation Finally, in the closing supplication Chapman prayed for converting power, that the poor old sinner who had spent all his life in sin might be converted, and added: 'Oh Lord, convert him now, and take him home from this sinful, distracting world to heaven!' To which the Judge responded, 'Amen; do, my good Lord, and that quickly, before Gen. Jackson is crowned King of the United States!'" The story does not relate the final result of all this effort.

The early bar of Todd County numbered among its members some of the most prominent members of the profession in this section of the State. Of the lawyers from Hopkinsville were Messrs. Sharp, Patton, Mayes and others; from Russellville were Hise, Macy and others; from Warren, J. R. Underwood, Henry Grider, and of later years W. V. Loring and W. L. Underwood. Of the Elkton bar some of the earlier members were J. M. Davidson, Thomas Johnson, W. W. Fry, Thomas M. Smith, Thomas W. Taylor, Charles S. Morehead, Cyrus Edwards, J. M. Strode, Burrus E. Pitman, Finis E. McLean, Francis M. Bristow, John Umblevany, Treadwell S. Ayres, Joseph A. Russell, Ninian E. Gray, William Landsdale, Benjamin T. Perkins, Sr., H. G. Petrie, H. G. Bibb, Samuel Kennedy, J. H. Lowry, G. Terry, etc. Of the earlier lawyers many left for a larger field after giving promise of some ability. Fry stayed here but a few years, when he left the State; Smith went to St. Louis, and subsequently published a volume of reminiscences, which was once found in many of the libraries here; Ayres went to Memphis and became prominent in legal circles. Finis McLean was one of the early bar who remained and gained both wealth and renown. He was a man of versatile talent, a fine debater and the great champion of the Whigs in this section. He was repeatedly pitted against the renowned Democratic speakers of the day, and never failed to bear off the laurels of the occasion. Before the court and jury he gained his cause with the same address, and for years was the leading member of the bar. He was elected to the lower house of the State Legislature in 1837, and would have been returned a second time had he pressed his claim, but he seemed to have satisfied his ambition in the single term. He was an earnest member of the church and a strict moralist in all his deportment, with a fatal exception. In later life he retired from the practice of his profession and turned his attention to farming, at which he seemed as prosperous as in his profession. He subsequently left the State, and a few years afterward died.

Succeeding him at the head of the profession here was F. M. Bristow. He came to the bar in 1826, after receiving a thorough education in the classics as well as English. He was well read in the law and rapidly acquired a large and lucrative practice. His great claim upon the respect and confidence of the people was the sterling uprightness of his character. This fact made him also a great power with a jury. Without eloquence or any attempt at rhetoric or meretricious accomplishment he became known as a great advocate. Before a jury he was always plausible and fair, and his earnestness did the rest. He was a lawyer of large resource, and while at first sight he was sometimes undervalued, he never failed to maintain the control of his case and rise equal to any emergency that presented itself. He " never failed," in the language of one who often met with him at the bar. Mr. Bristow was a great admirer of Burns, and it is said in a case where he was prosecuting certain patrollers for the unwarranted punishment of a negro, that he quoted " The Cotter's Saturday Night " in full to the jury, and with such effect that in spite of natural prejudices they gave his client a verdict. In the celebrated Lycurgus Leavell case, when some of the strongest legal talent of this part of the State was arrayed against him, and after several eloquent speeches the opposing counsel were confident they "had the jury," one of that counsel relates: " Bristow hung the jury with a quotation from St. Paul," and it may be added eventually won the case. Mr. Bristow was elected to the lower House of the Legislature in 1831 ; to the State Senate in 1846 ; as member of the Constitutional Convention in 1849 ; in 1853 was elected to Congress for the unexpired term of Presley Ewing ; and in 1859 was elected to the Thirty-sixth Congress. Few lawyers in southern Kentucky had more followers in his profession, several of the present bar having received their early legal instructions in his office. He died in 1864 at Elkton.

An early student in the office of Mr. Bristow was James A. Russell. He was admitted to the bar in 1837, and for two years was in partnership with his preceptor. He was a ready speaker and found ample opportunity to develop his natural gift of oratory. He was the stock speaker of this region, was repeatedly called upon to fill the appointment of some absent speaker, and no matter what the occasion, left no room for regret that the regular appointee had not been present. He represented the county in the Legislature during 1855–57, and is now serving his second term as Clerk of the Circuit Court. H. G. Bibb was a great little man; a man of small stature, but large natural ability. He came to Elkton without money or friends, his spare clothing in a handkerchief, and went at once into a tailor shop and learned the trade. In the meantime he borrowed law books and studied his profession, and was afterward admitted to the bar. With little culture, save what he found in his law books, he became a power in the county. He was elected in 1848 to the lower house of the State Legislature, and in 1851–55 to the State Senate. In 1854, John B. Thompson having resigned the office of Lieutenant-Governor, Bibb was on the ninth ballot elected Speaker of the Senate. His short but brilliant career was untimely closed by dissipation. Samuel Kennedy was another lawyer of this date; a man of strong will, great energy and power, and successful in his profession. He lacked the faculty of accumulating wealth, however, and died in 1880, with an inconsiderable portion of the property he earned in his practice. H. G. Petrie is the only one of the old bar in the active practice of his profession now. Deprived of liberal opportunities to study his profession, he borrowed legal text-books from Mr. Bristow's library and read them at night. In 1844 he came to Elkton from the country and entered the office of Mr. Bristow on salary, and in 1847 formed a partnership with his employer, which continued until the death of Mr. Bristow in 1864. The senior partner's political duties, and widely extended practice in other courts, gave Mr. Petrie an excellent opportunity to develop his ability in the practice of his profession, and on the death of his partner gave him the leading position at the Elkton bar, which he has since maintained. The members of the present bar are: H. G. Petrie, W. L. Reeves, G. Terry, B. T. Perkins, Jr., F. H. Bristow, W. B. Reeves, W. B. Harrison, H. F. Willoughby, and G. B. McClellan.

Cause Celebre.—The early practice in Todd County as elsewhere in Kentucky was largely confined to land litigation, and complications growing out of the institution of slavery. This practice involved a great deal of technical research, property of large value, and a long, determined contest, for which the fees were in proportion. The system of survey or lack of system was provocative of litigation. Patents for adjoining lands almost invariably showed a portion of the contiguous territory granted to both parties. The older patent established its owner's claim, but there arose an endless number of fine discriminations as to the settlement of the "lap," etc., etc. Much of the land in the county was originally patented by wealthy men, who fought opposing claims with great pertinacity, and some cases were continued for years, until the death of all the heirs closed the case. An account of the various litigations between Azariah Davis and Maj. John Gray would alone make a respectable volume, and these have been finally laid to rest only within a few years past. The statute of limitations, however, has long since taken this class of litigation entirely out of the courts. Slavery also contributed a class of cases similar to the land question in the character of the contests involved. A child was often given a slave which would be placed in trust. On coming to his or her majority, the natural increase or accumulation of wages would amount to a large sum, which the trustee was often unwilling to surrender. A case occurred in Todd County where a girl was given by her grandfather a female slave, who was placed with the grantee's father. The gift was lost sight of or unknown, and no claim was made for her property until some time after her marriage, when the fact of gift was established. Suit was brought for the recovery of some thirty slaves, the natural increase of the original gift, involving a large value. The complications of such a suit to gether with the large value at stake, entitled the successful attorney to a large fee, which was demanded and received. But the "logic of events" has closed all these cases. Criminal practice has never been large nor profitable in Todd County, but even this class of practice has felt the reducing influence of later political changes. The class of criminals are not now such as can pay large fees, and are generally defended at State expense. Perhaps no lawyer at the Todd County bar to-day finds the income from his practice sufficient for his ordinary expenses; all have business of quite as profitable a character in addition to their profession. The situation is strongly suggestive of that warning of the latter day, mentioned by Holmes: "When lawyers take (of necessity) what they would give." There have been but few cases, if any, in the county that have been even a "nine days' wonder." The contest over the will of Lycurgus Leavell, in which certain slaves were freed, and his property, amounting to some $150,000 bequeathed to his children by slave women, is perhaps the most celebrated. His relatives contested the will upon the remarkable ground that the testator was too morally depraved to make a proper and legal will. If such a plea is good in law, the evidence went very far to show the incompetency of the deceased, but after being tossed about in the courts for some twenty years, the will was sustained. A large part of the property was dissipated, however, by the administrator, and in the final settlement his securities suffered heavily. The Graves estate of some $75,000 was another case that involved considerable controversy and expense. There have been but three judicial hangings in Todd County, and these were of negroes. One of these was for attempt to rape a white woman. He was hanged solely on the woman's identification, which was of such a character as to lead all candid minds to believe that she was mistaken. However, in the excited state of the public, the jury thought it was sufficient, and declared him guilty. The others were for murder, the one of a fellow slave, and the other of his master. It is not to be inferred that this includes the whole list of murders in the county. A complete list of these would be a longer and sadder list. Violent altercations have been frequent, and have too often been attended with fatal results. The changed relations of the white and black races have been provocative of some fatal encounters. About 1876 there was a short reign of the Kuklux spirit. The negroes taking advantage of their new found liberty, began to find homes in quarters that were distasteful to certain of the whites. A secret organization of night marauders was formed, numerous negroes were cruelly whipped, from the effects of which some died, and others were shot. This sort of thing could not be tolerated by the law-and-order portion of the community, and a posse of some thirty or forty armed citizens, headed by the Sheriff, arrested certain parties engaged in this crime, and under the "Kuklux Act" of the Legislature, sent some five or six to the penitentiary. This summary action put a sudden and complete stop to the nefarious business.

The administration of Lynch law has found general denouncement among the older and solid citizens of this county, but there have been times when the ordinary course of justice has seemed inadequate to mete out the merited punishment to vicious criminals. In the early history of the county a band of horse-thieves infested the hilly country of this, Christian and Muhlenburg Counties, the operations of which became so bold and annoying that a general vigilance committee was formed of citizens in the three counties, and an end put to the gang. Several of them were killed in Todd County, but the chief scenes of this tragedy were in Christain and Muhlenburg Counties, an account of which will be found in the chapters on Christian County in this volume. A second vigilance committee sprang into temporary existence in 1882. A negro killed and outraged a white woman of the county. The crime was fixed upon the perpetrator, who was arrested, but while in the hands of the officers was taken by a crowd of infuriated neighbors and summarily dealt with. Led aside, his body was riddled with bullets, his head severed from it, and the trunk burned to ashes. The head was then placed upon a pole, and shot to pieces. The punishment, scarcely less barbarous than the crime, was somewhat palliated by the nature of the outrage; but such proceedings cannot be tolerated in any community with impunity. Within the past month (April, 1884), a third mob visited the jail in the county seat to execute illegal vengeance upon a negro who had made a nearly successful attempt to murder a white man who had ended a controversy by knocking the negro down. He had just been apprehended when word came to the authorities that it was intended to mete out summary justice at the hands of a mob. The County Judge at once issued an order for the removal to Russellville of the prisoner, who had been out of town but a few hours when the mob arrived. Finding their purpose foiled by the promptness of the officials, the mob quietly returned, and the county was saved a further addition to this unfortunate record. The demoralizing tendency of the free use of fire-arms is felt in Todd County as elsewhere in the State of Kentucky. Up to about 1840, while every man was trained to the use of the rifle and the hunting-knife, their use in personal encounters was forbidden by the unwritten law of the community. Since that time the knife and pistol have gradually grown into general use, until now scarcely one of that class to whom the possession is peculiarly dangerous is without them. This change in public sentiment, united with a degenerate spirit of chivalry which counts it more honorable to redress certain personal injuries by violence rather than law, gilds the ruffian with the romance of the knight, and makes ruffianism respectable. The responsibility for this state of things is with public sentiment, and not with the law. Stringent enactments against the carrying of concealed weapons, and for the punishment of crime, are found in the law of the land, and the courts give force to the penalties prescribed with commendable impartiality, but the people fail in their part. A long list of murders, shocking to every sentiment of justice, degrading to every feeling of true chivalry, and wholly demoralizing in their effect, could be compiled from the annals of Todd County. And yet, not one has been adequately punished by law, and few have received any *attempted* punishment. It would be unjust to the solid, law-abiding portion of the community to leave the impression that this state of facts existed without any protest on their part, or even that the lawless element counted a majority of the citizens of Todd County in its ranks. But this statement of the problem, which is undoubtedly correct, adds to the difficulty of its solution. Candid men everywhere acknowledge the existence, deplore the obvious tendency, and invoke the rigid enforcement of the law against this order of things, but it all ends in this and nothing more. These very men are unconsciously the great supporters of the evil they honestly deplore. Society throughout the State is imbued with an abnormal distaste for physical cowardice, which over-shadows all moral or material considerations. To this barbarous senti-ment there is a growing protest, which in time will effect a correction in this moral perspective, but not before the blood of its martyrs shall have sprung into full fruition. The recent tragedy at Mt. Sterling has brought the moral forces of society face to face with its responsibilities. A moral hero, the peer of any knight who gathered about King Arthur's table, or crossed a lance on the fields of Cressy or of the "Cloth of Gold," died for the emancipation of his fellow-citizens from the bonds of this latter-day chivalry. Every citizen who subscribes to the unwritten law of personal redress, shares in his "damnable taking off." Enlightened conscience re-pelled the demands of this social sentiment, but reason tottering from its throne, madly paid homage to the barbarous instinct, and sought to escape moral turpitude and social disgrace through the portals of his own life. In his, like great Cæsar's death—"Then I, and you, and all of us, fell down." But in the hour of a tragedy like this, the broad shadow of which covered the whole Commonwealth, how strong was the sentiment that slew him. His cause had no avowed champion. Apologists were numerous, whose best attempt was but to "damn with faint praise, assent with civil leer." But Judge Reid did not die in vain. His protest has already been taken up by the living, and the sentiment will grow, spreading from Christian homes to Legislative halls, until the moral shall overtop the physical characteristics of the Knight of the nineteenth century.

CHAPTER V.

SOCIAL DEVELOPMENT—FREEDOM OF EARLY SOCIETY—THE PECULIAR IN-
STITUTION—ITS MOLDING INFLUENCE—EFFECT OF EARLY ROADS—
IMPROVEMENT OF HIGHWAYS—RAILROADS—NEWSPAPERS—CHURCH IN-
FLUENCE—SCHOOLS.

THE early society of Todd County was derived from Virginia, North
Carolina and Tennessee. The natives of the latter State largely
preponderated in the northern part of the county, while the Virginians
and North Carolinians were found in about equal proportions in the southern part. The greater part of those who came here early were in limited financial circumstances, though the cheapness of the land and the
opportunity of profitable speculation attracted a few who were remarkably
well-to-do for that period. There were few, if any, of outward marks
of difference, and neighbors were too highly prized in the sparsely settled
community for society to exact too much in the way of credentials. There
was now and then a little disposition on the part of Virginians to assume
some superiority because of their possible connection with the "F. F.
V.," but then was so little opportunity to display this innocent vanity
that an aristocracy never gained a reasonably sure foothold. Society
here was very democratic, and those who persisted in asserting any other
pretension, found eventually that they had danced to an expensive piper,
and left the country poorer if not wiser. As a rule, there was little
"book learning" among the people, and schools were very slowly established. Public offices were filled for the period of "good behavior" by
the Governor, and once supplied there was no "rotation in office" to act
as a stimulant to the people to qualify themselves for places of trust and
honor. It accordingly became very generally accepted that some were
born to rule, and that the many were born to be ruled, and both parties
accepted this division of labor as natural and desirable. This was the
starting point with that harmless form of caste that has dubbed every man
of parts with a title. Respectful deference to elders or those in official
station was a marked feature of family training, though entirely unmixed
with anything of servility. Traditions of that chivalry which graced the
court of Charles I. and found its way to Virginia, had also an important
influence upon the early people here. But these influences found society

" in the rough " and while they made a lasting impression which may be traced even now, they did not work a marvel, transforming the backwoods-man into clumsy knights-errant. " Honor" became, however, a prominent word in the early vocabulary, and the habit of attaching an exaggerated importance to insult, a strong and universal custom. In close correlation with this feature was a marked courtesy in ordinary intercourse that approached the verge of gallantry. Friendships were warm and constant ; resentments were bitter and revengeful. With these variations, society here was similar to that always found where men and women are brought close to the leveling tendencies of a new country. Unbounded hospitality, which freely divided their rough fare with neighbor or stranger, and would have taken offense at offered pay, prevailed. Neighborhoods lived, worked, feasted or suffered together in cordial harmony ; families inter-married, so that every one was the natural ally of each one, ready to espouse his cause in danger, or to congratulate him in success. The limits of neighborhoods extended over a wide area, and a ride of several miles on horseback to pay a friendly visit was an unnoted and frequent occurrence. Nor was the social duty devolved solely upon the women, as in the Northwest. The habits and agricultural system of the region gave the men a large amount of leisure, which was employed principally in masculine gossip. On coming together, men disposed of each others' business projects and prospects with short shrift, and fell to discussing family genealogies, and politics. The pipe was almost invariably " an un-obtrusive third," the mild influence of which served to keep political talk well within friendly bounds. Short visits were neither desired nor made. The guest for the time was put in full possession of the resources of his host, whose domestic habits experienced scarcely a ripple of interruption by the temporary addition to his household. The entertainment was without ostentation, and the table, though rudely spread with coarse but substantial food, was large in its bounty. Court days were frequent occa-sions on which the male portion of the community gathered to the county seat in large numbers. On such days the farmer desiring to dispose of stock or other commodity brought it hither, where he found buyers seek-ing the thing he had to sell. If the sale was not effected in a private way it was sold under the hammer of the auctioneer. A certain quarter of the town early gained the name of " Trading Alley " where horse traders hitched their stock, and sometimes as high as forty or fifty ex-changes would be effected in a day. But few had business with the court, and, business done, the afternoon was given to the enjoyment of the social glass, the mellowing influence of which laid many a manly form in a shady corner to recover his senses. Young men of muscle stripped to the waist, frequently decided the question of superiority in an impromptu ring formed on the square. Not unfrequently a less deliberate fight ensued, when the object was more to take satisfaction out of each others' skin than to decide the championship. So general were these occurrences, that most men came prepared to stay to see the fights as a part of the regular programme of court day. An impromptu quarter race between some of the scrub-horses often served to vary the entertainment, and kept alive the traditional interest in this kind of sport, which flourishes more vigorously in the blue grass region.

The Peculiar Institution.—Slavery made its appearance in Todd County with the quite early settlement. Many of the pioneers brought slaves with them from their old homes, but the institution did not flourish here until society began to get out of the woods. As a matter of history it has proven unprofitable outside of rich agricultural districts, and the natural conditions found in Todd County soon relegated slave labor to the southern portion. The first settlers in the northern part brought their human chattels with them, but the niggard character of the soil forced its owners to the closest economy in its culture, and reduced the question to the alternative of starvation of the master or the removal of the slave. The latter followed, and divided the two sections upon the great question which agitated the whole nation for so long a period. The feeling of the people in the hilly country was not so much anti-slavery'as opposition to the slave-owner. It was not until about 1836–40 that slavery began to contribute largely to the wealth of the county. A large majority of the settlers were poor men, and, cheap as human chattels were at that time, but few could afford to buy them. There were a few slaves in the county held here and there as house servants or people of all work, and one or two wealthy pioneers had a number of hands. There was little or no buying or selling in this class of property until about the date mentioned. About this time the development of the cotton interest in the far South rendered slaves very valuable there, and this in connection with the panic of 1837 made the transfer of slaves from the older State of Virginia to Mississippi rather a brisk trade. Their passage through this region stimulated the desire for this kind of property; as one became able one or two were bought. It was very much the rule for a pioneer to save all his earnings and purchase a field hand to help him clear his farm, and master and slave worked together with many of the outward appearances of equals. The number purchased was comparatively small, and the number that eventually was found here was principally made up of the descendants of the first ones here. There was very little encouragement given to the negro-trader here. His business was generally despised, and while the laws gave it a legal standing, society viewed the man askance. It was the unwritten law of the community not to sell slaves out of the county, and it was very generally obeyed. Now and then for some especial reason a single one was disposed of, but such cases were exceptions.

In the settlement of estates slaves were by law sold at auction, but the heirs felt under obligations to this sentiment to purchase the old servants, and often seriously compromised themselves financially to do it. Negro traders often attended such sales, and bidding for the Southern market would bid the prices up to a point which no planter here could afford, and while he often got the slave, got the hearty detestation of the community. The institution was probably found in its best form in Todd County. Brutality was condemned, and not more than three or four masters in the county could be charged with cruelty in the management of their hands. With the development of the county the institution grew more profitable, expanded into larger proportions and embodied a large proportion of the wealth; and when the " logic of events " wrought emancipation upward of a million of dollars in value was destroyed in Todd County alone. Among the earliest effects of the institution of slavery upon society was the building up of a spirit of caste. A male slave was valued very early at about $400, but from 1850 forward the value increased to a sum varying from $800 to $2,000. Slaves therefore represented wealth; but in addition to this fact the owner of such property, exacting and receiving the utmost deference from his chattels, unconsciously demanded something similar from his less fortunate white brother. This was felt at once by the non-slaveholding class of the hill country, who did not object to slavery but to the "aristocracy of slave-owners." It was very apparent also that there was a bond of sympathy between the large slaveholder and the one less wealthy that did not exist between either one and the equally wealthy non-slave-owner. A reasonable cause for this was the fact that all slave-owners had a vital interest at stake in all the political agitation of the day as well as in all the local legislation with which the " domestic institution " was helped about. The non-slaveholder seemed as bitterly opposed to " abolition " as any one, but he manifestly had not the strong motive of the pocket to insure his loyalty in an emergency. The spirit of caste which thus gradually sprang into being became widespread and determined. The opening of profitable markets soon made slave labor enormously profitable, and led to the accumulation of large areas of lands in the hands of a single owner. This in its turn made the necessity for a large number of hands, and the large land-owners soon became autocrats of the neighborhood. This led also to a lavish state of living and a hospitality which copied in its extravagance that of the older slaveholding States, which in turn followed English models so far as circumstances would allow. Here and there natural penuriousness led to the reverse, but the majority expended their income in " riotous living " if not in " purple and fine linen." But little money was expended in surroundings, but lavish hospitality and prodigality of expenditure used up a revenue that would now be considered princely on the farm. All, however, were not of this type, but a majority of the planters in the more fertile part of the county lived a life of ease, and found no need for mental or physical exertion. Many who were not farmers owned slaves who were hired out by the year. The lessee provided food, clothing and maintained the slave, and paid a gross sum reaching as high as $200 per year for the services of a slave. Slaves of this character were very valuable property, and found ready employment. Many were trained as mechanics and were especially valuable to their owners. One man in Elkton had a large number trained as bricklayers, who was offered for them just before the war $60,000 and refused the offer. The royal road to wealth seemed to have been found, and idleness was bred in the dominant race. With many practical farmers the sons labored in the field with the blacks, but it was a frequent occurrence for them to leave the plow in the furrow on the impulse of a sudden whim.

The planter's was largely an isolated life. Large farms made neighbors somewhat far apart, and trained in later years by pride and natural indolence to find their pleasures within their own resources, they confined themselves to their own premises. Beyond visits to their especial friends, a ride to town on occasion, they were little abroad. This gave occasion for little interchange of ideas, and surrounded by negroes continually they even contracted their dialect and something of their primitive ideas. Situated thus, where there were none to oppose their views, and consorting principally with those of like mind when abroad, an intolerant spirit was engendered which, enforced by considerations of the pocket, gradually made them violent in their opposition to any independence of thought, and confined the vigorous intellect to philosophical speculations which, however, seldom took a high range, from the fact that such a flight must inevitably have brought them into contact with a subject which society was generally agreed should not be freely discussed. Such a state of things militated against liberal, popular education. A newspaper in such a society is handicapped, and in fact so far as Todd County is concerned, never had a vigorous existence. Schools, free and suited to the necessity of the common people, could not thrive if established, but they did not exist. Slavery could not exist beside such influences, and slaves were not only forbidden education by law, but the dominant class were also cut off from free schools by the demands of the institution. The natural result of all this training, a combination of pseudo-chivalry, intolerance and popular ignorance, could not fail to beget its natural offspring—violence. Like powder, with the ingredients brought together in proper proportions, it needed but the spark which whisky supplied to bring about a fatal explosion. Agitators did not supply in Todd County the fulminating power, nor was the subject of the " domestic institution " the direct origin of the deeds of violence so often perpetrated. It was sufficient that people brought up under this influence should get inflamed with whisky sufficient to lose the ordinary respect for others' rights to bring on a murderous altercation. County Court days were the frequent occasions for fatal shooting matches. Two or three would be shot, and those not disabled would almost invariably escape. To such an extent was this carried that a man was killed within a hundred yards and within hearing of a large crowd gathered about a patent medicine vendor on the square, without for a moment thinning the crowd or interrupting the sale. The officials did not ignore their duty in such cases, but public apathy was so strong that society looked upon the matter as one in which the criminal and officials alone were interested, and an officer's failure in bringing such cases to justice was never considered any evidence of his incompetency for the position.

Since 1865 a marked improvement has been gradually effected. The producing cause has been removed, " local option " has given the people the opportunity to express the preference of the majority, and violence has been greatly restricted. The disposition to shoot is not less strong, but the provoking causes are less abundant. Stringent laws against carrying concealed weapons have been brought to bear upon the subject, but without any apparent effect in reducing the number of pistols in the community. It is a frequent remark that every man carries one, and the negroes, imitating the superior race, increase the aggregate by substituting the razor for the pistol. The abolition of slavery was but one step toward the solution of this social problem. Notwithstanding the large pecuniary loss which emancipation occasioned this county, society felt the relief of a patient whose life is saved at the expense of a limb. Slavery had become unprofitable, and was yearly growing more so, to an extent more marked in Kentucky than in the far South. The institution was hedged about by humanitarian instincts and laws in this State that were unknown to the far South ; black labor, considering the total capital involved and the small returns received, was growing unprofitable in a rapid ratio, while the vast irreducible expense of the institution, the growing impoverished condition of the land under its *regime*, and its utter lack of adaptability to other pursuits, rendered ruin near and inevitable. And so, while the opposition to emancipation was unanimous and determined, when once it was effected the relief was immediately apparent and rejoiced in. The agricultural system has been vastly improved under the new order of things, farm labor is more profitable, the dominant class are more enterprising and vigorous, and the old slave caste is broken down and the last vestiges of it fast disappearing. But emancipation while an efficient remedy was not a panacea. The conditions effected by this radical change have been met with a creditable spirit by both races. Freedom found the negroes destitute of everything but the meager clothing in their possession. A number anticipated the final abolition of slavery in the border States by going into the army, but those who remained found themselves wholly unprovided for and without resources. In this condition the greatest misery might have followed had the masters cherished a vindictive spirit. A few did try their new found wings only to fail utterly in their first flight, and begged to be taken back upon the old place. A characteristic incident is told of two pampered men-servants whose duties consisted in supplying their master's table with game, feeding the poultry and bringing their master's horse to the house. They were maintained as his especial servants, were well dressed, were fed with the best that came from the family table, and whenever the master took his glass of liquor they were called in and joined with him in a social glass. This was a regular occurrence, and glasses for *their* use alone were kept with the decanter. When the Federal army came up the Tennessee River they took their first opportunity to escape, and shortly afterward begged in vain to come back to their old master. It is undoubtedly true that the physical condition of the freedmen here for the first year or two was worse than during the period of slavery, but the masters, partly from humanitarian sentiments and partly because they needed them, allowed their former slaves to remain. There was no necessity for so great a number, however, and large numbers found it to their interest to emigrate to Kansas and elsewhere. Those who remained found ready employment and considerate treatment. Many are doing well, many are doing but little better than under the old *regime*, and some are doing worse. This freeing a large number of ignorant negroes, whose whole training has taught them to lie, pilfer, to live improvidently and unchaste, has imposed upon society here a heavy burden of responsibility. Twenty years have passed since the war which set them free, but society has not yet adjusted itself completely to the new order of things. Neither race fully appreciate the full extent of the change that has been wrought, and the responsibilities which it imposes upon each. The negroes trained to an utter disregard of personal character in themselves have not yet learned that this must now be cultivated. The whites fail in the same respect. Negroes convicted of felony lose caste with neither race, and find employment at the hands of the whites as readily as the honest black. Women notoriously unchaste are readily employed by the whites as cooks or servants, and lose no standing in black society. This fatal lack of self-respect is encouraged by this heedless action of the whites, and so long as it exists is a menace against society and a fatal hindrance to the elevation of the race. Education to such a class is a dangerous power, and religion a sham. Both races need to learn in this respect. Under the old *regime*, no more responsibility was imposed upon the human chattel than upon a mule, and the dominant race has not awakened to the fact that this freedom can no longer be allowed. That it does exist arises from force of habit, and not from any ill-considered sentiment of humanity. Petty crimes, such as were winked at on the plantation, and offenses punished with severity, are dealt with in the same spirit now. The only remedy for the evil, which many see but do not entirely comprehend, is to put every man, black or white, upon the same responsibility before the law, and exact the same rigid obedience. Law admits no defense on the score of ignorance, and the result is that men inform themselves. The application of the same principle to the negro question will make the blacks better workmen, better citizens, and an advantage instead of a curse to society.

Early Means of Development.—The great hindrance to the development of pioneer society earliest felt, is the lack of ready intercommunication. A struggling settlement located on some convenient stream gathered about it the necessities of pioneer existence, and was in a large measure independent of the outside world. Several such isolated communities made up the county of Todd, and while visits were interchanged by families the only opportunity to come together in friendly emulation was on court days. But the nature of the early political status was such as to concentrate the vigor and executive power at the county seat, and the county really formed only one large community, which needed to come in contact with other county communities to beget that emulation which leads to rapid progress. Before the formation of the county the main road, which the first settler found only a trail, was a nearly direct route from Russellville to Hopkinsville. Roads from these points to Clarksville, Tenn., opened an outlet southward, and in the November term of 1820 the County Court ordered the road to Greenville laid out to connect with the one which led up to the county seat from Guthrie. Other roads were subsequently laid out for neighborhood convenience, but these two main lines of travel were the only means of reaching the outside world. With them opened, however, the community was practically fenced in by the difficulties of ordinary travel. The roads were narrow, a thirty-foot space only being allowed, which the elements soon converted into an impassable morass, under even the light travel of that day. Journeys were therefore undertaken only at the bidding of an obvious necessity. At a later day, when stores were established here, business paid tribute to this condition of things in a way that robbed the merchant of a considerable profit, and the consumer of many advantages. When the building of the line of railroad, now known as the Memphis Branch of the Louisville & Nashville road, was projected, Todd County took a lively interest in it, and petitioned the County Judge, according to law, to subscribe $300,000 to secure its passing through the county in a central direction. The majority for the subscription was only one vote, and the judge arbitrarily decided not to make the subscription. No legal measures being taken to reverse his action, the county lost whatever hope there was of speedy railroad connection with the world. In 1860 the railroad touched the eastern edge of the county, leaving the county still at the mercy of nine miles of bad road. In 1867 the line to Henderson, Ky., was built along the southwestern portion of the county with much the same result as the earlier railroad, absorbing considerable local subscription without materially benefiting the whole county. In the meanwhile progressive citizens had not been inactive. The county paper contained long articles by various contributors on the subject of road improvement, the building of pikes, etc.; representatives in the Legislature secured the passage of enabling acts, and about a mile of pike was built on each of the roads leading out of Elkton. In 1869 the aid of the railroad was again invoked, and $400,000 subscribed in aid of a road to be built from Greenville or some other point in Muhlenburg County on the Owensboro & Russellville Railroad, through Elkton to Guthrie. Hopes of success were high for a time, but it proved to be only a ruse of the railroad managers to stimulate Logan County to greater activity to retain the original project. Thus disappointed, the people quietly submitted again for several years to the exactions of the mud. In 1883 a stone pike was projected from Elkton to Allensville, but was defeated by the failure of the Elkton District to vote its support as required by the law. This, however, will prove no great loss to the county at large, as the active, persistent demand for better facilities for travel and shipping has crystallized in a new railroad project. This contemplates the construction of a road from Elkton to Guthrie, to be operated by the Louisville & Nashville Company. Its estimated cost is placed at about $40,000, the larger proportion of which is already subscribed. The route is fixed, and the preliminary work of the engineer nearly done, and sanguine friends of the enterprise predict that it will be completed in time to obviate the mud blockade of the coming winter. The advantages of such a road are weighty and apparent· All goods brought to the merchants of Elkton cost an average of 25 cents per hundred for wagoning, and even at this rate cannot be secured in certain times of the year without vexatious and sometimes expensive delays. Much business that would otherwise come to Elkton now goes elsewhere, while the merchants fail to get the benefit of the competition that a larger number of commercial travelers would create. All this the proposed road will tend to correct, but there will be still a large need for pikes. To make the contemplated railroad of the most benefit to the whole county, good roads should lead to the county seat as a central shipping-point, and this necessity will become more apparent when the railroad becomes a fixed fact. Good highways are a necessity to the prosperity of the county.

The Press.—Another powerful agency in stimulating progressive tendencies in a community is the newspaper. This unites the popular sentiment, leads to a rapid and widespread interchange of views, and acquaints all with the current history of each part. Russellville and Hopkinsville papers supplied this agency for Todd County until 1851, when the *Green River Whig* was established at Elkton. The checkered career of newspaper enterprises in this county is noted elsewhere. Local journalism has never been of the vigorous kind. Local happenings have found but slight and imperfect chronicle, and important questions have been discussed with an apologetic severity that has gained neither the consideration to which moderation is entitled, nor the respect granted to a candid but determined opponent. The community in Todd County has offered very few inducements to capital or ability to undertake this kind of work. The number who would support its subscription list is small; the official and business patronage is meager; and there are no compensating considerations to offset these fatal deficiencies. However, since the establishment of the first paper, with the exception of one or two considerable intervals, a paper has been published continuously in Elkton. The *Elkton Register* now occupies the field, but with so little vigor as to cause scarcely a ripple upon the placid current of events.

Early Church Influence.—The people who laid the foundations of society in Todd County were a religious people. The great revival movement which originated in Logan County in 1800, spread over the new settlements of the State like a prairie fire, and set the whole land in a flame of religious ardor. It was a time when pious ardor broke through the restraining forms of the church, and expressed itself in the wildest ecstasy and most extravagant manifestations. There were but few church buildings of any character in this region, and the people came together in large camp-meetings, where the Spirit of the Lord seemed to manifest His presence with almost the miraculous power of apostolic times. These manifestations, often bordering upon the ridiculous, baffle philosophical speculation. Men of rugged mind and physique, and women and children alike, succumbed to the "jerks, the falling or running exercises." In describing these scenes, the Hon. Urban E. Kennedy relates: "Many times I have seen them unexpectedly jerked flat on their backs, and the next instant jerked full length upon their faces. Ladies while sitting intently observant of the exercises, were jerked so violently that their bonnets, capes, handkerchiefs and loose apparel would be thrown clear away, and their long, beautiful hair, unrestrained by combs, fillets, etc., flowing down to their waists, would crack like an ox-whip with the violent vibrations of their heads and shoulders. Others would jump and run like an antelope, perhaps for fifty or a hundred yards, and then fall prone upon the ground and lie apparently lifeless, sometimes for hours. Some would say it was the chastening work of an Almighty God; others, that it was the work of the devil. You might see the skeptical high-flyers stand on the outskirts of the assembly, winking and making sport of these manifestations, and often, in five minutes, they would be screaming and howling like madmen. Once two old church members of great formality and incredulity visited a meeting of this kind to observe with their own eyes what they had heard and disbelieved of these manifestations. After critically scrutinizing the whole matter, they pronounced it heterodox, and left the ground. However, before reaching home they took the jerks and were thrown to the ground, giving utterance to piercing yells. After a time the unbelieving and ridiculing portion of the community became afraid to attend these meetings lest they should feel this supernatural power. But many even here, in the midst of ridicule and philosophical explanation of this subject, would be taken with the jerks and send for the ministers and Elders for instruction and relief. These experiences were not wholly confined to those of religious training, but to all the community. Most of those who were thus affected became members of the church, though some while not embracing religion abated much of their skepticism."

Methodist Episcopal Church.—The Methodist Church was probably about the earliest represented in Kentucky. At the conference of 1800 there were five circuits, to which six preachers were appointed, and a total membership in the State of about 1,741 communicants. At this point the remarkable revival of the time greatly added to its influence and numbers. During the following decade the membership was increased to 7,057, with such men as William McKendree, Lewis Garrett, Peter Cartwright and others as preachers, and Gabriel and Daniel Woodfield, Joseph Ferguson, John Graham, etc., as local preachers. The great revival began in 1799 under the preaching of John and William McGee, the former a Methodist and the latter a Presbyterian. Peter Cartwright and John Grahame were the only apostles of Methodism in Todd County up to about 1810, and their labors were carried on all over the county. Services were held in the cabin home of some member of the church, the class being guided by its leader on ordinary occasions, and preaching had when the pressing calls of the itinerant would allow. The King's business demanded haste, and services were not deferred until Sunday, but whenever a preacher arrived word was sent round and an audience convened. Church buildings were not constructed in Todd County by this denomination until some years later, camp-meetings in the meanwhile serving to bring the people together, where they could enjoy the continued services of the church conducted by the few but efficient men to whom this large field was given to cultivate. The earthquake of 1811 ushered in a great revival in this church in Todd County. The natural phenomenon announced itself by shaking the furniture until it rattled, knocking down stones from the chimneys, and with a deep muttering sound that to the superstitious pioneers was ominous of the end of the world. Those learned in the Scriptures quoted with telling effect, "Yet a little while and I will not only shake the heavens, but the earth also, and ye shall hear of wars and rumors of wars, and earthquakes in divers places." The times lent confirmation to the earthquake; the Indian war in Ohio was only a mask which covered the more dangerous struggle with Great Britain, and what was not supplied by the facts was made good by the popular imagination. The pioneers had more than the average amount of superstition, and the general expectation would have hardly been exceeded if a large portion of the unrepentant people had been swallowed by some yawning gulf. Near Bell's Chapel had been a dancing school, and here the excitement was intense. Prayer-meetings were inaugurated on the instant and held throughout the day, subsequent to every meeting. All churches profited by the event, and large accessions were received. The growth of the Methodist Church has been gradual, and did not have its usual early lead in numbers and influence in Todd County. It is probable the reason is found in the fact that other churches, which came as close to the common people, divided the field usually occupied entirely by the Methodists. At present this church has its organization in every village and center of population in the county.

Cumberland Presbyterian Church.—The Presbyterian Church was hardly second in its appearance in Kentucky. In 1796 James Mc-Gready, a Presbyterian minister, settled in Logan County and took charge of three congregations—Little Muddy, Gaspar River and Red River, the latter being situated near the line separating Kentucky and Tennessee. Mr. McGready was a native of Pennsylvania, but commenced his ministry in North Carolina, where he inveighed with great earnestness against slavery and formalism. On this account he became offensive to the church and immigrated to Kentucky, where his severity and earnestness had a different effect, and gave the initial impulse to what became the great revival of 1800.   Soon after his arrival in Kentucky several other ministers of this denomination came hither, among whom were William Hodge, William McGee and Samuel McAdoo, who entered heartly into the spirit of McGready's work.   There was decided opposition to their work from members of the church, which needed but a plausible pretext to grow into a formidable schism.   The demand for ministers for the work of the church was far in excess of the means of the church to supply according to their methods, and these earnest men advised certain congregations to select some pious and promising young men and encourage them to enter the work which so urgently called them.   They were not expected to undergo the usual educational preparation, and in a short time three young men were advanced to the ministry.   This summary action brought out a vigorous but ineffectual protest, and when these young men were allowed to preach after refusing to accept certain dogmas of the old church, the opposition became irreconcilable.   The difficulties were protracted through several years ; the progressive party considered themselves wronged, and when it became apparent that no redress could be had in the old church they determined to reconstitute the Cumberland Presbytery, which had been previously constituted and dissolved by the Synod of Kentucky.   The ministers who took the responsibility of thus defying the Synod were Samuel McAdoo, Finis Ewing and Samuel King. The Cumberland Presbytery was reconstituted February 4, 1810, and became the head and front of the Cumberland Presbyterian Church.   The character of church government and legal worship of the mother church was such as no intelligent man could much longer tolerate, and hundreds repelled by this and attracted by the position taken by the earnest leaders of the revolt, joined the standard of the new organization.   The system of camp-meetings was instituted by this church, and the first one held in Christendom was at Gaspar River Meeting-house in Kentucky.

Finis Ewing was an early settler in Todd County, and did much to give this church the ascendancy here.   A large number of the settlers were Seceders, and went into this organization.   Camp-meetings were regularly held at a point two miles south of Trenton, where afterward the Lebanon Church was erected, which was instrumental in bringing large numbers into the church.   A brick edifice was early erected here, and a seminary established which occupied this building.   Ewing, King, Cassitt and others, leaders of the church, were among the early ministers of this denomination in the county.   Some idea of primitive views may be gained from some of their church customs as related by Mr. Kennedy, so often quoted in these pages.   In relation to administering the Lord's supper, he says : " First, the minister would announce the times for his sacramental meetings, and Saturday, previous to the communion on the

Sabbath, they met as a day of preparation and prayer. I remember well my father's old buckskin purse of tokens, which I would then have thought sacrilegious to have touched with the tip of my finger. Every one that desired to commune must apply to the Elders for one of those tokens, simply made of bullets hammered flat to the size of a silver dime. If the bench of Elders believed him worthy, they would give the applicant a token, which would be pocketed cheerfully until they went to the table, which was erected clear across the church. Then they all took seats, and while the institution hymn was chanted, the Elders passed one on each side of the table and took up the tokens. If one happened to be present without this mark of his fitness, he was obliged to retire." Such formalities could not last long in a progressive organization, and, in fact, in the mother church, and were done away with many years ago. Ewing remained here some fifteen or twenty years. Toward the end of his stay here he was greatly annoyed to find the Baptist Church making rapid progress, and the culture of tobacco gaining popularity, both of which were distasteful to him. In 1821 he emigrated to Missouri, accompained by many of his followers. This broke up the church here, and he left the edifice by will or recommendation to the Baptists, who had occupied the land. In the meanwhile Rev. F. R. Cassitt had organized a church at Elkton ; Willliam John had organized another at Salubria Springs; James Barnett at Mount Hermon, and one at " Black Jack " by M. H. Bone and others. To these various churches the few members who remained were now transferred. Mr. Ewing died in 1842 ; he was one of the young men advanced to the ministry, and is considered one of the most important of the originators, if not the father of the church. Rev. F. R. Cassitt was prominent in the early history of the church as head of the school in this county, and subsequently the first President of the Cumberland College at Princeton, Ky. He was one of the originators of the *Religious and Literary Intelligencer*, and subsequently was for a number of years editor and publisher of the *Banner of Peace*, both papers devoted to the interests of this denomination.

The Baptist Church.—This church is also connected with the earliest settlements in the State. Its earlier history in Kentucky is marked by several important dissensions which caused divisions which greatly retarded the growth and influence of the church. Its largest strength came from the Old Dominion State, who were of the " Iron Jacket " or " Hardshell " school, as they were popularly known. This church profited also by the great revival of 1800, but their meetings were generally free of those peculiar manifestations known as the "jerks or rolling and running exercises." The early church grew rapidly until 1802, when a slight Unitarian schism occurred, which drew off a number of its members. In

1804 a schism which had its origin in the opposition of some to the institution of slavery occurred, which gave rise to the "Baptist Licking-Locust Association, Friends of Humanity." The Regular Baptists declared that it was "improper for ministers, churches or associations to meddle with the emancipation of slavery, or any other political subject," and the schismatics withdrew. This new organization had but a short-lived existence. In 1809 another rupture occurred, which originated in a negro trade between a minister and layman, which resulted in the withdrawal of a respectable number under the name of Particular Baptists. Notwithstanding these adverse events the regular organization continued to thrive. Drake Pond Church of this denomination was organized in 1802, and still retains its primitive doctrine. The church edifice was erected just south of the Tennesse line, near Guthrie, but draws a large portion of its supporters from Todd County. This was the only church in this immediate region for years, until the emigration from Virginia in 1815–20 brought large accessions of strength to the denomination. Among the early ministers of this denomination in Todd County were Philip Boel, Ambrose Bowen, Archibald Bristow, Richard W. Nixon, John Christian and others. The Lebanon Baptist Church was organized about 1820, and marks the first permanent progress made by this denomination here. The church has since developed with persistent effort, and in point of numbers ranks first or second in the county. It has organizations and good church edifices in each of the villages of the county, and divides with the Methodist Church the colored church membership of Todd.

Reformed or Christian Church.—This organization is an offshoot of the Baptist Church, and originated in the dissensions of 1829–32, under the guidance of Alexander Campbell. Rev. Barton W. Stone, a Presbyterian clergyman, was the great head of this reform movement in Kentucky, and the Presbyterian Church may properly be said to have contributed almost as much to the new organization as the Baptists. The dissensions of the general church were felt in Todd County as well, and in 1833 the Zion Christian Church was formed from the Lebanon Baptist Church. Until about 1842 the church was fostered here by itinerant preachers, but at this time Elder C. M. Day entered into the work, and may be called the chief of the early preachers of the denomination in this county. Mr. Day was born in Virginia and educated for the ministry at Richmond. He became interested in the reform, and without any special commission from the church began to labor in Todd County. His work was a labor of love, and done without pecuniary reward. He was a man of remarkable energy and industry, and supported himself and an invalid wife by teaching school at Trenton. His preaching was marked rather by forceful expression and logical deduction than by eloquence. He was not lacking in culture, however, and his earnest, powerful will seemed to control the minds and hearts of his hearers. His nature was such as resisted coercion with vigor, and yet could be led by persuasive reason most easily. In his church work Mr. Day was remarkably successful. He was eminent as an organizer, and aided by G. W. Ellery and John D. Ferguson, established churches at Trenton, Elkton, Daysville and Allensville. He became the settled pastor of the Trenton and Allensville Churches at once, and served them until his death, a period of about thirty-eight years, holding the undivided love of his parishioners to the end. After the death of his first wife, he married a lady of some wealth, and in his declining years was saved the extra exertion which he had put forth in earlier years to preach a Gospel "without money and without price." He died in Todd County at the age of seventy-two years. J. B. Ferguson was for a short time a prominent Elder of the church; he was a native of Virginia, educated at William and Mary's College, and came to Todd County at the age of twenty-two; he was a gifted speaker, his eloquence making him the idol of every community. But he lacked the more solid and substantial acquirements, and about 1855 drifted into spiritualism. Elder John T. Johnson, brother of R. M. Johnson, the Vice-President, and the hero of the battle of the Thames, was an eminent evangelist of the Reformed Church, and remarkably successful in Todd County. Mr. Johnson was well educated, and entered upon the practice of the law. He was a volunteer aid to Gen. Harrison, and at the battle near Fort Meigs, on May 5, 1813, had his horse shot under him. He represented Scott County, Ky., in the Legislature in 1814–18, and again in 1828. He was a member of Congress four years, 1821–25, and a Judge of the new Court of Appeals for nine months from December 20, 1826. He joined the Baptist Church in 1821, and in 1831 embraced the principles of the reform movement, and began preaching. He visited Todd County about 1860, and carried on his work here with his usual success. His political training colored his style of speaking, which was of the heroic kind. He had a large fund of effective anecdotes, which, with his deep earnestness and great personal magnetism, wrought wonders upon his audiences. At his meetings here he baptized as high a number as forty or fifty at a place, and was the means of adding great numbers to the church. The number .of baptisms performed by him is placed at 3,000. He went to Missouri and soon afterward died.

Other ministers of some note in this church in Todd County were Dr. Orville Collin, J. J. Harvey and W. E. Mobley. The latter is still serving the church in this county. He began his ministry in 1851, with but little educational preparation, but his natural ability marked him as eminently fitted for the service. His circuit extends from Roaring Springs in Trigg County to Berea in Logan County, the intermediate appointment being at Elkton. Save an interval of two years, Mr. Mobley has served these churches for thirty years, a longer pastorate than any other Elder in this church in Kentucky. One Sunday in each month he preaches where his services seem to be required, having no regular appointment. J. W. Gant is another cotemporary Elder of the church. He is agent of the Sunday-school and Christian Missionary Society. His duties are those of a home missionary agent, and as such he has been instrumental in establishing several churches in the county. The denomination has organizations at Daysville, at Mount Vernon in District No. 7, Kirkmansville, Cherry Hill, Hadensville, Trenton, and one about four miles north of Elkton. Save the last all have good places of worship: frame buildings, save at Trenton, which is a brick edifice.

Educational Interests.—Under the social influence described in these pages it will be easily understood that popular education must be attended by many difficulties. Its value and importance were certainly under-rated by all classes, and it gained a foothold in Kentucky only through the strenuous exertions of a far-sighted few. Education was at first entirely in the hands of the church, which established seminaries at various points, primarily for the preparation of the clergy for ministerial work, but which were at once accepted by the wealthy portion of the church membership as a convenient means to give their children such accomplishments as their social position demanded. It was to these institutions that the State first extended its fostering aid, an act of the Legislature in 1798 granting 6,000 acres of the public lands of the Commonwealth to each of five educational institutions then in existence. In 1805 and 1808 similar acts were passed making like provision for seminaries to be established in each of the forty-six counties then formed. In 1821 an act was passed providing that one-half the net profits of the Bank of the Commonwealth should be set apart as the "Literary Fund," to be distributed in just proportions to the counties of the State for the support of a general system of education, under legislative direction; and that one-half of the net profits of the branch banks at Lexington, Danville and Bowling Green should be donated to Transylvania University, Center College and Southern College of Kentucky respectively. Until the failure of the old Bank of the Commonwealth, this last appropriation yielded about $60,-000 per annum. About the same time a committee was appointed to confer with eminent educators, and report a plan of common schools to the Legislature. An able report was made, but the natural hostility to the equalizing tendency of popular education served to let the project die with the report. About this time also the Legislature requested the State

Representatives in Congress to advocate a bill for distributing the proceeds
of the sale of public lands to the older States, as had been done to the
newer States, " for the purpose of education," Kentucky claiming $1,000,-
000 as her share under the proposed distribution. It was not until 1836,
however, that any practical legislation resulted from this movement. At
this time Congress apportioned about $15,000,000 of surplus money in
the treasury to the several older States, in the form of a loan, Kentucky's
share being $1,433,757. No provision of the law imposed any obligation
to devote it to educational purposes, but it had originally been demanded
for such purposes, and it was generally expected that the funds would
find such employment. Only $1,000,000 of this amount was devoted to
this object, however, and this was subsequently further reduced to $850,-
000, which by the additions of the unexpended surplus has reached the
sum of $1,327,000. In 1838 the first law was enacted for the establish-
ment of a general system of common schools in Kentucky, but for ten
years the bill constituting the system was the most significant part of it.
The State was financially straitened, and the general lack of interest in
public education led the State officials to withhold the payment of interest on the school fund, claiming that it was a State debt which could be
repudiated without disgrace. Up to 1843 but $2,504 had been paid on
this account, while there was $116,375 of accrued interest unpaid. In
1845 the bonds which represented the school fund were delivered to the
Governor, and burned by order of the Legislature before the Auditor and
Treasurer of the State. Such unwarrantable spoliation of the school
fund aroused the resentment and activity of the friends of the public
school system, and under the lead of Rev. Robert J. Breckinridge a
proposition to issue a new bond for all arrears of interest due, and to levy
a tax of 2 cents on the $100 to aid common schools was submitted to the
people and carried. Not satisfied with this success, the friends of popular
education brought the subject before the Constitutional Convention of
the succeeding year (1849), and secured a clause in the present Constitution declaring that the school funds for which the State had executed its
bonds, together with all other funds thereafter raised for the purpose,
should be kept inviolate for the use of the common schools of the State.
The opponents of free schools continued their opposition, though successful only in retarding the growth of the system. In 1855 the *ad valorem*
tax of 2 cents was increased to 5 by a large majority of the popular vote.
After the war the friends of the common school sought to usher in the
new era by a thorough reform of the system of public education. A bill
presenting the best features of the school laws of the more advanced
States was framed, advocated and passed by the Legislature in the face of
a vigorous opposition. In 1870 a proposition to further increase the *ad*

valorem tax in aid of schools to 15 cents was carried by a good majority, and the draft of a school law presented to the Legislature for enactment. This was forced to run the gantlet of a thousand conflicting prejudices, and reached the goal with life, but shorn of many of the advantages which its models possess. Since then the cause has gradually but surely progressed. Prejudices have become more amenable to reason; schools for colored pupils have been established; white and colored pupils have been placed on equal footing in relation to the advantages of the law; the *ad valorem* tax has been increased to 22 cents, and a new law containing more advanced methods has just been passed.

County Schools.—The history of public education in Todd County is but a minimized repetition of that of the State. Common schools were rejected here by the class most largely to be benefited with contempt. They looked upon the district schoolhouse as an educational poor-house, and believed that to patronize them was to affix the stigma of a pauper to their children. The aristocracy, largely of the slaveholding class, disliked its tendency to bring all upon an educational level, and feared its influence upon the "domestic institution." Up to 1856, therefore, the cause made little progress in the county. About this time Elder Mobley was made County Commissioner of Schools, who took active measures to give the law its fullest efficiency in the county. Districts were formed and a few schools established under its provisions. The war succeeded, and society was in such an unsettled state here that but little progress was made. After the war a new element was added to the question which strengthened the opposition. Negro-phobia, which possessed the people for a time, led them to reject apparent advantages lest it should open the door for equal privileges to the freedman, and the overcoming of this prejudice has been a slow, tedious process, not yet entirely accomplished. The recent law, approved May 12, 1884, marks an advance in administration of the public school interests, and represents the system of Kentucky in its best estate. The County Commissioner of Schools is now termed Superintendent, and is required to "visit each district school of his county, and investigate and direct the operations of the school system, and promote, by addresses or otherwise, the cause of common school education." In addition to this he is to form one of three examiners to issue teachers' certificates to examine school buildings and see that improper buildings are condemned; to organize and attend teachers' institutes, and disburse all school moneys of the county. The Trustees are required to "employ a qualified teacher and agree with him as to compensation;" when a school begins, one of the trustees, within five days thereafter, shall visit the school, and thereafter once a month;" to take an exact census of the children of school age in the district, and take charge of the work of erecting new schoolhouses, repairs, etc.   Teachers are required to obtain certificates from the County or State Board of Examiners, and to attend the full session of the County Institute, which shall be not less than four days. Districts are to be laid off when necessary by a board consisting of the County Superintendent, County Surveyor, and a "discreet and suitable citizen" appointed by the County Judge.   No district is to contain an area of more than nine square miles, unless it be to secure the minimum number of children of the school age; no district is to contain over 100 children of school age, and not less than forty, save in cases of extreme necessity, and none with less than twenty.   When necessary to build a schoolhouse, it is provided that the trustees shall order a per capita tax not exceeding $1 on each male in the district over twenty-one years of age, and a tax not exceeding 25 cents on each $100 of taxable property. Where such a tax is not adequate to the building of a schoolhouse, or where it would be oppressive, it is the duty of the trustees "to warn in the hands liable to work on the public highways in such district to meet at the place selected for the schoolhouse, with such tools as they are directed to bring."   The house may be "built of logs, stone, brick or plank, but must be of sufficient size to accommodate the children of the district   *   *   *   * and have a property value of not less than $100."   The instruction "shall embrace spelling, reading, writing, arithmetic, English grammar, English composition, geography, United States history, and laws of health: *Provided, however*, that when there are as many as one-third in number of the pupils of any district who are the children of other than English-speaking parents, their respective languages may be added to the foregoing course of study."   It is provided that indigent orphan children may be supplied with text-books by the County Judge not to exceed the value of $100 in any county per annum.   No publications of a sectarian, infidel or immoral character shall be used or distributed, or said doctrines taught in the schools.   No school shall be deemed a "common school" or be entitled to State support, unless the same has been "actually kept by a qualified teacher for three months in districts having thirty-five pupils, or less; for four months, in districts having more than thirty-five and less than forty-five pupils, and for five months for districts having forty-five or more."   The support of the common school is derived from the funds mentioned in the preceding pages, from certain fines and forfeitures, and from local taxation.   The recent law provides that a county may vote a tax, or a school district alone may do so.

   Colored Schools.—In 1874 a system of schools for colored children was established, similar to that provided for white children.   The law provided that the trustees, teachers and scholars should be colored; that the schoolhouse for colored children should not be erected within one mile of the one occupied by white children, save in a town where they should be separated by a distance of 600 feet at least. The support of these schools was derived: 1st, from so much of the annual *ad valorem* State tax, and the State school tax as is paid by colored people; 2d, a capitation tax of $1 on each male colored person above the age of twenty-one (repealed in 1882); 3d, all taxes levied and collected on dogs owned or kept by colored persons; 4th, all State taxes on deeds, suits, or on any license collected from colored persons; 5th, all the fines, penalties and forfeitures imposed upon and collected from colored persons due the State, except the amount thereof allowed by law to Attorneys for the Commonwealth. In 1882 the two school funds were united in a common fund, to which both races are entitled in the same proportion. In Todd County the whites have fifty districts and forty-one schoolhouses. The negroes have eighteen districts and ten schoolhouses. These buildings are log, box, frame or brick structures. The "box" is made of planks and constructed without a regular frame. Teachers accept schools for the "per capita," which affords a revenue of $12.56 to $48.47 per month. There is no local taxation, and some teachers are obliged to rent a room in which to conduct the public school. This is the case in Elkton. Some excellent private schools are maintained in the county, but they do not supply the place of public education, which has not yet attained such development in Todd as to be of the greatest efficiency.

CHAPTER VI.

PATRIOTISM OF TODD COUNTY—REVOLUTIONARY PENSIONERS—THE STORY OF THEIR SERVICE—SECOND WAR WITH ENGLAND—"POLK, DALLAS AND TEXAS"—POLITICS AND CHIVALRY—THE WAR OF THE REBELLION—THE COUNTY'S CONTRIBUTION TO THAT STRUGGLE—B. H. BRISTOW—JEFFERSON DAVIS.

PATRIOTISM is the sum of social and political virtue; the tangible expression of a people's intelligent appreciation of worthy institutions. Founded upon a nation's civilization it rises like some fair temple, bounded by the wisdom of the statesman, towering with the aspiration of the people, and beautified with an unselfish devotion. In this virtue Todd County was early schooled. Coming into existence at the close of the Revolutionary war, and its people imbued with the chivalric sentiment of the Old Dominion State, love of country became an absorbing passion, and national affairs the absorbing theme of debate. Many of the early settlers were of that heroic stock that bore " the burden and heat of the day," and their precept and example serving to intensify the natural bent of the general mind, added an influence which has made Todd County, like every Southern community, a determined partisan.

Relics of the Revolution.—Among the active participants of the Revolutionary war earliest to settle here were Robert Acock, Sr., Michael Kennedy, Samuel Davis, Robert Harris and George Randolph. The latter served eighteen months under Capt. Shelton in Col. Matthew's regiment of the " Virginia Line," and was discharged by Gen. La Fayette. A little later came Charles Hamon and Charles Hounsler. The latter served under Capt. James Newenn in Col. John Montgomery's regiment. He enlisted on New River in Virginia ; marched thence to Long Island on the Halston River; thence to Big Creek and joined Col. Shelby ; thence the forces embarked for Chickamaugatown, Louisiana Territory; thence to Kaskaskia, and from there proceeded to a post at Koko. From this point the command ascended the Illinois River, and thence returned to Kaskaskia, where he was discharged. Mr. Hounsler then enlisted for three years or the war, and was stationed at the falls of the Ohio, where his company remained during the war. On the 7th day of June, 1832, Congress passed an act pensioning soldiers of the Revolutionary war, and the declarations required bring out the fact that quite a number of this class

settled in this county after the ones already mentioned. Conrod Lear
was one of these, and at that time was ninety-four years old. He enlisted
in 1775 with Capt. Ross, and served in the First Regiment of Horse
under Col. William Washington of the Continental Line. He served as
trumpeter to the Colonel during the whole time of his service. He was
discharged soon after the battle of Germantown, when he re-enlisted from
Lancaster County, Penn., and subsequently took part in the battles of
Boston, New York, New London, Conn., Princeton, N. J., and Brandywine. At the battle of Trenton his force aided in the capture of 500
Hessians. In the course of the campaigns of the army he marched
through Pennsylvania, New York, New Jersey, Vermont, Connecticut
and Massachusetts. Benjamin Pannell, aged seventy-five years, deposed
that he enlisted in 1778, and served in the army up to the surrender of
Yorktown. Ambrose Madison, aged sixty-five years, enlisted in 1776
under Capt. Benjamin Temple in the First Regiment of the Virginia
Line, and served eighteen months, taking part in the battles of Brandywine, Germantown, Amboy and Morgantown. He was at that time a
resident of King William County, Va. Peter Petrie, aged sixty-eight
years, enlisted under Capt. William Moore, and served eighteen months
in a regiment of North Carolina in the Continental Line. He enlisted
in 1782; was in the command of Gen. Green, but was engaged in no
important battles, though taking part in skirmishes at James Island and
on the Edisto River below Orangeburg. With his command he marched
from Hillsboro, N. C., to Orangeburg, S. C., thence to Guilford and
James Island, and was stationed subsequently near Charleston. Henry
Maben, seventy-six years old, enlisted in 1777, was subsequently taken
prisoner and held at Charleston nearly two years. He served under Gen.
Lincoln, but was in no general engagement. He enlisted from Chester
County, S. C. Jonathan Smith, seventy-four years old, was a resident
of Middlesex County, N. J., and was drafted into the army in 1776 or
1777. He served about seven years, but not continuously, his service
being chiefly in raiding and scouting expeditions, which allowed him to
remain at home when not in active service.

Samuel Gordon, seventy-one years old, was a citizen of York County,
S. C., and joined the militia of that State in 1779, under the command of
Capt. Latimore in Col. Neel's regiment. From the place of enlistment
the regiment marched to Philip's Fort in Georgia, where it was stationed
three months, and then allowed to return home. In the latter part of
the same year he was drafted into the army, and went to the "ten-mile
house" in South Carolina, where he remained until discharged at the
expiration of his term of service. Soon after his return home he was
again summoned to arms, and went out as a mounted volunteer in Col.

Walton's regiment, which proceeded to Mobley's Meeting-house in South Carolina, where a party of Tories was attacked, defeated, and a large number of them taken prisoners. Soon afterward a party of Americans under the command of Col. Brandon was defeated by the English at the stations on Fishing Creek. The next engagement was at Hill's Iron Works, where the Americans were again defeated and the works burned. About this time Col. Walton became discouraged and threw up his command, when Gordon with twenty-six others joined Gen. Sumter, who, uniting his forces with Col. Lock and Maj. Fall, attacked and defeated Moore at the head of 1,100 Tories, at Ransom's in North Carolina. From this point the American force marched down the Catawba and met the enemy under Beaufort Brown at Love's Ford, who was promptly driven out without the firing of a gun. The force then returned to Rocky Mount, where a spirited skirmish took place, and thence proceeded across the Catawba River to Hanging Rock, in North Carolina. Here this force joined the command of Major Davy, and had constant skirmishing with the enemy until the mouth of Fishing Creek was reached, where the Americans were brought to a stand and defeated. From the scene of this action the force proceeded to Biggen's Bottom, where they spent some time in recruiting their strength and numbers, and subsequently followed down the course of the Congaree River, skirmishing with the enemy at Wright's Bluff and at Congaree Fort, S. C. Making a long, tedious march from this point to Bratton's old field, the command again fell in with the enemy, who gave way after a slight skirmish, but was again overtaken and defeated on the Broad River. The command then marched to Shire's Ferry, and thirty of the force were ordered to worry Tarleton's force on the opposite side of the river. At Black Stocks, another skirmish took place. Gen. Sumter, who had been laid up with a wound, now rejoined his command, but being called by Gen. Greene to Orangeburg, his command was attached to that of Col. Wade Hampton. The united forces then turned toward Charleston, and defeated an outlying force of the British near that city. During the balance of Mr. Gordon's service the command was engaged in scouring the country, engaging in repeated skirmishing, out of which he came unhurt.

Gideon Thompson, aged sixty-eight years, entered the service in 1782, and joined the command of Gen. Sumter. He was engaged in no battles, though taking part in several skirmishes. Matthew Thompson, aged seventy-two years, enlisted from Bedford County, Va., in 1775. He served in the First Regiment of the Line, commanded by Col. George Washington, who was afterward made Commander-in-Chief. Thompson enlisted for three years, and joined his company at New London, Conn., where he received clothes and his bounty money. From New

London his command was marched about 250 miles down the sea-shore, passing through Richmond and Williamsburg. They returned to the latter place, and stripping the lead covering from Lord Dunmore's house melted it into bullets. From this point he was marched to North Hampton where the force was stationed for a time, and then marched to Little England.

Henry Boyd, aged seventy-four, enlisted from Halifax County, Va., in 1778, under Capt. Moses Fountain, and marched to Charlotte Court House, Va. The company was attached to Col. Parker's command at Petersburg, and joined the expedition against Savannah, where the Americans were defeated October 1, 1779. Retreating to Augusta, Ga., the army spent the winter, and in the spring joined the forces under Gen. Lincoln at Charleston. Here after a siege of forty days the American Army was forced to surrender to Gen. Clinton. Boyd remained a prisoner some fifteen months. At first, with others, he was put into barracks, but after three or four months so many made their escape, the prisoners were removed to the prison ships in Charleston Bay, where Boyd was confined some ten months. At the expiration of this time, in company with Joshua Hawthorne and William Thompson, he made his escape by swimming about two miles on planks in the night, and was not in the service afterward.

Ephraim Shuffield, aged seventy-eight years, was drafted into the service for three months from Duplin County, N. C., under the command of Col. James Kenyon. The command was moved to Cape Fear, where it remained till the expiration of its term of service. Shuffield was soon after again drafted for a term of three months, which he served under the same commander. The command marched toward Charleston, S. C., and erected fortifications on the Catawba River. While here a detachment of 100 men were sent across the river to dislodge some troops of the enemy, but the force was found too large, and only twenty of the Americans escaped. The command then began a retreat, the British forces closely pursuing till Cross Creek, North Carolina, was reached, when an engagement ensued in which the pursuers were beaten. After this battle Shuffield was discharged, but was at home but a short time, when he volunteered under Capt. Bowden and marched toward Charleston, S. C. Reaching a point about thirty or forty miles from that city, the detachment turned toward Rock Fish Creek, where it was stationed for a time. Shuffield was then sent to Kingston on the Neuse River, and was subsequently discharged. James Flack, aged seventy-one years, entered the United States service under Col. McDowell and Gen. Butler, in 1779, from Guilford County, N. C. He made a campaign of about four months under these officers, and a second one of about four months under Col.

Pacely, in 1780, as Ensign. In 1781 he took part in a third campaign of four months under the command of Cols. Pacely and Isaacs. In the first year the company to which he was attached rendezvoused at Guilford, N. C., and from there marched to Salisbury, and thence through Charlotte, across the Savannah River into Georgia, where they went into camp near Augusta. Remaining here but a short time, the detachment retraced their steps. They went toward Charleston, S. C., to reconnoiter the ground, but retired, and were discharged without any especial incident to mark their service. In the second campaign the same ground was passed over with the same result, the company being discharged at Mecklenburg. In the third campaign the company was engaged principally in Randolph County in the pursuit of Tories. Ephraim Porter, aged sixty-nine years, entered the army in 1777, at the age of about fourteen. He enlisted from the State of Maryland under the command of Capt. Charles Hammond, Col. Thomas Dorsey and Gen. Smallwood. His company rendezvoused at Elk Ridge Landing, and from there marched by way of Baltimore to the head of Elk Creek, where Lord Howe was expected to land. From thence the command proceeded by several marches to Brandywine, and took part in that engagement. Generals Washington, La Fayette, Wayne and Sullivan commanded the regulars. The Americans were defeated and badly demoralized, Gen. Smallwood's Brigade retreating to " Perkeomen." Proceeding from thence this brigade soon fell in with Gen. Wayne's command, and the united force marched toward Germantown. At the " White Horse," the enemy having learned the American countersign, marched in and attacked the unsuspecting camp, stampeding the whole force. The dispersed force rendezvoused at Jones' tavern and continued the march to Germantown. Here the American Army attacked the British early in the morning, under cover of a heavy fog. When approaching this point, Wayne ordered his command to lie on their arms on either side of the road, near a large stone mill. While here the Dutch battalion of riflemen passed through the ranks and opened the battle by attacking the pickets of the enemy. The battle became general and lasted until ten or eleven o'clock, the Americans having decidedly the advantage in the early part of the fight, but the failure of Gen. Stephanes to come up at the proper time forced the Americans to give way in disastrous rout. Retreat from this field was made at great loss, and a month later the volunteers were discharged. While on his way home, Porter enlisted in the regular service and was assigned to the horse troop of Col. William Washington. He enlisted at Perkeomen, and from there marched to Frederickstown, Md., where the troop went into winter quarters. Here the troop was engaged in constructing brick barracks and guarding Hessian prisoners of war. In the spring, the troop left Porter sick in the hospital, who was soon after discharged at the solicitation of his mother. He volunteered again, however, in the following April or May, and served five months, guarding the magazine at this place, and in the fall, 1778, was discharged. Overton Harris and Robert Sherrod were Revolutionary soldiers, but who gave no detailed account of their service. In 1840 there were still living here a number of pensioners of this war, of whom nothing more than their age at this date and name is known, to wit: Robert Acock, eighty-six years; John M. Boyd, seventy-seven; James Flock, seventy-nine; George Gibson, seventy-eight; Samuel Gordon, eighty-one; Benjamin Pannel, eighty-three; Peter Petrie, seventy-seven; Jonathan Smith, eighty-three; William Turner, eighty-five; Anna Boone, sixty-seven; Jeannette Mahon, seventy, and Elizabeth Quarles, seventy-five. These disconnected stories tell the simple tale of the Revolution. The pomp and pageantry of war lent little luster to that determined and patriotic struggle, where every man was a "hero in the strife." The limited resources of the public treasury forbade the maintenance of a large regular army, and every patriot was invited to "work over against his own door." The heroic spirit which possessed the men and women of that day is plainly portrayed in the prosaic sketches recited. Men planted and left the women to cultivate and harvest the crop; discharged at the expiration of one term of service, the loyal partisan on his way home re-enlisted, "nor cast one longing, lingering look behind;" and thousands held themselves ready to fly to arms to resist the enemy's advance, to curb the Tory's treason, or join the regulars in the sturdy conflict in the "imminent deadly breach." Such were the simple agencies which wrought the marvel of the age. Nor did their influence cease with the times that called them forth. "E'en in their ashes live their wonted fires," and circling round the blazing hearth, a new generation learned of these tales of patriot devotion the deeper meaning of fatherland, a stronger affection for its institutions, and a profounder respect for the duties of a citizen.

The Second Struggle.—The early settlement of Kentucky demanded every resource of the pioneer. For thirty-five years he was hunter, scout, warrior and farmer by turns, and even women were called from the distaff to seize the death-dealing rifle. Up to the close of the war of 1812 no hour came that did not bring with it the distant threat of war. The first fury of the Indian onslaught had hardly spent itself, when the national questions involved in the free navigation of the Mississippi River, and the treason of Aaron Burr, were added to keep up the general alarm. Then in close sequence came the agitation over England's high-handed outrages which culminated in actual conflict. It was amid such scenes that Todd joined the sisterhood of counties, and though remote from the threatening border, the interest of each became the duty of all, and this county freely sent forth her sons to do battle for the general weal. The West, with its thousand savages, sullen with defeat, offered an admirable theater for the action of the enemy, and the flame of war rapidly spread toward the wilderness of Ohio and Michigan. Kentucky entered the ranks with ardor, and on every field her sons were "where danger called or duty." The population of Todd was small, but it is said the Hon. Benjamin Reeves organized a company which served in the war. Nothing is definitely known of its career, or under whose command it served, but there were some from Todd County in Gen. Hopkins' command, and it is probable that Col. Reeves' company was in the same department. On the declaration of war between England and the United States, the martial spirit blazed forth with unprecedented vigor in Kentucky. Several thousand volunteers at once offered their services to the Government, and 1,500 were on the march for Detroit when the news of Hull's surrender induced them to halt. The military ardor of the State seemed to increase in the face of this disaster, and 2,000 volunteers responded to the call of the Governor for troops to march against the Indian villages in northern Illinois. These volunteers rendezvoused at Louisville, and set forth under the command of Gen. Hopkins. The march into the Indian country was a difficult undertaking. Provisions became scarce, and the ardor of the untried soldiers having had time to cool, they deliberately returned to their starting point in spite of the remonstrance of their commanders, without having accomplished anything. Many of these volunteers afterward did noble service under Gen. Harrison and some of the Todd County contingency took part in the battle of Tippecanoe.

War with Mexico.—The four greater wars of this country mark the four stages of its development as a nation. Of these, the first two were waged for its existence as an independent power, and the rights due such independent state in the high court of nations, objects which commanded the united support of the people. The Federal party in national politics did indeed make a vigorous protest against the war with England in 1812, on the ground that it gave ostensible support to the French Revolution, a political movement that in the name of liberty perpetrated the most horrible outrages against freedom ; but the intolerable assumption of England to impress American seamen, and with a paper manifesto to destroy the commerce of the world, aroused the war spirit of the whole nation. In the latter respect the commercial centers of the new world had quite as much reason to complain of France, but a sentiment of gratitude for her timely aid in the Revolutionary struggle served somewhat to palliate the offense of the latter nation, and outside of New England the universal voice was for war. And now that time has removed the temporary cause of aversion, the achievements of these struggles are prized as the rich inheritance of every American. The last two wars, however, hold a different place in the hearts of the people, and the impartial historian must ever note them as the mad fevers that follow the insidious poisoning of the nation's civilization. Their origin must be sought at the very fountain head of the national existence. Two distinct and dominant social elements were planted upon the virgin soil of the new world, the graceless Cavalier and the intolerant Puritan—the fateful legacy of the Stuart dynasty. These elements, antagonistic in every law of their being, under the old colonial *regime* found ample room to develop without coming into contact with each other, but with their consolidation into a nation, a mutual repulsion began which threatened to disrupt the State. " Mason and Dixon's line " for a time delayed the " irrepressible conflict," but the growing demand of the far South was for " more room." The Texan rebellion offered an opportunity to evade the direct issue between these warring elements, which was speedily seized by the one and reluctantly acquiesced in by the other. The Whig party in politics feebly opposed the measure on the ground that further extension of territory was undesirable, especially when it was gained on questionable pretenses that had no sure foundation in fact; but the dominant power in national affairs boldly launched the ship of State upon the turbulent billows of war. Allied by politics to the Whig party, and by its origin and civilization to the far South, Kentucky joined the cry for war urged by chivalrous rather than mercenary motives. The military spirit was excessively developed in Kentucky. The militia, authorized and provided for by law, drew its vigor from the chivalrous sentiment of the people, and in its rank and file were found the leading spirits of every community. The One Hundred and Second Regiment drew its strength from Todd County, and the annual muster at Elkton was the event of the year. The admission of Texas into the Union, May 1, 1845, fore-shadowed a contest with Mexico and fanned the military spirit to a fever heat. When the call for troops came in September of the following year the One Hundred and Second Regiment was assembled at Elkton, and paraded on the hill southwest of the village. Here it was addressed by James A. Russell and Finis E. McLean, who fired the heart of these holiday soldiers to the pitch of madness, and when the latter orator proposed that the Governor should be tendered the services of the whole regiment, the suggestion was greeted with a universal shout of approval. The call of the Governor, however, allowed the acceptance of but a single company from a county, and the regiment was subsequently formed in line of battle on the Russellville road, east of the village, and the orators, preceded by a band of martial music, paraded before the regiment amid the firing of guns, the rattle of drums, and the squeaking of fifes. One after another the recruits stepped out of the ranks and joined the procession which paraded up and down the front of the regiment, until the full complement was obtained. Unfortunately for the chronicler of this veritable history, all this "pomp and circumstance" of war ended in sound and fury. The tender of the company thus enlisted was declined, as the quota of the. State had been filled before it was received, and Todd County's military ardor "lost the name of action."

The Civil War.—The war which opened the vast area of Texas to the expansion of slavery proved a costly but vain experiment, and the cry for "more room" was soon heard as urgent as before. There was no expedient by which the issue which was fast hurrying on could be evaded. The tastes and habits of the people made national politics an absorbing topic, and while nothing here contributed to disturb the unanimity of sentiment, the popular sympathy was not wholly with either of the predominant political factions. Todd County was unanimously opposed to emancipation, a firm supporter of the principles enunciated in the famous "Resolutions of 1798," and remained to the last a devoted supporter of the Whig school of politics. On the triumph of the Republican party in the election of Lincoln, the general sentiment accepted it as the inevitable result of popular elections, and accepted the defeat in good faith. But the ominous mutterings of the "Cotton States" could not fail to awaken the liveliest concern in regard to the future. There were no elements of agitation here, but the popular sympathy was strongly with the radical measures adopted in certain communities to drive out the friends of emancipation from the State, and with the legislative efforts to intrench the "domestic institution." But with this was an overwhelming loyalty to the Union, and a desire to avert the threatening collision. In the celebrated "Peace Convention" which met in Washington February 4, 1861, Todd County was represented in the person of Hon. Francis M. Bristow. The attack on Fort Sumter and its surrender dispelled the fond illusion that war could be averted, and the Lexington speech of the Hon. John J. Crittenden, on April 17, voiced the popular feeling here. The sentiment was: "Kentucky had done nothing to bring the war about; she had not invited it; it was against her interests and she should do nothing to promote it, but by all the moral force of her position, should bravely hold on to the flag of the Union, and under its broad folds extend the hand of conciliation to both." The position, however logical, was impracticable, not only in Todd County but throughout the State. The partisans of either side strove to turn the popular tide to their own advantage, and the "moral force" of neutrality proved "a little more than kin and less than kind" to either faction. In Todd County the prevailing sentiment stood firm for the Union for some time, though intensely sensitive as to the final effect of the war upon slavery. This proved the weak point in her armor of neutrality. On every available occasion the great questions involved were discussed with an earnest eloquence which bespoke sincerity on the part of the participants. Although the old-time State-leaders of the people continued to counsel the giving of aid and countenance to neither the National nor rebellious cause, the nature and the training of the people were opposed to it. The chivalrous blood of the Kentuckian bounded through his veins at quicker speed, to think of the promise of heroic action on one side or the other. Too hot-blooded to be a cynic, he must act the partisan. Loyal to the teaching of the "Resolutions of 1798," the action of the leading State men was largely favorable to the rebellious States. In an address issued by the Union State Central Committee, composed of Harney, Prentice, Bullock, Speed, etc., their position was defined as follows: "What the future duty of Kentucky may be, we of course cannot with certainty foresee; but if the enterprise announced by the President should at any time hereafter assume the aspect of a war for the overrunning and subjugation of the seceding States—through the full assertion therein of the national jurisdiction by a standing military force—we do not hesitate to say that Kentucky should promptly unsheath her sword in behalf of what will then have become the common cause." Such language was unmistakably in favor of the rebelling States, and opposed to the assertion of the national authority by force of arms. Todd County was flanked on the west by the Union sentiment of Christian, and the violent rebellious sentiment of Logan on the east, and soon began to waver in its neutral position. Hon. James A. Russell gave the influence of his eloquence to the Southern cause, and declared his earnest convictions far and near with telling effect. In one of his earliest efforts in the court house at Elkton, with almost prophetic insight, he declared that if war ensued "the tramp of a negro soldiery will be heard in our streets, and the glint of their bayonets in this hall of justice." The cause of the Union was advocated with equal fervor by Hon. F. M. Bristow, his son, Benjamin H., and Judge Ben. T. Perkins, Sr., who declared that the war was waged solely for the maintenance of the National authority, and that if any attempt was made to interfere with the "domestic institutions" of a State, they too would be ready to take up arms in defense of their rights.

The hill country of the county was strongly in favor of the Union ; for a time even Russell, who was greatly respected, was not allowed to make speeches there, and the dividing line between the two factions in this county may be said to be the line dividing the rich farming district of the south and the broken, hilly country of the north—the slaveholding and non-slaveholding population of the county. Enlistments were rapidly going forward in the State without regard to the obligations of a neutral power, and by the middle of May a regiment of Kentucky troops, under the command of Blanton Duncan, had rendezvoused at Harper's Ferry, Va., in the interest of the Confederate cause. By July several regiments of Kentuckians were forming at Camp Boone, eight miles from Clarksville, for the Confederate service, and at Camp Clay, opposite Newport, and at Camp Joe Holt, opposite Louisville, four Kentucky regiments were forming for the national service. In August a Federal camp— Dick Robinson—was boldly established by Gen. Nelson in Garrard County, Ky., which called forth the indignant remonstrance of Gov. Magoffin through two commissioners. The President replied that this force consisted solely of Kentuckians in the vicinity of their homes, and was raised at the urgent solicitation of many Kentuckians, and declined to move it. In September the Confederate troops from Tennessee occupied and fortified strong positions at Hickman and Columbus, Ky., and Federal troops occupied Paducah. In the same month the Legislature passed a resolution demanding the unconditional withdrawal of the Confederate troops, and at the same time refused to demand the same of the Federal force, or to pass a resolution demanding both to withdraw. Thus even the pretense of neutrality was overturned with a leaning toward the National cause, but the policy of temporizing was still continued.

Military Operations.—About the middle of September Gen. S. B. Buckner moved with his troops from Camp Boone to Bowling Green, and issued his proclamation as an officer of the Confederate army, "to the people of Kentucky," that the force under his command "will be used to aid the Governor of Kentucky in carrying out *strict neutrality* desired by its people whenever they undertake to enforce it against the two belligerents alike." Notwithstanding this, the Confederates put forward the first act of war by burning the bridge over Rolling Fork, five miles west of Muldrow Hill. This occurred on the 18th of September, and on the following day the first clash of arms was heard, the Confederates attacking the *State Guard.* Federal camps at once sprang into existence in several places, and the Legislature, without breaking with the National Government, constituted a Military Board to enlist, arm and control a body of State troops, which very soon were turned over to the United States Army by act of the Legislature. United States troops began to pour into the State, and the reports of skirmishes between the hostile forces were heard at Smithland, Lucas Bend, Buffalo Hill and Grayson. In the meanwhile the Military Board had appointed recruiting officers in various parts of the State, Judge Perkins being appointed in Todd County. In a short time two companies were formed here, which were organized and mustered at Calhoun, on Green River. These were mustered into the United States service as Companies C and F, of the Twenty-fifth Regiment of Kentucky Infantry. Company C was officered as follows : D. M. Claggett, Captain ; Jesse Griffin, First Lieutenant; Walter Evans, of Christian County, and now Commisioner of Internal Revenue, Second Lieutenant. Company F was officered with E. B. Edwards, Captain; F. H. Bristow, First Lieutenant ; and S. H. Perkins, Second Lieutenant. Soon after being mustered into the service they were ordered to join Gen. Grant's command in Tennessee, and were present at the taking of Fort Donelson. They continued with this command to Shiloh, where the regiment suffered severely, as did all the troops engaged. After the battle the Seventeenth and Twenty-Fifth Regiments of Kentucky Infantry were consolidated, as neither was full, under the title of the former. The two companies raised from Todd, Christian and Muhlenburg Counties were consolidated as Company D, of the Seventeenth Regiment, with D. M. Claggett, as Captain ; F. H. Bristow, First Lieutenant ; and Ned Campbell of Christian County, as Second Lieutenant; the other officers retiring from the service save Lieut. Griffin, who was killed at Fort Donelson. The regiment as consolidated continued in service until December 29, 1864, when it was mustered out at Louisville. A considerable number of Todd County young men found their way into the Federal Army, but as there were no public early enlistments in the county, they went in squads of two or three to various organizations, of which there is no record.

The friends of the Confederate cause were much more prompt in making enlistments in this county. Early in the spring of 1861 a large company was formed by Childers and Edward Meriwether. They formed a camp at Trenton, and drilled for some time, organizing with Childers as Captain, and Meriwether as Lieutenant. Some difference sprang up in the company, when Childers with some twenty men left for Lee's army, and joined Duncan's regiment at Harper's Ferry, Va. They soon started to join the army of Virginia, and were only prevented by a land-slide from taking part in the fight at Manassas. The balance of this company repaired to Camp Boone, and were mustered into an infantry regiment with the understanding that when Meriwether should recruit sufficient numbers to form a company with them, they should be released for that purpose. They subsequently proceeded with Buckner's command to the northern part of the State, and circling south came to Hopkinsville. Here Meriwether demanded the carrying out of the agreement, and after some difficulty this was effected, the company under command of Meriwether forming a part of Forrest's cavalry. Capt. Meriwether was a gallant officer, and was killed early in the war, his company subsequently forming a part of Woodward's regiment.

At the Front.—The record of their service has been written by Hon. Austin Peay, as follows:

" At Oak Grove, Christian Co., Ky., on the 9th day of April, 1861, a company of cavalry was organized with Thomas G. Woodward, a West Point graduate, as Captain. Oak Grove is near the Tennessee line, and many Tennesseans anxious to become soldiers united their fortunes with this Kentucky company. The citizens around Oak Grove were ardent Southerners, and gave liberally of their means to mount, arm and equip the company. Lieut. Darwin Bell and Orderly William Blakemore were sent on a secret mission to Cincinnati for arms, and succeeded in purchasing enough fine Colt's revolvers with which to arm the company.

"It was the intention of the company to unite with the Kentucky State Guards, but the action of the State was so dilatory that on the 25th of June, 1861, it was mustered into the Tennessee service as an independent organization. It numbered 108 men and officers, and no finer body of men, or better equipped, ever sought or obtained service anywhere. It saw no active service for some months, but was drilled in camp at Boone, Cheatham and Trousdale.

" When the army invaded Kentucky, it led its vanguard, and penetrated as far as Hopkinsville, the home of many of its members, returning to Bowling Green in the early winter. At Bowling Green the company grew to such proportions that it was divided into two companies, and then merged into the First Kentucky Cavalry as Companies A and B, Capt. Darwin Bell commanding Company A, and Capt. William Caldwell Company B. Woodward was promoted to Lieutenant-Colonel. Ben Hardin Helm, a noble gentleman and chivalrous soldier, who gave his life for his country on the field of Chickamauga, was Colonel of the regiment. The regiment was 1,200 strong.

" Hard service, picketing and scouting through the hard winter of 1861 and 1862 characterized the company's history, and a few skirmishes, in which the men bore themselves well, and gave promise of the valor which afterward bore fruition upon many a hard-fought field. When the army retreated from Kentucky, the regiment was its rear guard, and with sickening heart followed its dreary march through the whole State of Tennessee, until once again it formed its lines and confronted the enemy at Shiloh. Then it was stationed at Florence, Ala., and gave Gen. Johnston accurate information of the advance of Buell's army, which precipitated the attack at Shiloh. After the battle, which but for the untimely death of that great soldier, Gen. Johnston, would have been the most complete victory of the war, the command followed the varying fortunes of the army in Mississippi and Alabama until in May of 1862, under Gen. Adams, it was sent on a raid in middle Tennessee. Here it was engaged

in several hard fights.   At Winchester, Tenn., Companies A and L, with
a fool-hardy courage, under orders of Capt. Cox, of Adams' staff, who was
in command, charged the court house filled with Federal infantry, halted
in its front, fired their guns and revolvers in its doors and windows in the
faces of the astonished foe, and then retreated under a murderous fire,
which left many of its best and bravest dead and wounded.   At Huey's
Bridge, the First Kentucky and some companies of the Eighth Texas,
charged a Federal regiment entrenched in camp, and killed or captured
every man of them, but with fearful loss of life among its officers and
men.   The advance of the Federal infantry drove Adams' command from
this portion of Tennessee across the river to Chattanooga.   Here on the
25th of June, 1862, the time of enlistment of Companies A and B expired, and they were mustered out of the service.   Some of the men re-
enlisted at once and joined a command which Forrest was raising for a
raid into Tennessee and Kentucky, but the greater number returned to
their homes within the Federal lines in the above-named States.

" On the 12th of July, just seven days after disbandment, Woodward
had returned into Kentucky, and in Christian County began the organization of a new command.   His old men almost to a man gathered
around him, new recruits flocked to him from Kentucky and Tennessee,
and he soon had a large regiment in the field.   The men were generally
not well armed, and like all raw recruits in the beginning wanting in discipline, but under Woodward's fine system of military tactics they soon
became disciplined and hardened to the usages of war.   They met the
enemy often, and with varying success.   Clarksville, Tenn., with Col.
Mason and its entire garrison, was captured with but little loss; Fort
Donelson was attacked, but the attack was repulsed with severe loss.   The
next morning the enemy, presuming upon the repulse of the day before,
followed to the Rolling Mills, and charged with a regiment of cavalry.
Woodward had had warning of their approach, and was ready for them.
The command was placed in position under the river banks, and in the
demolished works of the old mill, while the small four-pounder was in position at a bridge which was a little way in front.   The Federal cavalry
scarcely gave the command time to get into position before it charged in
column down the road.   On they came with headlong courage.   The
cannon was overturned after one discharge, and the cavalry with drawn
sabers swept down upon our position.   The tale was soon told.   The men
poured a terrible fire from both sides of the road into their serried column,
and the road was soon choked with dead and wounded men and horses.
Two front companies were annihilated, not a single man escaping to tell
the bloody fate of his comrades.   The rear companies never came through,
but turned and fled.   The command lost not a man in the action, and its
retreat was in safety to Clarksville.

"Woodward remained in Kentucky drilling and enlarging his command until after the battle of Perryville and Bragg's retreat from Kentucky. The Federals then sent Gen. Ransom with a large command into southern Kentucky to drive Woodward out. Near the little town of Garrettsburg, in September of 1862, the Federals struck Woodward's regiment in line of battle. The conflict was sharp and brief. Overpowered in numbers, armed only with shot-guns, and upon ground unfitted for cavalry fighting, the men were no match for the long range rifles of the trained infantry and artillery of the foe, and broke into disorder and fell back in great confusion, leaving a good many dead on the field, and carrying off as many more wounded. The next day Cumberland River was crossed, Kentucky faded into the distance, and the homes of our birth were left to the possession of the foe.

"Near Charlotte, in Dixon County, the command was camped for some time. The regiment was enlisted for one year's service, and here came the tidings that the Confederate authorities would receive no enlistment for less than three years' service, and it came coupled with the command to swear the men in for three years and place the regiment under the command of Forrest, who was then preparing to invade west Tennessee. At this time Forrest was as much feared and despised as he was afterward appreciated and beloved. So the men refused to submit to the terms proposed and the regiment went to pieces, as the night gathered clans of McGregor dissolved before the light of the morning.

"Woodward's work, before its full fruition, had come to naught. His disappointment was great, but nothing daunted, he gathered around him a company of 100 men, followed Forrest into west Tennessee and did yeoman service, participating in every engagement of that hard campaign, and winning the highest commendation for himself and men from his chief, that glorious old dead hero, who never said to his men, 'Go,' but 'Follow me.' In this campaign was killed Lieut. Joe Staton, a man of great vanity, but of courage as true as steel, of brilliant mind, and an officer gallant as ever drew saber or buckled a spur.

"When Woodward returned from the campaign in west Tennessee, for weeks his command was camped at Columbia, Tenn. His old comrades again flocked to his standard; there was no peace for them while their beloved South writhed in the grasp of the foe and fought for liberty. They came in troops and companies; to-day in squads of three or four, to-morrow in organized companies, mostly from Kentucky, but a goodly sprinkling of Tennesseans, most of whom joined Company A, commanded by Will A. Elliott, himself a son of Tennessee. Company C was composed entirely of Tennesseans, and its Captain, Tom Lewis, was as noble a gentleman and brave a soldier as ever lived or died. Soon once more by his indomitable exertions, Woodward had organized a fine, serviceable body of men.   Seven full companies answered at his roll-call and stood ready to follow him to battle: not sufficient for a regiment, yet it was received as such.   Woodward was elected to the command with the rank of Lieutenant-Colonel, and Thomas Lewis as Major.   Its companies were commanded and distinguished as follows: Company A, Capt. Will A. Elliott, about one-third Tennesseans; Company B, Capt. Given Campbell; Company C, Capt. Tom Lewis; after Lewis' promotion to Major commanded by Lieut. Jackson; Company D, Capt. Robert Biggs; Company E, Capt. John Crutcher; Company F, Capt. J. H. Harvey; and Company G, Capt. Joe Williams.   C. D. Bell was Adjutant and Edward Gray Sergeant-Major.

"Thus was organized and officered and constituted a regiment, and sworn into the Confederate service for the war.   It was the famous Second Kentucky, and if its country had a history its record should be written deep upon it.   But who can write its history?   It would take a volume in itself to contain it.   It cannot be done; its roll has been lost, and could it be called to-day more voices would answer from the further shore than from this.   The pen stands appalled at the magnitude of the task. How write the eulogies and elegies of its living and dead?   Its dead sleep in every State of the South, and not a stream that has not run red with their blood.   From the deep-moving current of Green River to the slumbrous waters of Cape Fear these veterans marched and fought.   From where the winds of winter sweep in shrill cadences over the hills of northern Kentucky, to where the warm waves of the ocean lave the sand beaches of Carolina, they followed the flag of their country with unfaltering devotion through victory and defeat, until with sorrowing hearts they saw it furled and laid away forever.

"Who can write its history, illustrate its devotion and call the roster of its dead?   How it followed a cause until 'lost' and dead; how it fought under Forrest, the most beloved leader of them all, in his numerous hard fights in many campaigns; in east Tennessee under chivalrous Kelly; and then to Chickamauga, where Forrest dismounted his men and led them into battle as infantry, and when the enemy were defeated and routed, he mounted his impetuous riders and pushed them right upon Chattanooga. Here Forrest, followed by Maj. William Caldwell, Adj. C. D. Bell and Lieut. Pack Edwards, daringly charged into the streets of the town, where Forrest's horse was killed.   After this battle the regiment, in spite of its prayers and tears, was taken from Gen. Forrest and with the First and Ninth Kentucky organized into a brigade, and placed under the command of J. Warren Grigsby, and assigned to Gen. Joseph Wheeler's corps of cavalry.   This was in obedience to new regulations from Richmond, putting regiments from same State in brigades together. Forrest was to be sent into west Tennessee, and was allowed some troops with him. He asked for the Second Kentucky and McDonald's battalion, but for some reason was refused his request.

"Wheeler, immediately after the battle of Chickamauga, gathered together his forces, and crossing the Tennessee far above Chattanooga, swept around the enemy's rear through the whole of middle Tennessee, leaving ruin and devastation for him wherever he marched. At Farmington was fought a battle in which the Second Kentucky lost heavily and bore the brunt of the fight.

"It would be an endless task to attempt to follow in detail the service under this distinguished general, the Prince Rupert of the Confederate army. After the raid into Tennessee and some further service in east Tennessee, the command was recalled to the main army, and Gen. John S. Williams sent to command the brigade, under whom it served until the close of the war. After the disastrous defeat at Missionary Ridge, Wheeler covered the retreat from Dalton to Atlanta, and after the battle of Jonesboro followed and captured Stoneman and his command in the heart of Georgia, and then again crossing the Tennessee River near Knoxville, made the circuit of the enemy's rear. On this raid Williams' brigade was separated from the main command, and being hard pushed returned by way of east Tennessee and Virginia, reaching Saltville in time to join in the battle there under Gen. John C. Breckinridge, which resulted in the total overthrow of the Federals, and the saving of those valuable works.

"Hood had invaded Tennessee, and Sherman was marching for the sea. Williams' brigade was sent to join Hampton, who was the only foe Sherman had in his front. This general was another Forrest, and fighting was hard, but how useless. A few cavalry, however great their valor, could not successfully check the countless hordes of Sherman, and hordes they were more pitiless than those of Attila and Genghis Khan, leaving fiery destruction in their march. Hampton fought them every step, and kept their plunderers from scattering too far from their line of march. On the plains in front of Columbia, S. C., Gen. Williams' brigade was engaged in the heaviest contest of the war for it, and the Second Kentucky left its best and bravest, dead on the field.

"Soon after the foe reached the sea the command joined Gen. Johnston, who was gathering the scattered fragments of Hood's army in North Carolina. History tells how those decimated veterans fought at Bentonville. Part of that history belongs to this veteran regiment. Hope had fled, death had thinned its ranks, but with unconquered resolution its men fought; and it is but truth and justice to say that they never met the foe in those last days but their battle-scarred banner floated in victory over his silenced batteries and broken columns. But the dread fiat which struck sorrow to so many faithful hearts had gone forth from the Lord of Hosts, and the cause was lost !

"President Davis dispatched to Gen. Johnston at Raleigh to send, as an escort for himself and the remains of the Government, a thousand of his best cavalry. Dibbrell's division, composed of Williams' and Dibbrell's brigades, was sent. The division reached the President at Greenville, and followed him in mournful march until about three days before his capture, beyond Washington, Ga. It was a mournful cortege that wound along over the hills of Carolina and Georgia in those memorable May days of 1865. The writer of this remembers on this march a scene one morning that made a strong impression on his youthful mind. An ambulance, which was in the train and near the front, had mired in the mud, or broken something, which caused a halt. Around it, with shoulder to the wheel on one side, was Judah P. Benjamin, Secretary of State ; on the other side was John H. Reagan, Postmaster-General, and looking on were the Secretary of the Treasury and Samuel Cooper, Adjutant-General of all the armies ; while a little further off, mounted and looking on, were President Davis and Gen. John C. Breckinridge, Secretary of War.

"The regiment was paroled May 9, near Washington, Ga., and allowed to retain their horses, but at Chattanooga the horses were taken from them and they sent to Nashville and lodged in the penitentiary until morning. In the morning its men were marched into the city, made to take the oath, and allowed to go to their homes sadder and wiser, if not better men.

"Such is but a cursory sketch of a command composed of the flower of the youth of Kentucky and Tennessee, and which did its duty in a great historic conflict. It is incomplete and imperfect, and it is not possible now, and never will be, to write an accurate history of its deeds. No history of Tennessee could be complete, or just, or honest, unless meritorious mention was made, even nameless though they be, of those gallant sons, who, merging their identity in this Kentucky regiment, gave their services and fought and died for the land and cause which they in common with their mother Tennessee loved so well. Some of them go through life dragging their poor wounded bodies, and no government administers to them with fostering care, while the graves of many more, who died in battle, dot the hills and plains of the South, and the finger of affection cannot find their last resting place. No monument rises above them, no cenotaph, perhaps, will ever have carved on its voiceful marble their glorious deeds ; but how useless are all of these, for marble and monumental brass corrode and fall into dust, but their memories live and flourish in the hearts of their comrades, green as the grass that grows above them, and in the traditions of their grateful country their heroic deeds shall live forever."

A few found their way to Morgan's command, and to other organizations in the Confederate Army. Most of these enlistments were made early in the war, there being little in the cause of either side to subsequently draw the more conservative element into the ranks of either army. As matters progressed, the folly of any attempt to maintain neutrality became more apparent. The Union sentiment secured and maintained control of the official machinery of the State, notwithstanding the short-lived attempt to establish at Bowling Green a provisional government to draw the State into the Confederacy. The temporizing policy, however, served to make Kentucky the battle-ground of the contending armies, and only the early success of the Union arms in Tennessee saved Kentucky from the most destructive ravages of war. Todd County was situated too far west to experience the effect of a campaign by large armies, but the community was kept in a constant state of insecurity by the scouting parties of both armies. It should be said, however, that the non-combatant adherents of either party acted with good faith toward each other. When detachments of either army appeared in the county, the friendly influence of the partisan of the dominant power was always exerted in behalf of his neighbors, and while none were safe from the indiscriminate plunderings of the guerrillas, or the arbitrary action of irresponsible subordinates, still the community here suffered comparatively little the ravages of war. Two slight skirmishes, on the western border of the county and at Coleman's bridge; a few dashes of guerrillas into Elkton, with the usual plundering of a store or smokehouse; and the occasional passage or temporary stationing of small bodies of troops in the county, were the sum of Todd County's military experiences.

Hon. Benjamin H. Bristow.—Besides its contributions to the file of either army, Todd County claims the nativity of two of the leaders in this contest, who according to the "eternal fitness of things" were arrayed on either side. On the side of the Union was Benjamin Helm Bristow. He is second in a family of four children, and was born at Elkton, Ky., in July, 1832. After gaining the rudiments of an education here, he was placed at an early age in Jefferson College, at Cannonsburg, Penn. After completing the course of study prescribed by this institution he returned to Elkton, and entering the office of his father, Hon. F. M. Bristow, began the study of law. In 1857 he removed to Hopkinsville, where he formed a partnership with Judge R. T. Petrie, and practiced his profession with some success until the breaking out of the civil war. During the unsettled state of things incident to the effort to maintain a neutral position on the part of Kentucky, his efforts were united with others in sustaining the Union sentiment against the eloquence of the secession orators, and when the question passed from the forum of debate, he promptly enlisted in the National army. He was mustered into the service of the United States as Lieutenant-Colonel of the Twenty-fifth Kentucky Infantry, Col. Shackelford commanding, and distinguished himself as an efficient officer and soldier in the battles of Fort Henry, Fort Donelson and Pittsburg Landing. Returning home in 1862 he became active in raising the Eighth Kentucky Cavalry, with which he again entered the service as Lieutenant-Colonel. This regiment found active service and made an honorable record on many a field, taking part in the pursuit and capture of John Morgan, under the command of Bristow as Colonel. In 1863 he was transferred from the army to the Legislature of his native State, being elected to the Senate from the Hopkinsville District. He served on the Committee on Military Affairs, and did loyal service for the Union during those eventful years of 1863–65. He then resigned his seat in the Legislature and located in Louisville, taking up the practice of his profession. In 1866 Col. Bristow was appointed Assistant United States District Attorney for Kentucky, and about a year later succeeded to the office of District Attorney. The office at that time required the courage of conviction to sustain the incumbent, and Col. Bristow discharged his duty with unflinching honesty and acceptance to both the partisans of State and National interests. In 1870 he resigned this position and formed a law partnership with Gen. John M. Harlin, which lasted less than a year, when he was called to the office of Solicitor-General of the United States. He was the first incumbent of this office, which he filled with approved ability for some two years, when he again resigned office and retired to private life and the practice of his profession in Louisville.

Col. Bristow's ability in his profession and success in his official career gave him a prominent place among his professional brethren in the State, and a foremost place in the bar of Louisville. When Attorney-General Williams was nominated for Chief Justice, Bristow was nominated to succeed him, but the failure of Williams to receive the confirmation of the Senate left no vacancy. On the resignation of Richardson as Secretary of the Treasury, President Grant called Col. Bristow to fill this position. Here he made his individuality appear by beginning a vigorous war upon the frauds which were being perpetrated under cover of the system of internal revenue. He carried forward his work against the most vigorous opposition of not only the victims of his prosecution, but by the unconvicted officials or accomplices in his department. He succeeded, however, in demonstrating the enormous character of the frauds, and in enlisting the enthusiastic support of the Nation. Coming on the eve of a Presidential election, it gaʋe Mr. Bristow a prestige which promised to bring him to the White House; but these fond anticipations failed, and recognizing that his work was accomplished, he again retired to private life and the practice of law at Louisville. He subsequently removed to New York City, where he is still practicing his profession, appearing occasionally as orator before political conferences, though not actively engaged in politics.

Jefferson Davis.—Among the earliest settlers of Todd County was Samuel Davis, an old Revolutionary soldier, who came from Georgia and settled in what is now Fairview, just east of the Christian County line. Here, in a log-cabin still standing, his son Jefferson was born June 3, 1808. Several years later the family removed to Wilkinson County, Miss., where the father became a cotton planter. Jefferson Davis was early placed at the Transylvania University, where he remained until his sixteenth year. In 1824 he received an appointment to the United States Military Academy at West Point, where he met Robert E. Lee, Joseph E. Johnston, Leonidas Polk and others who afterward became distinguished in the service of the Confederacy. Graduating in 1828, Davis was assigned to duty on the northwestern frontier, and in 1832 was advanced to the position of First Lieutenant. In the following year he was made Adjutant of a regiment of dragoons, and after serving through the Blackhawk war and other Indian disturbances, he resigned his commission and settled down to the life and retirement of a cotton planter. Eight years later he emerged from the seclusion of his plantation as a delegate to the State Democratic Convention, and in the following year "stumped" the country as elector. He championed the extreme "States' Rights" doctrine from the first, a dogma around which his political principles have at all times revolved. In 1845 he was elected to the lower house of Congress, where he rose rapidly in the estimation of his colleagues and constituency. He took a prominent part in the debates of the House, displaying an independence of action, a refinement of speech and a breadth of thought that brought him to the favorable notice of members of all parties. While serving in Congress he was appointed Colonel of the First Mississippi Regiment, enlisted for the Mexican war. He immediately resigned his seat in Congress, and with his regiment repaired to the Rio Grande in the summer of 1846. During his term of service he distinguished himself for gallantry and won the favorable mention of his superiors in general orders. In 1847 he was appointed by the Governor of his State to fill a vacancy in the United States Senate, caused by the death of Gen. Speight. He was afterward elected by the Legislature and served until 1851, appearing in the Senate to quite as great advantage as formerly in the House. At this time he resigned his seat at the request of his fellow-citizens to make a hopeless race for Governor, in opposition to the "Compromise of 1850," in which he was defeated. He was an ardent supporter of Franklin Pierce for the Presidency in 1852, and on his election was given the portfolio of Secretary of War in the new administration. While still holding his position in Mr. Pierce's Cabinet, he was elected to the United States Senate, and took his seat March 4, 1857. With the inauguration of Buchanan's administration began the political movements which ushered in the great civil war. In all the storm of debate which followed on the Kansas-Nebraska measures, Mr. Davis bore an active and leading part, as one of the exponents of the extreme States' Rights doctrine adopted by one faction of his party. His speeches were accepted as the authoritative expression of the position and determination of this ultra wing of the Democratic party, and created a profound sensation throughout the nation. On January 9, 1861, Mississippi passed the ordinance of secession, and on the 21st of that month he withdrew from his seat in the Senate. He was at once placed in command of the militia of the State, and proceeded to place it on a war basis. February 5, 1861, he was chosen President of "The Confederate States of America" by the convention of delegates from the seceding States assembled at Montgomery, Ala. In the same month he was inaugurated and formed his Government; and in the May following the seat of Government was moved to Richmond, Va., where it remained to the end. Mr. Davis remained to the last a sanguine believer in the eventual success of the cause in which he had embarked, notwithstanding the discouraging view of many of his associates from the beginning. The final collapse buried in its ruins all his hopes and ambitions; and unable, in the very constitution of his mind, to accept the logic of events, his occupation gone, he has placed himself in an attitude hostile to the best interests of that section of which he was once the foremost champion. "'Tis much he dared;" but unfortunately, he lacked the "wisdom that doth guide his valor, to act in safety." The "piping times of peace" that have intervened have brought great changes to Todd County. The enfranchisement of the negro has alienated many of the Union men from their associates of those "troublous times," and some of the bitterest opponents to the National party of politics are those who, in 1861, were stanchest in their devotion to the National cause. By the addition of the negro vote the Republican party is a vigorous minority, but the Democratic party bears unquestioned sway, *not* as adherents to the "lost cause," but as opposed to the rule of the great mass of ignorance and non-property holders of the county.

CHAPTER VII.

MAGISTERIAL DISTRICT No. 4—ELKTON—TOPOGRAPHY—FIRST ROADS AND BRIDGES—EARLY SETTLERS AND SETTLEMENT—JOHN P. BROWN—HAZLE PETRIE—THE EDWARDSES—MAJ. JOHN GRAY—JAMES KENDALL—FIRST ATTEMPTS TO FOUND THE SCHOOL AND CHURCH—VILLAGE OF ELKTON— ORIGINAL PLAT AND ADDITIONS—FIRST RESIDENTS—GREEN RIVER ACADEMY—THE PRESS—TOWN OFFICIALS—CHURCHES, ETC.

DISTRICT organization as formed in Kentucky is by no means similar to the township organization of the Northwest, and does not afford so reasonable nor obvious a division of the historical interests of the people. But in an attempt to supply the fullest details of the county's history for which there is any data, the necessity for some such division becomes apparent, and these arbitrary lines have been seized upon to aid in such systematic treatment as the best result seemed to demand. These lines, however, are expressive of something more than the convenience or whim of the authority by which they were run. Neighborhoods form natural centers of their own without reference to political divisions, and are earliest formed. Dividing lines are subsequently drawn to suit the tastes or conveniences thus created, and while the " district " lacks much in individuality, a community of interest is sufficiently developed to suggest the plan here followed.

The centralized character of county organization makes the county seat the seat of power and importance, toward which the activities of the whole county tend, and, with rare exceptions, to which commercial enterprise is attracted. This is eminently true of Elkton, and with the completion of the projected railroad from Elkton to Guthrie its predominance over other villages in the county will be more marked. The district known as No. 4, the lines of which are drawn about the county seat, is centrally located, but owing to the narrowness of the county, the village is placed rather in the western portion. On the east it extends to the Logan County line, where Daysville affords a voting place for those placed at an inconvenient distance from Elkton. It is bounded on the north by District No. 2 (Sharon), and District No. 7 (Bivinsville); on the east by Logan County ; on the south by District No. 6 (Allensville); and on the west by District No. 3 (Fairview). The surface is drained by Elk Fork of Red River, which rises in the northwestern portion of this district, flows generally in a southeasterly direction into the Allensville District and thence to the Red River. Besides this stream, there are two or three smaller creeks which flow into the main one. The surface is hilly in the north, rolling through the central portion, and comparatively level in the south. From the south extending toward Elkton, the general surface continues to rise, the land near Elkton, according to the recent railroad survey, being 113 feet higher than the surface near Guthrie. Along the banks of the creek the land is very low. The surface in the northern part of the precinct is considerably diversified, there being two or three ranges of hills with valleys between them. The soil of the valleys is composed of the red clay subsoil, over a limestone formation, and this characteristic is also noticeable in the soil of the central and southern portions of the district. The soil of the hills is mostly of a yellowish clay, and considerable surface is composed of the "clifty" limestone formation, which makes up a major part of the northern portion of the county. The timber in the district in an early day was mainly in the northern portion of the district, although in the south there was a very fine grove some two or three miles in length, by a mile and a half in width. The original timber was mainly of several varieties of oak, among which might be mentioned black, pin and red, with an occasional tree of white oak, also cottonwood, maple and an undergrowth of hazel. Through what was known as the "barrens," was a thick growth of "scrub" hickory, which almost every season would be burned to the ground. In an early day in the more open places in these "barrens" grew the most luscious of wild strawberries, and the early pioneer often made his daily meal from this most healthy appetizer. The first settlers in this district made their cabins in the timber and along the creeks, as they thought that starvation would be their reward if they settled in the "barrens," and thus it was that the richest portions of the county were settled later than the timbered land. To-day the once neglected "barrens" of this district form a part of the northern boundary of the area comprising the famous Clarksville tobacco district, which comprises the most valuable farms in southern Kentucky.

To the searcher after the curious and the wonderful but little of interest is presented in this district. In the northern part on the farm now owned by Mr. Gordon there is a cave of some note. It is entered by going down some ten or twelve steps, and it has been explored about one mile. There are two or three comparatively large caverns in the cave, and here the average height is about seven or eight feet. In one of them there is one column which has been formed by the dropping of the water from the roof. There seems to be no especial history connected with the cave, which is at present pursuing the even tenor of its way and is doing duty to the people of the surrounding neighborhood as a cellar. The early pioneers found, in plowing up their lands, many traces of the pre-historic races and early Indians in numerous specimens of arrowheads, tomahawks, stone knives, pestles, etc. On the farm now owned by William Hadden is a very perfect Indian mound, and in an early day the pioneer in plowing over this mound, it is said, uncovered the bones of a gigantic race of people. All the human bones found were very much larger than those of the skeletons of people of to-day, and in connection with the bones many interesting implements were also discovered.

We cannot, in commencing to write of the early settlers of this district, tell with certainty who was the first white man that made a home in what is now Elkton District. Some years ago Mr. Urban Kennedy published a series of sketches in one of the papers in Elkton. In looking them over we find that he refers to several persons as living here when his father settled just on the outer edge of this district in Fairview, in 1808. Of the names he mentions none live now to tell of their trials and hardships, and but few of their descendants are present to inform us of their nativity. In this connection we deem it best to use Mr. Kennedy's own words. He says: " A ditch field composed a part of the town of Elkton, extending from the court house to the creek, and there was a small cabin where the Rathburn House stood, and here a hunter by the name of McIntosh lived, holding the land for Gray. Gray and Garvin both claimed the land, and Gray saw fit to have a man live on it. Jesse Irvin lived on the creek west of Daysville. James Millen was on an improvement between Daysville and Elkton on the farm now owned by the Millen heirs. Here was a spring that had been used by buffaloes in an early day as a drinking place. On John Bell's farm, Andrew and John Mann were living, and a man by the name of Davis on land now owned by Aaron Williams, and there he died. Peter Furgerson came the following year after his father, but soon sold out to Robenson Burrus, the father of Col. Nat Burrus. Burrus was from Virginia, and wore his knee breeches and buckles, and was fond of his guns and hounds. William Daniel settled where Caleb Bell now lives. In 1811 Armstrong Bailey, Jesse Irvin and Farrow White were living where Daysville now stands." Thus briefly the first settlement of the district can only be noted. The first authentic settlement in this region that we have any record of was in 1809. In that year Henry Maben came to this district and settled on the farm now owned by his children Matthew and Elizabeth Maben, both of whom are now over seventy years of age. This early pioneer was born in Bellamony County, Ireland, in 1760. He came to the United States when he was nineteen years of age. He landed in Charleston, S. C., and lived there some eight or ten years, and then moved to Chester County, S. C., where he remained until his departure for the West. Upon his arrival here, he settled five miles south of Elkton in the fine grove of timber which still forms part of the Maben estate. He first entered 150 acres, which he afterward increased to 550 acres, and here he resided until his death, which occurred in 1840. While he was living in South Carolina, he enlisted in the Revolution and was under Gen. Washington. It is said that many were the hours he spent in relating stories of this great man to his listening children. Of his descendants but two are now living. A third child, Thomas Maben, was a soldier in the war of 1812, and was with Gen. Jackson at the battle of New Orleans. Returning to this county he resided here until his death in 1872.

Accompanying Maben to the then "Wilderness of Kentucky" were several other sturdy yeomen of South Carolina. They were Archibald Cogell, James McKee and Isaac Bean. Cogell and McKee were both natives of Ireland, and came to South Carolina with Maben. Bean was born in South Carolina. Cogell settled on part of the farm now owned by Matthew Maben, where he lived many years. Both he and his family have now passed away. McKee lived in the same neighborhood for twenty-five years and then moved to Ohio, where he remained a short time and then moved to Illinois, where he died. Bean settled on the farm now owned by Alex Chestnut, where he resided until his death in 1840. We have spoken of James Millen as living here in 1808, and in 1809 his two brothers, William and Archie, came here from South Carolina. William settled on land now owned by Baxter Porter, and here he ran a horse-mill for many years; some of his children are now residents of the Purchase. In 1810 Thomas Park made a settlement on land now owned by Ben Parish. He only lived there a short time and then moved to Illinois, where some of his children are now living.

In 1809 John P. Brown came to this district and settled on the farm now owned by T. Foster. This gentleman was born in Virginia, and was of English descent. After his arrival in this district he only lived on his first settlement for two years, and then moved to the southern portion of the district, settling near Pinchin, near the line between this district and Guthrie. Here he entered about 400 acres, a part of which forms the land now owned by the widow Wolf. In this district he resided until 1833, and then moved to Macoupin County, Ill., where he died. His son, Preston Brown, who was four years old when the father came here, grew to manhood in this district and then settled in the Trenton District, where he remained some time. He afterward moved to the Hadensville District, and sold goods there in 1838–39. Turning his attention to farming he resided in that district for many years, but is at present living near Elkton, at a hale old age. As early, probably, as 1810 Charles Russell of

Virginia came to this county. He had come to the State some years prior to this, and had been living in Logan County. After his arrival here he followed the trade of a shoe-maker, and never had any regular place of residence in the county. There are a number of his grandchildren still living in the southern portion of this district.

In a very early day, exactly when we cannot say, there were several settlements made in the northern portion of the district. John Harrison was one that was living here prior to 1812, and a grandson of his is still living on the same farm. Thomas Allender also came here quite early from Virginia, and settled on land now owned by Thomas Fox. On that farm he lived for many years, but finally passed away, and his children have all emigrated into other States. Thomas Fielding, a son-in-law of Allender, came here with him, and was a shoe-maker here in a very early day. In 1810 John Chestnut came to this district from North Carolina and settled on the farm now occupied by Franklin Chestnut. While engaged in building a house two years afterward he fell and was killed, leaving a widow and a large family of children, who are now with their children scattered over this county, and all unite in doing the old pioneer honor. We are not exactly able to state the time that Samuel Coleman came to this county and made a settlement in this district, but it was in a very early day. The farm on which he resided is now owned by the Bailey heirs. After residing here for many years he died, leaving two sons, James and John. The former continued to reside here until his death, and his children are still living in the district. John moved to Missouri, where he raised a large family of children, and in the late war five sons of his were in the Confederate Army under Gen. Price. Among other settlers who deserve to have their names enshrined in the annals of time were two brothers by the name of McKinney, Collin and Daniel, and their brother-in-law, Ambrose Douthitt. They lived here many years, and in about 1828 the three families moved to Texas. There Collin McKinney became one of the most prominent men of that new region. He was an officer in the revolution for independence from Mexico. In the first convention after the Republic had gained its independence he was a delegate, and upon its admission to the United States he was one of the first Members of Congress to represent that Commonwealth at Washington. To-day a county and a city both bear his name in the State of his adoption. Joshua Shreves came here also in an early day and settled on the farm now owned by Perkins and Terry. A son-in-law of his, Daniel Garton, settled on a part of the farm now owned by the Bailey heirs. About 1808, or perhaps a year or two later, Anthony New came to this county from Virginia, where for many years he had been a member of the Assembly of that State. Upon his arrival here he settled on part of the farm now owned by Mrs. Lucy E. B. Greenfield, building the house that she now occupies. Soon after the separation of this county from Christian he represented Todd County in the Legislature, and before this, when Christian and Todd were together, he went to Congress from this district. After a life of usefulness he died, and now lies buried on the farm that he settled over seventy years ago. His son, R. D. New, also represented this district in Congress later on. On the farm now owned by Peyton Simpson, two miles west of Elkton, John Standard and his son Sherard made a pioneer settlement. The latter was for many years the leading auctioneer in this part of the county. Probably the first physician in this region was Dr. Sappington, who made a settlement four miles northwest of Elkton and set out the celebrated "France" orchard, which was known far and wide through this portion of the State. Valentine Wolf is now living on the old farm. In 1824 the Doctor moved to Missouri, settling in Saline County. In that State he afterward became quite noted as the inventor and proprietor of "Sappington's Pills." Gov. Jackson, one of the first Governors of that State, married his daughter. In 1812 James Kendal came here and settled at the town of Newberg. This pioneer deserves more than a passing mention in the history of this district, and we deem it proper to insert the following brief notice of him at this point: He was born in the State of Virginia and came to Kentucky when a young man. Coming to this county he settled first four miles from Elkton; there he resided until 1816, and then settled near Newberg. Here he farmed and kept a hotel; the place being the half-way point between Russellville and Hopkinsville, the inn became quite an important point. In 1819 he came to Elkton and commenced running the Nick and Will House. He remained in this business until 1827, when he retired and resided in Elkton until his death in 1835. Elisha B. Edwards came to this district in 1816, having come from Nelson County to this point, and to that county from Maryland. After his arrival here he opened a grocery store at Newberg, at which point it was thought the county seat of Todd County would be located, it being in what is now the center of the county. He remained at this point but about two years, and then moved to Christian County. He settled near Garrettsburg, but only resided about one year, and upon the formation of the new county he returned to Elkton. He was elected the first County Court Clerk of this county, and served in this position until his death in October, 1823. Urban E. Kennedy is authority for the statement that Gideon Thompson came to this district prior to 1809, and settled about two miles and a half from Elkton, on the farm now owned by James Chestnut. This pioneer was a very plain, blunt sort of man, but withal was as sharp as the many sharp ones of that day. A rather good story is related of him, which we insert in this connection. Some time after he came here a bone was found on the farm near him and brought to the county seat. The doctors at this point pronounced it to be the bone of a child's fore arm, and it was immediately surmised that a murder had been committed. A special detective was about to be sent to the scene of the "find," when Thompson, who happened to be in town, took the liberty of looking at the bone, and upon examination he pronounced it to be nothing more nor less than the bone of a dog's fore leg, and so it finally proved. Probably in this same year Joseph Black came to this county, and settled two miles northeast of Elkton, on the farm now owned by S. K. Mallory. Here he resided for many years, but finally passed to his reward.

In 1809 Hazle Petrie came to this district and settled on the present site of Taylor's Chapel. This gentleman was born in Chester District, South Carolina, came to Tennessee in 1807, and subsequently came to this county. He lived on his first settlement only one year, and then purchased from Maj. John Gray a tract of land three miles southwest of the present site of Elkton. On this land he built a dwelling house, and resided there until his death in 1869. Mr. Petrie was a man widely known in this county. For many years he was a member of the County Court, and at one time represented Todd County in the General Assembly. He raised twelve children, four of whom preceded him to the grave. He left fifty-four grandchildren and forty great-grandchildren.

Probably the most important character in the early history of this district was Maj. John Gray, who came here in 1816. He was born on the eastern shore of Maryland, his ancestry being Welsh. He came with his father, Drakeford Gray, to this State in an early day. The latter settled on Corn Creek in Gallatin County, where he died. Maj. Gray came to Centerville in 1805. This point was at that time the county seat of Christian County. He was a lawyer and practiced his profession generally in southern Kentucky. In 1812 he came to Hopkinsville and resided there until he came to this district. Here he entered thousands of acres of land in this and other districts, and was one of the most important factors in early land speculations. He, however, turned his attention mostly to farming, and was considered to be one of the largest land-owners in the county. In the fall of 1820, soon after Christian and Todd Counties were divided and Elkton became the county seat, he laid out quite an extended addition to the town. Two years prior to this he commenced the erection of the Nick and Will House, which is still standing. In 1828 he commenced to run a system of stage lines all through southern Kentucky and northern Tennessee. Altogether he ran some ten different lines, and owned some 150 head of horses. Graysville in Hadensville District which bears his name, was the crossing of some six lines of stages, and here he built a large hotel and stables for the accommodation of the public. Maj. Gray was withal a very wealthy man, as well as a philanthropic one. It is said that he never let his right hand know what his left hand did. The following incident is related of him: In an early day there was a very great dearth of corn one season, but Gray had plenty. One day a man came to him and wanted to get some corn. Gray asked him if he had the money to pay for it, and the man replied that he had. Gray then told him that he could not let him have it, but told him to go to the next neighbor who would sell him some. He then gave his reasons for refusing to let the man have the corn. He said there were plenty of men in the county who were without corn, and who had no money to buy it with, and his corn was being kept for them. And it is said that he afterward gave hundreds of thousands of bushels away. He died here in 1833, after a long and useful life. In 1817 Charles Mann, Matthew Thompson, John M. Harns, Willis Hardwick and Joseph McBride all came to this district from Buckingham County, Va. They were all of English descent, and were as sturdy a set of pioneers as one generally finds. Upon their arrival here Mann purchased Park's improvement, and the latter moved West. The other families settled near Mann's improvement, and the descendants of these pioneers are still to be found in this neighborhood. When Mann arrived here, a man by the name of Pritchett was living on the farm now owned by Mr. Grumley, and a family of Brindles were living on the adjoining farm; both settlers and their descendants have now passed away, and hardly any trace of them is now found in this district.

In 1820 Benjamin Edwards came to this district and made a settlement one-half mile south of the present site of Elkton, on the farm now owned by Rev. Gill. This gentleman was born in Maryland, and in 1798 he moved to Nelson County, in the northern part of this State. In 1821 he wrote to William King, in Nelson County, describing his settlement here, and as it is a true picture of pioneer life in those days we reproduce it here. The letter is dated January 21, and he says: "There was not a bush cut down here in June. We have since cleared and cultivated thirty acres of land and built a brick house 60 feet long by 30 feet wide, with four good fire rooms about 18 feet square, and a passage 10x10, with two cellars 20 feet square, one of which is our kitchen, with a cellar in it, with a good closet. We have got two good fire rooms with one coat of plastering and all the joiner's work completed. We shall have another fire room completed in about two weeks, which we will call our dining room. The last year was the driest year I ever saw, or we should have made corn enough, but as it is I have; and still have, to buy nearly 200 barrels, I expect; and as the winter is so unusually severe, I fear we shall be much difficultied to support our stock with fodder. Corn blades now sell at 7s. 6d. per ct., and hay about the same, 6s. in the meadow, and pork from $3 to $4 per ct., about 4,000 of which I have bought. We have a good house of hewn logs, with shingle roof and brick chimney, planked below and above, with potato cellar under it, and also a good brick smoke-house, 14 feet square and 10 feet high, besides other small houses. We have 30 acres in meadow and also 10 acres on lot of 25 acres adjoining town. This detailed improvement will cost of about $4,000." Mr. Edwards continued to reside on that farm until his death, in about 1826. He was a brother of Ninian Edwards, the first Governor of Illinois, and lies buried on the farm he first settled. His son, Elisha B. Edwards, the father of Dr. Edwards, is also interred at this place. In 1820 Mike Mackey came here from Virginia and settled on a farm about a mile south of Maben's, and is still living there.

In 1821 David M. Russell came to this district and settled two miles southeast of Elkton. Mr. Russell was born in Scotland, and came to the United States about 1805 on a visit, but was not permitted to return on account of the Embargo act. He first settled down in Maryland, but coming to Kentucky soon after he made an improvement near Auburn, Logan County. He came to this county and district in 1821, as we have stated above, and resided here until his death, which occurred in 1852. Four children are still living, one of whom, James A., is the present Circuit Court Clerk.

Accompanying Mr. Russell to this district was Carl Mario, who was known in his day as the "best man in the county." He was born in Jutland, Denmark, and was for eight years the Secretary for that Government on the island of Santa Cruz. In 1809 he came to New Orleans, and being hindered from returning home on account of the Embargo act he finally started northward. In 1812 he drifted to Logan County, and meeting Mr. Russell a friendship sprung up between them, which lasted until the hand of death dissolved it. Upon his arrival in this district he opened a shoe-maker's shop in a building erected by Mr. Russell on the latter's farm, and lived there until his death in about 1840. He was a man of very fine education, speaking three languages fluently. He was also a fine conversationalist, and in every pioneer house in this district "Charles Murray," as he was called, was a welcome guest. Thomas Philips came here in 1820 with the Edwardses from the northern part of the State, and settled on the farm now owned by Samuel Coleman. He was a native of Pennsylvania, and came to Kentucky in a very early day. He was a silversmith by trade, but never followed his vocation after he came to this county. He died here in about 1840. A grand-daughter of his is still living in the person of Mrs. Dr. J. O. McReynolds.

In Mr. Kennedy's sketches a man by the name of William Blackwood is spoken of as being here as early as 1809, but as no trace can now be found of him we can simply insert his name in this connection. Mr. H. G. Boone, who is still living one mile north of town, came to Elkton in 1823, and found the following named parties living here, in addition to those mentioned above. As we can find no accurate date of their arrival we simply insert their names and locations : Hugh B. Wilkins was living four miles west on the Hopkinsville road, on the farm now owned by William S. Crouch. George L. Harrison was living on the north edge of the district on the farm now owned by his son, William B. Harrison of Elkton. John Taylor lived near Harrison on the farm now owned by the Campbell family. Taylor was an early magistrate here, and under the old Constitution was Sheriff of the county at one time. William Hopper and his brother-in-law Mr. Martin were also living in the northern part of the district. Hopper had a tan-yard, and made a fortune out of the business. Frank Whiting Drew was living on a farm adjoining Hopper, and was also running a tan-yard on the farm now owned by Mr. Miller. Brison Ervine was living north of town near the bridge on the Greenville road. He was also a tanner, and was engaged in that business for many years. James McCormick was living on the farm now owned by McCullouch. He was a native of Ireland and came to this county from Shelby. He was originally a weaver, but did not follow his vocation after his arrival here. David and Jones Stokes were living on the farm now occupied by their descendants, as were also Edmund and William Keeling, on a farm that is now owned by their heirs. Robert Baylor was living on the farm now occupied by Dr. Russell. He was one of the foremost men of early Todd, and was a Chief Commissioner and Trustee in laying off the town of Elkton. He married a daughter of Hon. R. B. New, but died in rather early life, and left a widow and seven children, all of fine character, but now scattered far apart.

In about 1820 Darvett Brockman made a settlement in this district about three miles northwest of town, where his son Isevel also lived for many years. The latter, however, finally died near town. In about 1821, John, Jephtha and Thomas Hollingsworth came to the district. John settled on the farm now occupied by S. H. Perkins ; Jephtha on a farm two miles east of Elkton, on the Russellville road, and Thomas still to the east of him. Jephtha was a Magistrate here for many years, and Thomas was Constable and Deputy Sheriff. All of the brothers have now passed away, but some of the family are still living here. About the same time William Omblevaney made a settlement two miles northeast of Elkton. He remained here for some years and then moved to Missouri, where he now has a large family of children living. William Hurt came here in about 1823, and settled on the farm now occupied by his widow. In 1824 Daniel France came here and settled on the farm which had previously been occupied by Dr. Sappington. There he lived for many years, and now lies buried there. In 1830 there were quite a number of immigrants came here from Tennessee. Among them were Mr. Trout, who settled on the farm now occupied by his son John Trout. Capt. Jack Munday came about the same time, and settled near the Highland Lick road. He was a soldier in the war of 1812, and after his arrival here he was one of the foremost citizens of the county, and now has passed to his reward. James Rickman was another one that came here about the same time, and is still living. The oldest man now living in the county is Pleasant Martin, who came here in 1833. He is still residing on the same farm he first settled, at the age of ninety-six. He was a soldier in the war of 1812, going out in a Virginia company. Rev. Thomas Porter, a minister of the Presbyterian faith, came to this county from Hopkins County, in 1839, and settled on the farm now owned by F. M. Byers, where he died the same year. His son Baxter is still living here. This is but a brief and meager sketch of some of the pioneer families who settled this division of the county. The list, no doubt, is very incomplete, as the means for obtaining the information of the "long ago period" are few, and year by year are becoming lessened. With all the disadvantages under which the historian must necessarily labor, it is not strange if many names together with important facts and incidents are overlooked or omitted altogether. The hard life of the early settler is a theme often discussed. There is no question but that they did live a hard life; but there were exceptions then just as there are now. There was then as now, great difference in the forethought and thrift of the people. Many, in even the early days of the county's existence, lived in generous plenty of such as the land afforded. True, the pioneers had to have powder, tobacco and whisky, but for everything else they could kill game. Meat of a superior quality and in varieties that we cannot get now, was within the easy reach of all. For hunting was one of the chief amusements of the pioneer. Game of all kinds abounded here. The first settlers tell of very pronounced buffalo trails that extended through this district from north to south, and running convenient to the "licks" that were situated along the streams, but no one ever heard a pioneer tell of having killed a buffalo. Bears were said to be plenty here in those days, and Daniel Garton, whom we have mentioned above as being one of the early settlers, was also a great hunter, and his dog and his rifle were his inseparable companions. Many people now living have heard this old hunter tell many a tale of rare sport and adventure. Deer were also found in abundance in this district, especially in the groves in the southern part, and many herds of them have been killed here. The early settler also found panthers here, and Matthew Maben, who is still living in the south part of the district, was chased a long distance by one when he was a boy.

There were many traces, very indistinct, through this wilderness in an early day, but probably the first road which was regularly surveyed through this district was what is known as the Highland Lick road. This road is known better as the Russellville and Madisonville road, and forms part of the northern boundary of this district. The next road of importance to be surveyed was the Russellville and Hopkinsville, which was a trace as early as 1798. Following the survey of this road, the next thoroughfare opened was the Greenville road, and in about 1820 the Elkton, Allensville and Keysburg road was opened, followed by what is known as the Davis Mill road. The first bridge probably ever built in the district was the one across Elk Fork, just north of town, on the Greenville road. The bridge on the Russellville road east of town was probably the next, followed by the one on the Allensville road across Elk Fork, and another across the same stream at Reeves & Bradshaw's Mill. At present there are no turnpikes in the district, although there is a project on foot to pike the Elkton, Allensville and Keysburg road, between Elkton and Allensville. As yet, however, nothing definite has been decided about the matter. As yet the district has no railroad facilities, but the prospects are that before a year has passed away trains will be running from Elkton to Guthrie. Some years ago a charter was granted by the State Legislature for the purpose of building a railroad between these two points as soon as $25,000 worth of stock had been subscribed. But it was not until last January that any definite arrangements were made for the promotion of this idea. Some time in that month several of the leading men of Elkton met at Judge Petree's office, and decided to open a subscription book and try to raise the amount necessary to build the road. This was accordingly done, and by April 20 a sufficient amount had been subscribed to comply with the requirements of the charter. On that evening a meeting of the stockholders was held for the purpose of electing the directors of the road, with the following result: Ben T. Perkins, President; H. G. Petrie, Dr. J. O. McReynolds, Willis L. Reeves, G. Terry, S. H. Perkins, A. F. Rogers, Directors, and John O. Street, Secretary and Treasurer. The amount of stock already subscribed to the enterprise is $35,325. At present a surveyor has already made two surveys for proposed routes, and is now making estimates as to the probable cost of each. As soon as the cost is ascertained and the right-of-way purchased, work will be commenced, and it is now prophesied that before next May trains will be running between Elkton and Guthrie.

Among the early settlers, corn was the chief grain that was planted, and almost as soon as the corn was in the ground, these pioneers turned their attention to the erection of a mill. These early mills were very crude structures, and the first one ever built in the district was that of John Carson, which stood on Elk Fork, where Reeves & Bradshaw's Mill now stands. According to Kennedy, it was standing there as early as 1809. It had only one pair of runners, and when wheat was ground the bolt was turned by hand. A jocular old fellow was the miller here. Once when asked how the new mill was doing, he said, "She is doing a brisk business, for as soon as she gets one grain smashed, she instantly hops on another." Carson sold the mill to David Bail, who ran it for many years, and then sold out to Reuben Ellison. This man was a blacksmith in Elkton in a very early day. He sold the mill in turn to Jesse Russell, and the latter disposed of it to David and Joseph Russell. These parties ran it for many years, and the mill finally came into the hands of Reeves & Bradshaw. These gentlemen some years ago put in steam power, and are still running the mill. As early as 1812 Joseph Robertson put a horse-mill on the Trenton road, south of town, on the farm now occupied by Tandy Foster, but it only ran a short time. About 1818 Thomas W. Garvin put up a mill on Elk Fork, near the bridge on the Russellville road. This stood probably until about 1823, and was then pulled down. Somewhere about 1825 some of the Russells put up a horse-mill near the Reeves & Bradshaw Mill. It was used for some years, and then becoming neglected soon rotted away. In 1840 Joseph Black built a horse-mill on the farm now owned by William Shanklin, and ran it for fifteen years or over. In 1880 George B. Lewis put up a steam flouring-mill at a cost of about $8,000. It is still standing, and is one of the finest in the county.

Of the early schools, their history in this district is but a repetition of the same in other parts of the county, viz.: the log-cabin schoolhouse, the illiterate pedagogue and the mischievous urchins. There have been numerous free schools held in the district in buildings that could be secured for the purpose, as according to the law the teacher was compelled to furnish room, fuel, etc., out of a very meager salary, and then teach only from a three to a five months' school. In fact, the free schools have been of so low a grade in this district that they are hardly worthy of mention. The last Legislature passed a new school law and appropriated a much larger sum for defraying the necessary expenses of a good school system, and it is to be hoped that under the new *regime* of the County School Superintendent, the free schools here will become a more potent factor in the education of the young. The main means of education has been through the subscription school. The first school of this kind in this district was the seminary in connection with the Presbyterian (Old School) Church, which was built in about 1827, north of town at the forks of the Greenville and Kirkmansv.lle road. Here a seminary was conducted for some years, one of the main teachers being John Peirce, who taught there about 1832. Soon after that the building was burned down.

Soon after that the Green River Female Academy was started in Elkton, and as that institution is still in existence, it will receive due notice in the town of Elkton.

Newberg.—As early as 1815 there was a little hamlet on the Russellville and Hopkinsville road exactly half way between those two points. As early as 1816 Elisha B. Edwards had a store there and ran it for two or three years; it was within a half mile from the center of what is now Todd County, and when the question of constituting Todd began to be agitated, it was thought that that point would become the county seat. In 1817 Maj. John Gray had a store there, followed by James Kendal, who kept store about 1817–18–19. The location of the county seat at Elkton in 1819 was the death-knell of this little town, which soon after ran down.

Daysville.—On the Russellville road, five miles east of Elkton, the town of Daysville was first inaugurated as early as 1833. In a very early day a man by the name of Day had a store there, and the little village was named after him. A Mr. Knight also had a store there about the same time Day was there. T. B. Bailey was about the next to do business there, followed by Lewis & Luck. At present the place has about 100 inhabitants, with two stores, one of which is kept by W. F. Cole, the other by J. W. Lucket. There are also two doctors there, and a blacksmith shop. This point is also one of the voting places of the Elkton District. Among the early pioneers there were many pious people who early turned their attention to the erection of a place of worship. About the first religious organization in this district was the Old School Presbyterian denomination. This society met at what was known as the old Rockbridge Church. This building was of logs and was built as early as 1812, and stood one mile north of town. Among the early members of this church were Thomas Hadden and family, James and William Paden and their families, and many others. In about 1822 a new brick house was erected on the Greenville road where the Kirkmansville road leaves it. It was two stories high, the upper story being used as a seminary, as we have mentioned above. This edifice continued to be used as a church for some years, and then was finally burned down.

In quite an early day the Cumberland Presbyterians used to hold camp-meetings at a place known as the Hebron Camp Ground, which was located about one mile west of where Daysville now stands. Here large annual gatherings were held for many years, and subsequently a society was organized at this point, and a church built which was known as the Hebron Church. This church continued to be used for some time, and then the society was finally moved to Logan County.

One of the earliest preaching-places in this district was at the residence of Hazle Petrie. Here, soon after he built his house, the Methodist preachers commenced holding class-meetings. Among the first preachers was Peter Cartwright, who was followed by Malone, Axley, Holliday, Thomas A. (afterward Bishop) Morris, Ogden and Lorenzo Dow. His house continued to be a regular meeting-place for some time, and then he afterward built a log-house. This was called "Petrie's Church," and here religious services continued to be held until about 1837, when Bell's Chapel was built, three miles west of the old church, near the residence of Rev. C. N. Bell, to which place the society of Petrie's Church was removed, and there the members continue to worship to this day.

Elkton.—On the 8th day of May, 1820, the county seat of Todd County was located at Elkton. With this the history of the town properly commences, although in March, 1819, Thomas Garvin and Thomas Jameson laid out the original plat of the town. This plat was recorded in the Christian County Court, and consisted of about eighteen lots. The first addition to the town of Elkton, after it had been made the county seat, was that of John Gray, which was made and recorded on Nov. 16, 1820. This addition lay west of the original plat, and consisted of 251 lots. It contained the grounds now covered by the major portion of the town of Elkton, including the public square. John Mann, Jr., and Charles Smith made another addition to the town two days afterward. It consisted of nine lots, and joined the original plat on the south. On the same day William Greenfield made a third addition to the town. It consisted of fifty-six lots, and lay to the east. At the last session of the Legislature a new charter was granted to the town of Elkton, in which the corporate limits were extended to a considerable extent, but as yet no survey has been made of the portion added, and no definite statement can be made as to the number of lots.

The first portion of the town originally lay near Elk Creek, hence the name "Elk Town," which in later days has been contracted to "Elkton." The first man, or at least one of the first, to come here was Thomas Garvin, who, as we have mentioned above, ran a mill here as early as 1817. It stood almost directly south of the present site of the Christian Church on Elk Fork. It was only in operation a short time. He was the same man who laid out one of the additions to the town. He left here in about 1823. About the first merchant here was Charles Smith.

He kept store in the building now standing on Main Street, at the forking of the Allensville road with that street. Here he remained until about 1826. William S. Logan was about the next person to engage in merchandising, probably about 1818. He ran a store here for a few years and then moved to the Hadensville district, where he farmed for many years. Near the town William Greenfield had been running a blacksmith shop for many years before the organization, and after the town sprang up several of his sons also engaged in that business. In about 1820 William Greenfield, Jr., began merchandising here, and did business at this point until about 1833, and then moved to Clarksville, Tenn. Some of the other members of the Greenfield family moved to Arkansas and are still living there. In 1818 Maj. John Gray, whom we have noticed above, built the Nick and Will House and hired his brother-in-law, James Kendal, to run it for him. This gentleman had charge of it until about 1827. Prior to this, however, Samuel Hadley had kept an inn on Main Street, opposite the place where the Allensville road comes into it. About the first persons to come to the new village were several hatters, among whom might be mentioned Edson Waters, Thomas Jameson and William Powers. All had their shops near the creek, and only remained here a short time. In an early day there were also several saddlers here; among them were Issachar Roberts, Thomas W. Pitt and William Gowl. The first two gentlemen were here only a short time, but Gowl remained here some time, and in about 1832 he built a mill in connection with his brother-in-law, Mr. Grooms, but it did not run very long. Probably the oldest building now in the town is the brick, now owned by Mr. Woolard, which was built by Mr. Edwards about 1817. The building has been put to different uses, but now is used by various artisans for their shops, and as living rooms by numerous families. The second story is used by the *Elkton Register* as an office, composing and press rooms. As early as 1820 Henry Roberts was keeping a hotel in a building that stood near where B. T. Perkins, Jr's., house is. John S. Wilson came here in about 1820, sold goods here a short time and then went West. About the next arrival here was Henry F. Roberts, who came here about 1822. He first opened a grocery store, but afterward a general store, and remained in business here for some time. About the same time Isaac Ayers came here and engaged in the grocery business; he remained here only a short time and then moved away. In 1823 Benjamin Logan came here and opened a store where Dr. Miles' drug store is now standing; he continued business here until about 1835, and was one of the most successful merchants of an early day. In the same year the widow Boone came to this town, accompanied by her family, from the Allensville District. This pioneer lady deserves more than a passing mention in the history of the district. She came to the county with her husband, Squire Boone, in 1815. This hardy old pioneer was a native of Virginia, a nephew of the famous Daniel Boone, and accompanied his renowned relative to this State in the second journey of the latter to Kentucky. He settled in Madison County, and there, in 1790, on the banks of Kentucky River, he married the lady who survived him. This was probably one of the first marriages ever performed in that part of Kentucky. Mr. Boone was in the famous battle of Blue Licks, and was shot through the thigh, the ball shattering the bone very badly. After his arrival in this county he settled within a mile of Allensville, where he lived only about two years before he was called to his reward. His son, Squire Boone, came to Elkton with his mother, and began merchandising the same year, continuing in business some time. Another son, H. G. Boone, began merchandising in about 1829, in the room now occupied by Hancock & Grumbley, and engaged in business there in partnership with Mr. Greenfield until about 1840.

In about 1827 T. W. Gray succeeded Kendal in the management of the Nick and Will House. He ran it for only a short time, and then John M. Cobinass, who in turn was succeeded in 1832 by Archie Buckner. After Buckner retired Jared Crab obtained possession of the hotel, and ran it for many years. He had originally come to the town in 1823, and had engaged in the trade of a silversmith for some time. In about 1827 Thomas W. Greenfield began merchandising near where Hancock & Grumbley's establishment now stands. He remained there only a short time, and then moved to Tennessee. In 1830 Squire B. Greenfield began to sell goods here in connection with Mr. Roberts. The firm remained here only about five years, and then retired. About 1832 S. H. Scott opened a store here. He had come here in about 1823, but had been acting as Constable up to this time. After entering business circles here he was a successful merchant for a short time, and then moved away. William McChristian was merchandising here with Mr. Scott for a year, having bought out Mr. Greenfield, but subsequently he received the appointment of Tobacco Inspector at New Orleans, and selling out his interests here, he went South to assume his new position. In 1834 Dr. James A. McReynolds came to this point, and as he afterward followed other vocations besides his chosen profession, and was withal one of the foremost men of the place, we deem it best to insert a short sketch of this gentleman. He was a son of Oliver and Elizabeth McReynolds, and was born in Campbell County, Va., in 1812. He was of Scotch-Irish descent, the family moving from Scotland to Ireland immediately after the conquest of Ireland by Cromwell. The grandfather of Dr. McReynolds came from Ireland to this country with his mother and one brother, soon after the siege of Londonderry, and from this small beginning the whole family of McReynoldses are now descended. The family first settled in Pennsylvania, moving thence to Campbell County, Va., where the grandfather married, and raised a large family, and of that number the father of James A. McReynolds was the youngest. Dr. McReynolds was raised and educated in his native county, receiving only such instruction as was given by the common schools of those days. In 1832 he moved with his father to Trigg County, Ky., settling near Cadiz, and two years afterward he came to this point. Upon his arrival here he began the study of medicine with Drs. Grooms and Venable. In 1835–36 he attended his first course of lectures at Cincinnati, and in 1836–37 he attended the Transylvania University of Medicine, at Lexington, Ky., which was at that time the leading medical college of the West, and ranked among the first in the Union. Returning to this town he began the practice of his profession. About 1842, his health being rather poor, he quit the practice of medicine and commenced reading law. But after about three years' attention to that profession he returned to the practice of medicine. In 1847 he was elected to the Legislature, and served one term. Returning to this point he continued the practice of medicine until 1867, when he was elected Cashier of the Bank of Elkton. This position he occupied until his death in 1869. In person Dr. McReynolds was very tall and spare, with light auburn hair, large light gray eyes, and in his address he was exceedingly awkward. His mind was strong and logical, and he investigated subjects slowly and carefully. As a practitioner of medicine he was cautious and careful. He was for a long time a prominent member of the Christian Church, and wielded a large influence, both by reason of the strength of his intellect and the force and purity of his character.

Probably no one has ever done any more for the town of Elkton than Jesse Russell, who was born in Virginia, and came to this district with his brother before the town was laid out. The latter was a brickmason, and engaged at his trade here. Under him Jesse Russell learned that trade, and afterward followed it. Coming to the county with nothing, but being possessed of remarkable energy, he succeeded far beyond the lot of ordinary men, and at the breaking out of the war he was the owner of negroes to the value of $85,000, besides a great deal of real estate. Most of the brick houses in Elkton were built and were at different times owned by him. But the vicissitudes of the war, however, swept most of his wealth away, and left him nothing but his real estate. He died here in 1883, and to-day his name deserves to be handed down to the coming generations.

In 1851 George B. Lewis came to this county, located at this point, and here he has since been engaged in merchandising. In 1844 James M. Thompson came to this point, and until his death, in 1873, he followed the trade of blacksmith and wood-workman. George W. Millen began the undertaking and cabinet business at this point in 1860, and is still engaged in the business. In 1859 John W. Lewis opened a general store here, which he now carries on. In 1862 E. Garth opened a grocery store here, but only engaged in that business until 1865, when he retired. In 1870 he opened a general store, and is still engaged in it. In 1873 Street, McReynolds & Co. opened a general store, but remained in business only a short time. In 1872 Russell & Bell began a general grocery business here; this firm continued in operation two years, when Russell retired, and Bell ran the store until 1881, when he sold out and engaged with Mr. Boone, under the firm name of Boone & Bell, in the dry goods business. In 1877 Felix G. Miles came to Elkton and formed a partnership with Dr. C. D. Lewis, in the drug business. In 1880 the latter retired, but Mr. Miles is still engaged here. In that year Edward M. Weathers also opened a drug store, which had been operated here by Jefferson & Perkins, and is still in general business at this point. In 1878 Douglas M. Miller began selling agricultural implements here, and is still conducting · his business at this point; and about the same time Joe C. Russell opened his grocery store, at the same stand at which he is still to be found. In 1879 Isaac Spillman opened a fine livery stable here, and is still doing an extensive business; and in the same year S. H. Perkins opened an extensive general store, and continued in business by himself until 1881, when he took in G. P. Street as partner, and subsequently associated S. H. Wells in the same business, and the firm is now doing a very large trade under the title of S. H. Perkins & Co. In 1880 John L. Mauzy & Bro. came here, and opening a tin shop, are still following that trade at this point.

Bank of Elkton was organized on March 5, 1866, with a capital stock of $50,000. At the first meeting of the stockholders the following Directors were elected: James T. Clark, John O. McReynolds, H. G. Petrie, G. B. Lewis and John W. Lewis. The Board chose James T. Clark as President. This gentleman was at that time one of the leading merchants of the place, and one of the finest business men in southern Kentucky. Milton Gant was also made the first Cashier; he was in turn succeeded by Dr. J. A. McReynolds. A few years after its organization the bank lowered the capital to about $23,000, but it has since been raised to the original amount. At present the Directors of the bank are H. G. Petrie, President; Dr. J. O. McReynolds, and John O. Street Cashier. The institution is at present in a flourishing condition and is doing a good business.

The following is a list of the gentlemen now engaged in business at this point :

Bank—Bank of Elkton.

Drugs—E. M. Weathers, William Terry and F. G. Miles.

General Stores—S. H. Perkins & Co., John Lewis, E. Garth.

Groceries—G. W. Lewis, Russell & Edwards, Joe Russell, Russell & Wilkins.

Dry Goods—Boone & Bell and L. J. Hancock.

Millinery—Miss Mary L. Russell, Mrs. Mary Hays, and Mrs. Elizabeth Hooser.

Harness Shops—William Tolbert, John A. Goodman.

Furniture Store—Millen & Millen.

Tinware—Mauzy & Bro.

Tailor—Caleb W. Bell.

Hotels—Kennedy House, Misses Kennedy; Nick and Will House, Mrs. Hunter.

At present the town contains about 900 inhabitants, and it is claimed that the size of it has not increased any for the past thirty years. It is to be hoped that with the advent of the new railroad the town will spring into new life, and that other citizens may be induced to locate here.

The newspapers of the town of Elkton have had a very precarious existence. Several different sheets have been started, but one by one most of them have died the death of the righteous. About the first paper issued for the gratification and divertisement of the people of this county as well as for the purpose of ministering to the finances of the editor was the *Green River Whig.* This paper, or at least its outfit, was brought here from Hopkinsville by James R. Abernathy, in about 1851. In the course of a year or two the paper changed hands, Mr. A. B. Stark purchasing the office. He also changed its name to the *Elkton Banner*, and made V. B. Morris the editor and publisher. This sheet continued in operation here until about 1857. From this time until about 1872 there was a dearth of newspapers, when the *Elkton Witness* was started by Dr. Cox. This gentleman ran the paper about three years, when he sold out to Bradley & Reeves, and under this administration the paper finally became extinct. In September, 1878, Maj. F. H. Bristow and H. F. Willoughby began the publication of the *Elkton Register.* These gentlemen were the proprietors of the paper until the summer of 1882, when S. D. Reese began the publication of it, and still issues the paper.

Town Organization.—The town of Elkton was originally incorporated and organized under charter, soon after the original plat and additions were made. But upon examination all the early records were found to be lost, and a statement as to the early officers cannot be made.

In 1867 a new charter was granted the village, and a new board was organized under it. The following statement shows the members of the board to the present time:

1867—G. Terry, J. W. Lewis, John A. Bass, J. D. Russell, J. O. McReynolds.

1868—G. Terry, W. A. McReynolds, G. B. Lewis, A. H. Millen and J. O. McReynolds.

1869—G. Terry, W. H. Roberts, J. W. Lewis, Berry Hurt and J. O. McReynolds.

1870—G. Terry, R. F. Allison, John R. Runsome, J. O. McGehee, H. G. Boone, Jr.

1871—G. Terry, John R. Runsome, R. F. Allison, James O. McGehee and H. G. Boone, Jr.

1872—R. F. Allison, W. A. McReynolds, J. F. Luck, John O. Street and W. H. Roberts.

1873—R. F. Allison, W. H. Roberts, W. W. Stinnett, John F. Luck and John O. Street.

1874—R. F. Allison, G. Terry, W. H. Roberts, G. W. Millen and H. G. Boone, Jr.

1875—R. F. Allison, G. Terry, John F. Luck, G. W. Millen and H. G. Boone, Jr.

1876—R. F. Allison, G. Terry, John F. Luck, G. W. Millen and H. G. Boone, Jr.

1877—R. F. Allison, G. Terry, M. L. Christian, S. L. Thompson and G. W. Millen.

1878—J. W. Lewis, G. Terry, R. F. Allison, G. W. Millen and Samuel L. Thompson.

1879—R. F. Allison, G. Terry, G. W. Millen, J. D. Christian and S. L. Thompson.

1880—R. F. Allison, G. Terry, G. W. Millen, J. D. Christian and S. L. Thompson.

1881—W. A. McReynolds, T. E. Thompson, J. F. Luck, H. G. Fletcher, G. W. Millen.

1882—E. W. Weathers, S. L. Thompson, J. F. Bell, Benjamin T. Perkins and A. H. Millen.

1883—J. D. Christian, J. F. Bell, T. E. Thompson, G. W. Millen and Dr. E. B. Edwards.

1884—E. B. Edwards, J. W. Bell, G. B. Lewis, G. W. Millen, G. Terry.

The free schools of the village of Elkton are something similar to those of the district, and from year to year continue to run in the same rut, as the old schools did fifty years ago. Last year the school was taught in a little old carpenter-shop that stands on Main Street, and was a fair sample of those that have been in existence for some years. Probably about the first subscription school in the town of Elkton was taught by William Moore, who came here as early as 1823. He taught for some years and was succeeded by his son, William H. Moore. Rev. William K. Stewart, a son-in-law of Moore, also taught school in this village, as well as at the Rock Bridge Church north of town, and followed his vocation for many years here.

Green River Female Academy, or, as it is now known, the Green River Academy, was built in 1835, its erection being cotemporary with that of the court house. The academy was founded and built through the instrumentality of a stock company, the leading members of which were H. G. Boone, F. M. Bristow, Finis E. McClaine and Willis L. Reeves. There was about $3,500 worth of stock subscribed, at the rate of $25 per share. The State also took $500 worth of stock in the new institution, and about the full amount subscribed was consumed in the erection of the building, which was of brick, two stories, and is still standing. The school was at first, as its name indicates, for ladies alone. The first teacher in the institution was Mrs. Sarah K. P. Failes. This lady taught the school some years, and was followed by J. R. Curry, who in turn was succeeded by William Dickey and wife. This worthy couple taught school here for many years. After them, Rev. Wiggins, a Baptist preacher, taught there some time, and he was succeeded by a Presbyterian preacher by the name of Lourey. In 1861, under Prof. Mariner, the school was opened to both sexes. Since then among the teachers who have been employed there might be mentioned Profs. Lofland, Williams, J. W. Hester, —. Hendrick and Rev. Gill. The present teachers are Prof. H. O. Snow and wife, and the school now has an average attendance of about eighty-five. A major part of the stock is now owned by Rev. Gant, who at present controls the school.

Elkton Methodist Episcopal Church was organized in about 1822. Among the very early members were Henry H. Roberts, Isaac Ayers, William Powers and Edward Shanklin. Soon after its organization a little brick church was put up on Main Street, a little west of the public square, and here services were held for many years; in 1851 the present brick edifice was built at a cost of about $4,000, and in 1872 the house was remodeled at an additional cost of about $2,000. At present the membership numbers about seventy-five. The present officers are : Stewards, H. G. Petrie and F. H. Bristow ; Trustees, H. G. Petrie, J. F. Bell, E. B. Weathers and D. B. Williams.

Among the pastors of the church might be mentioned: Dr. N. H. Lee, L. B. Davidson, L. B. Crenshaw, Thomas Bottlemy, Eli B. Crane,

John P. Perry, Silas Lee, Zach Taylor, David Morton, A. C. Dewitt, George R. Browder, Robert McCowan, James H. Lewis, E. W. Bottlemy, James C. Petrie, Dennis Spurrier. Since about 1845 a Union Sunday-school has been held in this town. The first Superintendent was Willis L. Reaves. In about 1870 the Baptists drew off, and soon after the Christians. Since that the Methodists and Presbyterians have continued the Sunday-school and now meet in the Presbyterian Church. The attendance is now about fifty. Present officers are: F. H. Bristow, Superintendent; Isaac Spillman, Assistant; John Weathers, Secretary; Treasurer, John Reaves.

Elkton Baptist Church was organized in the fall of 1825, in the village of Elkton. Among the early members of the congregation might be mentioned: Anthony New and wife, Benjamin Edwards and wife, John S. Wilson and wife, David Stokes, William Keeling, Mrs. Conner, and Moody Grubs and wife. The first meetings were held in the second story of the court house. In 1826 the society built the church now occupied by the colored Baptists as a house of worship. The building at that time cost about $500, and was erected through the supervision of Moody Grubs, one of the members. The congregation continued to meet at this church until about 1873, when the present handsome edifice on Main Street was erected at a cost of about $6,000. At present the society numbers about 100 members. The following list shows the different ministers who have acted as pastors of this church: John S. Wilson, William Warder, Robert Anderson, Robert Nixon, R. A. Massey, William M. Jordon, J. M. Pea, John W. Kendal and E. N. Dicken. The present pastor is Rev. W. H. Rials. The following gentlemen are now acting as officers of the church: Clerk, Dr. S. M. Lowry; Deacons, George B. Lewis, Dr. E. B. Edwards, H. G. Boone, Dr. S. M. Lowry, Thomas J. Wilson and John Holland. The regular church services are now held on the third Sunday in each month. A Sunday-school was organized in connection with this church under the pastorate of Rev. Massey. It has an average attendance of about forty. The present officers are: John M. Lewis, Superintendent; Dr. E. B. Edwards, Librarian; Dr. S. M. Lowry, Treasurer, and Thomas Pepper, Secretary.

Elkton Congregation of the Cumberland Presbyterian Church was organized in this village in October, 1824, by Rev. F. R. Cossett as pastor. Dr. Cossett was afterward President of Cumberland College, at Princeton, Ky., and still later President of the Cumberland University at Lebanon, Tenn. Subsequently he was editor of a paper called the *Banner of Peace*, but now known as the *Cumberland Presbyterian*, and published at Nashville, by the Board of Publication. Dr. Cossett in old age retired from regular work and wrote several books in the interest of the church, one of which is the "Life and Times of Ewing, one of the Founders of the Church." He died in 1859 at Lebanon, Tenn. The first Ruling Elders of the Elkton congregation were: Thomas Bryan, James Campbell, U. E. Kennedy, J. H. Hollingsworth, Samuel Ewing, W. L. Reeves and James H. Bone.

The congregation enjoyed general prosperity for several years under the pastorate of the following ministers: Rev. M. H. Bone, and his colleague, H. B. Hill, labored in the county and Elkton especially with great success. The latter moved to Tennessee, where he spent the flower of his life, and his ministry was crowned with great success. He died about the year 1863. The former recently died near Maysville, Ala., after a long and useful life. Rev. Silas Davis followed Bone and Hill, and his ministry was followed with almost unbounded success. He was a man of strong mind and uncompromising integrity, and when he left Elkton he left an unblemished name. The next pastor was Rev. J. M. Penick, a man of great energy, of earnest zeal, deep piety, and his labors were fruitful wherever he went. He died in Logan County a few years since.

Rev. W. L. Casky was his successor, who continued a short time, but who was a punctual and efficient pastor. He still lives, and resides in Christian County, Ky. In the fall of 1857 Rev. J. M. Gill was chosen pastor. He came from Tennessee, and took charge of the Green River Female Academy. Under his ministry the congregation has been in great harmony.

About four years ago the congregation erected a new house, which reflects great credit upon them and their pastor, who is still laboring as usual in the church.

Elkton Christian Church was organized in Elkton, Ky., on August 27, 1837, with the following members: B. C. Ritter, C. Cheatham, Alexander Cheatham, J. D. Garrod, R. Greenfield, Mary C. Bell, D. T. Smith, J. R. Perkins, Lawson Cheatham, Sarah Cheatham and Susan Kay. The meetings were first held in the second story of the court house. In 1850 the present church was erected on Main Street at a cost of about $1,500. Among the ministers who have watched over this flock have been Enoch Glascock, Job Harvey, George P. Street, John E. Furgerson, John N. Mulky, W. E. Mobley, C. M. Day and A. L. Johnson. Since 1878 W. E. Mobley has been filling a second pastorate very acceptably to the people here. The present membership is about sixty-five. The present officers of the church are: Elders, Dr. J. O. McReynolds and G. P. Street, and Clerk, J. O. Street. Preaching services are held on the second Sunday in each month. The present average attendance of the Sunday-school is about thirty-five. Present officers: J. O. Street,

Superintendent; S. H. Wells, Secretary.   Teachers: Mrs. Dr. E. P. Russell, Mrs. F. M. Perkins, Mrs. E. P. Street and C. G. Christian.

The colored people have two churches here—Methodist and Baptist—and both seem to be prospering nicely.

Vespers' Lodge, No. 71, A. F. & A. M., of Elkton, was first formed under dispensation on March 16, 1821.   Among the original members were Jephtha Wells, Archibald King, Thomas Bridges, William Gaul, Willis L. Reaves, R. B. New, John Belamy, Squire H. Boone, James R. Gray, S. W. Ewing, George L. Cabanis and Newton Fox.   In October of the same year a charter was granted to the lodge, signed by Henry Clay as Grand Master of Kentucky.   The first officers under this charter were: John S. Robson, M.; James P. Thomas, S. W.; Jac. Baird, J. W.; James Hammond, Secretary; Samuel Ewing, Treasurer; John T. Alderson, S. D.; Jasper Anderson, J. D.; William Bean, S. and T. After the building of the court house the sessions of the lodge were held in the second story of that building until about 1854, when a hall was fitted up over E. Garth's store, and here the lodge met for some time. At one time, especially just before the war, the lodge was very large, having over 100 members.   After the war it began to run down, and about 1873, owing to dissensions, it was found necessary to surrender its charter.

There was also an Odd-Fellows lodge here, but it was transferred to another point.—*F. S. Tyler.*

CHAPTER VIII.

MAGISTERIAL DISTRICT NO. 5, TRENTON—THE SOIL AND ITS PRODUCTIONS
—THE TIMBER OF THE DISTRICT—THE CREEKS—EARLY TRACES AND
ROADS—THE EARLY PIONEERS AND WHERE THEY CAME FROM—MAJ.
SAM MOORE—BREWER AND COL. BENJAMIN H. REEVES, ROBERT COLE-
MAN, MCFADDEN AND CARPENTER—THEIR TROUBLE WITH THE INDIANS
—LEBANON CAMP-MEETING—FIRST CHURCHES AND MINISTERS—TOWN OF
TRENTON—ITS EARLY MERCHANTS—CHURCHES AND SCHOOLS.

MAGISTERIAL DISTRICT No. 5, commonly known as Trenton,
lies in the southwestern portion of the county, and is the largest one.
It is bounded on the north by the Fairview District, on the east by Guthrie and Allensville Districts, on the south by Tennessee, and on the west
by Christian County. The topography of the district is somewhat varied.
In the south the land is quite flat, through the central portion it is rolling, and in the northern rather hilly. Here in several places the cavernous limestone comes to the surface. On the old Childs farm there is a
cave which has been explored about a half mile. This place in an early
day was a fine resort for frolics and picnic parties by the young folks.
The soil of the southern and central portions is of dark red clay, while
that of the north is of a lighter hue, and by no means so rich. In an
early day there was but little timber to be found in the district, except
along the banks of the creek and on the northern edge of the district.
Since the county has become somewhat settled small groves of timber,
consisting of several varieties of oak and some maple, are springing into
existence. Also in places in what were once known as barrens the scrub
hickory is now found, and wherever that is noticed it is an indication of
very rich lands.

Creeks.—The main creek of the district is the West Fork, which rises
in the northern part, flows generally in a southwesterly direction along
the Christian County line, and finally empties into Red River just on
the edge of the Tennessee line. The next creek in size is Montgomery,
named in honor of a man that in an early day settled at the head waters
of it. It rises in the northeastern portion of the district, flows generally in
a southwesterly direction and empties into West Fork on the farm of Hardin Wood. The other creek of importance is Rain's Lick, which rises
near the line between this district and Guthrie, flows generally in a south-

westerly course, and strikes West Fork near the State line. Of the early
roads but little can be ascertained. Probably the first one of any note
was the Hopkinsville and Nashville road, followed by the survey of the
Trenton and Clarksville road, and later on the Pond River and Gallatin
roads.

Pioneer Settlers.—Of the very early pioneers who settled in the district there are many whose coming we cannot locate. They were here so
early that there are no chroniclers now left to tell us of their arrival.
One of the earliest pioneers in this district was Maj. Sam Moore, who
came here some time prior to 1809, and he soon became one of the largest
land-owners of the county. At one time he owned nearly the whole of
the Trenton District. Land was cheap here in those days. When Mr.
Kennedy first came here in 1809 Moore offered him 200 acres of land
near the present site of Trenton for his saddle-horse, and all the land he
could buy at 50 cents an acre. At that time the land was the wildest of
barrens, and Kennedy thought that it was a case of starvation for him
to settle there, consequently he declined Moore's offer. It is also related
of Moore that he sold another farm of 300 acres to one of the early
pioneers for a couple of calves. Moore lived here for many years, and
was one of the leading men of the county.

The first authentic date of a settlement being made here is that of
1796. In that year Brewer and Martha Reeves came here from Augusta
County, Va., but in a few years after their arrival they both died. They
left four sons to do them honor in the early history of the county. Of
these, Col. Benjamin H. Reeves was the most noted. He was born in
Augusta County, Va., in 1787, grew to manhood and settled on the farm
formerly owned by his father. His first public service was representing
old Christian County in the Legislature in 1812. Soon after that he
made up a company for the war of 1812, was subsequently appointed
Major, and was one of the finest officers in that conflict. He afterward
moved to Missouri, and was elected one of the first Lieutenant-Governors
of that State. He returned to this county in 1835, and settled on the
farm now owned by Lewis Garth. Soon after his arrival here he was
elected a member of the Legislature, and served in that capacity from
1838 to 1840. He died here in 1849. Another son, Willis L., was for
many years both County and Circuit Clerk of Todd County, and a third
son, Ottaway, was a farmer here for many years. He was said to be a
man of fine intellect and good education, but did not in any way, as his
brothers had done, seek political notoriety. A grandson of Brewer
Reeves is still living in the district in the person of Crittenden Reeves,
who represented this county in the Legislature in 1879 and 1881.

Some time prior to 1809 Rev. Finis Ewing came to this district and settled four miles north of Trenton, where Henry Maynard now resides. In an early day he was one of the foremost men of the county. He was a minister in the Cumberland Presbyterian Church, and was the founder of the church in the county. He built a store on his farm, and had a postoffice established there, which he called Lebanon, and also undertook to build up a town. In 1820 he moved with his family and many of the members of the church to Missouri, giving as his reason for emigrating, that " the Baptists and tobacco were taking the county." After his arrival in Missouri he formed another Lebanon, which afterward became quite a town. Col. Thompson Ewing, a son of this worthy gentleman, grew to manhood in this district, and then settled down on a farm about three miles south of Trenton, on the Clarksville road. There in an early day he had a store and postoffice, and subsequently represented this county in the Legislature. In 1840 he moved to Missouri, where he died a few years since.

Living immediately around Ewing in an early day were several other Presbyterian families, among whom might be mentioned the Weirs, Berrys, Millers, Gillmoors, Doconers, McClures, Bryans and Rubys. It is supposed all these families moved to Missouri with Ewing, as hardly any trace can now be discovered of them.

Another settler of an early day whose arrival cannot be stated with accuracy was Beverly Stubblefield, who settled three miles southwest from Trenton. He came from Virginia, where he had been a soldier in the war of 1812, and an officer in that conflict. He died here in 1824, but his wife survived him for many years, and taught her children to respect and revere the name of their sturdy father.

Probably as early as 1800 the Harlow family first came to Kentucky from Virginia, and soon after this William Harlow settled in this county and district, where he lived for many years. His father, Elisha B., came from Ireland, and was a soldier in the Revolution, being killed while in the service. A brother of his, Silas, came to this State, and was afterward killed in the battle of Blue Licks. In this district there are only two or three grandchildren of this family now living, but their progeny are now scattered throughout the Union, and many of that name are now holding positions of trust and honor in this country.

About 1809 Lewis Leavell moved to this district, and purchased from Maj. Moore the land now in the immediate vicinity of Trenton. He was one of the largest real estate owners in the county, and was at one time a man of great wealth. In connection with the founding of Trenton he took an active interest.

In 1810 Elijah Garth came from Albemarle County, Va., and settled on the farm now owned by Webster Garth, a grandson. This pioneer was an intimate friend of President Jefferson, and a man of fine capabilities. Accompanying him to this county were his wife and eight children. He died here in 1816, and his son, William Andrew, inherited the home farm. The latter resided here until his death in 1843. Another brother, Littleton, emigrated to Illinois from this county, and settled near Peoria, where he died in 1853. Webster, a son of W. A. Garth, is the only one of the family now living in the district.

Accompanying the Reeves family to this district was a man of nearly as much note, namely, Robert Coleman. He came originally from Virginia to Hopkinsville, and at the latter point he practiced law for some time. Coming to this county he planted a small piece of land with corn that he had brought with him from Hopkinsville in his saddle-bags. This little piece of land now forms part of the farm owned by William Perkins. Coleman finally became one of the largest land-owners of the county, but like many others he did not seem to prize his possessions very highly, as it is said that he once sold the farm now owned by the Gray heirs, and which at that time consisted of about 300 acres, to the wife of one of the early pioneers for a piece of calico. Immediately after the organization of this county, Mr. Coleman was a candidate for the honor of being the first Representative to the Legislature from Todd, against John S. Anderson. The election was an old-fashioned one, and lasted three days. When the last vote was cast it was found that the election was tied. A subsequent vote resulted in the choice of Anderson for the position. Coleman died here in 1843.

Cotemporaneous with Coleman was John McFadden, who made a settlement on the farm now owned by Thomas Duson. He was a great fighter, and in an early day had many a brush with the red man. Up to a few years ago a tree stood on his farm that bore the impress of eleven bullets. Behind this tree McFadden had once stood, and by sticking out his hat had drawn the fire of the Indians when they were desirous of killing him. In an early day, west of Coleman's several families were living, of whom no trace can now be found. They were the Kenners, Bolingers, Fineleys and Norths. Up the creek from McFadden, in an early day, Henry Carpenter resided on the farm that was afterward owned by Rev. Reese. He was a full-blooded Dutchman, and as is typical of that race, very cool and phlegmatic. He would work in his clearing with his gun by his side and his pipe in his mouth. One day when chased by the Indians he dropped his ax and seized his gun, and started on the double-quick for the fort at Davis' Station, which was several miles distant on the Christian County line. And it is said that when he got there his pipe was found to be still smoking; he afterward built a block-house on his own land for his defense in a similar predicament.

In 1809 John Moore made a settlement two miles south of Trenton on the Nashville road. There he resided until a few years ago, when he died. Accompanying him to this point was his father, who was born in Augusta County, Va., and died in this county in 1832. Newton Moore, a grandson of the latter, is still living on the home farm. Another early settler here was Col. Jeffries, who made an improvement on the land now in the possession of his grand-daughter, Mrs. Barnes; he was a soldier in the Revolution and died here in 1820. Exactly when "Pouncy" Anderson, as he was called, came here cannot be ascertained, but in a very early day he settled down on the land now owned by Col. Sebree. He was a great deer hunter, and died here in about 1835.

In 1810 F. J. Sebree came from Albemarle County, Va., to this district, and settled about two miles south of Trenton; his people were of English-French descent. Soon after his arrival here he went to Missouri, and while prospecting there he had one-half of the present site of St. Louis offered to him for a mere pittance, but not liking the location he returned to this county; here he resided until his death in 1835; his son, Col. E. G. Sebree, was born in this district in 1817, and at the age of fourteen commenced life for himself at Trenton, as a clerk in the store of his uncle, Granville Garth; he remained with his uncle five years, and then commenced business for himself; he continued in business seven years, and turned his attention to farming; he first purchased about 400 acres at $11 an acre, and now owns about 1,700 acres where he now resides. He has also been extensively engaged in cotton and tobacco speculations. In 1853–54 he represented this county in the Legislature.

In 1812 Henry T. Burns came to this district from Orange County, Va., and made a settlement; he died here in 1825. Quite a large family of his children are still living here.

In 1815 a Mr. Carver, of Virginia, settled on the Clarksville road in this district, where he died in 1847. In the same year a Mr. Gillam settled on West Fork, near the Christian County line, and there resided for many years. A Mr. Henderson, a cousin of President Jefferson, also made a settlement in this district in 1815. The farm on which he then resided is now owned by Mrs. Williams. At one time he was a man of considerable wealth, and wielded a large influence in this section of the county. Two sons of his, Hudson and Charles Henderson, also grew to manhood in this county, but they too have now gone to their reward.

In 1816 Robert Durrett came here from Virginia. The first few years after his arrival he rented, but afterward settled on the farm now owned by C. Dickinson. He afterward moved to Christian County, where he remained a short time, but subsequently returned to this district. Here he resided until his death in 1835. A brother-in-law of

his, Reuben Mansfield, came to this county about the same time, and settled on the premises now occupied by Oscar Tandy ; he died here in
1840; he left a large family, but all of them except two have passed
away. Harrison Mansfield, a son, is now living in the Purchase, and Mrs.
Susan Camp, a daughter, is now living at Louisville. In 1816 James
Beazley also came to this district. He was accompanied by Thomas
McDaniel. Both settled about three miles south of Trenton. They were
both horse-fanciers and had a race-track kept up for many years. Here
in an early day the people for miles around came in large numbers to
view the races, which at that time were one of the institutions of the
county. In the same year John Massey made a settlement on the Sebree
farm, where he resided for many years. In 1819 James L. Tutt came
here with his father, Lewis B. The latter was a native of England, and
died here in 1820. James L. came here from Culpeper County, Va.,
and died here in 1833. His son, James F. Tutt, is still living here at a
hale old age. He is surrounded by a large family of children, who minister to his comfort in his declining years. Thomas D. Adams also came
to this district in 1819 from Fayette County, Ky. He was originally a
native of Virginia, and died here in about 1845. His son, William D.,
who was born in the upper part of the State, grew to manhood here and
resided in the district until his death in 1875. A large family of children are still living here. In about 1820 Dr. Fox came to this district
and settled near Trenton. Here he finally became quite a noted physician for his day and time. He was a magistrate of the district for many
years. In 1847 he was killed on the public road by some negroes, and
his loss was regretted far and wide. In 1822 Alexander McElwain came
to this district. This gentleman was born in the city of Cork, Ireland,
and came with his widowed mother to Maryland in 1790. In 1800 he
and his mother came to Logan County and purchased 1,000 acres ; in that
county the mother died. Mr. McElwain after his arrival here purchased
the land now owned by his son, and resided here until a good old age.
His son, James C., who was one year old when the father arrived in this
county, is still living here, and needs no mention at our hands. In 1822
W. C. Harrell moved to this county from Nelson County, Ky., and resided here until 1872, when he moved to Clay County, Mo., where he is
now residing. His son, Dr. George A. Harrell, who was born here, is
now practicing medicine at this point. In 1825 George W. Camp came
to this district from Virginia. He was a soldier in the war of 1812, and
died in this county in 1860. Edmund Ware was born in Franklin
County, Ky., came to Christian County in 1820, and in 1827 he came to
this county, where he resided for many years. His son, Charles Ware, is
still living here, and is one of the leading farmers and tobacco dealers in

the district. About this time Granville Waddill emigrated to this district from Shelby County. After his arrival here he settled on the farm now owned by Col. Sebree. He was well read, and was considered a very fine historian for his day and time; he died here in about 1852. In 1827 Edmund Turnley came to this county from Spottsylvania County, Va.; in this district he settled on the farm now owned by a Mr. Smith, on the Miller's Mill road. Here he resided until he passed to his reward in 1852. Another settler who arrived in the district about this time was Rev. William Boone, who had come to this county in 1817 with his father, Squire Boone, who settled in the Allensville District, and there died   William Boone afterward came to Elkton District and subsequently came here. He was first a preacher in the Baptist denomination, but subsequently joined the Christian Church, and became a leading preacher in that denomination; he died here in 1836. In 1827 Zachariah Billingsley came here from Virginia, and made a settlement on land now owned by Webster Garth. In 1828 Samuel Chestnut came to this district from Princeton, Ky. To that point he had originally emigrated from North Carolina in about 1819. Prior to that time he had taken an active part in the war of 1812; he died in this county in 1866. His son, William A. Chestnut, who came with his father, died here in 1879, leaving a large family of children to mourn his loss. About the same time Henry White also emigrated to this district from Virginia; he settled on the farm now owned by his heirs, where he died in about 1863. His son, Clay White, was a soldier in the late war. Another settler who arrived in this district in about 1828 was Dabner Smith, who settled on the farm now owned by his heirs, two miles south of Trenton, where he died in 1850. Still another pioneer, cotemporaneous with the above, was William B. Simms, who settled on the farm now owned by his daughter, Mrs. Stigger. He was a brickmason by trade, and put up a large number of the early houses in the district.

In 1830 William P. Arnold came to this district. He was born in Louisa County, Va., and came with his parents to Christian County in 1812, where the latter died. After his arrival here he taught school for many years, but subsequently turned his attention to farming; he also became one of the largest tobacco speculators in the county, and made and lost several independent fortunes in his operations. He is still living in Trenton with his son, Lycurgus H., who was born here in the year after his father's arrival. The latter began merchandising here in 1869, and of late years has been serving as Postmaster and Magistrate. Reuben Bradley also came to this county in 1830 from Virginia, and settled on the farm now owned by Mr. Hogan, where he died in about 1865.

About this time Thomas Waller, a native of Virginia, also made a settlement on the farm now owned by his children.

Roscoe C. Dickinson was born in Louisa County, Va., his father being a soldier in the war of the Revolution. The former came here in 1831, and settled in the south part of the district. Here he died in 1863; his son, Dr. Joseph S. Dickinson, who came here with the father, is still living, and is practicing his profession in this district.

Thus briefly, and perhaps hurriedly, we have gone over the settlements of this district. Many there are, probably, who have been omitted in the list of early settlers, and who are as deserving of mention as those whose names and deeds have been written here. Their actions and their lives are enshrined in a more enduring volume, the unwritten archives of the past that linger to-day in the minds of the people who are now walking in the footsteps so well and so plainly carved by the men of by-gone days.

All honor should be given to these heroes of the past, for theirs was a grand and a noble work, and the memory of their toil, privations and hardships will linger with the people here as long as time shall last. A lasting monument of their labor is seen in the agricultural prosperity of the district to-day. Truly, of the early settlers we can say:

> " Ye pioneers, it is to you
> The debt of gratitude is due;
> Ye builded wiser than ye knew
> The broad foundation
> On which our superstructure stands."

Mills of the District.—The early mills that were used by the people of this district were all water-mills, and stood on the banks of the West Fork. Some were in the edge of this county and some were just across the line in Christian County. They were all rude structures, and to the people of to-day they would seem very cumbersome and out of place, but to the sturdy yeomen of an early day they answered all purposes as well as our more modern concerns would. The first one of which any record has been kept was the Miller's Mill, as it was known. It was in existence as early as 1812, and was run for many years by a man by the name of Miller. Whether he built it, however, could not be ascertained. It was regarded as the finest in this portion of the county. It was finally bought by a Mr. Barker who ran it until his death. It is now owned by some of the latter's children, and is still in use. In about 1820 Coleman put up a mill on the same stream, which stood for many years. In 1830 another structure was put up and was also used for some time. Both have now finally rotted away. In about 1877 a Mr. Bacon put up a steam-mill in Trenton, which is still in operation.

Early Schools.—The education of the youth of this district received due attention in an early day, and there were many good teachers who here and there conducted their subscription schools. Probably the very first school in the county was what was known as the Lebanon Academy, held in the old Lebanon Church, which stood two miles south of Trenton. A school was probably conducted here about 1810, and from that on until 1821. It was under the supervision of the Cumberland Presbyterian Church, and among the teachers who were employed there were Prof. Allan and Mr. Grayson. One of the first teachers of whom we have any record was Other Graves, who was conducting a school at Reuben Mansfield's as early as 1825. He taught in different places in this district until about 1835, and he was considered one of the best teachers in the State. About 1830 William Arnold, whom we have mentioned above, came here and taught school for many years. Cotemporaneous with Graves a man by the name of Graham was teaching here. He lived on the Byers farm near Pinchem, and there ran a school for many years. In about 1827–28–29–30 Jack Tyler taught a school in and around Trenton. He afterward moved to Clarksville, Tenn., and subsequently became the leading teacher in Montgomery County. A son of his, Quintus M., is still teaching in Trigg County. In later years Prof. Aaron Williams was one of the leading and best-known teachers in the neighborhood of Trenton.

Rev. C. M. Day came into the county about 1842. He settled down at Trenton, and was pastor of the Christian Churches at that point and Allensville. He supplied the pulpits free of charge, and supported himself by his school-teaching for many years.

First Churches.—The pioneers of this district were men who to a great extent were religiously inclined. Among the very early settlers were many identified with the Cumberland Presbyterian Church. And to this denomination should be given the honor of holding the first religious services in this district. As early as 1809 a camp-meeting was conducted by these people two miles south of Trenton, on the place now known as the Reuben Bradley farm. It was on the edge of a large scope of open barren, but which is now heavily timbered. Here was the camp-meeting ground, with round-pole huts and camps. In addition to this were several huts made of bed-clothes, and a few wagons in which their provisions were kept. And to this camp-meeting people came from a distance of fifty miles, coming in their plain homespun garments, with their wallets and saddle-bags filled with meal. The stand was composed of a few rough slabs for the minister to stand on, and an altar in front, surrounded by a set of rough logs made for seats, covered over with green boughs, making an arbor to keep off the sun by day and the heavy dews by night. Here the preachers exhorted, sung and prayed for days and nights, hardly stopping for intermission. Here the anxious would crowd to the altar by scores for prayer. Among the ministers here were Rev.

Finis Ewing, whom we have mentioned above; Samuel King, of Tennessee; and Ephraim McLean, of Logan County : all ministers of the Cumberland Church. In 1810 this denomination, under the direction of Finis Ewing, built a church south of the camp ground about half a mile, near the old Lebanon Springs, where the late F. N. Child lived for many years. It was of brick, and was used for a church by this denomination until 1821, when, as we have mentioned above, Ewing and all of his followers left this county and moved to Missouri, where another Lebanon Church was formed. Soon after this a Baptist organization was formed here, and the church was used by them for many years. Among the early members of what was known as the Lebanon Baptist Church were Stokely Waggoner, Reuben Bradley, William Arnold and wife, and many others. It was at one time in a very prosperous condition, and had about 200 members. Among the early ministers were Jack Wilson, Reuben Ross, Mr. Warfield and Robert Williams. In 1859 the Trenton Baptist Church was organized, the constituent members being from the old Lebanon Church. The history of this new organization will be found in connection with that of the town of Trenton.

Mount Hermon Cumberland Presbyterian Church was organized more than fifty years ago by Revs. H. B. Hill, Thomas Bone and others, who were known as "Circuit Riders." The first Elders were Joseph Frazer, Samuel Chesnut, E. T. Porter and W. C. Harrell. The congregation was under the charge of Rev. Silas Davis for a considerable length of time. This good man's memory is cherished by the children and grandchildren of the people who heard him. He was a man of marked ability, and his ministry was very successful. He died at Princeton, Ky., in the year 1851. Rev. Casky was the next pastor, who labored successfully until he gave place to Rev. J. M. Gill in 1858. This gentleman's pastorate lasted for twenty years, during which time nearly all the present members were added. Succeeding him were Revs. M. M. Smith and B. M. Taylor, both of whom have done efficient work.

Zion Baptist Church was organized in about 1825. The church building was of logs, and stood on the Miller's Mill road, near the Mansfield place. Among the early members were the Tumleys, Dickinsons and many others. Rev. Boone was the first pastor. In 1833, when the Christian denomination first sprang into existence, a split occurred in this church, which resulted in most of the members joining the new faith and organizing a new church.

Zion Christian Church.—Among the early members were Rev. Boone and family, Mrs. Sebree, Mrs. Anderson Garth, Miss Jeffries, Henry Ewing, John Carver and J. Tutt. In about 1843 a new building was put up on the land now owned by Mrs. Sebree, which was afterward used by this congregation. About this time the name of the society was changed to *Corinth*, and by this title the church still continues to be known. In about 1865 the congregation was moved to Trenton, and the present house built at a cost of about $2,500, on land donated by Mr. Sebree. At present the society has about one hundred members. The present officers are : Elders, Dr. Ramsey, Mr. Graham and Ed. Webb; and Deacons, Charles Rutherford, Charles Crutchfield, Charles Burness and Mr. Cook. Rev. Boone was the first pastor. He was followed by Revs. Henry T. Anderson, Charles M. Day (who preached for thirty years), Jesse Furgerson, Miller, McChesney, Robert Carver and Waddell. A Sunday-school is at present held every Sunday, with Ed. Webb as Superintendent.

New Zion Baptist Church.—In 1833, after the split between the Baptists and Christians in the old Zion Church, some of the members drew off and organized a new church three miles from the old one, on the Clarksville road. Here a frame house was built at a cost of about $400. Among the early members were R. C. Dickinson, T. C. Waller, Thomas Watts and Edward Tinsley. In 1868 a new building was erected at a cost of about $800, and is still in use. At present the church has a membership of about sixty.

Town of Trenton.—The town of Trenton was laid out originally in about 1819, by Lewis Leavell. The plat consisted of fifty-nine lots lying immediately around the intersection of the Hopkinsville road and Clarksville Street. In 1867, after the coming of the railroad, Lawson & Colwell's addition of some thirty lots was added on the north and east. The Legislature of 1883–84 also increased the corporate limits of the town by about one-half. This latter addition has not as yet been laid off into lots. Mr. Leavell at first gave the name of "Lewisville" to the town in honor of himself. But there being another postoffice in the State by the same name, he changed it soon after to "Trenton." It was his desire to have the county seat located at this point upon the formation of the new county, and before the matter was finally decided in favor of Elkton, he and Maj. John Gray had a very severe contest in the matter.

Early Merchants.—Probably the first men to do business at the new town were Reyburn & Woods, who merchandized here until 1825, and then moved to Clarksville. Soon after the laying out of the town John H. Poston opened a store here. He engaged in business by himself until about 1825, and then took in as a partner Granville W. Garth. This firm continued in operation about five years, when the senior partner retired, and Garth continued the business here until his death in 1840. In 1822 Moore & Broadus opened a store here, and remained in Trenton until 1837. In about 1830 Stokely T. Waggoner came to this point. He first opened a tailor shop, but soon after turned his attention to merchandising, and until 1859 he was one of the leading merchants at this point. From here he went to Russellville, where he is still living. Henry Wisdom purchased Waggoner's store and continued operations here about ten years. He then went to Clarksville, where he was elected the Cashier of a bank. He afterward went to Paducah, where he is still engaged in business. In 1837 William H. Barksdale and Col. E. G. Sebree purchased the store of Moore & Broadus. This firm continued in business about two years, when Sebree retired. Barksdale continued in business until 1846, and then went to St. Louis. In 1840 Col. Sebree began merchandising again, and continued in business five years. In 1846 he sold to John Billingsley, who merchandized here until his death in 1869. In about 1845 Monroe Graves began merchandising here, but soon sold out. Samuel Brockman sold goods here from 1847 to 1850. Charles Ware purchased Wisdom's store, remained in business about eight years, and then turned his attention to farming and tobacco speculating, and is still living at this point. C. R. Rutherford began merchandising here in 1852, and is still engaged in business. He was first associated with his brother James Rutherford, and the two remained in business until 1867, when the latter died. In 1867 the L. & N. R. R. was projected through Trenton, and the village has since that time made consid·erable progress. Among some of the merchants who have been·engaged here might be mentioned J. Billingsley, who continued here until his death in 1873. In 1867 G. W. Center came here, and is still engaged here. James McElwain opened a store here in 1868, and is still merchandising. Webb & Bro. began here in about 1879, and continued here a short time. Logan Webb came here in about 1877, and remained here about five years. O. C. Hord began merchandising here in 1874, and continued here until his death in 1878. Hord & Talley controlled the business about four years, and since that time J. A. Talley has been carrying it on. P. A. Painter came here in 1877, and sold out to James G. Cavendish, who is still here. Russell & Chesnut came here in 1881, and are still here. Rutherford Bros. have been merchandising here for some time. In about 1871 Webb & Grady came to Trenton and began merchandising. In two years this firm was succeeded by Grady & Pendleton, and were in business about three years. They were succeeded by Cook & Pendleton, who remained here about two years. George A. Yost opened a drug store in January, and is still in business here.

In about 1854 Mr. Waggoner and D. Christian built a tobacco-stemmery here, which they ran for some years. It is now rented, and is still in use.

In 1874 the Bank of Trenton was organized. Among the original stockholders were Mrs. Stigger, Mrs. Perkins, Mrs. Simms, Col. Sebree and Charles Day. The original capital was about $50,000, which was afterward lowered to about $35,000. Philip Bacon was the Cashier. In 1881 the bank retired from business.

In 1878 the Trenton Academy was built. It was of brick, and cost about $5,000. It was built by a stock company, among which were Charles Ware, Dr. Dickinson and Elijah Garth. In 1881 Col. Sebree purchased a larger part of the stock, and is still running it. The first teacher was Philip Painter, who taught about three years, and he was succeeded by a Mr. Vineyard, who is still here. It is a subscription school, and has an attendance of about sixty.

Trenton Baptist Church was organized in about 1859, the members coming in from the Lebanon Church. Among them might be mentioned D. M. Christian, W. P. Arnold, S. H. Bradley, Z. Billingsley, Dr. J. S. Dickinson, J. C. Hancock, Newton Moore, J. M. Williams, Jack Williams and Henry P. White. A brick structure was erected at a cost of about $6,500, and is still being used. At present the church has about 170 members. The officers are as follows : W. S. Dickinson, A. H. Moore, C. D. Runyon and H. S. Lowry ; Trustees, C. W. Ware and Q. D. Waller ; Clerk, W. S. Dickinson. Among the Pastors who have presided over the flock have been Revs. A. D. Sears, S. P. Forgy, R. A. Massey, G. F. Bagley, Dr. W. W. Gardner, A. F. Pearson and R. H. Lockett. The preaching services are held here on the second and fourth Sundays in each month. A Sunday-school is also held in connection with the church, which meets at 9:30 A. M. It has about seventy-five members. The present officers are: H. S. Lowry, Superintendent; Austin Dickinson, Secretary and Librarian; Teachers, Mrs. J. C. Hancock, Miss Lou Arnold, Miss Brenda Vineyard, Mrs. M. A. King, Miss Lydia Lockett.

Trenton Methodist Episcopal Church South was organized in the spring of 1874. Among the constituent members were Andrew J. Center, Mrs. McGuire, Mrs. Gray, John Basford, Mrs. Tranum and J. J. Basford. The fall previous the erection of a church had been commenced, which cost when completed $2,025. The church at present has about thirty-five members. Preaching occurs on the first and third Sundays. The Ministers who have preached here might be mentioned Revs. William Alexander, Patten, Brandon, Virgil Elgin, Thomas Bottlemy, Frazier and Valentine Thomas. The officers are: Stewards, J. Basford, J. C. Dycus, Silas Bennett. A Sunday-school was organized a short time since with Mr. George Yost as Superintendent and Mr. McCowan Assistant Superintendent.—*F. S. Tyler.*

S. Dickinson M.D.

CHAPTER IX.

MAGISTERIAL DISTRICT NO. 6—ALLENSVILLE—TOPOGRAPHY—FLORA AND
FAUNA—PIONEER SETTLERS—REV. JOHN GRAHAM—BERNARD EDWARDS
—SAMUEL JOHNSON—JOHN BELLAMY—FIRST ROADS AND BRIDGES—
HORSE AND WATER-MILLS—PIONEER SCHOOLS—EARLY CHURCHES—OR-
GANIZATION AND SUBSEQUENT HISTORY OF ALLENSVILLE.

THAT part of this county now embraced in what is known as the
Allensville District, is probably one of the earliest settled portions of the county, and is bounded on the north by District No. 4, Elkton ; on the east by Logan County ; on the south by District No. 8, Hadensville; and on the west by District No. 5, Trenton. Except upon the
east, the boundary of the district is but poorly defined, being very irregular, and it is almost impossible for one to estimate the exact size of it.
Suffice it to say that the district is one of the largest in the county. The
name, Allensville, was given to this district as early probably as 1819,
when the county was organized, from the town by the same name which
originally stood at the crossing of the Russellville and Clarksville road,
and the Elkton and Allensville road, and which was first settled as early
as 1810.

Topography.—The surface of the district presents a rolling, undulat-
ing appearance in the main, but along the banks of the creeks there is
some lowland. The highest portion of the district is in the northwest,
and the ground from here gradually slopes in a southeasterly direction,
the lands being the lowest along the banks of Elk Fork, and then rising
gradually along either side. The soil is a red clay subsoil on a blue limestone basis. In the northwestern portion of the district the limestone
comes to the surface in several places, and forms very broken and unpro-
ductive land. The major part of the land, however, is composed of this
red clay, and forms the very best farming country. The district forms a
portion of the well-known Clarksville tobacco district, and some of the
finest tobacco in the State is raised in this portion of Todd County. Of
late years, however, the better class of farmers are devoting considerable
attention to general farming, especially to the culture of wheat; so that
at present probably not more than a fourth of the district is devoted to
tobacco farming. Some of the more advanced farmers are also at present

paying some attention to stock-raising, and are meeting with merited success. But little attention is paid to fruit culture, although the soil is of such a nature as to make a departure in this direction a success, and it is to be hoped that as the years roll on, much may be done in fruit-growing. At present about four-fifths of the district is under cultivation. When the pioneers first came here there was but little timber to be found. In fact, even the firewood had to be dug out of the ground, and what little underbrush could be found was used for fences. At present quite an amount of fine timber is growing here. Among the best known varieties of woods found might be mentioned, oak (several varieties, including black, white and red), hickory, maple, and along the banks of the creek, poplar. Of late years there is a thick growth of pine being formed in the lowlands.

Streams.—The Elk Fork of Red River is the main stream of the district. This creek enters from the northwest, flows generally in a southeasterly direction through the county, and crossing the Tennessee line empties into the Red River. The only affluent of this creek is Beaver Dam Creek, which rises northwest of Allensville on Demas Gill's farm, and flowing in a southeasterly direction empties into Elk Fork. This stream takes its name from the fact that in an early day a large number of beavers built their dams on the creek. In the northwest part of the district, on Elk Fork, there is one of the finest natural curiosities in the State. We refer to the sinking of the creek through a limestone formation, and its appearance again some two or three hundred yards below where it disappears. The water seems to sink some twenty feet from the base of a rocky promontory some forty or fifty feet high, and forms a very pronounced whirlpool as the water goes down. The rock through which it has forced its way forms part of one of the highest portions of the county, the cliff rising some hundred feet from the bed of the creek where it re-appears. What makes the place more interesting is the fact that at this day the old bed of the creek is still to be traced around this hill, and in the spring-time this also becomes filled with the overflow of water. There are two or more theories advanced to account for how this stream came to be thus changed from its original course. One of them is, that at one time there was an earthquake or volcanic eruption of some sort, and when affairs had assumed their natural state this new course was found. This idea seems to be borne out from the fact that the stream sinks out of sight some distance away from the base of the cliff, instead of disappearing under it. The other hypothesis for this *lusus naturæ* is, that the relentless wearing away and pressure of the water in the ages that have gone, have finally formed this latter course.

Traces and Roads.—Probably the first road ever surveyed through this district is the "Old State road" or the Russellville and Clarksville road, as it is now known. This was surveyed through as early as 1815, or perhaps even before. It was the old mail and stage route, and until the building of the Memphis Branch of the Louisville & Nashville road, it was one of the leading roads in southern Kentucky. The next road that was surveyed through this district is what is known as the Elkton, Allensville and Keysburg road. This thoroughfare was projected and completed as early as 1820. It crossed the Russellville and Clarksville road, and at this intersection the town of Old Allensville used to stand. Of late years this road has become unfit for travel, and a few years since the question of turnpiking the road was agitated ; it was finally decided to form a turnpike company, and that a turnpike be built from Allensville to Elkton. It was also decided to vote a tax for the building of this turnpike in each of the precincts, and the day was appointed for an election. When this time came around and an election had been held it was found that the people of Allensville District had voted a tax, while a majority of the people of Elkton District were against the project. Accordingly when the time arrived to collect the tax voted by the people of this district, some of the citizens here strenuously objected to the payment of it, as the people of Elkton District had not carried out their part of the contract. As a consequence the case is now in court, and is still undecided. Suffice it to say at this point that the aforesaid road is in a very deplorable condition, and sadly in need of repair and attention. About the next public road in this district to be surveyed was what is known as the Graham Mill road, extending from Allensville to the mill now owned by Mrs. Douie Gill. One of the last public roads opened is a short road that leads from the Russellville road to Allensville. It starts from Mr. B. D. Johnson's farm, and runs in a southwesterly direction to the town.

Bridges.—The first bridge ever built in the district was one across Elk Fork, on the Russellville and Nashville road. It was an old flat structure, and was put up there soon after the road was first surveyed. This bridge stood there until about 1849, when it was torn down, and the present covered structure erected. The next bridge built, and the only other one now standing in the district, is one across Elk Fork on the Graham Mill road. It was built in 1878, Mr. G. H. Gill being the means of engineering an appropriation from the county for the purpose.

Pioneer Settlers.—To what one of the brave pioneers who came to this portion of the county should be given the honor of first carving out a new home for himself, and then fighting out the possession of it with the savages and the wild beasts, cannot be ascertained by the present historian. The first settlement dates back so far that it is lost in the unrecorded annals of the past.   At present there are none of the descendants of those few brave men who first entered these unbroken wilds living in this district, and but little can be ascertained concerning them.   In 1808 Bernard Edwards came to this county, and found the following parties living here: George and Thomas Cross were living on the farm now owned by Dr. I. N. Walton.   George died here, and lies buried on the place he had settled so many, many years ago.   Thomas finally moved to Clarksville, where he died.   A son of his is now living in Elkton Precinct.   John Hill lived on Elk Creek on part of the farm now owned by Thad Coleman.   He lived here for a number of years, and raised a large family of children, but they too have passed away.   James Lowry had also made a settlement on land owned now by William Mimms.   Three of this pioneer's grandchildren are still living: R. M. Lowry in Christian County, S. M. in Elkton and Dr. Lowry in Texas.   Isaiah Boone, a nephew of the famous Daniel Boone, was living on the farm now owned by George Johnson.   A Mr. Bainbridge was also living in the district on land now owned by N. B. Penick.   He sold out his farm to Ben. Parish, who came here in 1810.   The latter resided here until his death, and now lies buried on that farm.   The estate was sold in 1847 to Nathan Penick, the father of the present owner of the farm.   A Mr. Valindingham resided on the north line of the precinct, between this district and Elkton.   A grandson of his is now living, in the person of Dr. Valindingham, of Owensboro.

Rev. John Graham was also living in this district on the farm now owned by Col. T. M. Adkins, of Clarksville.   This gentleman was a native of North Carolina.   He was a local preacher in the Methodist Church, and held services for a number of years in this and adjoining counties.   He died here in 1840, leaving a family of ten children, none of whom survive him.   We have mentioned above that Bernard Edwards came here in 1808.   This pioneer was born near Lynchburg, Va., and coming to this county settled on the waters of Elk Fork.   His improvement forms a part of the farm now owned by John Russell.   In about 1848 he bought the farm now owned by his son, P. G. Edwards, where he resided until his death.   He enlisted in the war of 1812, but subsequently hired a substitute and did not go.   He was the first Magistrate elected in this precinct, after the formation of Todd County.   In 1809, Estley and Horatio Muir, two brothers, came to this county from Fayette County, Ky.   Estley settled on the farm now owned by his son, John R. Muir.   Horatio settled on the old Hill farm.   Mrs. Maggie Wisdom, his daughter, is now living on the old home place within the corporate limits of Allensville.   In 1810 John Small came to this county and settled on the edge of the district between this precinct and Logan County.   He was a native of Maryland.   When a boy he came to Shelby

County with his parents, who died there. He continued to reside there until his removal to this county. While a resident of that county he ran flat-boats from there to New Orleans for a number of years, the return trip always being performed on foot. In 1815, when soldiers were being procured to send to New Orleans, he enlisted with troops that were being gathered in this county, but finally procured a substitute and did not go. He resided here until his death in 1840. At present a large family of his descendants are residents of this county. In 1815 there were several families that immigrated to this district. A Mr. Lumsden made a settlement on the farm now owned by his daughter, Mrs. Elizabeth Gill. George McClaine settled on the farm now owned by J. H. Johnson, and there resided until his death. Samuel Johnson also came to this district in that year. This gentleman was born in Maryland, and came with his parents when a boy to Fayette County, Ky. Coming to this district he settled on the farm owned by J. W. Johnson. He purchased from the Government an improvement of 400 acres, but only resided there two years when he sold out. He then bought the farm now owned by his son B. D. Johnson. He was a very successful farmer and at one time owned about 1,200 acres. Three of his sons are still living in the district. He died in 1861. Squire Boone, another nephew of Daniel Boone, was an arrival in the district in 1815. He did not live here long, his death occurring two years afterward, but several of his descendants are still living here. In 1818 the first pioneer of a family that to-day stands very high in this precinct, made a settlement here. We refer to James Gill. This gentleman was born in Culpeper County, Va., and came to Logan County, Ky., in 1815. While a resident of Virginia he enlisted in the war of 1812, and served as Captain in that conflict. Upon his arrival here he settled first near Allensville, and there resided until 1823, and then moved to the farm now owned by Milton Gill. Here he resided until his death, which occurred in 1843. In 1819 John Bellamy came to this district from Fayette County, Ky. He was originally a native of Dinwiddie County, Va., and came to the State in 1810. In Fayette County, Ky., he followed the carpenter's trade. While living in that county he was drafted into the war of 1812, but having procured a substitute he was permitted to stay at home. After his arrival in this district he turned his attention to farming. He also built a distillery in the Daysville Precinct, which he ran for a number of years. He also put up a distillery on Elk Fork, and bought the grist-mill which had been erected on that stream in an early day by George Cross. He followed both milling and distilling for a number of years, and was at the time of his death (which occurred in 1860) one of the wealthiest men of the county. He was for many years one of the Magistrates of the district, and at the time of the adoption of the new Constitution was next to the senior Magistrate of the county. In 1829 Joseph Watkins (from whom a large family of the people of this district now claim descent) came to this county and settled on the farm now owned by his grandson, J. H. Watkins. In his life-time he was one of the foremost men of the county. He ran a mill on Elk Fork for a number of years, and was otherwise engaged in promoting the county's prosperity. In 1837 three more settlers arrived here. F. A. Anderson came to the State in 1835, from Dinwiddie County, Va., and first settled in Logan County. After a two years' residence there he came here. James Bibb came here from Lincoln County, Ky., and settled near the depot. E. W. Hughes came here from Powhatan County, Va. All of these gentlemen are still living in the precinct, and consequently need no mention at the hands of the historian. This comprises the early settlement of Allensville as far as we have been able to learn, though there may be other names equally entitled to mention in these pages. Their early struggles and hardships and trials, incident to the pioneer's life, are but a repetition of those experienced by all settlers in a new and uninhabited region. Many daring deeds by these unknown heroes have passed into oblivion, and many of the foregoing list who labored hard to introduce civilization into this part of the country now lie in obscure graves unmarked by the simple epitaph. Those of the number who still live little thought, as they first gazed upon the broad waste of prairie, the unmolested grove, tangled with brush and brier, that all this wilderness in their own day would be made to blossom as a garden. Little thought had they of seeing beautiful homes, waving fields of grain, green pastures and grazing herds, where the bounding deer and crouching wolf then held unmolested sway.

"All honor to these gray old men,
For they've conquered stubborn soil."

Clustering around the settlement of many neighborhoods the historian finds incidents that form an interesting background for the hard struggles and many privations of the early settlers. In this precinct we find nothing of the sort. As it is remarked in the beginning of this chapter, the early settlers found but little timber, and the land being so rich they were early led to give their entire attention to the cultivation of the soil. The pioneers here were pre-eminently an agricultural people, so that we find the absence of the many startling incidents that are generally recorded in narratives of this character. Consequently the scenes of wild beasts and wild men that form interesting details in other histories are unrecorded here.

Early Industries.—The first improvement that the pioneer looks after, having procured a habitation for himself and family, is a mill, a piece of machinery that always accompanies civilization. Meal was first obtained by crushing the corn, when dry, in a kind of rude mortar, made by chiseling out a hollow in the top of an oak stump. The pestle was an iron block made fast to a sweep, and with this simple contrivance a coarse article of meal was ground. A still simpler means was resorted to before the corn had become hard enough to shell, namely, the common grater. The first mill that was probably patronized by the early residents of Allensville was an old horse-mill, that was built by John Small on his farm in about 1820. It was a crude structure but stood for a number of years. In 1830 John Graham put up a water-mill in the northern part of the district on the bank of Elk Fork. This mill he ran for a number of years, and at his death William Randol took possession of it. The latter sold out to W. J. Hooser, who in turn sold to Squire Lowry. This man took possession of it in about 1850, and while he had charge of it the mill fell into disuse. Soon after Graham put up his mill, George Cross built another one, five miles below on the same creek. It was this mill that John Bellamy bought and ran for so many years in connection with his distillery. He finally sold out to M. L. Lasley, who made some improvements on the old structure. This gentleman also ran it for a long time, and to this day it is known in the neighborhood as the Lasley Mill. In 1877 Mr. Lasley sold the property to Graham & Gill. This firm also made extensive improvements on the mill, and ran it until the fall of 1880, when Graham retired. Mr. Gill continued the mill in operation until his death in 1882. Mrs. Douie Gill is now carrying on the business, and it is now the only one in the precinct. After Cross sold his mill to Bellamy, he built another one about half way between the one he had first erected and the old Graham Mill. This mill was patronized some time and then ran down. In 1840 Charles A. Bailey put up another, above the Graham Mill, on the same creek. John Petree became the owner of this, in a few years' time, and he in turn sold it to John Chesnut. Under the latter's management it ceased operations a short time prior to the war. Joseph Watkins also erected a mill on the farm now owned by his grandson. This he ran for some time and then let it go down. In 1845 Estley Muir put up a horse-mill which he ran for some time. In about 1850 Green & Chesnut opened a tan-yard which they continued for a while, and then it ceased operations.

The Schools.—There were pioneer schools in those days, but very primitive in character, but meeting the great want of the people quite as fully, if not more so, than the schools of to-day. All were subscription schools, and about them were no great pretensions. A small room in some empty cabin was procured if possible, or failing in this, an outhouse was used. The first school in this district was taught at the old

Seceder Church, that used to stand in the northwest part of the district. Henry Porter was the first teacher and held a school here in 1830. Among the teachers that followed him were Alfred Waller, Brice Austin, James Hawkins, George Oldham and Charley Burr. The church was finally closed up and the school died out. The next school was built near the northern line on land formerly owned by Valindingham. Charles Brockman was about the first teacher here. Succeeding him, B. B. Edwards, Miss Mary Ann Howard and Miss Virginia Porter also taught here, the last school being held here in about 1855. In 1825 a schoolhouse was erected near a spring on land now owned by J. H. Johnson. A Mr. Faulkner taught here awhile, but the school was soon discontinued. In the north part of the district a log schoolhouse was built in about 1850. This building continued to be used until 1870, when what is known as the Russell Academy was erected. Among the teachers who have taught school there might be mentioned Miss Easter McGuire, Miss Lee Jones and John Thompson. In the new building the teachers have been Miss Mary Orr, J. A. Bone, Dr. J. H. Harris, Dr. Anderson, Miss Mary Smith, J. C. Baker. The present teacher is Dr. J. H. Harris. Besides this school Mrs. Dr. Morehead and Mr. Hooker are teaching schools in Allensville, and Miss Maggie Lanier is teaching south of the village. All of these schools are subscription schools, and we are informed by persons competent to testify on the subject that there is not sufficient money in the hands of the treasurer of the school fund to have one free school taught in the district. In fact, we are informed that the educational interests here are at a lower ebb than they have ever been before. This is certainly not as it should be. While the people of the county and neighborhood are making advancement in other directions the schools of the State are retrograding. It is a fact, that while Kentucky is keeping side by side with its sister States of the North in many branches of the onward march of civilization, yet it is noticed that the free school system is very inferior to that of Indiana or Illinois. The general masses of the people in this State are lacking in interest on this great subject of education. And, consequently, the schools in this district to-day are not much better than they were fifty years ago. And yet this manifest inactivity is not noticed in any other line of progress. There has been an upward tendency in matters pertaining to agriculture, commerce and religion, and there should be in the educational resources of the district as well. The people of Allensville should see to it that their children are afforded better educational advantages in the future than they have at present.

Pioneer Churches.—Among the early pioneers of Allensville were many pious men and women, and its religious history dates almost from the period of its settlement. The first preachers were Methodists, and came as one crying in the wilderness, and wherever they could collect a few together they proclaimed the glad tidings of salvation without money and without price. The first religious services held within the present limits of the district occurred at the residence of Rev. John Graham, probably as early as 1815. There was no regular class organized, but services continued to be held here for fifteen years. The first and only preacher of whom any notice has been kept, that ministered to these pioneers, was Rev. Peter Cartwright. This rugged itinerant preacher made this as one point on his circuit, which then extended from Bowling Green, Ky., to Dover, Tenn., about once a month. In 1820 what was known as the "Seceders" (who were one of the numerous branches of Presbyterians in Scotland that withdrew from the established church about the year 1773, and formed Secession Church, so called), built a church in the northern part of the precinct. It was the only church of that denomination in this part of the State, and consequently its membership embraced many families within a radius of twenty or thirty miles. Among some of the members were the families of Russells and Mayburns. James Russell was one of their early preachers. They continued to hold services here for upward of twenty years. There have been other churches and preachers in the district, but as the denominations have all become identified with the history of the village of Allensville, their history will be given later on in the chapter.

Old Allensville.—As we have mentioned elsewhere, almost as soon as the old State road and the Elkton and Keysburg road were surveyed, what is known as the town of Old Allensville sprang into existence at the crossing of these two thoroughfares. Most of the land where the town used to stand was owned by P. A. Wines, and now forms part of the land owned by his daughter, Mrs. Sallie Haddox. Exactly how the name Allensville came to be given to this little hamlet is not definitely known. In an early day there was a family of Allens living in the neighborhood, but whether any one of them was ever immediately connected with the town that now bears the family name cannot be ascertained. Probably the first man to have a store there was Ned Trabue. He did business here for some time. Clayborn Wooldridge was another early merchant at this point, also Edward Anderson and Charles Hatcher. At no time were there more than two stores doing business at once at this point. Aside from this there was a blacksmith shop and a collection of some four or five houses. In 1859 Spencer Small and D. B. Hutchings were doing business there. In that year the work on the Memphis Branch of the Louisville & Nashville Railroad was begun, and completed the year following. The railroad crossed the Elkton, Allensville & Keysburg road one mile east of Old Allensville, and as a natural sequence the new town sprang into existence almost as soon as the trains began running. The land now contained in the present limits of the town was at that time owned mostly by F. A. Anderson and E. W. Hughes. No regular lots were ever laid off or plat of the town ever made, but most of the land was sold to the people purchasing by F. A. Anderson.

First Merchants.—William Frazier was probably the first to put up a store here, on the site now occupied by Mr. Wooldridge as a drug store. Spencer Small also moved his stock down from Old Allensville, and built a store where John Adams' store is now. Hughes & Donalson put up a store next, on the opposite side of the street. E. A. Yost bought the store, and while he was running it the building was burned. During the war most of the merchants doing business here were compelled to suspend. Strangers came in, some from the North, others were Germans from Louisville. Soon after hostilities ceased these merchants went North again, and the former business men again assumed control to some extent. In 1865 Philip Hurshfield built the store now occupied by Mr. Yates, and did business here until 1879. John Adams came here about the same time, and began business in the store that had been built by Small & Wooldridge. Here he did business until 1878, when that building and several others were burned. Adams then began the erection of the brick he now occupies, finishing it the following year. Frazier & Winston soon after the war put up the building now occupied by Haddox & Riley. In 1869 C. W. Haddox purchased this store, and in the following year he took J. T. Donalson in as a partner. In 1871 he sold an interest to C. E. Haddox (Donalson having retired a short time before), and this firm continued in business until 1882, when C. W. Haddox died, and his brother continued the business by himself for about six months, and then took in N. B. Riley as a partner. This firm is also still doing business here. In 1871 O. M. Grinter ran a confectionery store here. About 1872 Dr. R. B. Richardson ran a drug store. In the following year he sold out to H. Q. Grinter, who afterward took in his brother, O. M. Grinter, as a partner. These gentlemen did business there only a short time, and then retired. In 1875, however, the latter started up in the drug business, and is also still engaged here. William Small has recently opened a harness shop here, and W. J. Yates came here in January, 1884, and is now running a dry goods store. J. N. Wooldridge is now running a drug store at this point in the room formerly occupied by his brother. R. D. Bellamy came here in 1866, and opened a furniture store and cabinet-shop, and is still doing business. From about 1880 to 1882 the little village of Allensville boasted of a newspaper called the *Gazette;* it was published by W. H. Frayser, and while in operation led a rather precarious existence. John T. Smith is the present Postmaster at this point, and his daughter, Miss Fannie, is running a millinery store, and another daughter, Miss Jennie, is running a hotel here, all in the same building. At present the town contains the following business houses : Two general stores, one agricultural store, one hardware store, one dry goods and clothing house, three drug stores, one furniture store, one harness shop, one millinery store; there are also two hotels, one tobacco factory, and three physicians.

W. W. Frazier was the first station agent at this point. He was succeeded by Newton Thomas, who attended to the business until January last, when Mr. Sublett assumed control, and is at present filling the position. The town at present contains about 300 inhabitants.

Mount Gilead Baptist Church was constituted in Old Allensville as early as 1815. Among the first members were Stephen Trabue, Squire Boone and wife, Mrs. Polly Bowen, Haskins Trabue, Aaron Trabue, Maj. Cheatham and family, John Hill and family, Isaac Wilson, Seth Wooldridge and Mrs. Elizabeth Hancock. The first services were held at the residence of Stephen Trabue. Soon after that organization a two-story brick house was built on land donated by Edward Curd near Old Allensville. This building was used as a place of worship until 1855, when a frame structure was built on the same site at a cost of about $2,000. In 1875 the church was moved to Allensville and the present brick edifice erected at a cost of about $8,000. The first pastor was Ambrose Bowen. He was followed by John Wilson, then Aaron Trabue, next Wilson Trabue. William Warder came next and preached for a number of years. James Lamb followed and then came F. C. Plasters. Under his administration, which lasted eight years, the frame was built. S. P. Forgy came next; he was pastor sixteen years, and through his instrumentality the church at Allensville was commenced. Since church has been held here, the pastors have been, W. W. Gardner, W. H. Williams and C. W. Dickey. The present pastor is T. W. Bibb. At the last meeting of the association, the society here showed 143 members. The present officers are : Clerk, J. H. Johnson ; Deacons, James Small, Dr. P. N. Walton, William Mimms and J. H. Johnson. Services are held here on the first and fourth Sundays in each month. For a number of years a Sunday-school has been held quite regularly. At present there are about forty members. The present officers are: Dr. I. N. Walton, Superintendent; William Mimms, Assistant Superintendent; Frank Johnson, Secretary and Treasurer.

Macedonia Congregation, Christian Church.—The first services of this denomination ever held in this district occurred under an arbor in Old Allensville in about 1844. A society was organized, among the members being Martin Hogan, John Colwell, Mrs. Betsey Watkins, Coleman Gill and family, Nathan Penick and family and William Edwards. Meetings were held in this arbor when the weather would permit, for three years. Then a frame church was built about a quarter of a mile southeast of the town. This building continued to be used as a place of worship until 1877, when the present frame church in Allensville was erected at a cost of $2,300. Henry T. Anderson was the first pastor. Rev. C. M. Day was the next, and occupied the pulpit for thirty-five years, followed by W. E. Mobley with a two years' pastorate, and James Fow with one. The minister now in charge is Rev. E. G. Sewell. Preaching occurs on the second Sunday in each month. At present the membership is about sixty. The officers of the church are as follows: Elders, E. B. Barnes, B. D. Johnson and Robert Carvell; Deacons, W. S. Gill and J. H. Watkins; J. H. Watkins, Clerk. A Sunday-school has been in operation in connection with this church for the past four years. The average attendance is now about thirty. The present Superintendent is B. D. Johnson; Assistant Superintendent, W. S. Gill; Secretary and Treasurer, J. H. Watkins.

Allensville Methodist Episcopal Church was organized in 1867 from the consolidation of two churches: one, a class that had met in Old Allensville, the other, the Bethlehem Church in Logan County. In an early day the Methodists used to hold camp-meetings in an arbor in Old Allensville, and afterward a class was organized which met for a number of years at Mrs. Covington's residence. At the organization there were about twenty members. Among them may be mentioned: David Sydnor, F. M. Anderson, Mrs. Estley Muir, E. W. Hughes and family, R. E. Coleman and Col. T. M. Adkins. The first meetings were held in a schoolhouse, but the church was built the same year at a cost of about $3,500. In January, 1884, the edifice was repaired at a cost of about $3,000 more. Among the ministers who have officiated there are: Revs. J. Moore, Hayes Petree, Bottlemy, Brewer, T. Lewis, Spurier, Ed Harrison, Emerson, Gooson, and the present one is Rev. Dr. Keene. The present membership is about seventy. Present officers: Stewards, John Adams, Washington Sydnor, Thomas Williams and Robert Coleman; Trustees, E. W. Hughes, John Adams and Washington Sydnor; Clerk, John Adams. A Sunday-school has been in operation here some time; it now has an average attendance of about sixty. The present officers are: Thomas Williams, Superintendent; William Shenick, Assistant Superintendent; John Adams, Secretary. The teachers are as follows: Rev. Thomas Hooker, Washington Sydnor, Mrs. Mattie Adams, Mrs. Anna Minor, William Shenick and Mrs. Robert Hooker.

Allensville Lodge No. 182, A. F. & A. M., was organized in about

1849 in Old Allensville. Among the charter members were Benjamin Barnes, M. S. Lasley, Dr. Garrett and a Mr. Waters. The first W. M. was Dr. Garrett, first Secretary Mr. Waters, and M. S. Lasley was the first Steward and Tyler. The lodge first met in a brick storeroom in the town, owned by Mr. Covington. In 1860 the lodge was moved to Allensville, and first met over Wooldridge & Small's store; next in Dr. Gill's drug store. After meeting there about four years they next moved to a hall over John Adams' store, and afterward met in Dr. Richardson's office. The lodge at one time had about sixty members, but now only about twenty-three are on the books. The last officers elected are as follows: W. M., Col. T. M. Adkins; S. W., Benjamin Barnes; J. W., Dr. Richardson; S. D., W. H. Adams; J. D., Joe E. Rust; Secretary, N. Thomas; Treasurer, John Q. Goodman; Steward and Tyler, H. Mitchell. Since January, 1884, no meetings of the lodge have been held, and the members are talking of surrendering their charter.

Allensville Lodge No. 163, I. O. O. F., was organized in 1867 in Allensville by Grand Secretary White, of Louisville. Among the charter members were F. Smith, Elisha Prince, Joseph Gill, R. D. Bellamy, S. S. Perkins, S. P. Forgy and George A. Payne. The first officers were : F. Smith, N. G.; Elisha Prince, V. G.; R. D. Bellamy, Treasurer; George A. Payne, Secretary; S. P. Forgy, Chaplain. First met over Wooldridge & Small's store, but afterward met in a hall which they fitted up over Coleman Gill's drug store. Stated meetings were held until 1870, when the charter was surrendered, lodge disbanded, and most of the members are now connected with the Keysburg Lodge.

Armstead Lodge No. 1432, K. of H., was organized at Armstead, Logan County, March 4, 1879. The charter members were H. B. Small, J. B. Small, F. M. Page, R. M. Wintersmith, T. F. Small, D. Darby and C. W. Roach. Dr. Kimbrough was the first Director. The lodge continued to meet at Armstead until January, 1884, when it was moved to Allensville, and now meets in Dr. Richardson's office. It now has a membership of about twenty-three. The present officers are: J. R. Young, Director; J. B. Small, Reporter; H. B. Small, Financial Reporter, and Joseph Wilson, Treasurer. The lodge meets on the first and third Saturdays in each month. From 1874 to 1879 what was known as the Pioneer Grange No. 1 was in operation at Allensville. At one time it had about forty members, and was in a very flourishing condition. It finally ran down, however, and the members disbanded. In 1872 John J. Hickman organized a Good Templar Lodge at Allensville, and at one time the lodge had about 140 members. Clay Hunter was the first Worthy Chief Templar. It continued to meet for about three years in the Odd Fellows' Hall, and then surrendered its charter.

In 1866 the village of Allensville was incorporated. The charter defined the corporation of the town as being "a mile square, and the limits extending a half mile in any direction from the depot." In 1878 the records of the town were burned, and, consequently, none but the present officers can be given. They are as follows: Board, C. E. Haddox, J. T. Young, John Adams, R. D. Bellamy and J. W. Small; N. Thomas, Police Judge.—*F. S. Tyler.*

CHAPTER X.

Magisterial District No. 8—Guthrie and Hadensville—Surface—
Barrens and Timber Land—Early Forts and Settlements—
Graysville—Old and New Hadensville—Guthrie—Its Original
Proprietor—Officers—Churches.

THE district of Hadensville, or Guthrie, which forms the subject of the following pages, is a somewhat level body of land lying in the southeast portion of the county. It is bounded on the north by District No 6, Allensville; on the east by Logan County, on the south by Tennessee, and on the west by No. 5, Trenton. The surface of the district is somewhat diversified. In the south, especially in and around Guthrie, it is swampy, and at one time a part of the district was under water. In the center it is rolling, and in the north it is somewhat hilly. The main portion of the soil in the district is of the red clay subsoil over a limestone basis. Originally a large amount of the surface of the district was in what is known as " barrens." But there were two or three groves of some size in the district, the main one being the Gabriel Roach Grove. The timber of the district consisted mainly of red oak, black oak and post oak. In the lowlands there were some pin oak and swamp oak, with an occasional tree of white oak, and in the barrens some scrub hickory was found. Scattered here and there were fine large meadows, in which the finest of strawberries were wont to grow, and these furnished many a hungry pioneer with food in an early day. It is stated by old settlers that there is more timber in the district now than there was in the early days. As an agricultural district this portion of the county stands at the head. Large crops of tobacco, wheat and corn are raised there, and of late years considerable attention has been paid to stock raising with merited success. Some slight notice is also being given to fruit culture. Two railroads, the L. & N., and the Memphis Branch of the same road, run through the district, and with two railroad points —Guthrie and Hadensville—within the boundaries. The resources have been developed by means of bringing its rich farming lands into easy communication with the outside world.

Creeks and Roads.—The main creek of the district is Spring Creek, which rises from a spring at the western edge of the district, flows generally in a southerly direction into Tennessee. It has several smaller branches, all bearing the same common name.

The first road in this district was the Clarksville, Elkton and Russellville road. Probably the next one was the Gallatin road, which ran from Port Royal to Trenton, and thence to Hopkinsville. This was probably surveyed as early as 1819, although many years before that there had been traces here.

Pioneer Settlers.—Collins in his "History of Kentucky" speaks of some settlements which were made near Elk Fork in what was then Logan County as early as 1785. Exactly where those settlements were, he does not say. But early pioneers tell us of a fort that used to stand within 100 yards of "Agent" Spring, only a little way northwest of Guthrie, and which was built in the very earliest settlements of this part of Kentucky. As this is the only fort of which any trace can be found in this region, we are constrained to make this fort the basis of the settlement referred to by Collins. And by so doing we claim for this place the name of being the earliest authenticated settlement in Todd County. To-day there are no traces left of a fort or any settlement in this region. In 1850 an old bronze medal was turned up by the plowshare, which was probably lost by some occupant of the fort. On the obverse side is an equestrian figure of Frederick the Great, with the legend, "*Fredrichs Rorusorum Rex, 1757,*" on the margin. On the reverse side is a battle sketch and the marginal legend "*Quo nihil majus.*" "*Rosbach, Nov. 5th, 1757.*" This is probably one of the medals commemorative of the victory which Frederick had struck from the metal of the cannon captured in this historic engagement and distributed among the soldiery. This suggests that some Prussian immigrant may have been among the early pioneers, but further than this nothing is known of the early community. Whether the settlement was continuous, or was driven out by the Indians, is also a matter of doubt.

Mr. Kennedy, whom we have quoted in the history of other portions of this county, has the following to say about the settlements in this district prior to 1809:

"The next mill below Carson (in Elkton District) was Smith & Laughlin's, on the Gallatin Road; then southwest of this mill lay the 'pony wood,' with much timber, where lived several worthy citizens—Henry Gorin, Gabriel Roach (father of John and James Roach), Elliott Vauter. The two last named men married Maj. John Gray's sisters, and in the neighborhood lived Uncle Jim Allen, the first Coroner of Todd County and auctioneer-general for all this country. He was of Irish origin, and cried all the sales for this new region. He would proclaim the sale and commence to sell with a bottle of whisky in his left hand and his cane in

G W Tahafer,o

his right hand. When he would rather stall he would cry the bid and say ' fair sale, gentlemen, and a dhram to the next bidder.' Now this was in very early times, and was the then custom and fashion of the early settlers.

" Now this beautiful barren limestone from the Russellville and Hopkinsville road was unsettled only where they could find a spot of timber, in which they would build their cabins. On Spring Creek, where it crossed the Nashville road, John Moore settled. He was the father of John Moore who yet resides there; also of Mrs. S. W. Taliaferro and Andrew Moore, deceased, and a brother of Maj. Sam Moore, who settled near Trenton."

In what is now the Guthrie District, Maj. John Gray owned a considerable portion of land, as he did also in other portions of the county. In 1812 he gave to Mrs. Kendal, his sister, what is known as "Leadwright," containing several hundred acres of land in the immediate neighborhood of Guthrie. The land had to be occupied before a correct and valid title could be secured, and so Mrs. Kendal, accompanied by her husband, came to this district, intending to occupy the land. Near the spring now known as "Agent" Spring, Maj. Gray had previously made a little cabin out of rails, and to this cabin Mrs. Kendal wended her way. When she reached the point she found the cabin occupied by men placed there by Ezeriah Davis, who claimed to own the title to this land instead of Gray. These parties refused to allow Kendal to settle, and the latter finally settled in the Elkton District. At that time Mr. Kendal states that a Mr. Byers was living on land now owned by Samuel Taliaferro, Joseph C. Frazier on land now owned by James Standard, and a Mr. Roberts on land now owned by Mr. Robert Frazier. In about the same year Col. Smith settled near what is known as the Graham Mill. He lived there for many years, and then finally sold out to a man by the name of Davis. George Isbell settled on the farm now owned by D. B. Smith, and a Mr. Ellis settled beyond Hadensville, on the place now owned by Mr. Hooser.

In about 1814 or 1815 there were several other families who settled in this district. Spottswood Smith settled near Graysville on Spring Creek; his son—D. B. Smith—was born here, and subsequently settled on the site of old Hadensville; he is to-day one of the leading farmers of the district, and in 1876–77 he represented this county in the Legislature.

Capt. Salmon came here from Virginia and settled on the place now owned by H. B. Salmon. Henry Jetter came probably from the same State, and settled on land now owned by Samuel Taliaferro. Squire William W. Terry settled on an adjoining farm on land now also owned by

Mr. Taliaferro. In an early day this worthy pioneer settler was magistrate, and finally succeeded by right of seniority to the office of sheriff. William Willis settled on land now owned by Mr. Lester. In an early day there were many other settlers here, but exactly when they came cannot be ascertained, as no clue can be given. Their coming however probably dated from about 1815 to 1820. The first one of these was Samuel Taliaferro, who settled on land now owned by Mrs. Taliaferro, and coming with him was Leroy Taliaferro, who settled on land now owned by his daughter. A Mr. Cooksy settled on land now owned by P. O. Duffy; Nicholas and William King settled on the farm now owned by D. B. Smith; John Roach, a son of Gabriel Roach mentioned above, grew up to manhood here, and became one of the magistrates of the district. Another early settler was Daniel Hooser, who settled on the farm now owned by his son, John Hooser, who is still living at the age of about eighty. Frank Eddington settled on land now owned by T. S. Mimms, and there a son of his, also named Frank, lived and died. Henry Meriwether made a settlement on land now owned by Mack Taliaferro, and John P. Bolon on the farm now owned by R. B. Kendal. One of the very earliest settlers here was Dr. Charles Meriwether, who made a settlement near the old town of Hadensville. Henry Barker, who came here from Virginia with Meriwether, built a house on the farm now in the possession of John Meriwether. Cotemporaneous with them was "Hock" Madison, as he was called, who settled on land now owned by Henry P. Williams.

About 1820 William Taylor settled on land now owned by his son— William F. Taylor, and William Kay settled on land now owned by Eli Webb. A year or two after Reuben Grady settled on land now owned by R. E. Adams. On the farm on which T. S. Mimms now resides, William Randol made a settlement in about 1822, and in the same year Andrew Coulter settled on the farm on which William Mackey now resides. Probably a little prior to this James Allan settled on the farm now owned by Richard Anderson. In about 1815 Elijah Haden came here from Virginia and settled on land now in the possession of D. B. Smith. In about 1823 John C. Harlan came here from upper Kentucky, and also made a settlement on Smith's land; this gentleman was a cousin of Judge Harlan, and came from one of the oldest families of Virginia, but that afterward became noted in upper Kentucky. He was a great trader, and probably the greatest hog-buyer in this part of Kentucky; he would buy a large drove of hogs in this section of the State, and then drive them on foot through to Alabama and Georgia; his homeward trips would be performed in the same manner, and he was entirely fearless. It is said of him that he was six feet high, straight as an arrow, and was one of the finest looking men in this portion of Kentucky.

Nathan Martin was another settler who arrived here about 1823; he settled on land now owned by Miss Taliaferro. In the same year Pouncy Anderson came here and settled on land now owned by Samuel Lawson.

Thus briefly have we gone over the early settlements of this district. Many more names probably deserve mention, but they and their ancestors have both passed away. Of those we have given our information is meager indeed, as the people now living here are all of them of a younger generation. It is our wish to give a full history of all the early pioneers, but in some cases as here we sometimes fail. For the facts regarding those given above we are very much indebted to Mr. Kendal, who is still living in the district at a hale old age. In speaking of the early settlements of this district we have but little of interest to record regarding the pioneer incidents of the settlers here. But few wild animals of any kind lurked among the few stunted trees of the barrens in early times. No stories of hunts of wild men and wild beasts greet our ears in talking over with the people of to-day. The pioneers here were purely an agricultural people, and turned their attention at once to the cultivation of the soil. The result of their early labors and perseverance we see in the waving grain and green pastures of to-day.

The Mills of the District.—The first mill ever put up in the district was built in about 1815 by Col. Smith on Elk Fork, in the southwest portion of the district. He ran it for many years and then sold out to Mr. Donnelly. The latter in turn disposed of it to a man by the name of Kimbrough, and from the last-named gentleman Robert Graham purchased it some years ago, and is still running it. It is now the only mill in the district, and is doing an excellent business. In about 1870 Powell & Phillips put up a steam mill in Guthrie. It continued in operation about two years, and then was destroyed by fire.

One of the early schools in the district was at Old Graysville. It was commenced in about 1850, and did not last long. Among the teachers were Dr. Richardson, Dewitt Farmer, who afterward became a Colonel in a Texas regiment during the war, and Smith Dulin.

Churches.—Drake's Pond Baptist Church, organized about 1807, is the oldest church in the county. Among the early members were Gabriel Roach, Richard McGowan, Elizabeth Wilcox, Mrs. Kendal and Mrs. Gray. The first meetings were held in a log-house that stood near a pond which bore the euphonious name of Drake, situated about half a mile from Guthrie, hence the name of the church. The log-house was used until 1825, when a frame was built at a cost of about $500. This was burned down in about 1835, and another log-house built within the next two years which was used by this congregation as a place of worship until

1866. In that year the present frame church was erected at a cost of about $700. The present membership is about twenty. The officers now in charge of the church are as follows: Deacons, L. B. Bryant and J. C. Parham. Among the ministers who have preached at this church might be mentioned Revs. Philip Boel, Dr. Watson, John Coonells, Archie Bristow, Rev. Munday, Thomas White and Needham Jones.

Hadensville Methodist Episcopal Church South was organized in about 1828, and was first called Ellis' Chapel. The meetings were first held in a log-house that stood near old Hadensville. Among the first members might be mentioned John Garrett, J. N. Barker, Jenkins Murphy, David Hooser and Robert Ellis. The latter was instrumental in having the church built, and hence it was called after him. The society continued to meet in the log-house until 1867, and then the present church was erected about a mile west of there on the Russellville road. It cost about $3,500, and is still being used. The membership at present is about fifty. Among the ministers who have acted as pastors over this charge have been Eli B. Crane, Thomas Bottlemy, L. P. Crenshaw, James Lewis, Ed Bottlemy, James Petrie and Dennis Spurrier. The present officers of the church are: Stewards, John Snadon, S. W. Taliaferro, J. H. Hooser and R. L. Smith. For some years a Sunday-school has been held in connection with the church. The average attendance has been about forty, and it is now held all the year round. The present Superintendent is John H. Hooser. Among the teachers are S. W. Taliaferro, Mack O'Brien, Mrs. John M. Roach, Dr. McClellan and Robert Kimbrough. The present Secretary is Robert Kimbrough.

Graysville.—In about 1833 Maj. Gray began running stage lines through the county. At the crossing of Elkton and Clarksville road with the Gallatin road, he put up a large hotel, and stables for the accommodation of guests, as some six lines all centered there. To this point he gave the name of Graysville. Besides the inn there were two or three stores there. John Brown and Thomas Allison both kept stores there, as well as James Brown, Ross Perkins and James Brenan. The stage lines only kept up a few years and then ceased running, and from that time the hamlet ran down. At present the hotel is occupied by several families of negroes, the rest of the buildings have gone to rack and ruin, and one blacksmith shop is all that reminds one of the old town.

Hadensville.—What is known as Old Hadensville originally stood about one mile from the present village of that name on land now owned by Mr. Smith, and here some of the ruins of the buildings can yet be seen. As early, probably, as 1815, Elijah Haden settled on this farm, and it being a crossing of two public roads, he commenced to merchandise there, and for many years he did an extensive business. He was succeeded by Dr. Burton, who had a store there in about 1821. Alexander Chesnut merchandized there in about 1830. John C. Harlan, whom we have mentioned above, also did business there for many years. About the last man to engage in merchandising there was Holland Uppenheimer, who continued in business until 1860. In that year the Memphis Branch of Louisville & Nashville road was run through this district, passing about a mile to the south of the old place. It ran through the land of Richard Hollins, who proceeded to donate land for depot and railroad purposes, and also proceeded to lay out a town. This gentleman had come to this district from Louisa County, Va., in 1837, and settled on that farm. After the town had been laid out he merchandized there until his death. His son, R. T. Hollins, succeeded him, and is still doing an excellent business there. Some years ago Dr. H. F. Randol started up a drug store there. In 1882 he sold out to R. Graham, Jr., who is still doing business. In 1866 W. L. Kimbrough opened a store there and continued in business for twelve years. This gentleman's father came to this district in 1819, and was for many years one of the leading farmers of the district, owning at one time about 1,000 acres. The village now contains about a dozen houses, and is at present one of the voting places of the district. Ed O'Brien is at present the Station and Express Agent.

Guthrie.—In about 1867 the Louisville & Nashville road, which had been building, drew near completion, and in the early days of 1868 the cars commenced running on it. The road passed through the land owned by Mr. J. C. Kendal, and he conceived the plan of having a town here, and also to have the shops of the road located here. He accordingly laid out a town to which he gave the name of Guthrie, in honor of James Guthrie, of Louisville, who was then President of the road and Member of Congress from that district. Mr. Kendal was born in Trimble County, Ky., and came with his parents in 1812 to this county, and settled in the Elkton District. In 1819 he began clerking in his father's hotel. He afterward carried the mail for some time between Russellville and Hopkinsville, and from 1832 to 1837 he merchandized in Elkton. He then went to Mississippi where he remained ten years; returning to this county he settled in this district, on land which he had inherited through his wife, who was a daughter of Maj. John Gray. On this farm he has continued to reside. A day of sale for the town lots was appointed, and it was advertised far and wide. On that day a large crowd gathered, and under brisk bidding it is said that over $10,000 worth of lots were sold. However, as time passed, the excitement died out, and from a half to two-thirds of the bidders never made their purchases good. The shops too, instead of being located here, went some place else, and the boom so fairly started very nearly died out. But in 1869 the track of the Memphis Branch of the

Louisville & Nashville, which had previously run through Tennessee below Guthrie, was taken up, and the village made the crossing of the two roads, and since then it has become a thriving little place.

About the first man to open a store in the new town was Thomas A. Carnell, who had been selling goods on his farm for some time before. He opened a store within the present limits of the town in 1866, but remained only a short time. William T. Spaulding came here in 1866, and until 1883 he was one of the leading merchants of the place. John Laninhan came in about 1868, but remained only about two years, and then moved to Irvington. Branch & White opened a store here the same year, and did business three years. Hughes & Bibb commenced merchandising at this point in 1870, but after one year's experience they retired.

In 1869 the Misses Grant opened a hotel and railroad eating-house at this point and are still engaged here. The hotel is at present the finest in the county and is having an excellent patronage. In 1872 White & Parker began to operate a hotel here, but continued in business only a short time. As early as 1868 Mr. Jeffcott opened a hotel here and continued in business here until 1874.

In 1873 T. P. Norris opened a store here, first with Mr. Bibb, then with Morgan C. Cunningham. This firm did business for about four years, when the store closed. In 1880, however, Mr. Norris commenced merchandising again with W. T. Tate. They are still doing business here under the firm name of Norris & Tate. In 1868 P. O. Duffy commenced selling goods here, and continued in business until the beginning of this year. In 1871 S. Platowsky opened a general store and is still here. From 1870 to 1872 W. W. Coleman merchandized here. In 1878 John Choat opened a hardware, furniture and implement store, and is still doing business. Mr. J. O. Linebaugh came from Logan to this point in 1877, opened a drug store, and is still here.

At present the town contains about 300 inhabitants, and is constantly improving. When the road from Guthrie to Elkton is completed it will become the leading point in the county, and bids fair to become a place of some prominence.

Town Organization.—We suppose that the town was first incorporated soon after it was laid out, but from the records we see that the charter was granted in June, 1879, and the trustees elected under it were W. T. Tate, W. T. Spaulding, S. E. Burbe, T. Covington, W. T. Kincaid. Since then the trustees have been as follows:

1880—Wesley Flood, C. W. Greenfield, S. E. Burbe, T. P. Norris, W. Lewis.

1881—N. Johnson, M. W. Worley, R. Waggener, J. I. Arrington and J. L. Phelps.

1882—A. F. Rogers, Robert Bigbee, Joseph Linebaugh, W. F. Tate and R. V. Williams.

1883—R. V. Williams, Robert Bigbee, A. F. Rogers, M. Hall and Thomas M. White.

1884—Thomas White, R. V. Williams, R. T. Barry, Joseph Linebaugh and A. F. Rogers.

Guthrie Baptist Church was organized in 1850 by Dr. Robert Williams. The first sessions were held at Old Graysville. Among the early members were Mrs. Kendal, Marion Carney, Reuben Manion, the Misses Grant, Mrs. Salmon, T. Covington, Frank Tate and several others. The church continued to meet at Graysville until 1873, when the present house was built at Guthrie at a cost of about $2,000. The membership is now about forty-five. The present officers are: R. O. Manion and Allan Bryant, Deacons; T. P. Norris, Clerk; and W. H. Salmon, Treasurer. Among the pastors of the church the following might be mentioned: Dr. Robert Williams, Sandy Holland (who was pastor at Graysville ten years), L. J. Crutcher (pastor when the church was moved to Guthrie), W. W. Gardner, Shannon, Marion Carney, John Kendal and Rev. W. H. Rials.—*F. S. Tyler.*

CHAPTER XI.

MAGISTERIAL DISTRICT NO. 3—FAIRVIEW—DISTRICT OUTLINES AND TOPOG-
RAPHY—PIONEERS OF THE EARLY SETTLEMENT—LATER DEVELOPMENT
—PROGRESS OF CHURCH AND SCHOOL—THE VILLAGE—BUSINESS DEVEL-
OPMENT.

THE early settlement of Todd County knew no method and observed no lines in fixing upon the site for a new home. The prejudice against the open country led the pioneers to seek the vicinity of
streams, and here they hewed out a farm from the stubborn forest, and
with laborious toil turned the wilderness into fruitful farms. Up to the
adoption of the present Constitution, the voting precinct was at the county
seat, but the inconvenience of this mode led to the organization of districts with some marks of individuality. As then formed district lines
served to mark the constituency of Justices of the Peace, which voted in
one or two places in the district. Fairview, or more strictly, Magisterial
District No. 3, is that portion of Todd County lying between the Davis
Mill road on the south, the Highland Lick road on the north, Elkton, or
District No. 4 on the east, and Christian County on the west, with voting
places at Tabernacle Precinct on the east and at Fairview on the west.
The Russellville and Hopkinsville road passes centrally through the district from east to west, and serves to divide, as elsewhere in the county,
the broken and less fertile soil of the north from the red clay subsoil of
the south. The principal stream of this district is the West Fork of Red
River, which takes its rise near the northern boundary and flows south-
wardly, forming a part of the boundary between the counties and passing
near Trenton. It receives several affluents from this district which have
received the general designation of "prongs," with the local designation
of east or west, one of which is of considerable size. There are no swamp
lands here, the streams affording good surface drainage. Along these
streams there is an abundance of good timber, among which is found the
various kinds of oak, a few walnuts, sugar maples and poplar. This attracted an early settlement, and subsequent tillage proving the value of
the land, the settlement has grown quite dense, the farms generally being
small, well improved and generously productive. The occupation of the
residents of this part of the county is exclusively agricultural, some of the
best wheat and tobacco lands in the region being found here. The

broken country is under good state of cultivation, the river valleys affording an important and valuable exception to the general character of this
region. "Forest Nursery," belonging to Downer & Brother, about
three miles southeast of Fairview village, is an important enterprise in this
district. The business was established in 1834 by John S. Downer and
consists of about eighty acres of nursery stock. Their agents are found
in all parts of the South and the firm ship annually over 250,000 apple
trees, 220,000 budded peaches, 20,000 pear, 15,000 plum and some
10,000 cherry trees, besides an endless quantity of small fruit, which is
their specialty.

Early Settlement.—The natural attractions of this locality were such
as to draw hither some of the earliest settlers of this part of the State.
As early as May 20, 1791, a tract of ten acres in the immediate neighborhood of Fairview was entered, the official document of which, now in
the hands of Dr. E. S. Stuart, is as follows:

> Edward Shanklin, assignee of Jacob Baire, enters ten acres, part of said Baire's war-
> rant for 1,000 acres, No. 17531, dated June 27, 1783, and desires to locate said same join-
> ing and between said lands of Edward Shanklin, Sr., and Perter Bolus and Black's land,
> with me.
>
> A. HERRING, *Surveyor, Kentucky County.*

From other papers in the possession of Dr. Stuart, an entry of sixteen
acres, on part of which Goshen Church now stands, was made under a
patent granted by Gov. Scott of Kentucky, dated January 31, 1809.
" In consideration (of a part of a reward) of a certificate No. 87, granted
by commission, 1796, agreeably to act of Assembly for encouraging and
granting relief to settlers, there is granted by the said Commonwealth to
David Logan, assignee of Edward Richey, a certain tract or parcel of land,
containing sixteen acres, by survey bearing date October 13, 1797." Two
hundred acres were similarly granted by Christopher Greenup, Governor of
Kentucky, to John Wilson, under date of June 12, 1808. This land lies
about one-half mile north of the present residence of John G. Wilkins.
Under date of May 19, 1808, 400 acres were granted by Gov. Greenup
to Edward Shanklin, which land is situated just north of John W. Petree,
near the village. Under the same date, fifty acres lying north of the
Goshen Church was granted by the same Governor to Shanklin. Previous
to any of these the celebrated Croghan's Grove, noted in the chapter on
Trenton, was granted to William Croghan, an old Revolutionary officer,
but never a resident of Todd County. The grove is a fine body of timber
comprising some 2,600 acres, and is situated partly in each of the districts
of Trenton and Fairview. These entries, however, did not necessarily
involve settlement, and the first settler of this district and probably of
the county was Justinian Cartwright. He came from Maryland, was of

Scotch-Irish descent, and built his cabin across the trail which is now the Hopkinsville road in 1792. In 1801 he sold the cabin to Robert Adams, and in 1809 it passed into the hands of Michael Kennedy. David Logan probably came to this district about the time of the survey mentioned above, and John Wilson and Samuel Davis about the same time. At least these men were living here in 1800. Of these earliest settlers but little is known. Davis, the father of the Hon. Jefferson Davis, was an officer in the Georgia troops during the Revolutionary war, and at the close of that struggle came to southern Kentucky ; whether he came directly to Todd County is not known. He was here in 1800 and remained until 1810 or 1812, when he removed to Wilkinson County, Miss. The cabin in which he lived in the village of Fairview, and in which Jefferson Davis was born, is still standing, and prized as a historical landmark by the citizens of the county. A few years ago Mr. Davis made an address before the Agricultural Society of Christian County, and during his stay in the county took occasion to visit his early home. A large crowd of admirers and citizens of the two counties assembled to greet him, and were addressed by the great Southern statesman from the door of this cabin.

The first definite account of the immigration to this district, however, is that of Matthew and David Rolston, Edward Shanklin, John Huston, and his sons, James and Granville, in 1800. These persons came together from Virginia, and all settled in Todd County, save David Rolston, who located over the line in Christian County. Edward Shanklin was a native of Shenandoah County, Va., and brought a family of several children. He lived here until his death in 1826. He was a man of very quiet tastes, domestic in his habits, and soon after his arrival here was elected Justice of the Peace, an office he held until his death. About 1802 George and Gideon Tilman came to this section. George located near the village on the place now owned by J. T. Smith, and Gideon settled in Christian County. In 1805 or 1807, a man by the name of Davis settled here, but stayed only a few years. He is chiefly remembered for the provident care of his buckskin breeches. Stock of all kinds ran unrestrained upon the wide range of open country. The tall grass in the morning was wet with dew, and the early settler who ventured into it before it was dried by the sun was treated to a very pronounced shower bath. This was destruction to buckskin breeches and uncomfortable to the wearer, and Davis was wont to obviate both difficulties by going after his horses without them. His intention was to get his horses up at an hour when his *dishabille* would not shock the sensitive portion of the community ; but where all were early risers and the range a wide one, it often happened that his calculations failed, but the necessity was such that repeated failure in this respect did not prevent his repeating the experiment regularly. About 1805, James Wilkins came to the district from North Carolina, and located about a mile and a half north of Shanklin, where he remained until his death in 1836. Of his four sons and three daughters four are now living here—William G., Harriet Rolston, Lucinda J. Brown and Matilda Tilman. Soon after the Wilkins family, came Solomon Scates and a man by the name of Craig. The latter located about three-quarters of a mile east of Col. Jesup's place on the Russellville road. Scates was a very severe master to his slaves and one of them once attempted to destroy his life. Mrs. Scates was a kind mistress and loved by the slaves, and the would-be assassin in trying to shoot his master was obliged to aim so high to avoid endangering his mistress, who stood near, that the master escaped. In 1809 Michael Kennedy bought the old Cartwright place and moved to the district. He came from Greenbrier County, Va., in company with forty or fifty families from that State under the lead of Gen. William Logan. Their journey was full of incidents and made in constant fear of savages, who prowled about the country ready to attack any who should become separated from the party. The family settled in the vicinity of Logan's Fort, and subsequently moved to the Hanging Fork of Dick's River. Here Kennedy remained until his removal to Todd County. His house here was quite remarkable for its kind, and was intended to be the finest one in the county. It was built entirely with such material as the country afforded and there was not a nail nor a pane of glass in the whole structure. Charles Mills settled here about the same time as Kennedy. He was a native of Virginia and located three-quarters of a mile south of Craig. He was an earnest Baptist, and reared a fine family of children ; one of his sons is now a member of Congress from Texas. Soon after these came the Manns, John, Elisha, Stephen and Jacob, brothers. About the same time came the Cowdrys, only one of whom, however, settled in the district. After these families came Thomas Murphy and three sons from North Carolina, and located about two miles south of Fairview. Henry Baire came about 1825, and was killed subsequently at Elkton. This brief review of the first settlers does not exhaust the whole list of those entitled to be classed as old settlers, but Todd County is unfortunate in the loss of many whose knowledge would have been invaluable in supplying these missing links. The most of the early settlers were blessed with large families, and their descendants for the most part make up the population of the district.

Pioneer Days.—The community thus established here found itself dependent upon the natural resources of the country for their whole support. What are now looked upon as the necessities of life and so common and cheap as to be overlooked in the estimate of household expenses, were then only to be obtained at a large expense of time, effort and money. Salt was one of these articles, and was only to be obtained by a tedious journey to the Ohio River. There was no well-marked road to guide the pioneer until the Highland Lick road was laid out. Coffee and sugar were obtained at Clarksville, or on the Ohio River, and mail at Hopkinsville or Russellville. Under such circumstances the ingenuity of the pioneers was tasked to the utmost to make the resources of the country supply their wants. In several places of the district maple trees were found in sufficient abundance to supply the fortunate possessor with a good supply of sugar. Wild bees furnished an abundant supply of honey, which was searched for by experts with abundant success. To these add the luxuriant growth of wild strawberries, grapes, plums, and persimmons, with nuts of all kinds, and one inclines to the belief that civilization has curtailed the luxuries of the table. Game was abundant, and after the first year or two pork and mutton varied the more substantial fare. The great want early felt, however, was the lack of good meal or flour. Mills were early established on the eastern side of the county and at Hopkinsville, but these were crude affairs, and at best slowly ground out a coarse quality of meal and no flour. Subsequently, when buhrs adapted to the grinding of wheat were obtained, flour was bolted by hand, and then was of a dark, inferior quality. But streams were abundant in this district and the demand for mills obvious, a condition of things which soon brought about their construction here. The uncertain character of the streams rendered steam power essential to the best success, and in 1840 a combined steam saw and grist-mill was built by Grooms & Gowel on the east " prong " of the West Fork of Red River. This ran but a short time when it was torn down. A second mill was erected a few years later by Slaughter Long about half a mile south of " Forest Nursery." It was only a cheap structure, had little business and soon rotted down. About 1846 John Hanna put up a similar mill about half a mile north of John G. Wilkins'. It ran a few years, but at the death of its proprietor it was moved to Simpson's Spring, and there falling into disuse it rotted down. About 1856 D. O. Day erected a steam saw and grist-mill just north of Col. Jesup's old place. A year or two later, however, it was moved away. In 1857 Joel Wallace erected a combined mill a little southwest of J. D. Tandy's residence, but it proved unprofitable, and after several years was moved away. In 1865 Reeves & Harrison erected another of these structures a little below W. H. Jesup's place, but it continued only three years when it was moved. Shanklin & Griffin put up another of these mills at a point on the west " prong " of West Fork in 1882, which is the sole survivor in this district of these country mills.

Later Development.—There is little to mark the gradual change from the early days to the present. The patient discharge of each day's duties, with the development of the surrounding country, has wrought the great change to be found everywhere in the country, and yet this has been accomplished by such slow progress that the closest observer will find little to mark its successive stages. The old trail from Russellville to Hopkinsville has gradually become a clearly defined road. In 1840 the old trail was straightened and some attempt made to pike it at State expense, but the project failed. A State road from Hopkinsville to Butler County was laid out, running northeasterly across the upper part of the district, and is now known here as the Butler road. The old road from Coleman's Bridge to Russellville by the main road through the county, uniting with it about three miles from Elkton, completes the main thoroughfares which connect the district with the outside world. The effect of good highways through a district is second only to a railroad, and should not be lightly estimated. They are prominent factors in its development, and enhance the value of all property, and stimulate enterprise to a degree that is almost marvelous to the uninitiated. It is to this fact that the village of Fairview owes its origin, while the early market at Hopkinsville and the growing market at Elkton, both made accessible by direct route, have had their impress on the success of the community. The development of the district has been marked by several incidents that, while not strictly confined in character to this locality, are worthy of note. This district probably takes the lead in suicides. A considerable number have occurred, induced principally by financial embarrassment. Besides these there have been several distressing murders, growing out of intoxication or the agitated period during the war. This district was prominent also as the scene of the Kuklux outrages. A band organized in Christian County for a time made nightly raids into this region, while one organized in Todd County added its disturbing influence. It should not be understood that the character of the community was of a savage disposition, but that it was more sinned against than sinning. The brutal murder of Mrs. Salmons, and the brutal punishment inflicted upon the negro perpetrator of the crime, fully noted elsewhere, found its scene of action in this district.

Churches.—The conservative influences of society were early established in the district, and while many unfortunate homicides have occurred within the limits of the district, the general progress of the community has been in the direction of law, order, and good morals. The Methodist Episcopal Church was among the earliest religious organizations in Todd County, and embraced within its membership many of the leading families of the community, including those of Elder Thornhill, Garland Bal-

Caleb N. Bell

lard, Thomas Greenfield and Hazle Petrie. Meetings were held at the residence of the latter for some time, but the church was soon enabled to erect a little log building, which served as their place of worship for many years. It was located in this district, and was known as Petrie's Church. The Rev. Caleb N. Bell came into the district December 25, 1822. He was a North Carolinian by birth, and had served as an itinerant preacher in Virginia. Upon his arrival here he at once identified himself with the church, and up to the time of his death, in 1872, was a most prominent figure in its councils, and for many years its most beloved pastor. The little log building soon became of insufficient capacity to hold the constantly increasing membership, and about 1832, under the active supervision of Rev. Bell, the services of a neighboring saw-mill were invoked, and a sufficient amount of timber hauled to enable the church to erect a small but substantial frame structure, which stood until about 1853, at which date it was superseded by the present brick edifice, and the old building was for some time afterward used for school purposes, and then torn down. The present structure, known as Bell's Chapel, was put up near the site of the old one, at a cost of about $2,200. It is in the Elkton Circuit, and its monthly appointments have been filled by the various pastors. The church has constantly grown in numbers and prosperity, and is noted also for its enjoyable basket meetings, which are always attended by large numbers.

The Methodists have another church in the district, known as the Tabernacle Church, located on the Butler road near Wyatt's store. It was erected about 1878, and served to supplant an old log-house which was built under the labors of David Moore and his sons Jordan, T. C. and Riley, exhorters in the early church. William Alexander, under whose pastoral care the present building was built, and Rev. Hobbs Morrison, have been the principal preachers at this point. The membership is small.

The history of the Cumberland Presbyterian Church in Todd County is noted at length in other chapters of the present work. The labors of Finis Ewing and others gave vigorous impulse to the new organization after its separation from the parent church, and it soon became a potent factor in the religious development of the county. Goshen Church in this district points its origin to a protracted meeting, which was characterized by a large number of conversions, which gave stimulus to the movement having in view the erection of a place of worship in this vicinity. A site was secured near Croghan's Grove, but for some reason work was suspended upon the erection of a single wall. Soon afterward, however, a log building was put up, which served the church purposes for some five or six years, when it was torn down, and the present frame structure erected at a cost of about $1,500. With some fifty or sixty members, the early meetings were held under the pastoral charge of Revs. McDaniel and Provine. Since the pulpit has been supplied by Revs. William Casky, Joel Penick, J. M. Gill and Frank Perry, and its present membership consists of about 100 souls, and is in a prosperous condition.

The Baptists have at the present time no representative church in this district. At a very early day the Close Communion branch of that denomination held comparatively largely attended meetings in a little log building which was called the West Fork Church. Archibald Bristow and the Rev. Plasters were among the early pastors. The organization ceased to exist about 1822, and became the parent to scattered congregations throughout the surrounding country.

The Christian Church has likewise no organization in this district at the present time. Philippi Church, founded by Nathaniel Burrus, was the result of its only endeavors to secure representation here. The little frame building was erected about 1847, but the organization was unsuccessful in its efforts to secure any considerable acquisitions to the membership lists, and the church building, falling into disuse, was torn down about 1871. Rev. C. M. Day preached occasionally at this place, but the church was most of the time under the pastoral care of Rev. W. E. Murphy.

Schools.—The natural opposition to the public schools was very pronounced in the district. Private schools flourished to some extent, and are still maintained supplementary to the public system. The first school of which there is any knowledge was taught by William Huston in a log-cabin near the residence of J. W. Petree. This was only for a single term. J. H. Shanklin taught a school for twelve months in the same cabin, and in the following year taught for a year in a log-cabin a half mile north of Fairview. Newton Payne, another of the early teachers, taught on the premises now owned by Benjamin Downer, for several years. In 1854 a school building was erected by J. E. Jesup, which was known by the high-sounding name of "Jesup's Academy." A teacher by the name of Shurtleff presided over the destinies of a school here for several years. Goshen school, held near the church of that name, was taught by a number of teachers. A part of the year the school was conducted as part of the common school system, and the rest of the time as a subscription school. In 1873 a frame schoolhouse was erected under the provisions of the school law at a cost of $500, in Fairview. Among the teachers at this point were D. C. Morehead, Baker, James Vick, Miss Brown and Mr. Robinson. A public schoolhouse was erected near the residence of J. G. Wilkins, and schools have been conducted here by Miss Mamie Jesup and E. B. Wood.

Fairview.—This little village, over which Todd and Christian Counties have for years striven to obtain the mastery, still lies where it always has, on the dividing line between the two belligerent counties, and situated on the main road from Russellville to Hopkinsville, about twelve miles east of the latter town. It was laid off on land belonging to Col. William Morrow in 1847, by act of the Legislature, approved February 7 of the previous year, Col. Nathaniel Burrus being the surveyor. The original plat, to which there have been no subsequent additions, consisted of twenty acres of land, lined off into forty lots of equal size, with twenty lots lying upon either side of the main road. The village was first named Davisburg, in honor of Samuel Davis, father of Hon. Jefferson Davis. It was for some time afterward called Georgetown, after, it is said, George Nichols, who was her first merchant. Nichols' principal business, however, was that of tavern-keeper, though he kept a small stock of groceries and general goods, generally on hand. Whisky, however, was the main article for sale, and this was dealt out in amazing quantities, and the place was always the appointed rendezvous of the fighting and riff-raff element of the early society. In such regularity was the occurrence of wholesale sprees and pugilistic encounters, that the daily programme was by common consent made to contain an act or two of this sort, and drunken hilarity and general villainy ran riot for a number of years. But this state of things finally gave way under the influence exerted by the steady improvement in the general morals of the community, and an improved condition of affairs inaugurated, which has ever since controlled the movements of the immediate society.

Fairview being incorporated and organized under what is known as the " Old Law; " the " city fathers " consisted of a body composed of five trustees, whose residence did not necessarily have to be within the corporate limits. The first board of such officers who presided over the destinies of the little village was composed of the following names: John W. Lackey. H. B. Wilkins, Wilson Shreeve, W. W. Darnall, J. S. Lindsay, L. T. Templeton and William Morrow. The village has from time to time been required to conform its municipal government to the various legislative enactments, but the principal change occurred in 1868, in which year it was reorganized under the new law. The present Board of Trustees is made up of Nelson Wade, Richard Vaughan, T. H. Shaw, John W. Yancey and A. C. Sayne; the two Magistrates of the district being W. B. Brewer and W. S. Wyatt.

A postoffice was established at this point soon after the town's incorporation, and it was named Fairview, and the same appellation was given the village, and still later the district. Col. William Morrow served as the first Postmaster, and he was followed successively by J. S. Lindsay,

Fayette Smith, J. C. Sims, F. H. Shaw, J. T. Smith, F. H. Shaw and W. B. Brewer, the present incumbent.

Fairview has always shown considerable activity in the mercantile trade, notwithstanding the fact that she has never enjoyed any railroad facilities. Her location commands the patronage of a considerable scope of good country, and her business career has been a comparatively bright and prosperous one. Among her first merchants were Morrow & Lindsay, who opened up at this point about 1847, and continued about six years. Shaw & Vaughan commenced business here soon afterward, and Mr. Vaughan is still "behind the counter," being now in partnership with a brother of his first partner. Sayne & Meacham and Tandy Bros. were early merchants in the grocery line, and following them were Jack Hightower and Smith & Stahl, the latter firm opening a dry goods store about 1850. Then came M. C. Kennedy & Co., and Brown & Meacham. The latter firm sold its stock of goods to M. H. Wood, who continued in business up to the time of his death from cholera, in 1867 ; Cason and Yates did business for some time at this point, afterward becoming partners, and upon the death of Cason the business was continued by Yates, and afterward by E. B. Walker, in the interest of Mr. Cason's widow. This is only a partial list of the early merchants of Fairview, but it contains the names of the principal ones, or those who remained here in business any considerable length of time. The business representatives at the present time are:

General Store—Shaw & Vaughan.

Grocery and Saloon—J. W. Yancy and John Everett.

Groceries—W. W. Ballard and W. B. Brewer.

Drugs—C. E. Tandy.

Furniture—Nelson Wade.

Blacksmiths—McGehee & Hawkins, and McGehee & Elkins, and one shop by J. Minns, situated outside the corporate limits. The resident physicians are Drs. Stuart, Armstrong and Browder.

If there was ever any brilliancy in the future for the general prosperity of Fairview, it was materially dimmed by the ruthless destruction, by the fire fiend, of Shaw, Vaughan & Hoy's fine brick custom mill, a monument to the energy and spirited enterprise of those connected with its erection. It was located near the east limits of the town, and was constructed at a cost of $18,000 about 1866. Its lease of active operation was short, its total destruction occurring but a couple of years afterward, with no insurance to reimburse its impoverished owners. It would have been of infinite benefit to the whole country and to the village, and, but for its untimely destruction, would have become a most potent factor in the town's commercial development and business prosperity. Several years previous to the destruction of the mill, Shaw & Vaughan sustained the loss by fire of their large frame store, with its entire contents. The loss was a total one in $30,000. The energetic proprietors rebuilt, however, the following year, a substantial brick building taking the place of the old one.

The Masonic fraternity is represented in Fairview by Lodge No. 214, whose place of meeting is situated in Christian County, and by Moore Lodge, No. 75, Royal Arch Chapter. This lodge received its charter October 16, 1860, with Absalom Brown, H. P.; T. H. Shaw, K.; and M. A. Fritz, Scribe, who with the following names made up the charter members: M. E. Kennedy, J. C. Lesher, E. S. Stuart, Rice Dulin, B. F. Rollins, R. Y. Pendleton and A. M. Dulin. The present officers are: E. S. Stuart, H. P.; M. D. Brown, K.; and H. E. Morton, Scribe. The lodge is not in a very prosperous condition. The I. O. O. F. was represented by a lodge organized here about 1855, but which did not survive the war.

About the earliest physician to locate near Fairview, of which there is any record, was Dr. Harrison, a botanical practitioner. He came about 1807, and locating in the north part of the county, practiced throughout the adjacent country. Following him many years later, was Dr. Fulcher, of the allopathic school. He located south of Fairview, about 1833, and practiced until his death in 1845. Since then the following physicians have either located here or practiced in this immediate vicinity: Drs. H. W. Darnall, Armstrong Stuart, Lesher, Ray, Richardson, Wilson, Dudley and Browder.

CHAPTER XII.

MAGISTERIAL DISTRICT NO. 1, KIRKMANSVILLE—INTRODUCTION—BOUND-
ARIES—TOPOGRAPHY—SOIL AND PRODUCTS—WATER-COURSES—EARLY
PIONEERS—WILLIAM REDDEN—PETER KIRKMAN—JOSEPH ALLISON—
THE POWELLS—MAJOR DODD—PIONEER INCIDENTS—THE HARPE FAM-
ILY—ALONZO PENNINGTON—FIRST MILLS—SCHOOLS AND CHURCHES—
KIRKMANSVILLE—ITS BUSINESS HOUSES—KIRKMANSVILLE LODGE.

IN gathering the histories of the different districts, we find that the
boundaries between them are indefinite and indeterminate, and often-
times in our mention of early settlers they have been credited to one,
when they should have been given to another. Especially in writing the
history of the northern portion of the county we are ofttimes at a loss
where to exactly locate an early pioneer. Consequently if in some of
the chapters names of settlers are found when they should have been
given elsewhere, the errors thus made may be assigned for the reason given above. Geographically, Kirkmansville District occupies the
northwestern portion of the county. It is bounded on the north by
Muhlenburg County, on the east by District No. 7, Bivinsville; on the
south by District No. 3, Fairview; and on the west by Christian County.
The name of the district—Kirkmansville—was derived from a little hamlet of the same name, and that in turn took its name from and in honor
of old Peter Kirkman, who in an early day made a settlement in this
district, near where the present town is located.

Topography.—The major part of the district is quite hilly, but along
the banks of the East Fork of Pond River there is considerable flat bottom land, and in this portion of the district the best farming land is
located. At present it is estimated that there is about one-fourth of the
surface of the district comprised in this bottom land. From a geological
point of view the soil of the district is made up of two formations, namely, the blue and gray limestone, and the free or sandstone. These are
very equally distributed over the district, both ofttimes being noticeable
in the same field. The gray limestone appears in several portions of the
district, and in an early day it was used to a considerable extent by the
pioneers for fire-places and fire-rocks, as it successfully withstands the
action of the heat. The soil of both limestone formations is the red clay,
and although it is not as dark or as rich as that found in the southern

districts, it forms the basis of the best farming land in the district. The sandstone is of three varieties, viz., the red, yellow and white. In the red sandstone quite a deposit of iron is ofttimes noticed. The soil of this formation is mostly of yellow clay, and it is considered very poor farming land. The soil, too, is not adapted to retaining fertilizers when placed upon it, and the whole is very soon washed away. Along the eastern edge of the district the sandstone formation appears in some very large rocks, bowlders, and a few very high, perpendicular cliffs, which afford some truly picturesque views to the admirer of the beautiful. Scattered through the district there are several caves in the limestone formations. On the farm of F. M. Pepper a cave was discovered some fifteen years ago, to which an entrance is obtained through a small hole in the surface, from which a person must drop some twenty feet before the bottom of the cave is reached. The height of the cave varies from fifteen to twenty feet, and it has been explored to the distance of half a mile. There are some very beautiful stalactites to be found, but aside from this nothing of interest is to be seen. On the farm of Mr. Keelin there is another cave, and there is also one on the Joe Martin farm. Both have been explored some considerable distance. The latter cave is at present serving the purpose of a cellar to the people of the surrounding neighborhood.

At present about one-sixth of the district is in cultivation. The rest of the area is very heavily timbered. But while the timber of the southern portion of the county has been on the increase, that of the north remains about the same. The most common varieties of timber to be found are white, black and swamp oak, beech and sugar tree. In an early day there were also considerable quantities of poplar and black walnut, but at present both have been nearly all cut off. In the bottom lands there is also a considerable growth of hazel brush springing into existence, and in the eastern portion of the district a growth of cedar has come up in the last few years.

Creeks.—The leading stream of the district is the Blue Lick Fork of Pond River, which rises in the Fairview District, flows into the district from the south, and then passes into Christian County. It enters the district from the west again, and flows north to the Muhlenburg County line. The East Fork of Pond River also heads in the Fairview District, flows generally in a northerly direction through the district, until it reaches the county line, where it unites with the Blue Lick Fork and forms Pond River. Cow Creek heads in the eastern portion of the district, flows generally in a westerly direction, and empties into East Fork on the farm of B. H. Johnson. Horse Creek rises in the district near the Mt. Tabor Church, and empties into East Fork near Kirkmansville.

Pioneer Settlements.—In an early day game of all kinds was to be found here in great abundance, and probably the first men to enter the confines of the district were the hunters and trappers. These men made no permanent settlement. Some of them perchance built a cabin of poles, which sheltered them from the heavy dews by night. But they were nature's true noblemen, and their time was spent in the pursuit of game. But this in time became somewhat scarce, and then gathering up their traps they moved onward toward the setting sun, leaving no trace behind. Hence, of their deeds we cannot speak with accuracy. We can only say that as a class they were brave, strong men, willing to bear the many privations and hardships of their class, and were worthy successors of Daniel Boone and Simon Kenton to mark out a way through the wilderness of Kentucky for the coming of the actual settler. The hunters found the timber to be plenty in the northern portion of the county, and water in abundance, and these two necessities of the early pioneer being found wanting in most places in the southern portion of the county, it follows perforce that here the first settlements were made.

The first one of the sturdy yeomen of whom any record has been kept is William Redden, who in 1794 secured a patent for part of the farm now occupied by F. M. Pepper. Here he made a settlement, and first entered 160 acres. He was originally from North Carolina, and was a man of very peaceable, quiet disposition. After his arrival here he sought no political distinction of any kind, but gave his whole attention to the cultivation of his farm. He died about 1825, leaving no children. His widow survived him about ten years, and then she, too, passed away. Willis Murdock, a cousin of Redden, accompained the latter to this county. He settled on an adjoining farm, and resided here until about 1825. He then emigrated to Missouri, where he subsequently died. A grandson of his is still living in Muhlenburg County. About the same time a Mr. Moore settled on the farm now occupied by M. L. Shelton, on the road from Elkton to Kirkmansville. He died there in a very early day, and left no record behind him. As early as 1800 William Kirkman came to this district from Virginia, and made a settlement on a farm now in the possession of Mrs. Peter Kirkman. In an early day he had a post-office established on his farm, to which he gave the name of Kirkman's, and served as Postmaster there for many years. During his life-time he was considered by his friends and neighbors to be one of the best men in the district. He died here in about 1850, leaving a large family of children. His son, Peter, was a magistrate in the district for many years, and died here in 1883. Another son, John, emigrated to Texas, where he subsequently died. A daughter of this gentleman returned to the district and afterward married Mr. Frank Bass. About 1805 Joseph Allison came to this district from Virginia, and made a settlement on the farm now owned by Mr. Grace. In an early day he was appointed a captain of the militia, and on muster days he was one of the drill-masters. About 1810 Collier Butler came here and made a settlement on the farm now owned by his son-in-law, John Johnson. He died here in 1859. A grandson of his, B. B. Butler, is at present acting as Sheriff of the county. In 1805 Daniel Morgan came to this district from Chatham Co., N. C., with his grandfather and uncle, Nathaniel and George Brewer, who settled in the timber in the northwestern portion of the district. Mr. Morgan was born in 1796, and is still living. His father and mother intended coming to this county too, but were taken sick and died a short time before the time for starting. After his arrival here he first made his home with his uncle, but over sixty-eight years ago he settled on the farm on which he has since resided. As early as 1805, and probably some years prior to this, Thomas Edwards came to this district from North Carolina, and made a settlement on Cow Creek. In an early day he manufactured considerable tar from the pine, which he brought from the clifts and subsequently burned. He died in about 1855. His son, H. B. Edwards, lived for many years on the farm now occupied by T. P. Sullivan. Accompanying Edwards to this unexplored country was Reuben Stark, who made a settlement on the premises now occupied by William Willis. Here he put up a horse-mill, which was probably the first one in the district. It continued in operation until about 1820, when it finally fell into disuse. Probably about the same time George, James and Levi Powell came here from North Carolina, and made settlements in the western portion of the district. The farms on which they lived and died are still in possession of their heirs. Joseph Long made a settlement cotemporaneous with those mentioned above, on the farm where Lee Cherry now resides. Here he died as early as 1825. In an early day, but exactly when we cannot state, John Roger made a settlement where his son, Burkett Roger, is still living. A family of Attaways came here also in an early day. They were hunters and moved elsewhere as soon as game had begun to be at all scarce, and their acts are now beyond recall by the people now living here. As early as 1815 Jacob Davis made a settlement on the farm now occupied by J. M. Graham. He was probably a native of Illinois, and was a soldier in the war of 1812. He died here in 1865, but his widow still survives him. About the same time Jacob Johnson came from North Carolina, and settled on the farm now occupied by his son, B. H. Johnson. It is said that subsequent to his arrival here he made sixteen trips to his native State on horseback. He died here in about 1840. Coleman Griffin also came here as early as 1815. He made a settlement on land now owned by Mrs. Sylva Powell.

He was a North Carolinian by birth, and died here in 1825. His son, J. J. Griffin, was a merchant at Kirksmanville for some years, and also magistrate. He died here in about 1880. In the same year Major Dodd came here from North Carolina, and settled on the farm on which he now resides at the advanced age of eighty-five. In the early days of State militia he was a Major, and commanded a battalion. Asier Shelton came here about the same time, and settled down on a farm adjoining Dodd's. During most of his life he was a school-teacher, and taught for many years. He was also a preacher of some note in the neighborhood. He was first a Methodist, then joined the Baptists, and finally espoused the Christian doctrine. He died here in about 1850. His daughter, Mrs. Nancy Murphy, is still living in the district, and a son, Christian Shelton, is still living near Sharon Grove. J. C. Bass arrived here in this county in 1820, and settled near Kirkmansville. He was born in North Carolina, and came to Christian County in about 1805 with his parents. He died in the county in 1880. His son, R. F., is still living on the farm on which his father had originally settled. Thomas Pepper was born in Virginia in 1794 ; came to Springfield, Tenn., in 1805 with his parents, and in 1815 he came to Christian County. He made a settlement near what is known as the " Old Lick." He came to this district in about 1825, and settled on the farm now occupied by his son, F. M. Pepper. He was elected magistrate under the old Constitution, but only served for a short time. He died in 1858. F. M. Pepper has served as Magistrate some eight years, and is one of the largest land-owners in the district. Another son, Noah Pepper, is also living in the district, and a third son is in Christian County. In about 1830 William Hammond made a settlement in the district, but subsequently moved to Christian County. In an early day, but exactly at what time we are not able to state with preciseness, Ben Panwell made a settlement near Maj. Dodd's, where he lived and died.

The settlements of this district may be classed among the early settlements of the county. Nearly ninety years ago homes were selected in this district by white people. This is a short period when considered in the world's chronology, but in the history of this part of the country it seems a long, long time. Many and startling events have transpired since then. Thrones and kingdoms have passed away, empires have risen, and flourished, and fallen, and the remembrance of their glory has almost faded from the minds of men as the waves of dark oblivion sweep o'er them and scarcely leave a track to tell us how or where or when they sank. Ancient palaces in whose spacious halls the mightiest ruler proudly trod show the ivy clinging to the moldering towers, and

" Victor's wreaths and monarch's gems
Have blended with the common dust."

In our county mighty changes have been wrought.   Human progress and human inventions have done more in these years than in ten centuries before.   The railroad, the telegraph and improved machinery of every kind and description attest the rapid progress of the age.   The early, simple settler little dreamed of what his short, simple span of life would witness.   As we have mentioned elsewhere, many of the early settlers here were hunters, and in an early day many stories are told of the wild beasts and wilder men that traversed these unbroken wilds.   But as one by one the pioneers and their families passed away these tales and stories have become almost extinct.   It is claimed by people who are still living in the district that in an early day the Harpes passed through the county from Logan County on their way West while they were trying to escape from the punishment of one of their crimes, and that one of them was shot in the northern part of the district by the pursuing party, and now lies buried on the land owned by Thomas Sullivan, but the following account taken from Collins' "History of Kentucky" seems to indicate that the above is a wrong supposition.   "There were two Harpes, brothers, one a large, athletic man named Micajah; the other small and active, named Wiley, but they were scarcely ever called anything except Big and Little Harpe.   Big Harpe had two wives, Little Harpe but one.   In the summer of 1799 Big and Little Harpe traveled through what is now Hopkins County.   The Harpes rode good horses, were well dressed and armed with rifles and holsters of pistols.   They stopped one night near the residence of a man by the name of Stiggall.   They passed him on the road, and at night the Harpes left their camp and went to the house of Stiggall.   Here over night a man by the name of Love was stopping, and entering the house they killed the stranger, Mrs. Stiggall and her child, took $40 in money and then set the house on fire.   That same night two men returning from a salt lick had also camped near Stiggall's.   About daylight the Harpes went to their camp and arrested them upon pretense that they had committed murder, arson and robbery.   They shot one and the other one finally escaped.   The Harpes went on their way, but the news of the murders spread among the scattered settlements, and an avenging party was organized and overtook the Harpes at their camp on Pond River, near the line between Hopkins and Muhlenburg Counties.   About a quarter of a mile from camp the two Harpes were discovered about to commit another murder on a traveler whom they had waylaid.   The Harpes taking the alarm fled, and the pursuers stopped to talk with the man they had rescued, taking him for an accomplice.   They soon followed, but the chase was a long one.   Big Harpe was finally overtaken near a stream where a big log had fallen across the path.   As he started to turn back one of the pursuers overtook him and shot him.   Harpe, however, did not fall, but rode on for some distance. His pursuers finally came up with him again and pushed him from his horse, Stiggall coming up at the time and shot Harpe through the heart. His head was cut off and hung up on a tree. This tree grew in what is now Webster County, and the place is known to this day as ' Harpe's Head.' Little Harpe escaped to Mississippi, where he was subsequently captured and executed for other crimes."

In an early day the noted outlaw Alonzo Pennington, of Christian County, built his house on the line between the two counties in this district. Here he for a time evaded the law by going from one county to the other. He was finally captured and hung at Hopkinsville.

There were traces in early days, mere paths through the wilderness. The early pioneer as he journeyed through the forests blazed the trees behind him that he might return. These were the first roads of any kind. But as the pioneers in one portion of the district visited others in another, and intercommunication became somewhat established, the necessity of well-established roads became apparent. Probably the first road in the district was the Elkton and Greenville road. This in turn was followed by the Hopkinsville and Greenville road. About 1851 what is known as the Mud River road was opened. In 1877 the Kirkmansville and Bivinsville road was cut through, and about two years ago the Kirkmansville and Fairview road was surveyed, but it has not been opened as yet. In early days the creeks were forded by the traveler, but later on bridges were built. Probably the first structure built in this district was the one across the East Fork of Pond River, on the Elkton and Green River road. It was probably built as early as 1830, and stood until about 1857, when it was undermined. A new one was built at a cost of about $1,500, and is still in use. In 1881 a bridge was built on the Kirkmansville and Bivinsville road across East Fork, at a cost of about $400.

Early Mills.—In order that his children might be fed, the pioneer soon after his arrival turned his attention to the discovery of some means by which the corn, which was then the staple article of food, could be made into meal. This led to the early establishment of a mill. These mills in an early day were very crude structures. Meal was first obtained by crushing the corn, when dry, in a kind of crude mortar made by chiseling out a hollow in the top of an oak stump. The pestle was an iron block made fast to a sweep, and with this simple contrivance a coarse article of meal could be manufactured. This form of a mill was superseded by the horse-mill ; that in turn gave way to the " over-shot " and water-mill, and the steam at last took the place of them all. Probably the first mill patronized by the early inhabitants of this district was a water-mill that was erected on the East Fork of Pond River by Samuel Coleman as early as 1830. After running it for a few years he died, and his widow took it up. She in turn gave way to her sons, who ran it for some years, and then the mill finally fell into disuse. In 1853, E. L. McClaine bought the grounds and built a new mill, which was burned down the following year. He immediately began another one, but that too was washed away before it was completed by the freshet of 1855. He then sold out to Murdock & Johnson, who began the erection of a new mill, but before the structure was completed they in turn sold to Kirkman & Bennett. This firm completed the mill and then ran it for about three years, when Bennett retired. Kirkman in turn ran it until 1869 and then disposed of it to M. W. Grissam. In 1879 this gentleman sold out to Butler & Rice, who added steam power to the mill and otherwise improved the structure. In the spring of 1884 H. H. Butler purchased Rice's interest, and is still running it. Joseph Allison had a horse-mill on his farm as early as 1825. It was run for some twenty-five years, and then finally rotted away.

District Schools.—The pioneers were as a rule a very illiterate, unlearned class of people. Their mode of life gave them no time to improve their minds. Their whole time was employed in ministering to the necessities of life. But while they were ignorant themselves their true love for their offspring made them wish that their children might be better able to meet the requirements of a civilized community. Thus it was that as soon as the more immediate necessities of life were supplied, the pioneer turned his attention to the erection of a rude structure in which the children might be taught in a very imperfect way the rudiments of an education. One of the first schools of this district was one that was erected on the farm of F. M. Pepper as early as 1825. Among the teachers there were Rev. Shelton and his son, L. W. Dulin, Albert Drake and Matt Mason. This building finally fell down, and in about 1845 another building was put up near the present town of Kirkmansville. Among the teachers here were P. C. Griffin, R. F. Bass, C. J. McGehee, M. W. Grissam, Miss Jennie McCullouch, Volney Clark and Mrs. Adeline Drake. In 1880 a new frame building was built at a cost of about $575. The entire community assisted in its erection, and the school does honor to the neighborhood. Mr. Girod is the present teacher assisted by Miss Mattie Major. The present average attendance is about seventy. The affairs of the school are managed by a board consisting of the following persons, viz.: J. D. Duncan, P. B. Robinson, J. N. Rice, J. W. Grissam and J. W. Bartlett. A school on the Howell Edwards farm has been in operation about eight years. Some of the teachers who have been employed there are R. F. Bass, J. C. McGehee, G. W. High-

tower and "Tobe" Hightower. In about 1870 a school was put up at the
Mt. Tabor Church. Here G. W. Hightower taught for some years. The
school on John Powell's land was built as early as 1857. Among the
teachers who taught there might be mentioned W. S. Simons (who had
formerly been Sheriff), Frank Bass, W. T. Griffin, Marion Powell and
Miss Octavia Lacey. There is also a school in the Hardison neighborhood. Among the teachers who have been employed there might be
mentioned Richard Sullivan, Miss J. L. Pepper, J. H. Faughender and
R. C. F. Hardison.

> Saw ye not the cloud arise,
> Little as the human hand,
> Now it spreads along the skies ;
> Hangs o'er all the land.
> *Old Hymn.*

From what a small beginning have the churches of this county sprung.
At first there was but a pioneer here and there who looked to the Father
above for the blessings in this life and the life to come. At first the early
settlers lived many miles apart, and the pioneer who wished to worship
God, did so around his own fireside. Occasionally some circuit rider or
itinerant would come, and gathering a few together, unfold to them the
mysteries of the plan of human salvation. In the summer time this little
handful of believers assembled under the shade of some spreading oak, for
the groves through all ages have been God's first temples, and in the
winter they gathered in some cabin. As the country became settled up
the necessity of some common place of worship became apparent, and thus
churches were established in the different neighborhoods. Probably the
first church in this district was the Mount Carmel Baptist Church. It
stood on the East Fork of Pond River, near where the Highland Lick road
crosses it. It was built as early as 1825, and among the first members
might be mentioned, Thomas Pepper and wife, John Christian, Maj.
Dodd and wife, Daniel Morgan and wife, Bennie Pannell and William
Pannell. This church continued in existence until about 1865. Among
the ministers who were stationed here were Revs. J. Christian, Williams,
Rutherford, Meacham, Nicholas Lacey, James Lamb and William Pannell.
At one time the church had about fifty members. Mount Moriah Baptist
Church was built in about 1868 ; it is a frame, and cost originally about
$400. Among the first members might be mentioned, N. D. Butler, J.
W. Hale and family, Mrs. Polly Ann Utley, E. F. Pepper and wife,
Isaac Walker, James F. Barrar and J. W. Kenley. The present pastor
is Rev. Whitson. The present membership is about thirty. The pres-
ent Deacons are, Isaac Walker, J. W. Hale and Ben F. Hale. Enberry
Chapel, North Methodist Episcopal Church, was built in about 1877, at a
cost of about $400. Among the members might be mentioned, Bradley

Davis, Mr. Hardison and family, Dr. A. Lewis, Mrs. Rowe. The present membership is about thirty. Rev. Enberry was the first pastor. Among the ministers who have been here since might be mentioned Revs. Davis, Powis, Gardner and Ford.

Town of Kirkmansville.—The first store in what is now the town of Kirkmansville was built in 1853 by E. L. McClaine, who ran it in connection with the mill. In about 1855 he sold the store to Lafayette Bennett. This gentleman took Peter Kirkman into partnership with himself and subsequently sold out the entire store to the latter. Mr. Kirkman continued the business until 1862. After the breaking out of the war, M. W. and J. W. Grissam started up. They engaged in business for some years, and then disposed of the store to Butler & Rice. The latter firm retired from business in 1878, and Dr. J. W. Guffey succeeded them. He only remained in business a short time and disposed of the store to E. Cannon. This gentleman also soon retired, and sold out to J. A. Elkins, who finally failed. In about 1867 R. F. Bass put up a store here and continued in business about three years, and then retired. About 1871 J. D. Griffin opened a store and was in business about four years. Edwards & Fritz also opened a store at this point in 1871. They remained in partnership a short time. Fritz soon sold out, but Edwards continued in business until his death in 1875. In 1876 S. E. Cash opened a store and continued in business a short time. In 1878 P. B. Robinson came there and is still in business. D. B. Yates opened a store there in 1883 and is still there. In about 1880 W. W. McCorpin began merchandising, and remained there two years. He sold out to B. F. Hill, who is still there. In 1882 Dr. J. W. Bartlett opened a drug store and subsequently added a grocery store, and is still in business. In about 1879 John McCowan opened a saddler's shop and soon after went into partnership with L. W. Rice. The latter bought the entire store in the spring of 1884 and is still in business. In 1882 M. W. Horton opened a cabinet shop and is still there. In about 1869 M. W. Grissam built a tobacco factory. Soon after Brennaugh & Merritt rented the house and ran it for some years. Grissam again assumed control of it, and took in F. M. West as a partner. In the spring of 1884 J. D. Duncan purchased it and is now running it. West & Sullivan have lately put up another factory and are also engaged in the business. In 1880 G. M. Babbitt put up a blacksmith and wagon shop, and is still engaged here.

The village of Kirkmansville shows considerable prosperity. The people are clever and hospitable in the treatment of strangers, and are ready to extend a hearty welcome to those coming into their midst. No community in the county has a class of more moral and law-abiding citizens, and those searching for a pleasant place to settle in will find the people ready to receive them with open arms.

The town was incorporated in March, 1882, and the following officers were appointed under their new charter: Trustees, J. W. Grissam, D. C. McGregor and P. C. Griffin; Marshal, E. E. Rice; and Police Judge, G. M. Babbitt (who has held the office continuously ever since). At the first annual election in 1883 the following officers were elected: J. M. Rice, W. H. Horton and B. F. Hill; Marshal, Thad. E. Williams; 1884, J. D. Duncan, D. D. Gates and W. W. Lacey; Marshal, L. W. Rice.

The village now contains about 150 inhabitants. P. B. Robinson is the present Postmaster.

Kirkmansville Lodge, No. 615, A. F. & A. M., was organized under dispensation in the summer of 1882, and a charter was granted to it in the fall of same year. The charter members were: J. M. Wilson, A. Lewis, W. W. McCorpin, J. W. Bartlett, P. B. Robinson, B. F. Hill, William Lacey and S. D. Pepper. The first officers were: J. M. Wilson, M.; A. Lewis, S. W.; W. W. McCorpin, J. W.; J. M. Bartlett, Treas.; P. B. Robinson, Sec.; B. F. Hill, S. D.; William Lacey, J. D.; J. K. West, Steward and Tyler. The lodge furnished up a hall in the second story of the school building and continued to hold their meetings there. The present membership is about twenty. The present officers are: J. M. Wilson, M.; R. F. Bass, S. W.; P. B. Robinson, J. W.; J. W. Bartlett, Treas.; C. J. McGehee, Sec.; H. Duvall, S. D.; G. W. Hightower, J. D.; J. W. Grissam, Steward and Tyler.

Bethlehem Christian Church was built in about 1857, on the Murdock farm. Among the early members of the church might be mentioned Daniel Gates, J. C. Bass and wife, W. P. Murdock, William McKinley and wife, Howell Edwards and family, A. J. Edwards and wife, and J. J. Griffin. The congregation continued to meet at this place until about 1870, when the place of meeting was changed to Kirkmansville, and the services are now held in the schoolhouse. The present membership is about sixty-eight. Among the ministers who have been here are: J. W. Price, W. E. Mobley, Thomas Weathers, Robert Dulin and J. H. Keith. The Elders of the church are: S. D. Pepper and P. B. Robinson; Deacons, P. C. Griffin and F. M. Weathers; Clerk, P. B. Robinson.

Kirkmansville Methodist Episcopal Church was organized in May, 1876, by Rev. Thomas M. Penick. There were twenty-nine constituent members, among whom might be mentioned John W. Grissam, Emma Grissam, Sarah M. Grissam, R. F. Bass, Mary Bass, J. W. Bartlett, Moody Bartlett, Eusebia A. Bartlett, E. H. Petree, Paulina J. Petree, Bettie Lacey, Mary Pepper, Mary B. Hill, W. W. Lacey, M. Spurlin, W. C. Spurlin and Moses Pace. Among the ministers who have been stationed here might be mentioned William Alexander, J. W. Griffin, J. W. Bunton, Hubs Morrison, W. I. Birchett; and Rev. Edwards is the present pastor. The society now has about twenty members. The present officers are: Steward, W. W. Lacey; Assistant Stewards, J. W. Grissam and John M. Rice; Class-leader, J. W. Grissam.

A Union Sunday-school is held every Sunday during the summer in the schoolhouse at Kirkmansville. At the last session the average attendance was about fifty, and the officers were as follows: John M. Rice, Superintendent; Assistant Superintendent, J. D. Duncan.—*F. S. Tyler*.

CHAPTER XIII.

MAGISTERIAL DISTRICT NO. 7—BIVINSVILLE—INTRODUCTION—CONFIGURA-
TION—THE CLIFFS AND THEIR LEGENDS—WATER-MILLS—EARLY SET-
TLERS—FIRST SCHOOLS AND PIONEER CHURCHES.

FEW studies are more interesting to mankind than that of the past
experiences, deeds, thoughts and trials of the human race. The
civilized man and the untutored savage alike desire to know the deeds
and lives of their ancestors, and strive to perpetuate their story. National patriotism and literary pride have prompted many in all time to
preserve the annals of particular people, but narrow prejudices and self-
ish interest have too often availed to suppress the truth or distort facts.
It is the aim of the present writer to collect and prepare in a presentable
and readable form some of the facts of the early settlements of the Bivinsville District, which furnishes the subject matter for this chapter. The
pioneers are worthy of remembrance, and their difficulties, sorrows,
customs, labors and patriotism should not be allowed to fall into oblivion.

Bivinsville District lies in the northeastern portion of the county and
is bounded on the north by Muhlenburg County, on the east by Logan
County, on the south by the Sharon Grove District and on the west by
the Kirkmansville District. The surface of the district is very broken
and irregular. On the north and south there are ranges of high
cliffs along the banks of the creeks, while through the center the
surface is somewhat rolling and well adapted to farming pursuits.
There are several ranges of cliffs, which from a geological point of
view present a most pleasing and instructive landscape. One of the
ranges of cliffs begins on the S. C. McGehee farm and extends in an
easterly direction to the Logan County line. Another range heads on
the Fritz Seers farm, near the Greenville road, and also runs to the line
of Logan County. Still another heads on the Shelton farm and also runs
east, while another, known as the Pigeon Roost Branch, begins near the
Muhlenburg County line and extends in a southeasterly direction to
Logan County. The cliffs in the southern portion of the district along
the Sharon Grove line are the highest and the most picturesque. The
scenery here is truly magnificent and people come here from many miles
around to visit the place. The height of the cliffs varies from 300 to 500
feet, and in many places are almost perpendicular. Through all the range

C14

of cliffs but one pass has been discovered through which the people can go
and come from one district to another.   This one route is very precipitous
and is but a simple bridle path.   Going down this pathway with the cliffs
rising in towering masses on either side, one is almost led to believe that
here in particular nature is wont to display her charms.   In some places
cliffs rising some fifty or a hundred feet extend at an angle of forty-five
degrees over the pathway and seem ever ready to crush the venturesome
traveler.   In other places the cliffs rise almost perpendicularly until their
tops are lost in the feathery clouds above.   Scattered among the cliffs are
many places of more than ordinary interest.   One, the Buzzard's Ball-
yard, is a huge column of rock that seems to stand all alone, the monarch
of all it surveys.   It is some fifty or sixty feet high, and is some thirty
feet broad on top.   The rock in some by-gone day was split in two from
the top, almost half-way down, by some internal action of the earth, and
the two parts seem to stand like twin sentinels guarding the secrets of
the place.   The name is derived from the fact that in the winter the
buzzards gather here, and bask in the sun for many hours at a time.
This place is also a much frequented point for picnic parties and pleasure-
seekers generally.

Another interesting place is the " dripping rocks."   Here a cliff extends immediately over the pathway, and from its surface it is said that
water has oozed and fallen drop by drop to the surface below for ages past.
Why or how it is, no one pretends to know, but that it is the case all who
have visited this interesting region will bear witness.   For many years
what was known as the " Garrett " rock was also a very interesting point.
Here a huge bowlder seems to be standing on its edge on the very
brink of one of the highest of the cliffs.   Here it stood for many years,
seeming ever ready to totter to the rocks below.   But one morning, by
some action of the earth's surface, the rock was precipitated to the ground
below, and broken into thousands of pieces.   It is stated by people living
in the neighborhood that the crash was heard for three miles around.   A
cave in what is known as the Big Cliffs is also an interesting point to
visit.   It goes by the name of " Saltpeter Cave " from the fact that in
the cave a very large deposit of this mineral is found.   The mouth of
the cave is some two hundred feet wide, and it extends back some fifty
feet.   In an early day it is claimed that the mineral was refined and dis-
tilled to a great extent.   One man who it is claimed worked here in an
early day was Jack Roger, and the cave in honor of this man is also
called " Jack's Peter Cave."   In the mouth of the cave up to a few years
ago, the huge iron caldrons in which the mineral was refined, stood, and
also the boards used in drying.   The " Big Cave," on the Horton farm,
has also been explored to some distance.

The rock composing these cliffs is mostly sandstone, and, consequently, the soil of the district is mostly of the light yellow, clayey texture, although in some of the valleys a light red clay is found. The soil in the main is quite fertile, and agricultural pursuits are followed very profitably. Under the cliffs along the banks of the creek there is a strip of very fertile land, and this of late years has been utilized to a considerable extent, and some very good farms are in process of cultivation in these almost isolated places. In an early day the district was heavily timbered; among the varieties being found here might be mentioned white, black, red and chestnut oak, chestnut poplar, sugar maple and black walnut. In the last few years an immense quantity has been cut down. Of late years the utilization of this timber has been quite an item to the people here. Thousands of dollars of valuable timber has been cut down and floated down the creeks to Mud River, thence down the Green River to Evansville. One of the leading operators in this direction has been Mr. Buie, who has netted thousands of dollars by his ventures.

There are several creeks in the district. One, Clifty Creek, heads on the Fritz Seers farm, flows generally in an easterly direction to the Logan County line, and finally empties into Wolf Lick. Piney Creek rises on S. C. McGehee's farm, flows generally in an easterly course, and finally empties into Green River. Pigeon Roost Creek heads on the Noah Martin farm near the county line, flows in a southeasterly course, and empties into Piney Creek. Long Creek rises on the farm of William Brown, flows generally in a northwesterly course to the Muhlenburg County line, and empties into Pond River.

The first road in the district was the Greenville and Elkton road, which passes along its western edge. In about 1840 the Mud River road was surveyed through the district. In later years the Jericho road and the Kirkmansville and Bivinsville road have been established. The name, Bivinsville, has been given to the district from the family of Bivins, which settled here in quite an early day.

We have mentioned elsewhere that there were two things the early pioneer looked for in making his settlement: one was plenty of timber, the other plenty of water. The first requisite was found here in abundance, but the second was only obtainable at the creeks, and these in most cases were walled up on either side by high cliffs. There were no springs in the district, and the early pioneer had yet to learn that water might be secured by digging for it. Hence it was that the settlement of the most of this district was made many years after the rest of the county had become quite thickly peopled. There was a great amount of game in the district, and the people from other portions of the county ofttimes came here to hunt. They found scattered here and there some isolated settlements, but the few pioneers who were then living here have all passed away, and not many of their children are yet living, so we were unable to learn much concerning them. We can simply state where they were living in an early day. Wilson Chappell settled on the farm now owned by his widow; here he died in 1878. William and Tom Powell came here from North Carolina, and settled on the farms now owned by John Asher and John McIlvain. They lived here only a few years when they emigrated further West. A Mr. Harper made a settlement on the Amos Bivin farm. There is a tradition here that this man was a counterfeiter, and in an early day received his just punishment. A Mr. Bivin made a settlement on the farm now owned by Amos Bivin. He was quite a noted man in his day, and left a family of four sons, one of whom, Charles, is still living. Sam Blake, a North Carolinian, was another pioneer here, and made an improvement on the farm now owned by S. C. McGehee; he was a preacher. Noah Slaughter came here from North Carolina about 1830, and settled where his widow is now living. And about the same time John Chappell made a settlement on the premises now occupied by his son John H. He was a great hunter, and many stories are told of his prowess with the rifle. Dillard McGehee came to this county in 1827 from Virginia. He first settled in the Elkton District. There he resided until 1835, and then came to this district, and made a setttlement on the Blake farm, where his son S. C. is still living. He died here about 1870. In about 1840 Gabriel Shelton came to this district, and is still living here. James Greenfield came about the same time, and is still living here. Abraham Shelton came here a few years after his son had arrived, and made a settlement near the latter; he died only a few years since. About the same time Stewart Carneal moved up here from the south part of the county, and made a settlement where his family still resides. Soon after this Brinden Jessup came here from Logan County, and settled near where Mr. Buie is now living. In about 1845 Archie Stinson came from Logan County, and settled where Albert King is now living. In an early day Joseph Driskill moved into this district from that of Sharon Grove, and made an improvement on the farm now occupied by William Bivin. In about 1830 he left the county, and moved to Saline County, Ill., where he died a few years after. Also in an early day three brothers, Abraham, Moses and Lewis Hurb, made settlements on the Greenville road near the head of Cow Creek. A son of Abraham Hurb is now living at Elkton. Another early settler here was John Pace, who made a settlement where George Shelton is now living. In about 1845 Jack McIlvain made a settlement on the farm now occupied by Riley Blake.

One of the first schools in the district was one that was put up in a very early day on the Bivin farm. It was of poles and stood only a short time. Among the teachers here was Richard Foster. The house of the West Clifty School, as it is called, was also one made of poles. In 1845 a log-house was built by William Gray. Among the teachers here were Gabriel Shelton, James McGehee, Briton Drake. A short time after Mc-Gehee taught there, the school was moved to S. C. McGehee's farm. Here Miss Lou Petree and Kenley Shelton taught. The building was subsequently moved, this time to the farm now owned by Gabriel Shelton ; Miss Fannie Shammle and Nannie Dowdy both taught here. In about 1878 a new schoolhouse was built. Among the teachers who have taught here are mentioned : Monroe Gant, Misses Rebecca Lamb, Maggie Jackson, Lou Pogue and Anna Gant. The New Harmony Schoolhouse on the Bivin farm was built in about 1860. Among the teachers who have been employed here have been Noah Martin, Misses Asher and Mitchell, Jane Dowdy and Mr. Clark Turner. The Asher Schoolhouse was built in about 1878, on Riley Asher's farm. Some of the teachers who have been employed here have been Miss Rebecca Lamb, Miss Pogue, Mr. Foulks and Miss Asher.

One of the early mills of the district was on the farm of Mr. McCorpin. It was in its time the only mill in this portion of the county. It was for the purpose of getting to this mill that the pathway through the cliffs that we have spoken of above, was made by people living on the other side. This mill was in operation for many years. In about 1875 James Steele put up a steam-mill on Mr. Shelton's farm. It was both a grist and saw-mill, and was run until 1882. In about the same year Mr. Mack Chappell put up a water-mill on Piney Creek, which is still in use. On Pigeon Roost Branch Mr. Moore put up a water-mill, in about 1877, which is still in operation.

As early as 1850 the Baptists had a church at the New Harmony Schoolhouse. Among the members were the Mayes family, John and James Bringham and Jesse Hinton. Among the ministers who have preached here have been Mike Cameron, J. Stinson and James Wilson. In 1878 the Christian denomination, which had up to this time been holding services in the neighboring farm houses, built a frame church near Bivinsville. Among the constituent members here might be mentioned Gabriel Shelton, James Steel, John Heltsley, John Hancock, James Greenfield and George Shelton. Among the ministers who have preached here have been Victor Davis and John Gant. The present membership is about 100. The present officers are : Deacons, John Heltsley and Thomas Edwards, and Clerk, Gabriel Shelton. A number of years ago Hancock & Ware put up a store on the west side of the Greenville and Elkton road just on the edge of the district. They did business here for a few years and then sold out to Bellamy & Young. This firm, after running it a short time, in turn retired and the store was run by D. Gates.   In about 1882 Mr. Cathcart began business there, and is still merchandising.   In about 1870 a store was put up almost opposite the one now used by Cathcart by Frank Duncan.   He ran it for some years and then disposed of it to William Ragsdale, who then sold out in turn to George Glenn, and the latter disposed of it to John Petree.   He did business there until about 1879, and then retired. Soon after he quit merchandising the building was torn down.   In about 1879 John Hester put up a store one-fourth mile north of where Cathcart is now doing business.   He merchandized there until 1884, and since that time David Watson has had a store there.—*F. S. Tyler.*

CHAPTER XIV.

MAGISTERIAL DISTRICT No. 2—SHARON GROVE—DESCRIPTION—CONFIGURA-
TION—FIRST SETTLERS—WHO THEY WERE AND WHERE THEY CAME
FROM—COL. HARDIN, JOHN DRISKILL, JACOB SELLERS, JOHN CHRISTIAN,
AND SAM SHAMMLES—PIONEER MILLS—CHURCHES AND SCHOOLS.

IN date of settlement, Sharon Grove District occupies a foremost rank
among the districts of Todd County. Its pioneer settlements were
made very early, and to undertake to give an exhaustive and detailed
account of the interesting and varied scenes and occurrences incident to
the time thereto, would be a most difficult task as well as one demanding
more space than can be allotted to it at this time. The study of man is
a most proper one for the present and future generations, and it is one
that is calculated to give rich returns to any thoughtful and inquiring
mind that will undertake it ; and in the lives of our forefathers we
see that they sacrificed their own comforts and interests, and ofttimes
their own lives for the benefit of those to follow them. The generally impoverished circumstances of these men, the hardships, privations and positive dangers immediately surrounding them, the formidable obstacles with
which they were almost daily called upon to contend, all are conditions
of life under which not many of the present day could live and make progress. So we say that the careful study of the lives and times of our
pioneers might well be the ambitious work of one's life, and how invaluable would such a work be.

Sharon District, to the history of which this chapter is devoted
abounds in historical happenings of great interest and importance. It
lies on the eastern side of the district, and has the following boundaries :
On the north by Bivinsville, on the east by Logan County, on the south
by the Elkton District, and on the west by the Kirkmansville and
Fairview Districts. The surface of the district is somewhat diversified.
The major part is rolling, along the north quite hilly, and in the southeast
quite flat. From the Bivinsville District the cliffs extend over a short
distance in the northern part, and here the sandstone is found. The soil
here is the yellow clay. Along the banks of the creeks the limestone formation appears. This in some places is surmounted by a rich black loam,
and in other points the white clay. On the east along the Logan County

line there is some flinty limestone, and here in some places a red clay soil appears, but which is inferior to that of the south part of the county. On Briton Sherrard and Sam Shammles' farms there are caves which have been explored to some extent. Also one on the widow Gilbert farm. Here in an early day it is said a counterfeiter's furnace and other tools were discovered, but by whom they were used in the days gone by re- mains a mystery. At present from a half to two-thirds of the district is under cultivation. The timber of the district is mainly made up of pop- lar, white, black and red oak, maple and in some places walnut. In the southeast there is also some chestnut. Of late years an immense amount of timber has been cut down and floated down the creeks and thence down the Green River to Evansville.

On the farm now owned by Charles Christian a coal bank was discovered many years ago. At first the pioneers simply mined it for their own use. John Christian used it almost exclusively for fuel for many years. In the last few years it has been mined quite extensively. For four years William Brockman used it almost exclusively to run his mill, and in the last two years Charles Christian has had miners at work there almost all the time, and it has been hauled to Elkton and other points in quite large quantities. Some very pronounced lead formations have also been dis- covered, especially along the banks of Clifty Creek are they quite prom- inent. It is stated that in an early day Mr. James Sherrard mined it to some extent on his farm, and made his bullets almost entirely from the lead which he got here. He, however, never informed any one of the exact location of the metal, and since that time no one has ever paid any attention to the mining of the mineral. East Clifty Creek heads in the eastern portion of the district, flows generally in a northerly direction into the Bivinsville District, where it empties into the Middle Clifty. This latter stream heads on the Fritz Seers farm, flows generally in a northeasterly direction through the Bivinsville District and empties into Wolf Lick Creek.

Early Roads.—Probably the first road in the district was the Russell- ville and Greenville road, which was in operation for many years, but was finally fenced up. About 1830 the Elkton and Greenville road was sur- veyed, and in about 1840 the Coal Bank road, as it is known, was opened. Within a year or two afterward the Morgantown and Hopkinsville road was first made a public thoroughfare, followed soon after by the Elkton and Mt. Sharon road. In 1800 John Driskill came here from Ruther- ford County, N. C., and made a settlement near the coal bank. He lived there for a few years, and then moved to the farm now owned by his son, John Driskill, Jr. Here he died in 1843. When he came here he stated to his son that he found the following parties living here: Col. Hardin, as he was known, made a settlement on the waters of Clifty, on parts of the farm now occupied by J. Driskill, Jr. He lived on his first settlement for some time, and then moved to a farm within a half mile of there, where he afterward obtained a patent of 200 acres. In the early days of his settlement here he had many severe encounters with the Indians, and at his request was granted a Colonel's commission and the power to raise men to repel the attacks of the savages. Through all his residence here he was a very prominent man, and was looked upon as the leader and master spirit of the settlement. His word was law, and all questions of dispute were referred to him. In an early day two men were caught stealing horses. Hardin was sent for. He came immediately, and being told of their crime turned and without a word shot them down. About the same time a Frenchman came through this portion of the county selling gunpowder to the Indians. Hardin having heard of it followed the man to his camp among some Indians and also shot him. Soon after the settlements became somewhat numerous here Hardin moved to Missouri, where he lived to a good old age.

On the creek immediately below Hardin, Jacob Sellers lived. He had originally come here from North Carolina. He was a great hunter and was regarded by all as a very peaceable and inoffensive citizen. A Mr. Hall, a brother-in-law of Sellers, was living where his grandson, James Hall, now resides. He was a great deer hunter, and spent nearly all of his time in the chase. He answered his country's call in the war of 1812, and served as a good and faithful soldier all through the conflict. After the war was over, he became quite an extensive farmer here, and at one time was quite wealthy. He died in about 1855. Mr. Roger was living on the farm now occupied by Squire Shammles; he raised a large family of children, all of whom were considered somewhat dissolute, and were among the greatest fighters of the day. A grandson, Burkett Roger, is still living in the Kirkmansville District, and is a very exemplary citizen. Sam McMullen lived on the farm now owned by Berry Tomlinson. He spent most of his time in hunting the game that then abounded here, and killed more bears, it is said, than any other two men in the district. He lived here for many years, and finally passed to his reward. He raised a large family of children, but they too have nearly all passed away. One daughter, Mrs. Dr. Mahone, is still living in the Bivinsville District. Robert Sherrard was living on the farm now occupied by his son, Samuel Sherrard; he came here from North Carolina, and was a faith doctor; he died here in about 1838.

As early as 1803 John Christian came here and made an improvement on the farm now owned by Joseph Carneal. He was a preacher in the Baptist Church, and died here a short time before the late war. A son,

John, is now living in St. Louis; James, a grandson, is now living at Elkton. In an early day, but when we are not able to state with accuracy, Samuel Shammles came here from Virginia and settled on the farm now owned by William G. Shammles; here he died in about 1860. James Shammles, a brother of the above, made a settlement where his grandson, Mark, now resides; he died in about 1826. James G. Shammles, a son of Samuel, was born here; he was for many years one of the magistrates of the district, and in the early days of musters and militia he was the Captain of a company. He died here in about 1880.

About 1810 James Garrel came here from Virginia. The farm on which he first built his little cabin is now in the possession of Marshall Meadows. Besides farming he also followed teaming and had a mill on East Clifty Creek. He was a very resolute, stern man, and was in an early day a great Indian fighter. About the same time James Glenn made a settlement here. He was one of the early Magistrates, and ran a horse-mill here for many years. He died here in about 1826; his son Robert became quite a prominent man in the early history of the county. He was a member of the lower House of the State Legislature for three sessions. He was subsequently elected to the Senate; he served in this capacity until the breaking out of the war, when, owing probably to the many cares devolving upon him, he sickened and died while still at his post of duty. In the early history of the county he was also a Magistrate, and at one time he was the Sheriff. The duties of his office were however, mostly performed by his son, George F.

Probably about 1815 Robert Acock came to the county and made a settlement in this district. He was a native of North Carolina, and was a soldier in the Revolution. He died here in about 1847. His son, Robert Acock, Jr., was one of the early Sheriffs of the county, and subsequently moved to Missouri, where he died. William Seers came here from Logan County, in about 1815, and settled where his son Fritz is now living, on the head waters of Clifty. Here he died in an early day. In about 1830 Patrick Carneal came here. In early days he was a school teacher, and taught here for many years. As early as 1835 John Lyon came here from Virginia and made a settlement on the farm now in the possession of his grandson, William Lyon, who is now keeping a store at Sharon Grove. Cotemporaneous with the arrival of Lyon, Jesse Robinson came here and settled on the farm now owned by William Gant. Soon after his arrival in this district, he put up a store on his farm, and merchandized here for many years. He was also quite an extensive buyer of tobacco. He moved to Illinois in about 1861, where he afterward died. In 1838 Russell Whitesides came here from Tennesse, and is now living near Sharon Grove. In about 1840 Andy Richmond also moved into this district from Tennessee and is still living here. He was for some years a merchant. Alfred, Joseph and John Gant settled here in about 1840. They came from Marshall County, Tenn. Of the three, John is now living in Elkton, and is a preacher of the Christian Church. Alfred is farming near Sharon Grove, and is a Methodist local preacher. Joseph died here about 1880; his son William is still living on the home farm. The days of yore in this district were very like the same days elsewhere—a time of home-made clothing and limited educational facilities, such as the present generation know but little about. Six yards was considered an extravagant amount to put into one dress, which was made plain. Bonnets were made from splints, and occasionally among the more aristocratic a leghorn hat was seen. The clothing of the women was hung upon wooden pegs around the walls of the house. They had none of the ruffles, silk hats, curls and jewels that adorn the young lady of this period. Reared in simplicity, surrounded by poverty, cared for by brave parents, their lives were one long dream of sunshine, unbroken by a single storm cloud poured out as a shameful libation to dim the horizon of their happiness. Corn bread and wild game were the principal articles of food. Wheat bread was a luxury which few possessed.

Before mills were built different plans were adopted to manufacture corn into meal for bread. While the corn was yet soft, it was grated into corn meal by rubbing over a piece of tin punched full of holes, to make it rough. Mortars were made by cutting off a tree about three feet from the ground, and burning a hole in the top of the stump, about a foot in depth and diameter. Into this the corn was placed, and a hard hickory pestle or an iron wedge attached to a spring pole was used to pound it fine. This was probably the first rude attempt at a mill. As the country became somewhat settled up, the horse and water-mills came into general use. Probably the first mill in the district of which any record has been kept was one built by James Glenn, on his farm. After his death Robert ran it for some time. It was a horse-mill, and a very crude one at that. In about 1830, George F. Glenn moved the mill to another part of the district, and ran it for many years. William Harrison put up in an early day a horse-mill at the head of Pond River, which was run for some time, and then finally fell into disuse. In 1830 Mr. Garrell put up a water-mill on East Clifty Creek. It continued to be used until about 1850, when it finally rotted away. In 1875 Gray put up a small steam-mill near where Glenn's Mill originally stood. He operated it for a short time, and then sold out to Trout. In 1879 the latter put up a flour and saw-mill, which is still in use. In about 1875 William and Henry Richmond put up a water-mill on Clifty Creek, which is still standing. Some years ago Francis Davis put up a steam-mill on Wolf Lick, in the eastern edge of the district, which is now doing a good business.

Early Schools.—One of the first schools in the district was one that was put up on the Shammles farm as early as 1830. Mr. Carneal was among the teachers employed here, and taught for many years. Another school was built in about 1835, on the Sherrard farm. It was taught by William Sherrard, who was a cripple. In 1845 a school was built near Mt. Sharon. Jonathan Carr was a teacher here. The first building stood for about twenty years, and a frame was then erected which is still in use. Among the recent teachers here have been John De Vard, Miss Sue Courcy and Miss Lou Courcy. In 1860 another schoolhouse was erected on the Shammles farm. Here William Shammles, Miss Frankie Shammles, Mark Rouke and Gail Craig have all taught. The Missionary Ridge Schoolhouse was built in about 1873. Among the teachers here might be mentioned Misses Anna Gant, Rebecca Lamb and —— Pidcock. The Campbell Schoolhouse, on the John Campbell farm, was erected in 1878. Frankie Shammles has been one of the teachers. A schoolhouse was built at Sharon Grove in about 1860, and a new building was put up in 1876. Here Prof. McGuire is the present teacher.

Pioneer Churches.—The Antioch Baptist Church was organized in about 1820. Among the first members were John Driskill, Thomas Sherrard, Mr. Johnson and family, Absalom Moore and William Donks. Meetings were first held in a log-house. In about 1850, a frame was built which is still in use. The church has about 100 members; the Deacons are John Driskill, Jr., and Andrew Seers; Clerk, John Link. Among the ministers who have been employed here have been R. V. Christian, John Walker, William Trabue, Jacob Bowers, Aleck Malone. Rev. Jenkins is the present pastor. The Mt. Sharon Methodist Church was built in about 1830. Among the pioneer members were Uel Gilbert, Samuel Shammles and James Shammles. In about 1870 a frame house was built, which is still used as a church. The membership is now about 250. Among the ministers here have been Revs. Alexander Griffin and Thomas Penick. Rev. Crandal is the present pastor.

The voting place in the district is at Sharon Grove. Here William Lyons and Marion Tomcilin have general stores, and F. Galbraith a drug store.—*F. S. Tyler.*

MEMORANDA

—OF—

HISTORICAL EVENTS

OCCURRING SUBSEQUENT TO THE PUBLICATION
OF THIS WORK.

BIOGRAPHICAL SKETCHES.

KIRKMANSVILLE PRECINCT.

DR. JOSEPH W. BARTLETT was born July 27, 1833, a son of Joseph S. and Amanda F. (Porter) Bartlett. His father was a native of Massachusetts. In early life he was a teacher, later a minister in the Methodist Episcopal Church South, and for many years a missionary among the Cherokee Indians. He came to Kentucky after the war of the Rebellion, and died in Todd County in 1875, at the age of seventy-eight. The mother was a native of Virginia, and removed with her father to middle Tennessee, when a child. She was first married to Elisha Zachariah, who died September 9, 1826. March 12, 1828, she married Joseph S. Bartlett, and died September 21, 1866, aged fifty-seven years. She was a life-long member of the Baptist Church. Dr. Bartlett was born in Williamson County, Tenn., and on reaching manhood he attended Medical College at Nashville and St. Louis. On leaving school he began the practice of his profession in Todd county, where he is still engaged. For the past three years he has had an interest in a mercantile business carried on by his son, Walter E., who has a flourishing trade. Young Bartlett is a gentleman of rare business qualifications, and bids fair to become one of the solid men of the county. The Doctor is the oldest practicing physician in the northern part of the county, with a wide-spread patronage. In his leisure, he has gathered about him the evidences of liberal culture, and dispenses the cordial hospitality of a home surrounded by the mark of thrift, business and comfort. Dr. Bartlett was married to Moody A. Sullivan of this county, June 16, 1859. Her parents are Caleb and Betty (Roper) Sullivan, natives of Tennessee. Mr. and Mrs. Bartlett are parents of six children ; Eusebia A., Walter E., Carrie T., Susie E., Willie L. and Joseph W. The parents and five of the children are members of the Methodist Episcopal Church South. Eusebia A., is the wife of Dr. P. S. Anderson, of Woodburn, Warren Co., Ky. Dr. Bartlett is a member of the Masonic order.

R. F. BASS. Among the well-to-do farmers whose solid acquirements and cordial hospitality have done so much to make the social features of the whole South celebrated, none is more worthy of honorable mention than the subject of this sketch, R. F. Bass, who was born October 24, 1844, in this county. His parents were J. C. and Sarah Bass, both natives of Kentucky. The father was a farmer. His death occurred November 27, 1880, aged seventy-three. The mother died May 28, 1882, aged sixty-seven years. Both parents were members of the Christian Church. These parents had three children: William H., John N., and R. F., only one of whom is now living. Wm. H. died in 1853, aged twenty-two years. John N. was a graduate of Jefferson Medical Institute, Philadelphia. He had practiced medicine for twenty years, located in Elkton. He married Miss Ellen, daughter of Dr. L. B. Hickman, of this county. Dr. Bass died July 21, 1880, aged forty-five years. At the age of twenty-two, R. F. Bass engaged in merchandising which he continued four years. Later he took to farming and stock-raising, which business he still continues with reasonable success. He now owns 400 acres of land, and is located one-half mile southeast of Kirkmansville. His home, without being pretentious, is crowned with the graces of a cultivated taste, and is the source of a genial hospitality, which, to the happy wayfarer who comes within its precincts, is "like the shadow of a high rock in a weary land." He was married July 14, 1867, to Miss Mary J. Kirkman, daughter of John M. Kirkman, a native of Texas. This union has been blessed with one child—Ellie. Her death occurred March 21, 1873, aged five years. Mr. and Mrs. Bass are members of the Christian Church and Mr. Bass is a member of the Masonic order.

BENJAMIN B. BUTLER, Sheriff of Todd County, Ky., was born in this county August 8, 1850. His parents were H. D. and Permelia C. (Carey) Butler, both natives of Kentucky. The father was born in Todd County; was a farmer, well and favorably known in his county. His death occurred May 3, 1884, at the age of sixty-six years. He had been a member of the Baptist Church for many years. The mother still lives in this county at the age of sixty-two years. She is also a member of the Baptist Church. Sheriff Butler began his business career at the age of sixteen. He followed farming until about the age of twenty-five. He then opened a general store at Kirkmansville, which he carried on with good success. Next he bought the business of M. W. Grissam, his only competitor. In the same year he bought the flouring-mill in the place and conducted the business of both until 1881, when he sold his store and has since conducted the business of the mill. Mr. Butler was elected Constable and discharged the duties of his office with credit to himself and satisfaction to his constituents. He was elected Sheriff in 1882, and will be a candidate for re-election the coming fall. It is generally conceded that he has made an efficient public officer. He owns a farm of 130 acres which he has acquired by his own unaided industry. Mr. Butler was married March 12, 1884, to Miss Nannie E. Heltsley, daughter of J. H. Heltsley, of Muhlenburg County. Mrs. Butler is a member of the Baptist Church.

JACOB B. DAVIS was born February 21, 1834, in Todd County, Ky. His parents were Jacob and Polly (West) Davis, both natives of North Carolina. The father settled in Todd County at an early day. His death occurred in 1865, aged seventy-five years. He was a member of the Cumberland Presbyterian Church. Our subject, the eighth of thirteen children, began for himself at the age of twenty-one years. He had nothing in the start but his own energy and perseverance. In addition to farming he has worked some at the carpenter trade. He has been tolerably successful in business. He owns 250 acres of land, much of which is improved. His outlook is encouraging. He enlisted October 1, 1861, in Twenty-sixth Regiment Kentucky Volunteer Infantry. He participated in the battles of Shiloh, Perryville, Stone River, Salt River, etc., besides many dangerous skirmishes. He was in the Thirteenth United States Army Corps, under Gen. Thomas. His discharge dates July, 1865. He served nearly five years. He was wounded in the Shiloh battle in the left arm, and in a skirmish he was shot in the left jaw and left leg at the same time. He was disabled by these wounds some two months. He carried the ball in his jaw from 1864 to 1883 (nineteen years), when it came into his left nostril and was taken by him from his mouth. The ball knocked out two molar teeth on the left side and one on the right, and then glanced upward toward the eyes. The ball that gave him the wound in his left limb he still carries, and from these wounds he has much discomfiture to this day. He has received a pension the last six years. He had a spell of yellow jaundice in 1862, and on convalescing from that he took the typhoid fever which disabled him three months. Mr. Davis is proud of his army record, but does not care to make another. He was taken prisoner when wounded, but was paroled the same day. Mr. Davis was married in 1861, to Miss Mary J. Rainwaters, of Logan County, Ky. Their children are Judidah B., Jacob C. (deceased), Jerome F. and Benjamin R. Judidah B. is the wife of M. S. Heltsley, of this county. Armon D. is their child. Mr. Davis is a minister in the Methodist Episcopal Church. Mrs. Davis is a member of the Cumberland Presbyterian Church.

W. H. DEASON was born in 1840 in Todd County, Ky.; his parents are James N. and Eliza J. (Tucker) Deason, natives of Kentucky. The father was a farmer; his death occurred in 1864, at the age of forty-seven years; the mother is living in this county, at the age of sixty-five years. These parents have eight children all living in years of maturity (a very uncommon thing). W. H. began for himself at the age of twenty years; he farmed on rented ground for fifteen years, when he bought 150 acres, located on the East Fork of Pond River; he has a nice farm and is a good farmer, responsible and well-to-do. His principal product is tobacco, having raised 4,000 pounds the past year; his farm raises good corn and wheat, and is especially adapted for the latter; it can hardly be excelled for wheat land. He was married in 1861 to Mrs. Mary V. (Tucker) Powell, of this county. These parents have six living children, viz.: Emma J. (the wife of T. N. Cathcart, of Tenn.), W. H., G. W., Mary A., Mida F. and Benjamin C. The parents and two of the children are members of the Baptist Church.

JAMES D. DUNCAN, tobacco merchant, was born in 1845, in Montgomery County, Tenn. His parents were D. H. and Mary L. (Brake) Duncan, natives of Tennessee. The father was a tobacco merchant, a member of the Christian Church and of the Masonic order. The mother's death occurred in December, 1873, at the age of fifty-four years. She was a member of the Presbyterian Church. Mr. Duncan began business for himself at the age of twenty-five years. Previously he had been interested with his father; he has been a resident of this county since 1871; he bought 135,000 pounds of tobacco the past year; he has been moderately successful in business, and takes rank among the good citizens of the county. He owns two lots with a comfortable dwelling in Kirkmansville, and at present has an encouraging outlook. He was married in 1874 to Mrs. Susan E. Boyd, daughter of Edmond and Elizabeth

(Mitchel) Boyd, of Christian County, Ky. Louis, Forrest, Florence and Mallie are their children. Mrs. Duncan was first married to Richard Boyd, of Christian County; his death occurred February 19, 1871. Wallace, Lulu and Henry were their children.

P. D. FRANCIS was born April 10, 1829, in this county. He is a son of Stephen and Nancy (Martin) Francis; both parents were born in Virginia. The father died in 1839, aged seventy. The mother died in 1849, aged sixty-eight. Our subject was raised on his father's farm where he remained till the age of twenty-one; he then lived on a rented farm two years, after which he bought a farm of 200 acres, where he remained about four years; he then sold that farm and came to his present locality; the first year he worked at the tannery; he then returned to Elkton Precinct and worked on his farm till February, 1871, when he came to his present farm, where he has since resided. He owns 200 acres where he lives, also fifty acres land elsewhere. He was married in 1850 to Susan Stokes, daughter of Armstrong and Susan Stokes of Todd County; these parents had eleven children—eight of whom are now living—six sons and two daughters. Mr. Francis is a member of the Baptist Church.

LOUIS N. GIROD, teacher, was born August 24, 1859, in Hopkins County, Ky. His parents were John and Sarah K. (Coffman) Girod, the father a native of France, the mother of Kentucky. The father was a merchant at Henderson, and later at Ashbysburgh, Ky. He came to this county in 1855. His death occurred in 1863, aged forty. The mother is living in Webster County, Ky. These parents had three children— Sophie A., the wife of W. H. Weir, of Hanson, Ky.; Louis N. and Charles (deceased). Mr. Girod attended public school until the age of fifteen. The next three years he clerked most of the time. He then attended school one year in Hopkinsville under Prof. Bramham. He attended at Lexington the Agricultural and Mechanical College two years, taking a special course. He then began teaching and has taught two years, giving general satisfaction. He has taught the past year with good success the High School in Kirkmansville, where he is now located. He is said to be a fine scholar and an efficient teacher, rendering good satisfaction to those concerned. He was married November 18, 1880, to Miss Nannie H. Dean, of Lexington, Ky. One bright child—Hazel Deane— gladdens the home. Mr. and Mrs. Girod are members of the Christian

Church. The family, Girod, in Kirkmansville is, so far as known, the only one in the United States.

P. C. GRIFFIN. Among the genial, hospitable and worthy citizens of the precinct, Phillip C. Griffin, our subject, deserves mention; his birth dates November 27, 1845. His parents, James J. and P. C. Griffin, and he as well, were natives of this county. The father was a farmer, later a merchant, who died February 15, 1880, at the age of sixty-six years. The mother makes her home with her youngest child, Mrs. Lacey, aged sixty-four years. The father was, and the mother still is, a devoted member of the Christian Church. At the age of eighteen Phillip C. began on the farm for himself. Four years later he taught, and continued teaching with good success for four years. He took kindly to the profession, but declining health gave notice of the necessity of a more active life; he sold goods then in company with his father, the firm name being J. J. Griffin & Son. This partnership continued six years, when he engaged in his present business, dealing in produce, in which he has been reasonably successful. October, 1870, he married Miss Lucy, daughter of George and Nancy Foughender, residents of Muhlenburg County. Six children have blessed this union, viz.: Robert B., Mina L., Effie M., Katie, Ella and Maud. The parents are members, the former of the Christian and the latter of the Baptist Church.

JOHN W. GRISSAM, produce merchant, was born April 11, 1832, in Christian County, Ky. His parents were J. W. and Sarah W. (Wells) Grissam. The father was a native of South Carolina; he managed the farm for many years and served the county for some years in an official capacity; he was Deputy Sheriff, Tax Collector and Constable, all under the old Constitution. It was generally conceded that he gave good satisfaction in his official work. He departed this life December 7, 1861, at the age of sixty-four years; he with his wife were for many years worthy members of the Methodist Episcopal Church South. The mother was a native of North Carolina. She came to Muhlenburg County at an early age, and is still living, with powers of mind and body unimpaired. These parents had twenty children, eight of whom died in infancy. The remaining twelve were raised to advanced years. John W. began for himself at the age of twenty-two years. Owing to a large family he had no moneyed assistance. He has been engaged variously at farming, milling and merchandising; he now owns a nice home in Kirkmansville, and is numbered among its respected and responsible citizens; he was married in 1865 to Miss Emma C. McCown, of Muhlenburg County. These parents have had six children, two of whom, John L. and Mary E., died in childhood. The living children are: Malvina F., William C., Micajah W. and Samuel C. The parents are members of the Methodist Episcopal Church South.

JONAH W. HALE was born October 14, 1824, in Todd County, Ky. His parents were Thomas and Nancy (Pittman) Hale. The father was a native of North Carolina, and died in March, 1855, aged about sixty years. The mother died about the year 1826. Mr. Hale began for himself at the age of nineteen years; he rented for many years, then bought 183 acres, and since has bought 157 acres; he at present owns 340 acres, and is clever and well-to-do. He was married, February 6, 1848, to Martha E. Utley, daughter of James and Fanny (Grace) Utley. The latter died August 22, 1869, aged sixty-five years. James Utley died June 22, 1880, aged seventy-six years. They were life-long members of the Baptist Church. The children of Mr. and Mrs. Hale are: James T., born November 24, 1848; William H., born December 9, 1849 (deceased); Jonah W., born January 18, 1851; Nancy E., born November 3, 1852 (deceased); Marial, born January 9, 1855; Benjamin M., born November 1, 1856; Fannie J., born June 26, 1858 (deceased); Jessie G., born May 2, 1861; John H., born March 26, 1863 (deceased); Alice B., born January 10, 1865; Otis C., born March 6, 1867; Charles A., born January 29, 1871; Mary A. L., born June 23, 1872; Crawford H., born March 20, 1875 (deceased). The parents and five children are members of the Baptist Church.

RICHARD C. HARDISON, teacher, was born February 3, 1858, in St. Mary's Parish, Louisiana. His parents are Richard B. and Elizabeth Hardison. The father is a native of Kentucky; he is a minister in the Methodist Episcopal Church South; he preaches and teaches in the public schools; he owns a farm of 100 acres in Muhlenburg County, Ky., which is carried on by himself and his son, John C. He has been a minister for about eight years, and a teacher for nearly thirty years. The mother is a native of Virginia. She also is a member of the Methodist Episcopal Church South. These parents have five living children, viz.:

May, wife of Benjamin F. Hill, elsewhere mentioned; Richard C., John C., Nellie R. and Lafayette B. Our subject left Louisiana and went with his parents to Illinois in 1861, Hamilton County. There the family remained four years, then came to Todd County, Ky. He worked on the farm in summer, and attended school in the winter, under the supervision of Prof. McGregor. Later he taught penmanship for two years; subsequently taught public schools, in which business he is still engaged. He expects to make teaching his profession; he has given general satisfaction where he has taught; but few teachers in the county have a better reputation for advancing pupils and giving satisfaction to parents, patrons and all concerned. There are but few persons of his age who have a better outlook for a life of usefulness and devotion than has Mr. Hardison, the subject of this sketch.

BENJAMIN F. HILL, merchant, was born in 1848, in Muhlenburg County, Ky. His parents were Perry and Nicey (Wells) Hill, both natives of this State. The father was a farmer. His death occurred in 1879, at the age of sixty-four years. The mother's death took place in 1877, at the age of fifty-four years. She was a member of the Christian Church. These parents had seven children, five of whom are now living. Our subject, the fourth child, began business for himself at the age of twenty-six years. He had previously learned and worked at the blacksmith business; the latter occupation he continued eight years. He then engaged in the mercantile business, and in this he has continued ever since. He keeps a general stock of groceries, dry goods, nails, etc. He owns a house and lot in Kirkmansville, including store and grounds. By his fair dealing and courteous manner he has built up a large and increasing business. He has been very successful and has an encouraging outlook. He was married in 1875, to Miss May B. Hardison, daughter of R. B. & E. Hardison (elsewhere mentioned), of Muhlenburg County, Ky. Mrs. Hill is a member of the Methodist Episcopal Church South. Mr. Hill is a member of the Masonic order.

DR. AUGUSTUS LEWIS was born May 15, 1839, in Trigg County, Ky. His parents were Leonard and Lydia (Withers) Lewis. The father was a native of Virginia; born July 4, 1796. He was a farmer and taught in public schools for thirty years. He came to Kentucky in 1818, and cast the first Republican vote ever cast in Muhlenburg County. It was for Gen. Fremont, in 1856. His death occurred October 13, 1881. He was a member of the Methodist Episcopal Church South since 1848. The mother was a native of Kentucky; born December 15, 1815; she is still living with powers of mind and body well preserved. She has been a member of the Methodist Episcopal Church for more than forty years. Our subject began for himself at the age of eighteen, by teaching school; this continued four years, and the latter three of these four he studied medicine at the same time. He enlisted in the United States Army in the Eleventh Kentucky Infantry in 1861; he served as Sergeant three years. He took part in battles of Perryville, Murfreesboro, in the Atlanta campaign and with Sherman in his grand march to the sea. He was in all the engagements of the Twenty-third Army Corps, under Schofield. He was on duty every day from the commencement of the Atlanta campaign until the coast was reached at Savannah. His discharge dates December 16, 1864, having served three years, three months and sixteen days. He received a severe wound in the right cheek, at the battle of Murfreesboro, and was disabled three months from the wound. He had typhoid fever in 1862, lasting two months, which caused him to miss the battle of Shiloh; he refused promotion twice, that of Sergeant-Major, also of Hospital Steward of the regiment. He often assisted in amputating, dressing and caring for the wounded. On returning, he began the practice of medicine in Christian County. After two years he went to Muhlenburg, and practiced two years. Since that time he has been actively engaged in the practice near Kirkmansville. He has been quite successful in business; he now owns a farm of 160 acres, and still continues in the practice of his chosen profession. Dr. Lewis attended the Nashville Medical College, and graduated therefrom in the class of 1879. He was married November 8, 1865, to Miss Sarah C., daughter of Francis and Mary (Mullens) King, natives of Tennessee. Mr. King died in Novenber, 1873, aged sixty-three. Mrs. King died in September, 1881, aged sixty-five; both were members of the Methodist Episcopal Church South. The Doctor's children are : Henry C., Frelinghuysen, Erasmus E. and Frances; both parents and two of the children are members of the Methodist Episcopal Church South. The Doctor is a member of the Masonic order.

CHARLES J. McGEHEE was born December 8, 1840, in Todd

County, Ky.; is the son of Carr and Lucy (Tate) McGehee—both natives of Louisa County, Va. The father was a farmer, and soldier in the war of 1812. He first furnished a substitute and later volunteered; his death occurred in 1852, aged fifty-five. The mother died in 1852, aged fifty-one. They were both members of the Methodist Episcopal Church. The parents came to Todd County in 1825, and settled in the southern portion of the county, where Charles J. was born and raised; he remained there till 1861; he first owned 109 acres, which was a part of the old homestead; this he afterward sold and located on this farm, consisting of sixty-five acres, where he now resides. His location and surroundings are among the nicest in this part of the county. He can raise on this farm almost anything that can be produced in this latitude. He was married October 12, 1865, to Mrs. Sarah J. (Edwards) Martin. She is a daughter of H. B. and Elizabeth Edwards, of this county; both Mr. and Mrs. McGehee are members of the Christian Church; the former is a member of the Masonic order, Kirkmansville Lodge, No. 615.

ROBERT H. McKINNEY was born November 26, 1845, in Todd County, Ky. His parents are William W. and Rebecca (Griffin) McKinney, natives of Kentucky. The parents of William W. were John and Naomi (Ridgedill) McKinney, natives of South Carolina. John died in 1834, aged sixty-five. His wife died in 1824, aged about 50 years. Of their eleven children, Nancy Rector, of Texas, and William W. are all who survive. The latter is one of the respected, good farmers of the county, owning at present writing 300 acres of land. His first marriage, to Rebecca Griffin, August 25, 1840, resulted in the birth of seven children, viz.: Mary E., John C., Robert H., Dicey A., Rebecca C. (deceased), Elizabeth E. (deceased), and Nancy J. (deceased). The mother's death occurred February 13, 1870, aged about forty-nine years. She was a lifelong and devoted member of the Christian Church. Mr. McKinney was married next, in 1871, to Mary E. Grissam. Jennie, William W., Jr., Elizabeth and Naomi are the children. Both parents are members of the Christian Church. Robert H., our subject, is a farmer and stock dealer. He owns 100 acres of improved land under good cultivation. He raises wheat, corn, tobacco and grass. He has been quite successful in business and has an encouraging outlook. He was married November 11, 1869, to Miss Melissa L. Shelton, daughter of N. J. and Polly Shelton, the former late of this county. They were honored and worthy citizens. N. J., the father, died June 20, 1876, aged fifty-eight years. The mother is still livi g in this county. The father was, and the mother still is a worthy and devoted member of the Baptist Church. The marriage of R. H. and M. L. McKinney was blessed in the birth of one child—William Henry—an interesting and lovely boy, who departed this life October 3, 1875, at the age of five years. His sickness lasted only three days. Both parents have been acceptable members of the Christian Church for many years.

DANIEL MORGAN was born December 23, 1796, in Chatham County, N. C. His parents were William and Milla (Brewer) Morgan, both natives of the same State. They both died of a fever the same day in 1804. They are buried on Hall River, N. C. Our subject came to Christian County, Ky., in 1805, with his grandfather and uncle—Nathaniel and George Brewer. Daniel is one of the two oldest men in this part of the county, James Wilke being the other. Father Morgan had five brothers. These brothers never lived together after the death of their father, and so far as known, he is the only brother living. He was the second child, and started without means. He now owns 500 acres of land, which he has divided among his children. He was married to Abarilla Martin, of this county, November 18, 1817. She died in 1847. She was a member of the Baptist Church. In 1848, he married Rebecca Tucker, of this county. She died in 1860. She was a member of the Baptist Church. She left four children, viz.: William D., James A., Nannie E. and Mary E., all of whom are living. Nannie E. is the wife of Samuel Cowan. Their children are Samuel F. and William D. In 1862 he married Susan Leveritt, of this county, but a native of South Carolina. She died in 1872, aged fifty-seven years. She also was a member of the Baptist Church. Father Morgan has been a member of the Baptist Church the past fifty years, and a Deacon in that church nearly forty years.

JOHN W. MURPHY was born August 26, 1846, in Todd County, Ky. His parents are William and Nancy (Shelton) Murphy, both natives of this State and still living. The father is a member of the Baptist and the mother of the Christian Church. The mother was previously married to Joseph Allison, who departed this life in November, 1836. By him she had four children. Our subject began for himself at the age of twenty-one. His start was one horse. Farming has always been his business. He is now comfortably situated and owns 100 acres of land located one mile from Kirkmansville. About sixty acres of this land is well improved. Considering his small start he has been quite successful in business. He holds the office of School Trustee. He served ten months in the Confederate Army. He was married, in 1871, to Miss Vashti Martin, of this county. These parents have had seven children, two of whom died in infancy. The surviving children are, viz.: William I., Charles L., Lulu O., James A. and Frances M. Mr. Murphy is a member of the Christian, and Mrs. Murphy of the Baptist Church.

CHARLES M. POWELL was born March 19, 1823, in Todd County. He is a son of Levi and Nancy (Brewer) Powell. The father was born in North Carolina; he died in 1856, aged seventy. The Mother was born in Virginia; she died in 1854, aged seventy. In about 1818 the family came to this country, and settled at Blue Lick Fork; after a few years they moved to Kirkmansville Precinct, where the parents died. Charles M. then bought out the heirs and carried on this farm till January, 1872, when he came to his present locality. Mr. Powell began life without a dollar, and by perseverance, industry, and strict attention to business, he has acquired a competency. He has owned over a 1,000 acres of land, a portion of which he has given to his children; he now ownes where he resides 200 acres of land, also a grist and saw-mill, also 187 acres elsewhere in this precinct, and fifty-seven acres at the Blue Lick Fork. He was married in 1844 to Mary Shelton. She was born in this county. These parents have had nine children, seven of whom are living. They are life-long and devoted members of the Baptist Church.

PINKNEY POWELL was born August 1, 1829. His parents were Isaac and Tebithie (Lacey) Powell, both natives of North Carolina. The father came to this county sixty-four years ago. He is still living at the advanced age of eighty-eight years. The mother died in 1864, at the age of about seventy years. These parents were for many years members of the Mount Tabor Baptist Church. Our subject began for himself at the age of twenty years. He knows exactly how every dollar of his wealth came, as he has earned it by hard labor and good management. He now owns 450 acres of land besides live stock. He has been very successful in business. He was married in 1849 to Miss Lettie Shelton of this county. Twelve children have blessed this union, of whom the following are living : Julia A., Betsey J., Melinda M., Isaac S., Virginia E., Mary O., John H., Lorenza J., William M., Pinkney A. The parents and five of the children are members of the Baptist Church. Mr. Powell is well respected in his county. He has a comfortable home and happy surroundings. Betsey J. is the wife of John Powell. They have five children. Julia A. is the wife of James Williams. They have three children. Melinda M. is the wife of George Henderson. They have four children. Isaac S. married Mary J. Cowan, and is the father cf three children. Mary O. is the wife of Fatal Daniel. John H. married Emiline Cowan. They have four children.

JOHN M. RICE, farmer and miller, was born in 1845, in Muhlenberg County, Ky. His parents, M. M. and S. A. Rice, were born in Kentucky. The father is a farmer, living in Muhlenburg County, at the age of sixty-six years. He is a member of the Cumberland Presbyterian Church. The mother died in 1872, at the age of forty-five years. She also was a member of the Cumberland Presbyterian Church. These parents had four boys and five girls, eight of whom are now living and members of the church. Our subject on arriving at majority, began for himself at farming. He still continues in that business. He sold goods for himself in Kirkmansville for two years. He farmed in Texas in 1879–80, making two crops of cotton, corn and wheat. He went to Texas more especially on account of health. On regaining that he returned and has been running his mill and farm ever since. He has been quite successful in business. He now owns 100 acres of land, besides a town residence and mill property. He has been very successful and has an encouraging outlook. He was married October, 1866, to Miss Mary A. Butler of this county. Benjamin B., John H. and Eura are their children. Both parents and two children are members of the Methodist Episcopal Church South.

PRESLEY B. ROBINSON, Postmaster of Kirkmansville, was born May 3, 1844, in Christian County, Ky. His parents were Harvey and Elizabeth (Thompson, Grant) Robinson, both natives of Christian County, Ky. The father was a farmer and a highly respected pioneer settler of his county. He with his wife were devoted members of the Baptist Church.

The mother died August, 1845, at the age of thirty-one years. The father died November 25, 1876, aged sixty-nine years. Our subject began for himself without anything in the way of finances, at the age of nineteen years. He began farming and continued that sixteen years. He then began in the mercantile business in a store in Kirkmansville, styled "P. B. Robinson's Store." He continued in that business five years, when he sold to Mr. Gates. He continues in the store clerking, and serving as Postmaster. He owns one among the nicest dwellings in the town, also ten acres of ground with the store-house and lot. He is a successful business man and his outlook encouraging. He was married October 19, 1864, to Miss Eliza A. Griffin, of this county. James H., Frank T. and Carrie T. are their children. Both parents are members of the Christian Church. Mr. Robinson is a member of the Masonic order.

DR. VIRGIL T. SHELTON, practicing physician in Kirkmansville, Ky., was born November 7, 1836, in Todd County, Ky. His parents are Crispin and Polly B. (Dodd) Shelton. His father is a native of Kentucky and a resident of Todd County since his seventh year. He is now a farmer, of robust health, in his seventy-seventh year. Dr. Shelton's mother is still living at the age of sixty-six years, with powers of mind and body well preserved. These parents had seven children, five of whom are now living. His brothers, W. Ira and W. Bell, are practicing physicians. Two brothers are farmers in Kentucky. Dr. Shelton worked on the farm and gained the rudiments of education until his fifteenth year, when he began teaching school and studying medicine, which he continued for five years. He then went into the Keokuk, Iowa, Hospital where he remained four years. He subsequently formed a partnership with Dr. S. L. Comer, and three years later removed to Greenville, Ill., where he remained twelve years. He then removed to St. Louis where he practiced two years, and then removed to Kirkmansville, where he has been eminently successful in his practice. Mr. Shelton is a graduate of the Iowa State University, and notwithstanding the exacting demands of a large practice, has maintained his love for and study of the literature of the day. He was an active member in the Illinois State Medical Association, and still continues his lively interest in the advance of his profession. He was married, in 1856, to Miss B. J. Hearn, of this county. Seven children have resulted from this union : John F. (deceased),

Egwert T., Ira D. (daughter), George W. (deceased), Vivian T., Juliette, Vituria T. The last three live at home. Egwert and Ira are at Alton, Ill.; the former a miller, and the latter, a teacher in the city schools. She is a teacher of five years' experience, and has a good reputation as a successful instructor.

GEORGE SIMONS was born March 28, 1841, in Todd County, Ky. His parents were George and Susan (Allison) Simons. The father died November, 1869, aged sixty-five years. The mother was born in Virginia in 1803, and is now living with her son James H. They were among the earliest settlers of the county. In 1861, George enlisted in Company D, Twenty-fifth Regiment United States Infantry, and afterward consolidated with the Seventeenth Regiment. He served three years and three months. He took part in the battles of Shiloh, Chickamauga, Missionary Ridge, the Atlanta campaign and others. While in the army he contracted a disease from which he is a continuous sufferer, and will be more or less all his life. He was married May 7, 1865, to Martha Rager of this county. Four children—Amos, aged eighteen years; Inus, aged sixteen years; Andrew, aged fourteen and Oren, aged seven years—have blessed this union. Four years after marriage they moved to Missouri where they remained five years. They then moved to Illinois where they stayed nine months. In 1875 they returned to Todd County and located on his present farm, consisting of 127 acres; about fifty acres of this farm are improved. This improvement was done by Mr. Simons himself.

K. L. TERRY was born December 29, 1841, in Muhlenburg County, Ky. William A. and Elizabeth (Hay) Terry were his parents. The father was a native of Virginia, the mother of North Carolina. The father was a farmer; his death occurred in 1844, aged twenty-four years. The mother is still living at the age of sixty-six years; the parents were members of the Baptist Church. These parents had two children, K. L. and William B. The latter is a druggist in Princeton, Ky. K. L. began for himself at the age of twenty-six. Previously he had assisted his mother on a farm. He enlisted October 1, 1861, in Company K., Eleventh Kentucky Regiment, United States Infantry. He participated in the battles of Shiloh, Stone River, Rural Hill, and the 100-days battle or Atlanta campaign. His discharge dates December 17, 1864, having served three years two mo..ths and seventeen days.　He was afflicted by being vaccinated by "virus vaccine" and did but little army service afterward, except keeping records and official duties as First Sergeant of the company.　The effects of that "doctored vaccine" are till carried by Mr. Terry and will be through life.　On returning from the army he worked on the farm for his mother until 1867, since which time he has been doing for himself.　He was elected Constable in Muhlenburg County, Ky., which office he held from 1875 to 1879; he kept a boarding house in Greenville from 1879 to 1881, since which time he has been farming, and meeting with moderate success.　He is nicely located on what is known as "the bend."　He was married first in October, 1867, to Miss Laura E. Martin of Muhlenburg County.　To Mr. and Mrs. Terry were born two children viz.: Mary A. and Bettie B.　Mrs. Terry died September, 1875, aged twenty-six years.　She was a member of the Baptist Church. Mr. Terry was next married January 22, 1878, to Miss Dicey A. McKinney, of this county.　Gano E. and William Mc. are their children.　Both parents are members of the Baptist Church.　Mr. Terry is also a member of the Masonic order.

LEVI TUCKER was born March 13, 1828, in Todd County, Ky. His parents were Joshua and Betsey (Powell) Tucker, both natives of North Carolina.　The father was a farmer, and died March 3, 1884, at the age of eighty-six years.　The mother died many years since; she was a member of the Baptist Church.　Our subject on reaching his majority began for himself without a dollar.　He has raised a large family and now owns nearly 400 acres of land; success has attended his labors.　He is well known and duly respected in his precinct; he was married in 1849 to Miss Mary Powell of this county.　James and Mary Powell were her parents.　To Mr. and Mrs. Tucker were born six children, viz, Matilda, Urzula, Beriah M., James J., Mary E. and Delia J.　All the children are living with their parents at home.　Matilda is a member of the Baptist Church.

JAMES A. UTLEY was born in 1851, in Muhlenburg County, Ky. His parents were William J. and Caroline (Vinston) Utley, both natives of Kentucky.　The father was a farmer.　His death occurred in 1854, aged thirty-six.　He was a member of the Baptist Church.　The mother died of typhoid fever, the same disease which proved fatal to her husband, her death occurring two weeks later than that of her husband. Her age was thirty-two. She also was a member of the Baptist Church. These parents left two children—Fannie F., now the wife of George M. Bobbitt, and James A. The latter began for himself at the age of eighteen years. He ran a saw-mill for seven years, principally for Miller & Robinson. He then began farming, which business has engaged his attention ever since. He has been very successful in business considering that he began without means. In this county he owns 205 acres of land. In Muhlenburg County he controls 208 acres. He has a nice home and a happy and encouraging prospect. He is one of the responsible, well-to-do men of the county. He was married January, 1874, to Miss Martha A. Shutt, daughter of Jefferson and Angeline Shutt, of Muhlenburg County, Ky. Floyd R. is their child. Mr. Shutts' death occurred July 8, 1860, aged thirty-five years. Mrs. Shutts' death occurred July 5, 1861, aged twenty-eight years. Both were members of the Christian Church. Mr. and Mrs. Utley are members of the Baptist Church. Mr. Utley is a member of the Masonic order.

SHARON GROVE PRECINCT.

T. W. GALBRAITH was born in Tennessee, December 27, 1858, and is the son of W. G. and L. A. (Morton) Galbraith, also natives of Tennessee. W. G. Galbraith was educated in his native State; is a mechanic and has followed his trade in connection with farming, which latter is his principal occupation. He lived for two years in Kansas and also two or three years in Illinois, but at present resides in his native State. T. W. Galbraith, our subject, received a good education in Kentucky, to which State he immigrated when quite young. He was engaged on the farm until 1877, when he engaged in the dry goods and grocery business near Sharon Grove, in which he remained until August, 1883, when he closed out. In February, 1884, he embarked in the drug trade at Sharon Grove, and is now doing a good business there. He is a devoted member of the Methodist Episcopal Church South and is one of the leading business and influential young men of the county.

G. E. PORTER was born in Todd County, Ky., July 17, 1861, and is a son of W. R. H. and Anna (Dowdy) Porter—the former a native of Kentucky and the latter a native of Mississippi. W. R. H. Porter was reared and educated in Todd County. He has followed farming, his principal occupation, all his life, with the exception of some seven or eight years, when he was engaged in the mercantile trade. He is now living in Elkton District engaged in farming. He has filled the office of Constable. He is a member of the subordinate lodge of the I. O. O. F. at Elkton, and he and wife are devoted members of the Baptist Church. G. E. Porter, the subject of our sketch, received a good education in youth. He remained with his parents until about the age of twenty-three, when he left home, going to Nashville, Ill., where he worked at the carpenter's trade six months; he then returned to Todd County, Ky., where he engaged in business in a store of general merchandise at Trout's Cross Roads, where he is doing a thriving business. He is one of the prominent business men and influential citizens of the district and county.

W. H. SARVER, son of Henry and Mary O. (Rice) Sarver, was born in Sumner County, Tenn., near Gallatin, March 1, 1835. His father was a native of North Carolina and of German-Scotch descent. His mother was a native of Tennessee and of Scotch origin. His father was educated at the pioneer schools of his day. In early life, by his own natural abilities, he became a skillful millwright and followed this calling in connection with farming. During his life he owned several mills; at one time two mills, a carding machine and pottery, doing an extensive business. He was a member of the Masonic order, the lodge meeting at his house for a number of years. Both Mr. and Mrs. Sarver were devoted members of the Methodist Episcopal Church South. He was one of the noted campers at Fountain Head camp-meeting ground. W. H. Sarver received an excellent education in his native State and graduated at the University of Medicine at Nashville, Tenn., in 1856. He began the practice of his profession in Logan County, Ky., in 1856, and remained there until 1871; from there he went to Montgomery County, Tenn., remained some six years and then removed to Sharon Grove in Todd County, Ky., where he now resides, and practices his profession, in which he is very successful. He is also largely engaged in tobacco and live stock. He was married August 6, 1857, to Miss Fannie S., daughter of William F. Gaines, and a native of Tennessee. Six children bless their union—two sons and four daughters—all of whom are living. The Doctor is a member of the Blue Lodge, A. F. & A. M., No. 177, at Adairville, Logan Co., Ky. Both Mr. and Mrs. Sarver are devoted members of the Christian Church. He is a Democrat in politics and one of the leading citizens and prominent physicians of the county.

F. H. SEARS was born December 25, 1814, in Todd County, and on this farm. He is the son of William and Susan M. (Howks) Sears. The father was born on the Potomac River, Va., in 1779; he died May 28, 1852. He came to Logan County, Ky., with his parents in 1792. There he was married, and in February, 1804, came to this farm. He died May 28, 1852. The mother was born in Frederickstown, Md.; her death occurred April 19, 1867, aged seventy-one. Our subject was born and reared on this farm, which he owns, consisting of 222 acres, and is the oldest resident in this precinct. He was married January 18, 1837, to Louisa J. Driscoll; she was born in Livingston County, Ky., March 10,

1820 ; this marriage was blessed with nine children—five living : James, John W., Jefferson R., Susan N., and Frank P. Mrs. and Mrs. Sears are members of the Cumberland Presbyterian Church.

W. B. SHELTON, by occupation a physician, was born in Todd County, Ky., October 20, 1843, and is a son of Crispin and Polly B. (Dodd) Shelton, both natives of Kentucky—the former of Scotch-Irish and the latter of Irish descent. Crispin Shelton was born August 3, 1807, and his wife was born in 1819. In youth he learned the carpenter's and cooper's trades and followed them in connection with farming, his principal occupation. He has held the office of Jailor of Todd County, and he and wife are devoted members of the Christian Church. W. B. Shelton was reared and educated in his native county, and in 1865, began the study of medicine at Hamilton, Ill. He began the practice of medicine in Greenville, Bond Co., Ill., and was there some two years. He then went to Stanton, in the same State, and remained there some eight years. He then returned to Todd County, Ky., and located in Sharon Grove, where he is doing a leading practice. He was married November 28, 1872, to Alice, daughter of Selby Snell, of Illinois ; four children bless their union : Tillie Bell, Harry Eugene, Charley Crispin and Fanny Jane ; all are living but Harry Eugene. The Doctor was in the Federal Army, in the Eighth Kentucky Cavalry, Company D, under Bristow. He is a member of the A. F. & A. M., No. 587, at Daysville, and the I. O. O. F., No. 67, at Trout's Cross Roads. He and lady are consistent members of the Christian Church. He is a Republican in politics and one of the leading physicians and citizens of the county.

FAIRVIEW PRECINCT.

WILLIAM R. BEARDEN, one of Todd County's leading farmers, tobacco and stock traders, was born January 1, 1833, in Montgomery County, Tenn. He is the second of five children—four boys and one girl —four now living, born to Benjamin B. and Elizabeth (Majors) Bearden, natives of Montgomery County, Tenn., of English descent. The father is the son of William Bearden, born in England; the mother is the daughter of James and Sarah (Weekly) Majors, who was reared in Montgomery County, Tenn. Subject's early educational advantages were poor; he attended school about two years in all, and has by his own efforts succeeded in getting a fair business education; his grandfather Bearden was a farmer; his grandfather Majors, taught school for a considerable time. Subject was reared on the farm and lived with his parents until he attained his majority, when he engaged in farming for himself. He was married April 20, 1858, to Miss Susan M. Norman, of Todd County, Ky., a native of Simpson County, Ky., daughter of William H. and Dorothy (Turnel) Norman, natives of Simpson County, of English origin. Subject had born to him, by this union, two children, both dead; one was named Henry. Mrs. Bearden died February, 1861. On February 2, 1865, subject married Dooha A. Patton, of Todd County, daughter of Robert and Emaline (McKinney) Patton, natives of Virginia and Muhlenburg County, Ky., respectively of English and Irish origin; to this union were born two children—Dorothea A. and Emma. In June, 1870, Mr. Bearden was again left a widower. On November 18, 1874, he was married to Sarah Armstrong, of Todd County, daughter of Charles and Eda (Stinnett) Armstrong.

WILLIAM M. BELL, "Roseheath." The subject of this sketch is a native of Todd County, Ky., and was born in his present residence, June 25, 1840. His father, Rev. Caleb N. Bell, was born in 1788, in Beaufort, N. C.; was an itinerant Methodist preacher in Virginia; removed to Kentucky in 1820, and died here in 1872, having been a useful minister of the Gospel for sixty-two years. He was thrice married, and his children are : Martha A. (Greenfield), John W., Ma:y S. (Clark), Eliza J. (Mills), Caleb M. and subject, who received a classical education t Emery and Henry College, of Virginia. Subject is a farmer by profession, having 300 acres of first-class land near "Bell's Chapel." His brick residen e was built in 1828 by his father, by whom the place was originally clearer and improved. In 1862 Mr. Bell was accidently crippled in such a manner as to disable him for life, and he consequently employs much of his time in literary pursuits, being one of the most extensively read and well posted men in the county. Being unmarried, his fine farm and books claim his chief attention. He is a member of the Grange; in religion is a Methodist, and in politics is identified with the Democratic party. Mr. Bell's portrait appears elsewhere.

COL. M. D. BROWN is a native of Christian County, Ky., born March 15, 1838, the youngest member of the famous Brown family, which consisted of fifteen children, twelve of whom lived to be grown. His parents were Thomas and Rebecca (Stuart) Brown. He was reared on the farm, and had in his early career no advantages of an education, and through life has relied on his own individual efforts to attain positions of social worth and of business prominence. A considerable portion of his time, since he attained the age of seventeen, has been spent as a teacher in the schools of this vicinity and also in Illinois, and many certificates granted him by the State Board and other examining Boards of Education attest his ability and scholistic proficiency as a public instructor. During war times he acted as recruiting officer, and captained a small company of calvary in the Confederate ranks. He was appointed a Colonel by Gov. Blackburn, and holds a commission as Colonel in the State militia and as aid-de-camp to the Governor. Returning from the war the Colonel took up his residence in Todd County, giving some attention to farming pursuits, but, taking up the study of law, his energies were bent in the interest of his new calling, and removing to Fairview about 1873, he was soon afterward admitted to the bar at Elkton, and given legal access to the higher courts of the State. He has served as Police Judge of Fairview for several terms, and in 1876 and 1880 was a Democratic Presidential Elector. He married, in 1862, Miss Sallie A. Daniel. The family consists of seven children: Hollie F., Minnie T., Lenna D., Mattie R., Mittie R., Littie R. and Arthur D.

CHARLES C. BRUMFIELD, one of Todd County's enterprising young farmers, was born on March 11, 1856, in Christian County, Ky., and is the third of five children—three boys and two girls—born to Wiley N. and Pernecy (Wood) Brumfield, natives of Virginia, and Christian County, Ky., respectively, of English descent. Subject's father was married twice, his first wife having been Margaret (Watwood) Brumfield, by whom he had six children—four boys and two girls—five now living. Subject was reared on a farm ; his parents died when he was quite young, his mother on November 23, 1861, his father on February 11, 1863. Subject received a good common-school education and made his home with his half brother till he became of age, when he commenced the struggle of life for himself, farming and attending school. He attended school at Trenton, Todd County, for one year and a half. He taught school near Kirkmansville in 1879 and 1880 ; was census enumerator of Kirkmansville District in 1880. Subject married, January 14, 1880, Alice J. Brumfield, of Todd County, Ky., daughter of Edmond and Verdilla (Canon) Brumfield, natives of Virginia and Tennessee respectively, of English descent. Subject and wife's people are among the first settlers of Todd County. This union is blessed with two children—Dennie and Vader. Subject's grandfather was James Brumfield.

THOMAS J. CAMP, farmer, was born June 15, 1851, in Todd County, Ky., and is the third of nine children born to William and Emily (Lewis) Camp, natives respectively of Hart and Todd Counties, Ky., of English descent. His early advantages for an education were poor, never having attended school for more than three months in all. He was reared on a farm and lived with his parents until of age, when he started in life for himself at farming. He was married on May 28, 1873, to Mary Annis McClelland, of Todd County, a native of Christian County, and a daughter of John and Hannah (Donoho) McClelland, natives of Christian County, Ky., and Sumner County, Tenn., respectively, of English descent. To Mr. and Mrs. Camp were born three children— John Thomas, William H. and Tina May. Subject lives with his mother-in-law on 126 acres of land. He and wife are members of the Presbyterian Church. Mrs. Camp's grandparents were David McClelland and Dimos Donoho.

BENJAMIN DOWNER was born August 10, 1819, in Todd

County, Ky., and has continued to reside here to the present time. He is the son of Benjamin Downer, Sr., a native of Spottsylvania County, Va., where he was born in 1782, and in 1809 removed to Todd County, then a part of Christian County, Ky., where he died in 1826. His wife, Elizabeth, daughter of John S. Slaughter (of Revolutionary fame), was born in Culpeper County, Va., in 1782, and died in Todd County, Ky., in 1862. From this union sprang Susan (Eddins), Frances (married first to Clark and afterward to Bradshaw), John S., William W., Mary S. (Lackey), Ellen (Casky), subject, Elizabeth (Hutchinson), Henrietta (Gibson), Adaline (Reno) and Julia (Hancock). Subject's early educational advantages were such as the schools of the community afforded in his youth, but he has greatly improved his opportunities by careful reading of standard works and current literature. On December 20, 1847, he was married to Miss Emily L., daughter of John and Frances (Thompson), Pendleton, of Christian County, Ky., and to them were born William K. (dead), Addie, Frank N., James W., Lizzie, John P., Carrie, Emily L. and Benjamin R. Mr. D. is a farmer, owning 337 acres of very good land in first-class condition, and in fine state of cultivation. In religion he is a Methodist, in politics a Republican, and was a Union man during the late war.

JOHN S. DOWNER, son of Benjamin Sr. and Elizabeth (Slaughter) Downer, was born in Woodville, Culpeper Co., Va., June 19, 1809 ; married Miss Elizabeth W. Cabaniss (daughter of George L. and Catherine Cabaniss), at Princeton, Ky., November 19, 1832; died while on a visit to his son, L. A. Downer, of Barren County, Ky., February 10, 1873. Subject's mother was a daughter of Col. John Slaughter, of Revolutionary days. John S. was one of eleven children who arrived at maturity, and when but a child was brought by his parents to Christian County, Ky. At an early age he evinced a fondness for horticulture ; this culminated in after years in his becoming an eminent pomologist and nurseryman, in which capacity he did valuable service in correcting the nomenclature of fruits, as well as producing and introducing new varieties. Though a great lover of flowers, and a thorough botanist, he gave most attention to apples, peaches, and strawberries, of which the popular Charles Downing and Kentucky strawberries are results of his labor. He was a ready and forcible writer, and was favorably known throughout the United States by pomologists, and was highly esteemed among his own people. To him and wife were born four children, all now living. The eldest, Lerond A., married Miss Mary E. Bradley, and had six children, viz.: Jennie, Maude, John S. Jr., Lela, Louis B. and Bert. The second, Preston E. (see sketch). The third child and only daughter, Cloantha E. married Aaron F. Williams and had five children, all girls, viz.: Bessie (who married Thomas W. Long), Jennie (who married Thomas Rodman), Ida D., Cloe and Sada. His fourth was Robert W. (see sketch). In religion our subject was a Baptist, and during the rebellion was loyal to the stars and stripes.

PRESTON E. DOWNER, Fairview. The subject of this sketch is a native of Todd county, Ky., having been born near the place of his present residence, September 22, 1837. He is the son of John S. and Elizabeth (Cabaniss) Downer. In youth he was favored with a good English education, and is an extensive reader, especially of pomological works and literature. On December 10, 1863, he was united in marriage to Miss Mary E., daughter of John S. and Angelina (Sasseen) Long of Todd County, and to them have been born three children: Nonnie, born November 14, 1870; Leslie, born August 8, 1873, died August 8, 1874; and Robert J., born February 22, 1875. Mrs. Downer was born October 21, 1839. Subject is a farmer and nurseryman, owning 600 acres of valuable land, and the firm of Downer & Bro. sell extensively in different States. He is a Baptist and a Democrat.

ROBERT W. DOWNER, son of John S. and Elizabeth W. Downer, was born February 3, 1843, on the place where he now resides in Todd County, Ky. Subject was married January 29, 1867, to Miss Sada K. daughter of Rev. Robert and Jane A. (Fuqua) Williams, of McCracken County, Ky., and to them was born one child—Preshie (deceased). Subject is a nurseryman by profession, and together with his brother, is extensively engaged in the nursery business, under the firm name of Downer & Brother, successors to their father, who established the business in 1834. They have at all times eighty acres of nursery stock, and graft or bud annually over 250,000 apple, 200,000 peaches, 20,000 pears, 15,000 plums, 10,000 cherries, with small fruit, ornamental trees, and other things in proportion. He is also a farmer, owning 550 acres of very valuable land in a high state of cultivation. In religion he is a Baptist and in politics a Democrat.

BENJAMIN D. EDDINS was born in Todd County, Ky., November 4, 1841, where he still retains his residence, though about one-third of his farm lies in Christian County. His father, Dulany Eddins, was born August 14, 1800, in Orange County, Va., and died in Todd County, Ky., July 24, 1864. He was a member of the Bethel Baptist Church. The family are thought to have been of Scotch origin. Subject's mother, Susan S. Downer, of Culpeper County, Va., was born June 14, 1806, and died in Todd County, February 11, 1874. Her grandfather, Col. John Slaughter, of the Revolutionary war, was a grandson of Francis Slaughter, who settled in Orange County, Va., prior to 1730. Subject was educated at the select schools in the neighborhood, until the war seriously interfered with the prosecution of his studies. He has read many good books, and is also well versed in the current literature of the day. By vocation he is a farmer, owning 300 acres of valuable and productive land, which he manages with success in the cultivation of tobacco, wheat, corn and stock, and it has been remarked by his neighbors that the products of his farm command the highest market price. He was married, October 1, 1874, to Miss Clara M., daughter of Rev. Samuel Baker, D. D., of Russellville, Ky. She was a graduate of the Evansville, Ind., High School, and died July 2, 1875. Subject is a member of the Blue Lodge, and of the Moore Chapter of Royal Arch Masons, of Fairview, Ky. He is also a member of the Grange; and while the organization existed, was a Good Templar. In religion he is connected with the Bethel Missionary Baptist Church, and affiliates with the Democratic party in politics.

JOHN R. FINCH was born in Caswell County, N. C., in 1820, and came with his parents to Todd County, Ky., in 1839, where he still retains his residence. His father, Adam Finch, the son of John, was born in Charlottesville, Va.; was a soldier in the war of 1812, and died here in 1860, at the age of eighty-five years. His wife, Jennie (Ruder), died in 1870, aged eighty years. To them were born Richard, subject, Elizabeth (Massie) and William. Subject's educational advantages were limited, but he is a constant reader of current literature. He has never married. Mr. Finch is engaged in the profession of farming, owning 1,000 acres of valuable land in a high state of cultivation. He is also a dealer in livestock. Politically, he is a Democrat.

JOHN W. FULCHER was born September 13, 1826, in Goochland County, Va.; removed with his parents to Lexington, Ky., in 1831, and to Todd County in 1832, where he still resides. His father, Dr. Alexander Fulcher, was born in Richmond, Va., 1791; was a soldier in the war of 1812, and died at this place in 1853. He was the son of Philip Fulcher, of Virginia, who served seven years in the war of Independence, and died about 1828. Alexander's wife was Sallie B., daughter of Tavnor W. Wisdom, of Spottsylvania County, Va., born in 1796, and died in 1873. To them were born: Joseph J., Emily W., George W., subject, Lucy A. (Fulcher), Caroline A. (Nelson) and Alexander. Subject's education was limited, but he has greatly improved his opportunities by constant reading. He was married, October 15, 1850, to Miss Lizzie H., daughter of Edward C. and Lucy G. (Wisdom) Humber, of Montgomery County, Tenn. He has 214 acres of good land, in a high state of cultivation. In religion he is a Baptist, and politically was an Old-Line Whig.

JAMES H. HALL was born September 28, 1848, in Todd County, Ky., where he has always resided. His father, John E. Hall, was born in 1824, in West Virginia, and died in Texas in 1879; and mother, Mary E., daughter of Mrs. S. A. Tandy, of Todd County, Ky., was born February 29, 1828, and died May 18, 1849. To them was born one child, our subject, who is engaged in farming, successfully cultivating corn, wheat, tobacco, and raising and dealing in stock. Subject was married, June 28, 1871, to Miss Henrietta, daughter of Maj. Levi and Martha A. (Layne) Darnall, of Todd County, and to them have been born Annie and William Davis. Maj. Darnall was a soldier in the war of 1812. He was born September 20, 1795, and was the descendant of an old and wealthy English family, who emigrated from the mother country with their kinsman, Lord Baltimore, in 1629, bringing with them the material for the erection of their ancestral halls, built at what was then known as the Old Wood Yard, on the banks of the Potomac, where they remained in good preservation till 1862, when they were destroyed by fire. After having amassed quite a fortune, he moved to Todd County—then Christian—in 1847, where he married and resided till his death, September 23, 1873. John E. Hall's father was Edward Hall, an early settler in Todd County. Subject is a Baptist and his wife a Presbyterian.

JOHN H. HINKLE, one of Todd County's intelligent and enterprising young farmers, was born December 12, 1849, in White County, Tenn. He is the third of four children, two boys and two girls, born to Isaac N. and Martha C. (Holland) Hinkle, natives of Georgia and White Covnty, Tenn., respectively. The father was of German and the mother of Welsh-English descent. The father moved first to Tennessee and then to Christian County, Ky., about the year 1854. Two years later he moved to Todd County, where he was very successful. He died in 1874, at about the age of sixty years. He was the son of John and Sara (Smith) Hinkle, natives respectively of Germany and England. Subject's mother was the daughter of John and Mary (Lewis) Holland, of English and Welsh origin. Subject received a fair common school education; was reared on a farm; lived with his parents during their lifetime; moved where he now lives in December, 1879, and purchased 106 acres of land, seventy-five of which are in a good state of cultivation. His house is located about one-half mile off Pilot Rock. With the exception of one year, 1883, engaged in the mercantile business at Greenbriar Station, Tenn., Mr. Hinkle has always been connected with farming. By his integrity, good management and industry, he has made life a success and is a highly respectable citizen.

JOHN HOLLAND, retired, was born February 4, 1799, in Cabell County, W. Va. He is the fifth in a family of eleven children born to Michael and Aggie (Ward) Holland. The father was a millwright and farmer; he died in 1825, aged about sixty-five. The mother died in 1810, aged about forty. John and a brother are the only survivors of this family. John came to Todd County in February, 1820, and located in Sharon Grove, where he remained two years, after which he moved to Pond River and remained one year. He then returned to Sharon Grove and there stayed eight years. In 1831 he came to his present locality. He then bought 100 acres and has since added until he now owns 240 acres, about 150 of which are improved. His sight has been failing him the past ten years; he is now totally blind. He was married November 20, 1821, to Mary Tharp Humphrey. She died February 11, 1879, aged seventy-eight years. These parents were members of the Baptist Church. They had six children, all of whom are deceased. Mrs. Holland was daughter of James and Elizabeth (Hopper) Humphrey, natives of Virginia. Father Holland has been a credit to his generation. He forms a link which binds the past to the present; he is richly deserving such an eulogy as should be given to the faithful, tried and true.

GEORGE W. JESUP. The gentleman whose name appears at the head of this sketch is one of the active, energetic and naturally intelligent citizens of Todd County, Ky. He is a native of Fayette County, in this State, where he was born February 10, 1823, and in 1829 removed with his parents to Todd County, where he has since resided. His father, Col. Samuel B. Jesup, was born in Orange County, Va.; immigrated to Kentucky in 1793; was a gallant soldier in the war of 1812; was once a member of the House of Representatives, and eight years a member of the Senate of Kentucky, and died in 1866 at the age of seventy-three years. His father, James E. Jesup, was an Englishman, and his brother, Gen. Thomas S. Jesup, is well known in history. Subject's mother, Catherine, daughter of Jacob Cidner, of Bourbon County, Ky., was born in 1796, and died in 1872. To her and Samuel B. Jesup, her husband, were born : Eliza A. (Yancey), W. Thomas, Margaret J. (wife of Dr. Tandy), James E., subject, Caroline (Cash) and Virginia (Crouch). Subject's educational advantages were limited, but he has long been a reading man. On April 30, 1857, Mr. Jesup was married to Miss Susan, daughter of Richard and Mary (Mosley) Brame, of Christian County, Ky. Subject is a farmer, owning 250 acres of very valuable and productive land (a part of the Croghan Grove tract) in a high state of cultivation, and in fine condition, which he successfully cultivates in the staple products of the country. In politics he is identified with the Democratic party.

WILLIAM H. JESUP. The gentleman whose name appears at the head of this sketch is a resident of "Jesup's Grove," (formerly known as "Croghan's Grove," in honor of the famous "Hero of Sandusky," who entered this land). Mr. Jesup was born near this place, April 26, 1843, and at the commencement of the late war, entered Company H, First Kentucky Cavalry, in which he served two years. In 1867 he engaged in the tobacco business here and at New York, in which he continued seven years. His father, William W. Jesup, was born in 1796 in Washington County, Ky., served in the war of 1812 and died in 1844. His father's brothers were Gen. Thomas S. Jesup (son-in-law to Maj. Croghan), and Col. Samuel B. Their father, James

E. Jesup, was scalped and left for dead by the Indians, but recovered again. William W. Jesup's children are: Judith (Rodgers), Ann O. (Layne), John F., Virginia E. (Danforth), Sarah F. (Hollingsworth), Caledonia (Talkington), and subject, who was favored with a good English education. His mother is Sarah H., daughter of William Martin, of South Carolina, born in 1812, and is now drawing a pension. Subject was married, February 6, 1872, to Miss Nannie M., daughter of Chiles and Mary (Hutchinson) Barker, of Christian County, Ky., and to them have been born Barker and Sallie C. Subject is by profession a farmer, owning 600 acres of first-class land in fine condition and high state of cultivation; and is also a successful live-stock dealer. On his place is one grove of 100 acres, on which are many thousands of stately sugar maples. Mr. Jesup is a prosperous and successful man.

SAMUEL H. JONES, an enterprising farmer of Todd County, was born April 15, 1827, in Christian County, Ky. He is the youngest of ten children, five boys and five girls, born to Amos and Barbara (Henderson) Jones, natives of Chatham County, N. C. His father was of Welsh-German and his mother of English descent. Our subject's early educational advantages were poor, never having attended school but ten months in all; he has by hard work been able to acquire a good business education. He was reared on a farm, and lived with his parents till their death. His mother died in November, 1844; his father January, 1851. Samuel H. (our subject), was married January 21, 1851, to Mary Jane Wilkins, daughter of John and Mary (Marrow) Wilkins, the former of Irish and the latter of Scotch descent, natives of North Carolina and Kentucky, respectively. This union was blessed with two children: John H. and Martha Jane; the latter married M. W. Martin. Mrs. Jones died in May, 1855. She was a member of the Methodist Episcopal Church. March 31, 1864, subject was married to Mrs. Mary McColpin, of Todd County, daughter of John and Martha (Lacy) Lindsey. (See biography of Romulus A. Lindsey as to genealogy.) This union was blessed with seven children: Amanda B., Louella, Cornelia, Charles D., living; Elizabeth, Lotta and Barbara, deceased. Mr. Jones takes a great interest in the education of his children. Since his marriage he has always resided in Todd County. He owns fifty-eight acres of land, and he and wife are members, respectively, of the Christian and Baptist Churches.

Mr. Jones is considered one of the live and wide-awake men of his community, and is well respected.

ELIJAH N. JONES, a prominent and enterprising citizen of Todd County, was born October 26, 1837, in Fairview District, Todd County, Ky. He is the second of thirteen children—five boys and eight girls—ten still living, born to Isaac H. and Anna (Wilkins) Jones, natives of Indiana and Todd County, Ky., respectively, the mother of Irish descent. Subject's early advantages for an education were poor; he attended school about two years in all. He was reared on the farm and lived with his parents till his marriage on December 23, 1858, to Miss Harriet A. Lindsey, of Todd County, daughter of John and Martha (Johnson) Lindsey. Ten children were born to this union : Martha Jane, now the wife of T. M. Harned, William H., Lucy B. (deceased), Mary A., the wife of L. D. Brusher, Cittie A., Ida E., Thomas E., Hattie E. (deceased), Dora May and Daisy. Mr. and Mrs. Jones are members of the Baptist Church. The former has been clerk of the church for the past ten years; has also been Deputy County Clerk by appointment for about fourteen years. He located after his marriage where he now resides on fifty acres of land given him by his father. He has had uniform success during life ; he now owns 330 acres, 200 in a good state of cultivation. The land was timber. By his own hand he has cleared and raised it to its present condition. Mr. Jones has made all by his own industry and is a highly respected citizen and neighbor. His grandparents, on both sides, were among the first settlers of Christian and Todd Counties, Ky.

THE KENNEDY FAMILY. In the year 1809 Michael Kennedy, Eleanor (McCaffrey) Kennedy his wife, and their six children : Thomas, William, James, Betsey, Paulina and Urban E. removed from Lincoln County, Ky., to Todd County (then Christian). Michael Kennedy was a coppersmith by trade, and was brought up in Dublin, Ireland. He came to America about the beginning of the Revolutionary war, in which he served as a soldier. At the close of that glorious struggle for liberty, he took up his residence in Virginia as a hunter and pioneer, and was there married in 1785. The following year, and shortly after the birth of their first son, the family packed up their small effects, and in company with some thirty other families, set out for the far-famed Kentucky, under the guidance of Gen. William Logan. The journey was made with pack horses, and was necessarily a most fatiguing and dangerous one. The whole country was infested with savages of the worst type, and it was necessary that the little pioneer train should be guarded both day and night by the most vigilant and experienced men of the party. They arrived, however, in safety, and most of the band settled in Lincoln County, near the present site of Stanford, while the Kennedys with a few other families located about eight miles from Logan's Station (now Stanford). The pioneers immediately set about erecting forts and block-houses for their protection. Here the Kennedys resided until 1809, and here their remaining five children were born. At the latter date all removed to Todd County, as before stated. Thomas Kennedy was a house carpenter; went to New Orleans in 1805; studied medicine, became a practicing physician; was a Judge in the courts and died in October, 1837, his wife, Mary (Kellem) Kennedy, following him in November of the same year. They left no children. William and James Kennedy volunteered and served under Gen. Hopkins, in his campaign against the Indians, being engaged at Tippecanoe and Fort Harrison in Indiana. After the war the two brothers located in Gibson County, Ind., where William died September 14, 1815, leaving his wife, Ann (McRee) Kennedy, and two children : Seneca W. and William. Seneca W. died in 1846, having married Mary Petrie, who bore him six children, only one of whom survives—Sarah P.—who married John Feland, of Hopkinsville, Ky. James Kennedy engaged in the horse trade, taking many droves by land and boat to New Orleans and Mobile. He lost his health from much exposure, and went to Hot Springs, Ark., to recuperate, but died there among strangers. Betsey Kennedy married Francis McCarroll, of Montgomery County, Tenn., and reared a large family of children. She died about 1830. Paulina became the second wife of Hazel Petrie. She bore him four children, and died at the age of sixty-nine years. Urban E. Kennedy was apprenticed to the tanner's trade, and served two years under William Hopper, after which he went with his brother James to Mobile, Ala., with a drove of horses, and visited his brother Thomas in Louisiana, who persuaded him to remain with him two years, giving him a captainship on one of his coasting schooners. Here Urban learned to use the compass, and was enabled to make a large amount of money, which was spent, as he himself says, in "foolish sport and high living;"

but it had a good effect upon him, in so far as it caused him to stop and consider his way, which was the means, together with his mother's special prayer, of bringing him into the fold of the Savior, having publicly professed religion in the fall of 1822. March 18, 1823, he married Lavinia Bryan, daughter of Thomas Bryan. She was a very handsome and refined lady, and was highly esteemed for her loving temperament and Christian piety. She died October 13, 1844, the mother of nine children : Angelina, married Rev. J. T. Johnston, a minister of great ability ; James T., married Miss M. Rutherford, daughter of John Rutherford ; Eliza J., married George D. Park ; Urban C., now a resident of Evansville, Ind.; William Mc., died in childhood ; David L., now of Hopkinsville, Ky.; Mary E., widow of the Rev. James H. Nickell; Michael R., served in the Federal Army in the war of the Rebellion, losing an arm at Dallas, Ga.; Theodore F. C., served in the war under Col. Shackelford ; married Kate M. Knight. Urban E. Kennedy afterward married Achsah H. Knight, who bore him four children. Mr. Kennedy was prominently identified with the religious interests of this county, being an active member of the Cumberland Presbyterian Church, from the time of his conversion to that of his lamented death, which occurred April 21, 1879. He was a member of the State Legislature in 1865–67. James T. Kennedy was born October 21, 1825, and has always resided in Todd County. He received his early education here, and has devoted his energies to farming pursuits, having a present farm of 220 acres, located some five miles east of Elkton. He is a member of the Masonic Fraternity. Mr. and Mrs. Kennedy are the parents of seven children : Lavinia J., Hiram A., Thomas H., Elizabeth E. (deceased), Mary E., James M., and Henry R. (deceased). Michael R. Kennedy was born July 22, 1842; obtained his early schooling here, and is a most respected resident of the county. His present farm of 111 acres lies adjoining the old homestead in the Fairview District. He married Miss Belle K. Wilson, and has two children: Nellie M. and Urban R. Mr. Kennedy is a member of the Cumberland Presbyterian Church.

G. W. LATHAM, a wealthy and prominent farmer of Todd County, Ky., is the eldest of six children—three living—born to John and Susan (Brock) Latham, natives of North Carolina and South Carolina, respectively, of English descent. His grandparents on his mother's side were

David and Betsey (Gibson) Brock. Subject's early education was neglected, never having attended school in his life. He was reared on a farm; his father died when he (subject) was but fourteen years old, hence the care of the family devolved upon him. He hired out by the month and worked this way till he was married, September 17, 1849, to Miss Emily L. Gibson, of Todd County, Ky., daughter of Nicholas and L. (West) Gibson, natives of South and North Carolina, respectively, of English descent. Subject had born to him by this union thirteen children, viz.: George N. T. (second), Ledona (now Jones), John W., Fannie S., David S., Emily B. (now Shanklin), Georgiana (deceased), Robert A. (ninth), Richard T. (deceased), Lovina (deceased), Tilford M., Alexander T., Edda J. W. (deceased). Mr. Latham takes a deep interest in the education of his children. After his marriage he commenced farming for himself, and has continued so doing ever since. He is now owner of 750 acres of land, 300 under cultivation, improved with comfortable buildings, etc. Starting in life without a dollar, he has by hard-earned efforts accumulated a fair fortune. He has had charge of the County Farm for ten years. Mr. and Mrs. Latham are members of the Methodist Episcopal Church.

ROMULUS A. LINDSEY, a native of Todd County and an enterprising farmer, was born September 1, 1839. He is the fourth of eleven children—four boys and seven girls—nine now living, born to John and Martha (Johnson) Lindsey, natives of Christian County, Ky., of Irish descent. Subject's father is the son of Archibald and Jane (Meacham) Lindsey, son and daughter respectively of John Lindsey and John and Lucy (Brewer) Meacham. The Lindsey family first emigrated from South Carolina to Virginia, thence to Christian County, Ky., about the year 1805 or 1806, where they entered lands and endured the privations of a life in the wilderness. They were of English descent. The Meacham family came from South Carolina to Christian County about the same time as the Lindsey family. These families established the first mills on Sugar Creek and Little River. Subject of this sketch was reared on a farm ; received a fair common school education. He lived with his parents till the age of twenty-six years, when he was married, January 25, 1865, to Miss Martha E. McColpin, of Todd County, Ky., daughter of Charner and Martha (Jones) McColpin, natives of South Carolina, of

German extraction. This union was blessed with three sons, namely: Frankey E., Thomas H., and John William. Mr. Lindsey takes an interest in giving his children a good common school education. Subject and wife are members of the Baptist Church. Subject's wife's father was a son of Joseph and Nancy McColpin. Subject, after his marriage, first located one and one-half miles east of where he now resides, on what was called the Mabery farm. In 1861 he purchased and located where he now lives, on 135 acres of land, 110 acres in a good state of cultivation, with comfortable buildings and good orchard. Is also the possessor of 180 acres two miles north of where he now lives, on which he lived about seven years. In the fall of 1883 he returned to where he is living, five miles northeast of Fairview. Subject received a legacy of $400 from his father when first married. He has by close application and industry met with uniformly good success during his life. Mr. Lindsey enlisted in defense of his country, August, 1862, in Company A, Eighth Kentucky, under Capt. Samuel Johnson, and Col. Bristow commanding regiment. Participated in several skirmishes, and was discharged on account of disability, May, 1863; returned to active farm life. Has several times been elected and appointed Trustee of his school district. Subject is respected as a good citizen and neighbor.

BARNET McCOLPIN, farmer, was born October 22, 1820, in Todd County, Ky., and is the youngest of seven children born to John and Phebe (Franklin) McColpin, natives of South Carolina. Subject's mother died October 22, 1820; his father about the year 1846. Subject's early educational advantages were not good, though he learned to read and write; he lived on a farm with his uncle and aunt, Joseph and Nancy (Franklin) McColpin, natives of South Carolina, till he became of age, when he began life for himself. He was married in November, 1843, to Nancy Black, of Todd County, daughter of William and Margaret (Armstrong) Black, by whom he had five children: William W., Martha H. (now Carpenter), Mary E. (now Rolston), Margaret Ann and Josephine L. Subject and wife were both members of the Baptist Church. Mrs. McColpin died in March, 1855, and in the fall of 1858 subject married Sarah Hill, of Todd County, daughter of John and Margaret (Gibbs) Hill, by whom he had four children: Nancy J., Sarah R., John D. and Fannie B. Mrs. McColpin is a member of the Baptist Church. Subject owns

206 acres of land in a fair state of cultivation, improved with a comfortable residence and outbuildings. His only ally has been his wife. He has made all his property by careful management and perseverance; he has always enjoyed good health and bids fair to live many years in the community, where he is highly respected.

CHARNER A. McCOLPIN, an enterprising citizen and farmer of Todd County, was born May 25, 1843, on the farm where he now resi !es ; he is the sixth of eleven children—fouɪ girls and seven boys—three boys and three girls now living, born to Charner H. and Martha (Jones) McColpin, natives of North Carolina and of Irish descent. Subject's father was a son of Joseph and Nancy (Franklin) McColpin. Subject received a fair common school education ; he was reared on the farm and lived with his parents till twenty-five years of age, when he engaged in mercantile business ; he spent two years at Bivinsville, Todd County, one year at Elkton, and two in Lovelaceville, Ballard County, Ky. He then returned to farming, which he now continues on 350 acres of land, 175 of which are in cultivation. He was married February 25, 1874, to Bettie A. Stephens, of Graves County, Ky., daughter of Isaac N. and Bettie A. (Wilson) Stephens, natives of Graves County, Ky. The father was a son of Harvey and —— (Washburn) Stephens; the mother a daughter of Samuel and Isabella (Davis) Wilson. This marriage was blessed with five children : Wallace E., Viola, Ora May, Martha E. and Edgar (deceased). Mr. McColpin is a strong advocate of good common schools. He was made a Mason in Lovelaceville Lodge, 157, and is an honorable and upright citizen. He and his wife are both members of the Baptist Church.

ELDER WILLIAM E. MOBLEY. Few among the deserving citizens of Todd County are more worthy, genial and intelligent than the gentleman whose name appears at the head of this brief sketch. He was born in Todd County, Ky., March 2, 1824, and has always retained his residence here. His father, Claburn Mobley, was born near Columbia, S. C., in 1787; removed to middle Tennessee in childhood, thence to Todd County, Ky., about 1807, where he died in 1867. He was the son of William Mobley. Claburn's wife, Elizabeth (Ellison), was born in Georgia, 1795, and died in 1862. Their children are : subject, Nancy (Harris), Reuben J., John F. and Claburn, Jr. In youth, subject was favored with good educational advantages, and is a man of general and extensive reading, especially in the department of theology. He was married in 1849 to Miss Mary E., daughter of Henry T. and Nancy (Daniel) Burrus, of Todd County. She was born in 1825. The result of this union is Mary S. (Kenner), Ella J. (Smith), Luther, Bettie H. and James B. Subject is an honored member of the Masonic fraternity. He has never taken an active part in politics, but was an unequivocal Union man during the late struggle. In 1851 he became a member of the Christian Church, and has been an active and useful factor in that energetic denomination. In 1852 he commenced preaching, and has been pastor of Roaring Springs Church in Trigg County nearly twenty-six years; of Elkton Church about thirty years, and of Berea Church, in Logan County, twenty-four years. These churches have occupied three Sabbaths in each month, and the remainder of the time has been applied to missionary work, somewhat extensive in its nature. Parson Mobley has received many disciples into the church, has married many people, and has once only been hindered from work by sickness.

H. EDGAR MORTON was born on the place where he now resides, November 5, 1835, and has retained his residence here all his life. His father, George, was born in 1795, in Orange County, Va.; removed to Todd County, Ky., about 1832, where he died in 1882. He was the son of John, who was the son of Elijah Morton, of Scotch descent. Subject's mother was Amanda, daughter of Henry and Elizabeth (Adams) Tandy, and to her and husband were born: Ann E., subject, Hulda F. (Tandy), and John G. Mr. Morton was favored with a good English education, is a reading man and has remained unmarried. He is by profession a farmer, having 280 acres of first-class land, which he successfully cultivates in wheat, corn and tobacco. He is an acceptable member of the A. F. & A. M. and I. O. O. F.; he is also a Baptist and a Democrat.

AARON VIRGIL O'DANIEL, one of the enterprising young farmers of Todd County, was born September 12, 1845, in Christian County, Ky. He is the second of seven children—four boys and three girls—three still living, all boys—born to Joshua and Nancy (Colvin) O'Daniel, natives of Christian County, Ky., and of Irish origin. Subject's grandparents, Joshua and Susan A. (Grissam) O'Daniel were natives of North Carolina, and emigrated to Christian County about 1812, and engaged in farming.

Mrs. Susan A. O'Daniel is still living, and is ninety-three years old. Our subject's early educational advantages were poor; he attended school but little on account of weak eyes. He was reared on a farm and lived with his parents till of age. He was married May 2, 1866, to Miss D. Lindsey, of Todd County, Ky., daughter of John N. and Martha A. (Johnson) Lindsey, natives of Christian County, Ky., the former of English and the latter of English-Welsh descent. Their union has been blessed with six children, viz.: Louana (married to Lafayette Marian Bearden), William P., Nannie H., Lanor, Jonnie Elizabeth, Archa J. Mr. O'Daniel has held the office of School Trustee or Director for the past four years. He owns 107 acres of land in good state of cultivation, improved with comfortable buildings, etc. Starting in life without a dollar, he has met with uniform good success; by careful management and industry has established a comfortable home. Mr. and Mrs. O'Daniel are members of the Baptist Church.

JOHN W. PETREE, a leading and enterprising citizen and farmer, was born November 27, 1830, about four miles east of Fairview, and is the third of five children—three boys and two girls—three now living, born to John and Sythie (Mobley) Petree, natives respectively of South Carolina and Johnson County, Ga.; the father of Scotch-Irish descent and the mother, on her father's side, of Irish origin. Subject's father was born in May, 1806; emigrated to Todd County, Ky., in an early day and settled near Elkton, where he lived till about 1871, when he moved to Kansas, where he still lives. Subject's grandfather, Hazel Petrie, died about 1870. Our subject attended the common schools and received a fair education. He was reared on a farm and lived with his parents till the age of twenty-two, when he went to the Iron Works of T. G. Welch & Co., on the Cumberland River, where he was engaged as general manager, contracting for wood and furnishing coal, etc. There he remained two years. In December, 1854, he returned to Fairview, Christian County, where he engaged in blacksmithing and wool-carding, in which business he was engaged, with good success, till 1863, when he sold his business to T. H. Harned, and engaged in farming 260 acres of land on A. J. Brown's farm. He has speculated considerably in cattle, and at farming has met with good success. He now owns 450 acres, one-fourth mile east of Fairview; his farm is embellished with one of the finest brick residences in the county. Starting with about $30 in money, he has by good management and industry established one of the best homes in the county of Todd. On February 19, 1856, he married Miss Mary Ann Harned, a native of Christian County, and daughter of John and Mary (Carroll) Harned, natives of Virginia and Christian County, Ky., respectively, both of Irish descent. This union was blessed with ten children, all living: William S., Mary E. (now the wife of J. C. Terry), Joseph E., Charles B., Thomas L., Abilene, John W., Hazel, Paul and Harry. Mr. Petree takes special interest in giving his children a good education. He and wife are both members of the Methodist Episcopal Church. He was formerly a member of I. O. O. F.; was also a member of the Grange. Possessing a strong constitution and an iron will, Mr. Petree bids fair to spend many years of usefulness in the community where he is an honored and upright citizen.

ASBURY STAMPER REESE was born December 16, 1829, in Shelby County, Ky.; removed with his parents to Todd County in 1833, where he grew to manhood and still retains his residence. His father, Rev. Thomas G. Reese, long a minister of the Methodist Episcopal Church, was born on the line dividing North Carolina and Georgia, in 1799, and died here in 1881. He was the son of James Reese, who died in this county in 1837. Subject's mother, Susanna (Demaree), was born in Shelby County, Ky., and died in 1850. To her and husband were born: subject, Jane C. (Tyson), William McK., Samuel F. D., Mary C., B. P'Pool, Thomas M. and Susan A. (Willis). Subject was favored with a fair education, and is a considerable reader of current literature. In 1865 he was married to Miss Sarah B., daughter of Rev. Fountain E. Pitts, of Tennessee, and this union was blessed with Pitts D., Martha S., Juliet M., Stonewall J., Fountainella, Asbury S. and Samuel T. Mr. Reese is a successful farmer, owning 550 acres of valuable land in general good condition. He is a member of the Masonic fraternity ; a Methodist and a Democrat.

PAUL H. SALMON was born September 25, 1814, in South Carolina. His parents are George and Elizabeth (West) Salmon, the father a native of Virginia, the mother of Maryland. The father was a teacher, merchant and farmer. He died in Marshall County, Miss., in 1865, aged eighty-seven. The mother died in South Carolina in 1829. Paul

H. came to this county in 1844. Six years previous he had been engaged in the cotton mills. He sold goods in Elkton six years, and in 1850 he came to the farm on which he now resides. After the death of his father-in-law, he bought the farm. It is known as the " Jefferson farm "; it contains 360 acres, about half of which is improved. He has a good liberal education ; he has the finest library in this neighborhood, and is very fond of reading; consequently is well informed. He is an ordained minister of the Methodist Episcopal Church South, and has been preaching the past ten years. He was married in 1859 to Miss L. J. Jefferson, born in 1828 in Virginia. She is the daughter of I. Randolph Jefferson and Louisa J. (Peyton) Jefferson, old Virginia stock. Mr. and Mrs. Salmon have six living children, viz.: George Randolph, who was married to Miss Ellen Stokes, now deceased ; Evaline, the wife of Harlan Lucaus (John H. is their only child); Lewis Jackson, married to Miss Rosa Montlow (William H. and America A.—deceased—were their children) ; Martha J., Paul H: and Mary Ann.

MRS. SARAH A. TANDY was born in Spottsylvania County, Va., October 28, 1809, where she was reared, and on the 16th of December, 1824, was married to Henry, son of Henry Tandy, of Orange County, Va., who was born in 1800 ; removed to Todd County, Ky., 1825, where he died in 1848. To them were born: John H., Mary E. (Hall) and Oscar E. Subject's father, John Davis, was born in Virginia; died 1826, aged forty-eight years. His wife, Mary (Pendleton), was born in Virginia; died 1844, age sixty-nine years. Their children are: Subject, as above, and Mary E., wife of Dr. N. M. Tandy, of Todd County. Mrs. Sara Tandy is engaged in farming, having 306 acres of good land on West Fork. She is a member of Bethel Baptist Church.

JOHN DAVIS TANDY. The subject of this sketch was born January 23, 1837, in Todd County, Ky., where he still retains his residence. His father, Nathaniel Mills Tandy, was born in 1810, in Christian County ; he removed to Todd County, Ky., in 1834, where he died in 1881. He was the son of Mills Tandy, who was born in Virginia in 1780 ; moved to Barren County in 1808, where he remained six months; moved to Christian County in 1809, and died in Christian County, Ky., in 1861. His father was Henry Tandy, of Virginia. Subject's mother, Mary E., daughter of John and Mary (Pendleton) Davis, was born in 1815 and died in 1843. To her and her husband, Nathaniel Mills Tandy, were born : Olivia (deceased) and our subject. To Nathaniel Mills Tandy and his second wife (Margaret J. Jesup), were born : Samuel R., Jesup M. and Charles E. Subject secured a good education and is a general reader of standard books and current literature. He was married October 23, 1860, to Miss Catherine, daughter of Preston L. and Elizabeth A. (Jesup) Yancy, of Crittenden County, Ky., and this union has been blessed with : Preston E., Robert M., Mary D. and Clarence. Subject is by profession a farmer, owning 700 acres of good and valuable land, which is finely improved and in a high state of cultivation. He is prudently turning his attention largely to the growth of the grasses, thereby maintaining and improving the fertility of his already productive farm. He is enterprising, energetic and public spirited. He is an honored member of the Masonic fraternity, a Baptist and a Democrat.

CHARLES E. TANDY, one of Todd County's young and enterprising farmers and stock-breeders, was born November 12, 1860, in Todd County, Ky. He is a son of Dr. N. M. and Margaret J. (Jesup) Tandy. The latter was a daughter of Col. Samuel B. Jesup, born November, 1792, died August, 1866, and Catherine Jesup, born March 1795, died July, 1870. Subject's father was born 1810, died July, 1881 ; his mother born 1819, died August, 1877. Parents were natives of Christian and Todd Counties respectively. Our subject received more than an ordinary education, having attended Fairview and Olmstead Academies two years and Bethel College one year, after which he engaged in farming at home. In November, 1882, he located where he now lives on what is called Col. Jesup's farm ; it consists of 250 acres of which 150 are in a good state of cultivation, improved with buildings, etc. Mr. Tandy is engaged in general farming and in breeding and training the best of Mambrino horses. Has a track on his farm and is energetic and active in procuring the finest quality of trotting stock. He was married November 23, 1882, to Miss Clara B. Layne, daughter of Alexander and A. M. (Elgin) Layne. This union is blessed with the birth of one child—David H. Mrs. Tandy is a member of the Methodist Episcopal Church.

NELSON WADE, a leading citizen and merchant of Fairview, was born in northeastern Todd County, Ky., March 23, 1825, and is the third

of ten children—seven boys and three girls—nine living, born to Brunt and
Easter (Carr) Wade, natives of Virginia and Todd County, Ky., respectively.
The father was of Welsh-English and the mother of Irish descent.   Subject's grandfather Wade was a native of Virginia ; his grandfather Carr,
of Ireland.   Subject's father was born in 1793, and served one year in
the war of 1812.   When he became of age he emigrated to Todd County,
Ky., where he rented land and engaged in farming and teaming, and succeeded in accumulating 100 acres of land.   He died in 1867.   Subject's
mother was born in 1797, died March, 1883 ; she drew a pension of $8
per month after her husband's death.   These parents were members of the
Presbyterian Church.   Our subject's advantages for an education were
poor.   He attended school in all about two years.   He was reared on a
farm and lived with his parents till he was twenty-two years of age, when
he commenced to learn the cabinet trade, which business he has followed
ever since.   He started in Elkton, where he remained two years ; thence
came to Fairview in 1850, where he has remained in the business ever
since.   Mr. Wade has made life a success ; commencing with nothing,
he has by industry succeeded in accumulating, till he now owns a good
furniture store, business lot and blacksmith-shop, also a good residence
and twenty-five acres of land at Fairview.   He has been Trustee of the
village of Fairview for the past fourteen years, and has been a member of
the Masonic fraternity for twenty-five years.   On May 25, 1854, he was
married to Miss Susan E. Smith, daughter of Zachariah and Sarah D.
(Snelson) Smith, of English extraction.   This union was blessed with
four children: Emma L. (deceased) who married Rev. M. A. Maxey,
Walter D., Thomas H. and Richard Lee.   Mrs. Wade died May, 1877;
she was a member of the Methodist Episcopal Church.   Mr. Wade's
second marriage was December 15, 1881, to Miss Mittie V. Evans,
daughter of Hugh V. and Martha (Dunaven) Evans, of Hopkinsville; her
father was born in Birmingham, England; her mother in Christian County,
Ky.

   BENJAMIN T. WYATT, an industrious and respected citizen of
Todd County, was born October 26, 1839, two miles south of where he
now resides.   He is the third of five children—two boys and three girls—
three now living, born to Finis W. and Catherine (Brock) Wyatt, natives
of Todd County, Ky., and North Carolina.   Grandparents were Thomas

and Mary (Neadham) Wyatt, natives of Virginia, and David and Nella (Norton) Brock. Subject's early education was neglected; he never attended school more than three months in his life. He obtained knowledge of books by hard study at home. He was reared on a farm and lived with his parents until his marriage on May 27, 1861, to Mary Jane Kirkman, a native of Todd County, Ky., of English descent. Two children were born to this union : Bennie (now dead), and Willie May. Mr. and Mrs. Wyatt are members of the Methodist Episcopal Church. He has been engaged in the tanning business since 1862. The tannery is owned by himself and brother; it is one of the oldest in the county.

WILLIAM S. WYATT, one of the wide awake farmers and leading citizens of Todd County, was born June 26, 1844, in Todd County, Ky. His parents were Finis and Catherine (Brock) Wyatt, natives of Todd County, Ky., and North Carolina respectively, and of English descent. Subject's advantages for an education were not good ; he was unable to write until after he became of age, but by his shrewdness and activity has made life a success. He was reared on a farm, and with the exception of the seven years he worked in a tan-yard has been engaged in farming, also in tobacco trading. He has a store near his residence for the accommodation of the community in which he lives; he owns 245 acres of land, mostly improved, with comfortable buildings, etc. Mr. Wyatt was married January 17, 1867, to Altegara J. Tatum, of Todd County, Ky., a native of Christian County, and daughter of William and Jurinda (Siveley) Tatum, natives of Culpeper County, Va. The grandparents were Joseph and Lydia (Hill) Tatum, of English and German descent, respectively, and Joseph and Elizabeth (Harry) Siveley. To this union were born eleven children, eight living: Barbara L., Ida C., Thomas E., Rosa A., Finis S., Gertrude, Harry Field, Maggie F.; of the three dead one received a name—Marvin. Subject and wife are active members of the Methodist Episcopal Church. He has been superintendent of the Sabbath-school for the past eight years. He takes great interest in educating his children, and in cultivating a happy home. His hospitality is unexcelled.

ELKTON PRECINCT

D. L. BAILEY, farmer, living in Elkton Precinct, southeast from Elkton, Todd County, was born April 1, 1850, on the farm where he now lives. This family, which is one of the most extensively known in the county, is spoken of by a previous writer as coming to Todd County as early as 1809. The father of D. L. Bailey, whose name was Charles A. Bailey, was born September 2, 1798; attained his manhood in Todd County, and married Elizabeth L. Jones; then settled on the farm now owned and occupied by the subject of this sketch. Here in this desirable spot they lived and labored, soon opened up an extensive farm, to which they added as they were able; and here, too, they died; she, September 27, 1856, and he, October 27, 1874. Elizabeth L. was born in Casey County, Ky., December 31, 1809; her mother, Ann C. Jones, was born August 12, 1788, and died at the residence of C. A. Bailey, September 24, 1856. Charles A. Bailey was noted for his upright life, and his death was mourned by a large circle of friends, who admired him for his many noble qualities, and by the Masonic order, of which he was an honored member for many years. His wife, Elizabeth L. Bailey, was an acceptable member of the Christian Church. These parents had a large family of children, the two first-born being twins, that died in infancy. Thomas A. Bailey was born September 27, 1825; he married Miss Kate Edmonds, and died at his home in Todd County, June 14, 1880. He was a very successful farmer and a Mason of high order. John A. Bailey died at the age of thirty years, unmarried; he was a graduate of the Nashville College, and served this county as Surveyor. Ann S. married Clinton Halsell, and died in 1883, leaving three children; Beersheba died in early womanhood, unmarried. Elizabeth married Elliott Halsell, and died in Missouri, in 1882, leaving six children; James Bailey died in early manhood; Emma is the wife of James C. Riley; S. A. Bailey, a farmer in Christian County, married Miss Lizzie Lane; D. L. Bailey, whose name heads this sketch. D. L. Bailey was reared on the old homestead; married November 25, 1875, Miss Ella R. Edwards, daughter of Peyton

G. and Mary S. Edwards (*nee* Graham). Ella R. was born May 5, 1855. They had one child—Laura—born May 2, 1877, and died December 25, of same year. Mr. Bailey is an energetic, practical farmer, an extensive stock dealer, and owns a farming interest of 1,000 acres of land. He also is a member of the A. F. & A. M. and both he and his wife are members of the Reformed Church. Of the ancestors of Mrs. Bailey mention is made in the history of Allensville Precinct.

JOHN F. BELL, merchant of Elkton, Ky., is a son of J. W. Bell, and Sarah H. Bell (*nee* Browder). He was born February 11, 1851, at Bell's Chapel in Todd County, where his father died September 2, 1884. John F. received the advantages of a common English education, in his native county, and in the Browder Institute of Logan County. In 1872, he came to Elkton and for one year was employed as a salesman in the business house of James Russell; he then effected a partnership with Mr. R. M. Russell in the grocery trade, which partnership was terminated in 1874, by the retiring of the latter, he having sold his interest to Mr. Bell, who continued in this line of trade until 1881, when he closed out his stock to engage in the dry goods business; he then, associated with B. E. Boone, opened their present line of business, in which they are very successful, both being young men of pronounced business ability. Mr. Bell was married in Elkton, November 26, 1879, to Miss Emma, daughter of H. G. Petrie. She was born in Elkton, August 25, 1855. Their children, two in number, are Mary Lucille, born September 19, 1880, and Hazel Bell, born November 21, 1882. Mr. Bell is a member of the Board of Trustees of Elkton, and both he and his wife are members of the Methodist Episcopal Church. His father, John W. Bell, died September 2, 1884, at his home at Bell's Chapel. He was a son of Rev. Caleb N. Bell, who was born in 1788, in Beaufort, N. C. Caleb Bell was for several years a traveling minister in the Methodist Church of Virginia, and for many years a local preacher in this State. He died in 1872 ; he was three times married; first, to Judith H. Moore; second, to Jane Browder, and last to Mary Greenfield. John W. Bell was born in Virginia in 1817, came to Kentucky with his parents in 1821, and to Todd County the following year. He was twice married; first in 1845, to Miss Sarah C., daughter of William and Sallie Browder, of Logan County; she was born in 1826, and died in 1855, John F. Bell being the youngest of their three children. Mr. Bell's widow, to whom he was married in December, 1855, was Mrs. Mary F. (Reeves) Todd, by whom he had two children, Joseph J. and Mattie Bell. C. N. Bell's portrait appears on another page.

ROBERT BRADSHAW, farmer and miller, two miles south of Elkton, Todd County, was born in Halifax County, Va., on the 22d day of May, 1834, and is the son of Benjamin and Lucy (Wilkinson) Bradshaw, who came from Virginia to Kentucky in 1840. They settled in the southern portion of Todd County, purchased a farm, on which Benjamin died, and where his widow is now living. They had a family of seven children, as follows: James, Robert, Joseph, Benjamin, Martha, Richard and Charles Bradshaw, the latter ot whom is deceased. The subject of these lines, Robert Bradshaw, attained his manhood in this county ; was reared on the farm, meantime attending the common schools. In early manhood he learned the carpenter's trade, at which he labored for a few years, since which time he has devoted his time to agriculture, combined with which he owns and operates a flouring-mill. This mill is noticed in the history of Elkton Precinct. Mr. Bradshaw, in 1861, married Miss Fannie Link, daughter of William and Martha Link, one of the old and honored families of the county. She was born in Todd County, April 9, 1844. Their children, six in number, are as follows: Ida, Charles, Vertie, Claude, Herbert and Melrose Bradshaw. Mrs. Bradshaw and the older children are members of the Cumberland Presbyterian Church. No mention in this work of the Bradshaw connection is necessary to establish their reputation for honor, as they are respected, wherever known, for their sterling worth as citizens.

ELIJAH C. BROWN. Mention has already been made of this gentleman's ancestors, and will be found in the chapter devoted to Elkton District. He is a son of Preston and Rosena Brown, and was born near Hadensville, Todd County, on the 30th day of October, 1845. He was reared on his father's farm, meanwhile attending the common schools, after which he attended school in Clarksville, Tenn. In the fall of 1861 he enlisted as a soldier in the Confederate Army, and followed the fortunes of his command to the close of the war. He was first a member of an independent cavalry company, under Captain Biggs. After the service of the first year the company was made the body-guard of Gen. Breckinridge, and in the fall of 1863 was attached to Gen. Wheeler's command,

with whom it remained until the close of the war.   Mr. Brown participated in the battles of Fort Donelson and Stone River, was made a prisoner
of war on the bank of Cumberland River, between Clarksville and Nashville, Tenn., in the early part of 1864, and was retained until the end of
the war, principally in Camp Morton and Fort Delaware.   Since the war
Mr. Brown has turned his attention to farming, in which he has been
successful.   He owns a valuable farm of 350 acres, located one mile south
of Elkton.   On the 2d of November, 1868, he married Miss Sallie R.,
daughter of James M. and Adeline (Atkins) Graham.   She was born in
Todd County March 4, 1847, and both father and mother are deceased.
They have a family of three children, viz. :   Rosa A., Walter T. and
Seymour H. Brown.   Mr. Brown is a member of the I. O. O. F.

    F. M. BYARS was born in Todd County, Ky., January 18, 1847,
and is a son of T. A. and Harriet (Eddington) Byars ; the former born
May 5, 1816, the latter born September 10, 1823, and died in 1854.
They were both natives of Todd County, Ky.   T. A. Byars was
reared and educated in Todd County, Ky.   His father emigrated from
Albemarle County, Va., to Kentucky ; about the time of the organization
of Christian County, he settled in what is now Todd County, near Hadensville.   T. A. Byars was married about 1840.   Four children were added
to this union, of whom F. M. was the second.   Both he and wife were
devoted members of the Methodist Episcopal Church South.   F. M.
Byars, the subject of our sketch, received a good education in his youth ;
he remained with his parents until December 28, 1869, when he was married to Miss Nannie, daughter of I. R. and S. A. Jefferson and sister of
the Honorable Dr. Jefferson.   She is a native of Todd County, born
October 3, 1847 ; her parents and grandparents were natives of Virginia.
Six children bless their union: Jennie, born November 13, 1871 ; Alexander T., born October 28, 1873 ;   Wirt, born May 22, 1876, died September 10, 1876 ; Nannie, born April 17, 1877 ; Manie, born March 20,
1879 ; Frank M., born August 15, 1881.   Mr. Byars follows the quiet
but industrious life of a farmer ; in 1870 he settled on the farm on which
he now lives ; it consists of 300 acres, 250 of which are under a high state
of cultivation.   It is located one and one-half miles from Elkton, on the
Trenton road.   Mr. Byars and lady are consistent members of the Methodist Episcopal Church South, and one of the leading families of the county.

FRANKLIN M. CHESNUT. Among the names of the first settlers in the vicinity of Elkton, is that of John Chesnut, who came from
South Carolina in 1810, and settled in 1812 in Todd County, on the
farm now owned and occupied by Frank M. He had a family of eight
children, including five sons, among whom was John Chesnut, the father
of Franklin M. He was born July 25, 1796, in South Carolina; came
to Kentucky with the family, and here in Todd County married Miss
Maburn, who died after bearing him three children, viz.: Jane, Mary E.,
who married J. Duncan, and A. W. Chesnut. The first two are dead;
the last named now resides near Paducah, Ky. John Chesnut next married
Miss Ruth Vance, a native of Todd County, and daughter of John Vance,
of North Carolina. As the result of this union eight children were born:
John W., who died in Ballard County, Ky.; James A., Samuel Mas-
sena, who died in 1865, in early manhood; Franklin M., Martin Luther,
of Paducah, Ky., married to Miss Laura Beaty; Underwood P., married
Miss Ollie Morrison, and died leaving four children: Sarah Ellen, wife
of Robert Coleman, and Margaret Jane (deceased), was the wife of Capt.
Charles Connor, of Tennessee. Mrs. Ruth (Vance) Chesnut died at the
old homestead January 1, 1873, and her husband, John Chesnut, at the
same place just two weeks subsequently. They were members of the Old
School Presbyterian Church, in the faith of which they were peacefully
gathered to their fathers. Frank M., whose name introduces this sketch,
was born on the farm where he now lives, on the 23d day of February,
1845; there grew to manhood, meantime receiving a common-school education. He was married October 6, 1870, to Miss Josephine, daughter
of Capt. Samuel W. and Lucy (Diuguid) Drake. Josephine was born
near the city of Richmond, Va., and her parents are now residents of
Jefferson County, Ky. The marriage of Mr. and Mrs. Chesnut has been
blessed with four children, viz.: Lula Ruth, Walter F., Samuel W. and
John Elgin Chesnut. Mr. Chesnut is a practical, progressive farmer,
and owns a farm of 212 acres of improved land, including the old homestead. He is an honored Elder of the Cumberland Presbyterian Church,
and his wife is a faithful member of the Baptist Church.

W. F. COLE was born in Todd County, Ky., January 1, 1856, and
is a son of Samuel and Sarah A. (Day) Cole, both natives of Virginia,
and were of English descent respectively. Samuel Cole was born in 1811

in Virginia, where he was reared and educated, his father being a teacher. On emigrating to Kentucky he settled in Daysville, named in honor of his wife's grandfather, the first settler in the village. He was a mechanic but followed farming principally; both Mr. and Mrs. Cole were life-long members of the Christian Church, he being a Deacon and leading member. He departed this life about the year 1876. His wife ended her mortality about the year 1879. W. F. Cole, the subject of our sketch, received a good education in his native county; he remained with his parents until four years ago, when he left home and was engaged as a local writer on one of the Elkton papers, continuing in this for a short time; he then engaged in the mercantile trade at Daysville, where he is now handling a complete stock of general merchandise, meeting the wants of the entire community, and is doing an extensive business. He is an enterprising young man, a prominent member of the Christian Church, a leading citizen and one of the influential business men of the village and county.

DR. ELISHA B. EDWARDS, Postmaster at Elkton, Ky., was born in Elkton, Todd County, February 2, 1824. He descends from one of the first families of the county, in point of settlement, and from one of the first in the State in point of honorable and intelligent men. His parents were Elisha B. Edwards, Sr., and Martha F. Upshaw; the former a son of Hon. Benjamin Edwards. Elisha B. Edwards, Sr., was a brother of the Hon. Ninian Edwards, so noted in the early history of Kentucky and Illinois, and was born in Maryland, May 11, 1781. He came from his native State to Kentucky with his father's family in 1800, and with them settled in Nelson County. In February, 1810, he married Lucy Richardson, who bore him a daughter, Mary B. Edwards. She became the wife of Judge L. Lindsay and died in Texas, in December, 1882. Lucy Edwards having died, Elisha B., Sr., in August, 1811, was married to Martha F. Upshaw, near Hopkinsville, Ky., by Rev. Peter Cartwright. He came to Elkton at the time of the organization of Todd County, and was elected the first Clerk of the infant county, an office he held until his death, on the 13th of October, 1823. His wife was born in March, 1792, in Essex County, Va., and died September 22, 1854. They had a family of four children: Martha M., wife of H. C. Boone; Margaret L., who died unmarried in February, 1883; Tazewell

N., died in infancy, and Elisha B. Edwards, Jr. Dr. Edwards received an English education, which he completed in Princeton College of Kentucky in 1840. He began the study of medicine with his uncle, at Alton, Ill., and continued his studies afterward in St. Louis; began practice in his native county, with which he combined a general practice of dental surgery, to which he finally gave his entire attention. On the breaking out of the Civil war, he entered the Federal Army as Captain of Company F, of the Twenty-fifth Kentucky Regiment. After the battles of Donelson and Shiloh, in both of which he participated, his regiment was consolidated with the Seventeenth Kentucky, and the law of seniority governing such cases, deprived him of his command. In 1864 he was appointed Deputy Provost-Marshal of Todd County, holding the position until the close of the war. In 1867, he received the appointment of Assistant Assessor of Internal Revenue, which he held until the office was abolished in 1873. Since the latter date he has served in the office of Postmaster at Elkton. Dr. Edwards was married in Elkton, November 20, 1849, to Miss Sarah B., daughter of James W. Porter. She was born in Fauquier County, Va., October 7, 1822. Of eight children born to them, but two are living, viz.: James H. and Cyrus Edwards. Mr. Edwards is a Mason of high order, and member of the Baptist Church. James H. Edwards, son of Dr. Elisha B. Edwards, was born August 22, 1850, and has served the county of Todd as Deputy Sheriff, and was enumerator of the census in 1870. He is a practical business man, and at present engaged in the grocery business on the south side of the public square in Elkton. He was married in Louisville, Ky., December 21, 1883, to Miss Mary E. Morton, daughter of the Rev. David Morton, a minister of the Methodist Episcopal Church, and present Secretary of the Board of Church Extension, and located in Louisville.

J. ROBERT FOSTER was born October 12, 1819, near Oak Grove, Christian Co., Ky., and while young removed with his parents to Todd County, Ky., where he grew to manhood and at present resides. His father, John Foster, was born January 8, 1785, in South Carolina, and died 1873. His wife, Elizabeth (Hill), was born 1781, and died in 1863. They were married in 1809, and the union was blessed with four sons and four daughters. The parents were both acceptable members of the Baptist Church. Subject was married September, 1840, to Maria, daughter of John and Mary Waugh, both natives of Virginia. She was born January 29, 1817, in Hopkinsville. To her and husband were born: Anna, September 22, 1842; Robert Ellen, June 16, 1845; Georgie E., February 28, 1848; Mary W., November 23, 1850. Subject is a farmer by profession, having settled on his present place in 1840, where he owns 135 acres of good land in fair state of cultivation. Mrs. Foster is a member of the Baptist Church. Subject, who was the second son, lives within sight of the old homestead, where his parents died. This was comparatively a new country when they moved here, with plenty of wild turkey, deer, etc., all driven away before the advance of civilization.

EGBERT GARTH. In 1812 Elijah Garth came from Albemarle County, Va., to Kentucky, and made settlement near Trenton, in Todd County, on a farm now occupied by Webster C. Garth, and which he had but fairly begun to develop, when (in 1815) he died. He was twice married, first to Miss Fretwell, and second to Miss Elizabeth Wait, and as the result of each union, had four children. None of these are now living, but among their immediate descendants are some of the most worthy families of Todd County. Paschal L. was a son of Elijah Garth, and was born in Albemarle County, Va., and removed with his father's family to Kentucky. He was here reared to maturity; returned to Virginia and married Miss Lucy E. B. Garth, who was born in 1813, in Albemarle County of that State. They settled on a farm long known as the "Dunheath" farm, where Paschal spent the remainder of his days, which terminated in 1865, and where his aged widow is now residing. Their union was blessed with twelve children, five of whom are deceased; four of the surviving ones being residents of Todd County. Paschal Garth had served as a county officer in Todd County, and was a member of the Christian Church. Egbert Garth, whose name heads this sketch, is the third child of Paschal and Lucy E. B. Garth, and was born in the county May 18, 1835. He grew to manhood on his father's farm, or until sixteen years old, when he began his career in mercantile life, first as a salesman in a dry goods house. He was thus employed until he opened a business for himself in 1862. From the year 1865 to 1870 he was retired from business, but in the latter year again embarked in business which he still continues. He owns a good double brick store-room on the south side of the public square, where he has a complete stock of goods of a general character. Mr. Garth is a good business man; has served as Police Judge, and is an esteemed citizen. He was married near Elkton, in December, 1880, to Miss Laura Sumpter, daughter of William C. and Mary Sumpter. She was born in Todd County January 23, 1857. Mrs. Garth is a member of the Methodist Episcopal Church South. Mr. Garth has one child, named Paschal Lee Garth, born May 21, 1884.

DANIEL E. GOODMAN (deceased) was a native of Hart County, Ky., where he was born June 7, 1838. He came to Elkton, Todd Co., with his parents, John A. (deceased) and Sarah E. Goodman (deceased), when a boy, and he was here educated and grew to manhood. For many years his father kept the only hotel in the village of Elkton, the building now owned by Dr. J. L. Woollard, known as the Elkton Inn. Daniel E. was the eldest of a family of twelve children, born to these parents. In early life, Daniel began a mercantile career, in which he was quite successful, first as a grocer, but later in life engaged in the furniture trade. In 1876, he went to Louisville, Ky., to engage in business, but in consequence of lost health was compelled to abandon this, and he returned to Elkton where, on September 25, 1878, he died. Mr. Goodman was a worthy member of the I. O. O. F. and of the Christian Church, and was universally esteemed for his pure life. He was married in Logan County, Ky., March 9, 1859, to Miss Antha L. Posey, daughter of Anderson N. and Mary A. Posey (nee Barker). Her father, Anderson Posey, was born near Bowling Green, Warren Co., Ky., August 13, 1808. His life, which was characterized for noble deeds, was spent on the old homestead farm, and terminated January 18, 1867. Mrs. Goodman's mother was born near Richmond, Va., in 1808, and came to Kentucky in childhood, and is still living. She is the mother of seven children. Mrs. Goodman is the fifth of this family and was born August 12, 1840, and is at present a resident of Elkton. To Daniel E. and Antha L. Goodman were born eight children, viz.: Charlie B., born December 22, 1859; Kate L., born April 27, 1862, and married to J. G. Algea, of St. Louis, Mo., November 28, 1880; Wright T., born July 12, 1864; Posey, born December 4, 1866; Rosa, born February 22, 1870; Sallie E., born May 23, 1873; Lou–Raney, born February 18, 1875, and Max D., born July 13, 1877. The three elder sons, now just developing into true men, are engaged in office work, in the city of St. Louis, Mo.

DR. WALTER B. JEFFERSON is a son of Isham R. and Sarah
A. (Mansfield) Jefferson, who came separately to Todd County in 1833,
from Abermarle County, Va. The father was a native of that county,
and was there reared by his uncle, Thomas Jefferson, the famous author
of the Declaration of Independence, and third Chief Executive of the
United States, Isham's father, Randolph Jefferson, being the youngest
brother of the President. The father of our subject married first a Miss
Henderson, and afterward a Miss Peyton. He located, on coming to Todd
County, upon a farm in Jesup's Grove, removing afterward to within a
mile south of Elkton, where he died in 1862. His third marriage occurred
in this county. He wedded Miss Mansfield, and the union was blessed
with the following children :   William A., James M., Walter B., Susan
M. (deceased), Nannie, wife of F. M. Byars, and Wirt, who died in 1875,
in early manhood. Dr. W. B., the subject of these lines, obtained his
early schooling in Elkton, and began the study of medicine under Drs.
James A. and John O. McReynolds. He attended the University of Virginia, and afterward the University of Nashville, graduating from the latter institution in 1862, since which date he has practiced his profession in
Todd and Logan Counties and in Paducah, Ky. He married, in 1863,
Miss Mamie, daughter of Judge Ben. T. Perkins. She died in 1877,
leaving one child, Anna M. His second marriage was with Mrs. Eve-
lyn A. Taylor, a daughter of Edwin Johnson, of Montgomery County,
Tenn. Dr. Jefferson is a man of ability, and of high standing with the
community. His sunny nature and high social worth attract to him a
large circle of acquaintances. He was elected to the Legislature of 1883,
and is now serving in that body, and was elected a delegate to represent
the Third District in the Democratic National Convention held at Chicago.

JAMES T. KENNEDY. (See history of Kennedy family under
head of Fairview District.)

GEORGE B. LEWIS is the eighth of a family of eleven children,
born to Williamson V. and Clarkie Lewis (nee Bell). These parents were
each natives of Chatham County, N. C., where they grew to maturity
and were married. They removed to Tennessee and settled in Robertson
County in 1819. There the mother died August 4, 1831. The father
died in Weakley County, Tenn., in 1874, at the age of eighty-three years.
His second marriage was to Sarah P. Freeman, by whom he had eight

children. George B. was born in Robertson County, Tenn., February 8, 1824. He was reared to manhood in his native county, and after a residence of a few years in New Providence, Tenn., he removed, in 1851, to Elkton, Todd County, which has been his home most of the years since. He is now engaged in the mercantile business on the north side of public square, and is the owner and proprietor of the Elkton City Mills. He was married in 1852 to Miss Lizzie Kennedy, daughter of Esq. W. T. Kennedy, who was born in Todd County in December, 1830. Their family consists of seven children, viz. : Anna B., Mary C. (wife of Robert B. Kendall), Mattie P. (wife of B. E. Boone), Emma G., Laura T., Lizzie J. and Herbert G. Lewis. Robert B. Kendall was born in 1843, in Mississippi. He was united in marriage to Mary C. Lewis, which union has resulted in the birth of four children : Flora Bell, Lizzie K., Jessie and George Lewis Kendall.

JOHN W. LEWIS, merchant at Elkton, Ky., was born in Robertson County, Tenn., November 19, 1829, and is a son of William V. Lewis and Clarkie Lewis (*nee* Bell). He was reared to the age of seventeen in his native State, after which he spent a few years in Illinois, coming thence to Elkton, Ky., in October, 1851. For about eight years he was employed as salesman in mercantile business, and in 1859 opened a stock of goods for himself, since which time he has been in active business life in Elkton. He is now located on the north side of public square, where he has a handsome stock of dry goods. Mr. Lewis was married in the town of Elkton, in November, 1859, to Miss Octavia Kennedy. She was born in Todd County, July 18, 1836. They have two children : Charles K. Lewis, born June 12, 1869, and Mary Lula Lewis, born June 4, 1871. In politics Mr. Lewis is a Democrat, and he is a faithful member of the Baptist Church and Superintendent of the Baptist Sunday School.

WILLIAM R. LINK is an extensive farmer in Elkton Precinct, in which he was born. His parents, William and Martha (Bradshaw) Link, were born, reared and married in Virginia, from whence they came to Todd County, Ky. They improved a farm a short distance south of Elkton, where William Link died many years ago. Their family consisted of six children : John B., Fannie (wife of Robert Bradshaw), Leathy, William R., Martha (deceased) and Winfield. William R. and his brother, Winfield, now own and occupy the old Ephraim Porter farm, consisting of 480 acres of desirable land, and constituting one of the best stock farms in Todd County.   They are engaged in general farming, principally in the pr oduction of wheat, and are paying some attention to raising improved stock.   Both of these gentlemen are thorough, practical farmers and valuable citizens.   Their mother, Martha Link, is still living and resides with these sons.

DR. S. M. LOWRY was one of a large family of children born to Squire M. and Sarah L. (Cherry) Lowry.   His grandfather was of Irish origin, and was born at sea.   He became a resident of North Carolina, and subsequently moved to Todd County, Ky., at a very early day, where Squire M. was born.   The latter died in 1853, leaving a wife and nine children, of whom but five now survive.   Mrs. Lowry was a native of North Carolina, but was reared in Tennessee.   She died in 1880, at the age of seventy-six years.   Dr. Lowry was reared upon the farm, but was afforded excellent educational advantages.   He prepared for college at the school of James Ross, in Montgomery County, Tenn., and then attended Bethel College at Russellville, Ky., where he completed the course in 1859.   He began reading medicine the same year, entering the Jefferson Medical College at Philadelphia, Penn., and graduating in the spring of 1861.   He began the practice of his profession at Elkton and continued it for ten years, when he abandoned it to engage in farming. For the past twenty years he has been extensively engaged in the purchase and sale of tobacco in the county, in which he has been eminently successful.   As authorized agent for the Elephant Warehouse of Clarksville, Tenn., he has been prominently identified with the tobacco interests of this and adjacent counties, putting up from 200 to 500 hogsheads of the staple article annually, the prizing being done at various points.   The Doctor is a man of public spirit and generosity, his substantial and unqualified support to all enterprises calculated for the lasting good of the people being forthcoming on all occasions.   He is an active member of the Baptist Church, with which he has been connected since fourteen years of age, and of which his mother was a member for forty years.   He is also a member of the A. F. & A. M. and K. of H. fraternities.   In 1867 he was married to Miss Lucy G. McLean, daughter of Hon. Finis E. and Lucy A. (Gray) McLean.   She was born in 1850, at Elkton.

Mr. and Mrs. Lowry have one son, Thornton Henry, born in 1871. John Henry Lowry (deceased) was born in Todd County, Ky., October 12, 1831, the second child born to Squire M. and Sarah L. (Cherry) Lowry. He was a bright boy, and as early as possible he was placed in school. Laying the foundation of his education at the academies of Allensville and Elkton, he subsequently entered the Cumberland University at Princeton, Ky., and was graduated from the literary course by this institution in 1853. He then took charge of his father's interest in a lumber business on the Cumberland River, but served in this capacity only a year or two. In 1856, he entered the Law Department of the university at Lebanon, where he completed his legal studies. He returned to Elkton and began practice, and soon achieved a wide-spread reputation. In August, 1858, he was elected County Attorney on the Know-Nothing ticket, serving four years, and was then elected to the Lower House of the Legislature on the Union ticket. In 1864, he made a race for Congress against H. C. Grider, and was defeated by a bare majority. In 1866, he met with a seemingly slight accident while riding a horse, but only a few weeks afterward he was suddenly stricken with paralysis, and for ten years following, was obliged to wheel himself about in an invalid chair. This sudden and direful affliction, however, did not serve to abate his natural power and force as a speaker, and though so unfortunately handicapped, he still retained his leading position at the bar, and his practice during this period was the most lucrative of all his legal experience. In 1876, a slight accident rendered his partial paralysis complete, and his death, which soon followed, ended a career that had once promised to lead to the loftiest achievement. Mr. Lowry left a daughter, Hannah G., as his sole survivor; he had married in 1857 Miss Hannah Brown, a native of Lebanon, Tenn., and a niece of Gov. Neal S. Brown of that State; she died in 1864.

J. W. LUCKETT, son of A. D. and Martha M. (Lumsden) Luckett, was born in Clarksville, Tenn., May 3, 1848; his father was born in Virginia March, 1806, and his mother in 1813. His father emigrated from Virginia in early life, and after traveling about for some time settled in Elkton, Todd County, Ky., where he remained ten years; he then spent some twenty years of his life on a farm between Elkton and Allensville, where he died April 14, 1882. His wife ended this life January 24,

1879. In youth he learned the painter's trade, followed mercantile pursuits, and lastly agricultural industries. He was a member of the I. O. O. F., and both he and lady were consistent members of the Christian Church. J. W. Luckett was educated in Todd County, Ky., to which place he emigrated with his parents when six months old. He remained with his parents until the death of his mother, when he left home and was engaged on a farm for some three years, after which he commenced as a merchant in Daysville, Todd County, where he is now doing a profitable business. He is a devoted member of the Christian Church, and one of the prominent citizens and influential business men of the village and county.

DR. ALVA T. McKINNEY was born November 14, 1856, at Roaring Springs, Trigg Co., Ky. His father, Dr. Guy W. McKinney, was a native Kentuckian, and was born March 12, 1816, descending from Irish ancestors. For over forty-five years he was a practicing physician of more than ordinary ability, and was a graduate of the Medical College of Columbus, Ohio. His wife, whose maiden name was Rhoda Shilton, was born in 1821, in Trigg County, Ky., where she now resides. She descends from French ancestry, and is the mother of fifteen children, four of whom died in infancy. Those attaining maturity are: Dr. Bunyan H., Mary E., Albert E., Dr. Guy L., Bell V., James W., Robert C. (dead), Dr. Alva T., Mattie A., Ida E. and Henry H. McKinney. Dr. Alva T. was educated in his native county, and in Lexington, Ky.; studied medicine under his father, graduated in March, 1880, from the Physio-Medical College, of Cincinnati, Ohio, and began the practice at Roaring Springs, Trigg County, from whence he came to Elkton in November, 1881, where he now has a prosperous practice. Dr. McKinney was married October 4, 1881, in Toledo, Ohio, to Miss Nellie S., daughter of Dr. D. A. Wright, a native of Ohio. They have one child—Bessie M. McKinney.

DR. JOHN O. McREYNOLDS, of Elkton, Todd County Ky. is one of the prominent physicians of southern Kentucky and was born in Appomattox County, Va., November 30, 1827 ; he descends from Scotch-Irish ancestors, who were first represented in the United States by James and John McReynolds with their widowed mother. They settled in Pennsylvania, but soon after removed to Virginia, from whence have emanated the numerous families of that name. The parents of Dr. McReynolds,

James C. and Mary B. McReynolds, emigrated to Kentucky in 1833, settling in Trigg County, where they died, the mother in 1837, and the father in 1844. In 1846, John O. came to Elkton, Todd County, and studied medicine under Dr. James A. McReynolds; entered the Jefferson Medical College of Philadelphia in 1847 ; graduated therefrom in 1849 and at once entered upon the practice of his profession in Elkton, where, with slight exceptions he has since practiced; he enjoys the confidence of a large circle of friends, who appreciate him for his many manly qualities, as well as for his ability as a physician. He has been twice married, first to Miss Julia P. Gorin in 1853, who died the same year ; second, in 1859 to Miss Ellen, daughter of Clark Reeves, who has borne him four children, viz. : Mary B., wife of his partner, Dr. Zarecor; James C., a law student in the University of Virginia; Robert P. and Ellie R. McReynolds. Dr. McReynolds is an Elder in the Christian Church of Elkton, and one of its oldest members.

FELIX G. MILES, druggist, Elkton, Ky., is a son of Elisha F. and Eliza J. Miles of Logan County, Ky. He was born in that county, near Russellville, August 4, 1854; was reared on his father's farm and educated in Cottage Home College of his native county; he is the second of a family of nine children, all of whom are yet living. The parents are natives of North Carolina, from whence they came to Kentucky in 1850, and settled in Logan County, where they still reside. Mr. Miles came to Elkton, Todd County, in 1877, and formed a copartnership with Dr. C. D. Lewis, in the drug business. This connection existed three years, and terminated by the retirement of the latter-named gentleman. Since that time he has prosecuted this line of business and now has a good thriving trade, located on the south side of public square. He was married to Miss Elva B. Willoughby, January 12, 1881. She is a daughter of Frank and Maria Willoughby, and was born in Montgomery County, Tenn., June 30, 1856. They have two children, viz : Frank Willoughby, and Lawrence A. Miles.

JAMES T. PENICK was born in Todd County, Ky., April 30, 1848. He is the eleventh of a family of thirteen children, born to Nathan and Nancy H. (Caldwell) Penick. His father was a native of Virginia ; was born in 1807, and was brought by his father, William Penick, to the State of Kentucky in 1814. This family located in Green

County, where Nathan grew to manhood, and where his father, William Penick, died. About 1828 Nathan married Miss Nancy H. Caldwell, and they remained residents of Green County until 1847. At the latter date they came to Todd County, and settled on the Allensville road, five miles from Elkton. Nathan Penick there engaged in agricultural pursuits until his death, which occurred in April, 1864. Nancy H., his wife, was the daughter of Beverly Caldwell, who removed from Green to Christian County, and who died in Todd County, at the residence of Nathan Penick. Nancy H. was born in Green County, Ky., in 1809, and died at the Penick homestead, Todd County, in 1869. Of the thirteen children, eight sons are now living, viz.: William B., Thomas H., John R., Isaac N., Nathan B., James T., Creed H. and Joseph C. Penick. James T. has devoted himself to merchandising and the pursuits of the farm. In 1878 he removed to Elkton, where he now lives, being that year elected to the office of Tax Assessor of Todd County, to which office he was re-elected in 1882, and which he now fills with acceptance. He was married December 20, 1870, in Green County, to Miss Mattie M. Hancock, daughter of Burrell and Elvira Hankcock (*nee* Cabell). Mrs. Penick was born in Green County, on the 18th of November, 1851. Their children—five in number—are: Minnie M., Nora, Irene, Ellis C. and Walter J. Mr. Penick is engaged in the agricultural implement trade; in politics is a Democrat, and both he and wife are worthy members of the Christian Church.

SEYMOUR H. PERKINS, of the business firm of S. H. Perkins & Co., Elkton, Ky., is a son of Judge B. T. Perkins, Sr., and was born November 7, 1844, in Elkton. He was reared in his native village, which has ever been his permanent home. In 1861 he enlisted as a member of Company F., Twenty-fifth Kentucky Infantry, and in the organization of the company was elected to the commission of Second Lieutenant. He shared in the service of his regiment until shortly after the battle of Shiloh, when, on the account of loss of health, he resigned his commission and returned home. After regaining his health sufficiently, he was appointed as Deputy Clerk of the Circuit and County Courts, which position he occupied until 1870, when he was elected to the office of Clerk of the County Court; re-elected to the same office in 1874, serving fully eight years or two terms. He also served the county as

Master Commissioner of the Circuit Court, to which he was appointed by Judge Rodgers, holding this position for about twelve years. He commenced his mercantile career in Elkton, in 1879, and is now engaged in a prosperous and extensive business, associated with S. H. Wells and George P. Street. Mr. Perkins was married in Todd County, June 6, 1866, to Miss Minerva J. Weathers, daughter of E.W.Weathers, of Elkton.

BENJAMIN T. PERKINS, JR., lawyer, was born September 12, 1846, in Todd County, Ky. The family is of English origin, and was among the early emigrants from the mother country, who took up their residence in Virginia. They remained in Virginia but a short time, when, following the general drift of the population westward, they found themselves in the wilds of Kentucky. His grandfather came to Kentucky some time prior to the year 1800. His son, Benjamin T. Perkins, Sr., and father of the subject of this sketch, was born in Todd County, in 1818, became a prominent lawyer, and is now Judge of the County Court, and one of the most esteemed citizens of the county. Benjamin T. Perkins, Jr., received a liberal education, though his later study was somewhat interrupted by the results of the Civil war. He chose for his life pursuit the one in which his father had already achieved distinction, and in the winter of 1866–67, he became a student in the Law Department of the University of Virginia; and after taking a course in that institution, entered the Law School of Louisville, Ky. He graduated with the degree of that school in 1868, when he was admitted to practice. He then returned home, and immediately rose to more than local reputation in his profession. After two years' practice, his ability was recognized in his election to the responsible position of Commonwealth's Attorney, which position he filled with marked ability for four years. In 1875 he was appointed Aid-de-camp to the Governor of the State, with the rank of Colonel. He was appointed by the State Convention a delegate to the National Democratic Convention, held at St. Louis, Mo., in 1876. Mr. Perkins was married on the 31st day of October, 1867, to Miss Roxie Weathers, daughter of the late Thornton Weathers, of Nelson County, Ky. Mr. Perkins possesses genuine talent as a lawyer; is a man of fine personal appearance, tall, well proportioned, and dignified in his bearing; of a cheerful sunny nature, and is esteemed by a large circle of acquaintance.

HAZEL G. PETRIE, (some of the family spell the name Petree, others as above, which is the original and correct orthography), is a descendant of Peter Petrie, who was born in Scotland, of Scotch-Presbyterian parents. When in his seventh year, Peter attended a school taught by a Presbyterian minister, somewhat distinguished for his rigid enforcement of the rules. For some real or fancied infringment of the rules of the school, the Scotch schoolmaster chastised Peter, who fled for refuge to his mother, who, unfortunately for Peter, was of the same stern stock as the schoolmaster. She accordingly administered a second whipping and started him back to school. This happened near a shipping port, and Peter, failing to find refuge in his native land, took passage on a sailing vessel which landed him in Charleston, S. C. He never again heard of his tutor, mother or any of his Scotch kin. In South Carolina Peter grew to manhood, having spent part of his youth as a soldier in the Revolutionary war. About 1783 or 1784, he married a Miss Hardwick, in Chester District, S. C. By this marriage he had two children: Hazel and Jemima. After the death of his first wife he moved to east Tennessee, where he married a Miss Wilson. He subsequently moved to Todd County, Ky., where he died in the fall of 1841, at an age between eighty and eighty-five years. His second wife died, and a few years before his own death, Peter married an old lady by the name of Franklin, who survived him several years. Jemima Petrie married Andrew Colvin. They resided in Chester District, S. C., and reared a large family of children. Hazel Petrie was born in Chester District, S. C., July 8, 1785, where he lived until he was grown. August 20, 1805, he was married to Sallie Mobley. In 1807, he removed with his wife and one child to Tennessee, and in 1809, he came with his wife and two children to what was then Christian County—now Todd. He lived one year near the present site of Taylor Chapel, and the next (1810), he purchased from John Gray a tract of land three miles southwest of where the town of Elkton was subsequently located. Here he lived continuously until his death, January 29, 1869. By his first wife, Hazel Petrie had borne to him twelve children: John, William, Peter Cartwright, Edward M., Mary S., Eliza J., Lucy A., Hazel G., Garland A., Richard T., Sarah A., and Henry L., all of whom lived to be grown. March 25, 1830, he was married to Paulina Kennedy. Of this marriage there were four children: James C., John

Summerfield, Newton C., and Harriet N., all of whom lived to maturity. Of his sixteen children only four preceded him to the grave. He left fifty-four grandchildren, and forty great-grandchildren. He was widely known in the county; for many years was a member of the County Court, and once represented Todd County in the General Assembly of the State. H. G. Petrie was born in Todd County, July 5, 1820. He spent his early years on the farm, in the meantime gaining such education as the school at Elkton afforded. Later he borrowed law books and studied them at home after the work of the day. In 1844 he entered the office of Hon. F. M. Bristow, at Elkton. In 1847 he became a partner of his preceptor, a relation which continued until the death of Mr. Bristow in 1864. May 16, 1854, Mr. Petrie married Miss Mary M. Bristow, daughter of Francis and Emily E. Bristow. His children by this marriage are: Emma, now wife of John F. Bell; Frank (deceased 1861); Mattie, now wife of T. B. Morton, of Louisville, Ky.; Sally and Benjamin B.

BAXTER C. PORTER is a son of the Rev. Thomas Porter, an early Presbyterian minister of Hopkins and Todd Counties, who was born in Virginia, May 12, 1788. Thomas Porter came in childhood to Logan County, Ky., where he attained his manhood, and where in June, 1808, he married Nancy Lawrence, who before her death in December, 1831, bore him three children, none of whom are residents of Todd County. In February, 1833, he married Jane H. Lawrence, a sister of his deceased wife. This union resulted in the birth of three children, B. C. Porter being the youngest. He was born in Hopkins County, Ky., on the third day of December, 1838, and in the early part of 1839 his parents removed to Todd County, settling on the farm now owned and occupied by F. M. Byars. There the father died in 1839, and soon after his widow purchased 125 acres of land, where B. C. Porter is now living. To this place she removed, superintending the cultivation of her land until her son was of sufficient age to assume its control. She died on this homestead June 12, 1871. Baxter C. was therefore reared to the pursuits of the farm, to which he has adhered. He received the advantages of a common school education, and on the 25th of January, 1866, in Todd County, was married to Miss Henrietta, daughter of John L. and Gillie (Edwards) Atkins. She was born on the 4th of September, 1843, in Arkansas, and came with her parents to this county in child-

hood.   Her mother died in this county, in 1845, and her father is still a
resident of the county.   Mr. Porter now owns a beautiful farm consisting
of 375 acres, mostly under cultivation, on which he produces tobacco,
wheat and corn, and is giving some attention to stock raising.   Their
family consists of six children, viz.:   Carrie Bell, born November 9,
1866; Herschel G., born July 22, 1870; John T., born August 1, 1872;
Bessie, born August 27, 1875 ; Virgil, born January 3, 1879 ; and Thusa
G. Porter, born September 16, 1880.   Both Mr. and Mrs. Porter are
worthy members of the Mount Hermon Cumberland Presbyterian Church.

WILLIS B. REEVES is a son of Willis L. Reeves and Margaret
Edwards.   They had four children : Willis B., Haden E. (now in Texas)
and two who died in childhood.   Willis B. Reeves was born near Elkton,
Ky., June 19, 1835, and was reared and educated here, which has been
his permanent home since.   In early life he began the study of law with
Hon. F. M. Bristow and H. G. Petrie, was admitted to practice, which
combined with agriculture, has occupied his time.   He has served Todd
County in the capacity of County Attorney, and two terms as Judge of
the County Court.   Mr. Reeves was married in Russellville, Ky., in
December, 1859, to Miss Priscilla G. Davidson, daughter of Col. James
W. Davidson.   She is a native of Kentucky, born in 1836.   They have
been blessed with eight children, viz :   Ellen T., who died in early childhood ; Mary G., John D., Hattie G., Willis, B., Jr., Fannie, Beall E.
and Anna McReynolds Reeves.   The family are members of the Cumberland Presbyterian Church of Elkton.

THE RUSSELL FAMILY.   In 1806 David N. Russell, of Lin-
lithgo, Scotland, came to this country, on a visit, and in consequence of
the embargo affecting the transportation between the United States and
Great Britain, during that troublesome period, he was hindered from
returning to his native country, and about 1807 or 1808 settled in Logan
County.   He was born July 12, 1782, and married shortly after coming
to Logan County, Ky., Miss Lydia McElwain, who was born in Londonderry, Ireland, June 17, 1780 ; her mother, Frances McElwain in company with her children, eleven in number, came from Ireland in the beginning of the present century, and for one year located in Annapolis, Md.
They then removed to Kentucky, settling first in Warren County, moving
thence to near Auburn, Logan County, where Frances McElwain spent the

remainder of her life and died at the age of eighty-three years. The exact date of the marriage of David N. Russell and Lydia McElwain is not known; but they settled in Todd County in 1821, improving a farm a short distance southeast of Elkton, now owned and occupied by their son, Charles M. Russell. Here they lived and labored, surrounded by the hardships and privations of pioneer life. The days of weary toil, the individual struggles and sacrifices, will ever form an unwritten page, yet hopefully they looked into the future, and lived to see the reward of their labor, in developing the wilderness into a home of plenty and of happiness; happiness which was heightened by the reflection that they had lived upright and useful lives, besides rearing a family of children to emulate their noble examples. They were members of the old Scotch-Presbyterian Church, in the faith of which they trustfully died; the father, David N., January 17, 1853, and his wife, August 12, 1861. They reared a family of five sons and one daughter. Charles M. Russell, Sr., was born January 29, 1825, on the farm where he now lives, being the one settled by his father, David N. Russell. To him no spot on earth is so dear as this old homestead farm; along its brooks and through its groves he listlessly wandered in childhood with mind free from life's cares, and happy in the possession of loving parents. Here, too, his parents rest in the quiet of the family burying-ground, while he now occupies the proud position of the head of an interesting family. Mr. Russell was married, in 1862, to Miss Gillie M. Atkins, daughter of John L. and Gillie G. Atkins (*nee* Edwards), Her father, who is now a resident of Elkton, Todd County, was born April, 1812, came from Tennessee to Kentucky in early life and has since been a resident of Todd County, with the exception of a short residence in Arkansas. Her mother died in Todd County, shortly after the birth of Mrs. Russell, which occurred October 22, 1845. To Mr. and Mrs. Russell have been born seven children as follows: John Bernard, born September 2, 1863; David Nimmo, May 23, 1865; George Lee, November 20, 1866; Nora Lydia, born July 23, 1870 and died March 14, 1874; Charles Ephraim, born February 25, 1873; Cora Ann, born December 23, 1875, and Mary Todd born December 7, 1879, and died August 27, 1880. Mr. Russell's farm now consists of 425 acres of land, and he is one of the most extensive wheat growers in his county. He is a member of the Elk Fork Grange, and of the A. F. & A. M.

Mrs. R. is an honored member of the Mt. Hermon Methodist Episcopal Church.

GEORGE R. RUSSELL, son of Jesse and Huldah (Standard) Russell, is a native of Elkton, where he has spent his life thus far. His father came to Todd County, when the site of Elkton was a brushwood, and for the many years, until his death, which occurred in August, 1883, was a prominent factor in the history of the county and especially so of Elkton. When quite young he married Miss Huldah Standard, who was a native of the county, and who at the time of marriage was but fourteen years old. She was the mother of four sons, and died in Elkton, in the year 1867. George R., in early life, learned the trade of brickmason, under his father, which has been his life employment and with which he has combined agriculture. He is now engaged in the manufacture of pressed brick, and superintends his farm, which consists of 480 acres of land near the town of Elkton, 100 acres of which are now planted in orchard trees. He is also associated with John Wilkins in the grocery business, on the west side of the public square. Mr. Russell was married near the city of Hopkinsville, Ky., December 22, 1862, to Miss Emily K. Elliott, a native of Christian County, and daughter of Rezin Elliott, and early settler and highly respected citizen of that county. Mr. Russell and wife are members of the Cumberland Presbyterian Church, and have a family of three children : Jesse R., Lula B, and Charles B. Russell. The family residence is on Clarksville Street, Elkton.

JOE C. RUSSELL, grocer, Elkton, Ky., is a native of Todd County, and a son of Jesse Russell, deceased, and the third of his family of four sons. He is justly entitled to the term native, as he was born and bred in Elkton, which has constantly been his home. He early began a mercantile career, first as salesman and manager of his father's store. In December, 1878, he opened a business house for himself, and is now engaged in a thriving grocery trade on Clarksville Street, south side of public square, in Elkton. Mr. Russell was married in Logan County, Ky., in May, 1874, to Miss Eva Merrell, daughter of Mrs. P. A. Merrell, of Williamstown, Grant County, Ky. She was born October 21, 1854. Both Mr. and Mrs. Russell are members of the Christian Church. They have two children : Sinclair M. and Stella L. Russell, the former born June 9, 1878, and the latter June 7, 1882.

DR. E. P. RUSSELL. This gentleman, who is a prominent physician of Elkton, is a son of John M. Russell and Sallie (Porter) Russell, an old and respected family of Todd County, where both parents died, the father in October, 1860, and the mother a few years prior. The Doctor was born in this county September 21, 1843, and here spent most of his boyhood days. He attended for some time the Cottage Home College of Logan County. After the breaking out of the war, in the year 1861, he entered the Confederate Army as Lieutenant of a company, which was subsequently placed in the Second Kentucky Cavalry. He was enlisted for one year, but served until September, 1863, when disability rendered his resignation necessary. Returning home, he read physics under Drs. McReynolds for a time, then entered the Jefferson Medical College of Philadelphia, from which he graduated in 1866. After a short residence in Decatur, Ill., he located in Elkton in 1867, which has been the scene of his labors since, and where he enjoys a handsome practice. In February, 1867, he married Miss Jennie, daughter of Dr. James A. McReynolds. She too, is a native of Todd County, is descended from Scotch ancestors, as is also the Russell family. Her parents were among the early permanent settlers of this county, and are now deceased. Dr. Russell is a member of the Masonic fraternity, and both he and his wife are members of the Christian Church. Their children, two in number, are Sue and John Russell.

THOMAS B. RUTHERFORD. One of the very earliest to locate in Todd County was John Rutherford, the father of the gentleman whose name introduces this sketch. He was born January 7, 1802, and in early life located on land that now forms a part of the farm owned and occupied by Thomas B. He afterward moved into the house where the latter now lives, where he spent many years and where, on the 3d of March, 1857, he died. He was married, December 24, 1822, to Miss Jane Morrow, and reared a family of eight children, viz.: James H., now of Logan County; Thomas B., the subject of this sketch; Carrol B. (deceased); Ellen O., wife of H. H. Gordon; Martina, wife of J. P. Kennedy; John W. (deceased); Emeline, deceased wife of Marion Woolridge, and Elizabeth, deceased wife of William Cheatham. The mother of this family, Jane Rutherford (*nee* Morrow), was born in Logan County, Ky., on the 12th day of December, 1797, and died in June, 1859. Thomas B. was born January 4, 1825, where he now lives, and on the farm that has ever been his home. He has devoted his life to the farm, and is now the owner of 600 acres of land. He was first married in 1844, to Miss J. H. Knight, who died, leaving two children: John B., and Phillip T. Rutherford. He then contracted a marriage with Miss Agnes Johnson, of Todd County, who soon after died without issue. His present wife was Miss Jane E. Gordon, which union has resulted in the birth of three children, viz.: Elizabeth, deceased wife of Edward Curd; William T. and Benjamin F. Rutherford. Mr. Rutherford is an enterprising man, of advanced views, and a member of Daysville Lodge, No. 587, A. F. & A. M.

J. M. SIMPSON is a son of Peyton and Jane (Waugh) Simpson; the former was a son of William and Nancy (Hawley) Simpson, the grandparents of our subject. William Simpson was born December 3, 1769, and died June 9, 1854. His wife Nancy was born June 19, 1785, the time of her death is not known. Both she and her husband were natives of Virginia. Peyton Simpson, the father of J. M. was born September 22, 1799, in Virginia. In youth he learned the cooper's trade and followed it for many years. On November 23, 1828, he started over the mountains to Kentucky. After making short stays in Madison, Fayette, and Christian Counties, he is the fall of 1834 bought a farm three miles west and south of Elkton, where he settled in March 1835, and is still living at the same place. He has been married twice; the first time to Caroline J. Foster, who ended this life August 30, 1840; his last wife was Jane A. Waugh, a native of Christian County. She ended her mortality January 4, 1883. Mr. Simpson is nearly eighty-five years old, hale and hearty, with memory far above the average for one of his age. He is a stanch Democrat and one of the oldest men in the county. J. M. Simpson, the subject of our sketch, was born in Todd County, Ky., July 21, 1847. He was engaged on his father's farm until January 11, 1877, when he was married to Mrs. Elizabeth Poickron, a native of Kentucky. Four children bless their union, namely: Arthur, Lewis and Lula (twins), and Frank. J. M. Simpson has followed farming all his life. He is a member of the Christian Church, his wife a member of the Baptist Church. He has a farm of ninety-six acres, on which he has now nice improvements, all by his own hand. He is a Democrat in politics and one of the influential citizens of the county.

ISAAC SPILLMAN is a son of James and Nancy (Paul) Spillman, who are now aged residents of Hardin County, Ky. His father, James Spillman, was born in 1800 in Kentucky. His grandfather, Jacob Spillman, was born in Maryland and moved to Oldham County, Ky., where James was born and grew to manhood. James in early life learned the trade of a cabinet-maker, and went to Hardin County, Ky., where he followed his trade for many years, and where he now resides. He was there married in 1833 to Miss Nancy J. Paul. She was born in 1803, in Nelson County, Ky. To these parents were born five children, of whom Isaac is the third, and of whom three are now living. Isaac was born in Hardin County in 1838, and there grew to maturity, beginning the trade of carpenter at the age of seventeen. From that time until 1870, he was employed at his trade, with the exception of the time spent in military service. In 1861 he entered the Confederate Army as a Sergeant of Company F., First Kentucky Cavalry. He shared in all the vicissitudes experienced by his command with the exception of a period of imprisonment from August, 1862, to April, 1863, during which time he was held on Johnson's Island. Since coming to Elkton in 1879, Mr. Spillman has been conducting the livery businees. He was married in Muhlenburg County, Ky., in 1873, to Miss Margaret M. Morgan, daughter of Thomas Morgan and Sarah J. Morgan (*nee* Earl). She was born in Muhlenburg County, Ky., in 1842, and is a member of the Cumberland Presbyterian Church. Mr. Spillman is a member of the Methodist Episcopal Church, and of the A. F. & A. M.

WILLIAM PINCKNEY STEPHENSON was born in what is now Alexander County, N. C., and is a son of William L. Stephenson and Lavinia Smith, both of whom were natives of North Carolina, the former of English and the latter of Welsh ancestry. William P. was born July 20, 1823, and in 1839 came to Kentucky with the family, who settled in Logan County, where, in February, 1840, his mother died. His father afterward removed near Hopkinsville, Christian Co., where he lived for many years, and where he died, January 28, 1882, at the age of eighty-four years. William P. is the third child of a family of ten born to these parents, of whom seven are still living. He was reared to the pursuits of the farm; married on October 3, 1852, to Miss Sarah Campbell, daughter of William and Mary (McLain) Campbell. She was born

March 30, 1820, in Logan County, Ky. They have been blessed with five children, viz.: Mary S., Susan L. (deceased), William T., Victoria A. and Helen, wife of George T. Dickerson. Mr. Stephenson located on the farm where he now lives in 1852, it being the first tract of land ever entered in the county, which entry was made by William McDowell. But one opinion is entertained of this family, who enjoy the esteem and confidence of an extensive circle of acquaintances. They are members of the Christian Church, and we deem it but justice to say that the word of Mr. Stephenson is regarded by all who know him as equivalent to his bond, and that he has, in fact, proven himself an example of " God's noblest work."

WILLIAM W. STINNETT, son of Noel N. and Margaret (Winders) Stinnett, was born in Todd County, September 16, 1838, and is the second of a family of eleven children, born to these parents. His grandfather, Benjamin Stinnett, was a native of Ireland and came here when young, to what is now Todd County, where he married and reared his family, and where he spent his life. He was a Baptist minister, with the duties of which he combined agriculture. His son, Noel N. Stinnett, was born in this county, of which he is now an honored citizen, and as above noted, married Margaret Winders, by whom he had eleven children. William W. was reared to the pursuits of the farm; was married in Christian County, February 19, 1862, to Miss Sarah B. Fourqurean. She was born, February 14, 1841, in Logan County, Ky. They have a family of five children, viz.: Ella B., born December 25, 1862; Willie A., born February 8, 1870; Charley W., born January 1, 1872; Ida May, born July 14, 1874; Maggie Booth, born September 2, 1876. Mr. Stinnett was elected to the position of County Constable, in which office he served five years; then served for two years as Deputy Sheriff, and in 1874, was elected to the office of Sheriff of Todd County, re-elected in 1876, serving two terms, since the expiration of which he has served two years as Deputy Sheriff. He is now Marshal of the town of Elkton; is a member of the Baptist Church, I. O. O. F. and Masonic order.

GEORGE STREET, who settled in the eastern part of Trigg County, Ky., soon after its formation, came from Richmond, Va., where for several years he had been a prominent merchant. In Trigg County he opened an extensive farm, and spent the remainder of his life in that place, devoting himself to the pursuits of agriculture. He had a family of several children, among whom was one son—George P. Street—who became a minister of much prominence in southern Kentucky. George P. Street was born in Virginia, in March, 1814, and when of sufficient age went to Illinois and obtained a collegiate education in Jacksonville, the educational center of that State. Returning to Kentucky he completed his education in the Princeton College. Having early in life became a member of the Christian Church, he determined to devote himself to the ministry, a calling for which he was eminently qualified. Being possessed of a fine education and unquestioned purity of character, he soon endeared himself to a wide circle of acquaintance. His ministerial labors extended over several counties, and he is still remembered as a man remarkable for reasoning power, maturity of thought, and for the wholesome influence of his spotless life. He was married three times, first to a Miss Waddell, of Trigg County, who soon after died ; second to Miss Jane McReynolds, of Christian County (now deceased); she was the mother of two children, both of whom died in their childhood, as did the one child born to him as the issue of first marriage. His third marriage was to Miss Susan H. McReynolds, younger sister of his former wife, and is now a resident of Elkton, Todd County. Rev. George P. Street was a man of more than ordinary energy, and aside from his labor as a minister looked after the interests of his farm in Christian County, and also spent much time in teaching, establishing a private academy, where was obtained the rudimentary education of several men who have become prominent in the State. Mr. Street died on his farm in Christian County in September, 1871. By last marriage he reared three sons and one daughter : George P. Street, Jr., John O. Street, Edwin C. Street, who died in early manhood, and Miss Fannie B. Street. George P. Street, Jr., was born in Christian County, November 15, 1848; received the advantages of his father's school, and in 1866, began his business career as a salesman and book-keeper, in both of which he soon developed much proficiency. In 1873 he became a member of the firm of Street, McReynolds & Co., of Elkton, since which time he has prosecuted a successful business, a portion of the time in Guthrie, later in Hopkinsville, returning to Elkton in 1881. He is now a member of the firm of S. H. Perkins & Co. In the early part of 1882 he was appointed to the office of County

School Commissioner, to fill an unexpired term, and in November of the same year was elected to the office. Mr. Street was married in Elkton, in 1876, to Miss Lillie, daughter of Judge Benjamin T. Perkins. She was born in Todd County, in December, 1853. They have one son—Benjamin Seymour Street. Both Mr. and Mrs. Street are members of the Christian Church, in which he holds the office of Elder. He is also a member of the A. F. & A. M. John O. Street, the second son of George P. and Susan (McReynolds) Street, was born February 22, 1851, and was reared to the age of eighteen on his father's farm, in Christian County. In 1869 he accepted a position as clerk in the bank of Elkton, and a few months later was elected to the office of Cashier of that institution, a position which he now occupies and which he has filled with credit to himself and acceptance to all concerned. He is a highly respected gentleman and a member of the Christian Church. In November, 1877, he was married to Miss Willie Clark, a native of Todd County, and daughter of Judge James T. Clark (deceased). They have one son, Edwin Clark Street. Mrs. Street is a member of the Baptist Church of Elkton. Her father came to this county from Virginia, was for many years a merchant in Elkton, and at the time of his death, in 1869, was Judge of the County Court.

L. P. TRABUE was born in Old Allensville, Todd County, Ky., August 2, 1857, and is a son of Dr. B. M. and F. E. (Sale) Trabue, who are now living at New Allensville, in Todd County. Our subject received an excellent education in youth in his native county, and at a proper age attended the City Hospital College of Medicine, at Louisville, Ky., one of the most thorough institutions in the country. He commenced the practice of his profession June, 1880, at Allensville; and on the 14th of April, 1881, opened an office at Daysville, four and a half miles east of Elkton, where he is now located, and is doing an extensive practice. He is of a family of physicians, his father and grandfather being leading men in the profession. He is a devoted member of the Christian Church, industrious and enterprising, and bids fair to soon be among the leading ones of his calling.

SAMUEL HORACE WELLS, County Clerk of Todd County, was born December 25, 1850; is a son of William H. and Mary (Porter) Wells, and a native of Todd County. His father was also born in this county October 23, 1822; was a son of Jesse Wells, and descended from an old Virginia family, which was represented in the State of Kentucky at a very early day. William H. married Mary E. Porter, daughter of Samuel Porter, once a resident of Elkton. She was born February 11, 1827, in Todd County, and died September 26, 1872. William H. Wells was a member of the Presbyterian Church, of the I. O. O. F., and of the Masonic fraternity. He served the county as Deputy County Clerk, and was elected to the first clerkship of the county, under the new constitution, and held the office at the time of his death, which occurred on the 30th of April, 1854. To William H. and Mary E. Wells were born three children: Mary B. (wife of B. H. Milliken, of Paducah, Ky.), Samuel H. and William H. Wells, of Elkton, Ky., the latter of whom is the present Deputy Clerk of the County Court. Samuel H. received a common English education, and when quite young was employed as salesman in a mercantile house, in which he was employed until 1870, when he entered the office of Clerk of the Circuit and County Court, as Deputy under Judge B. T. Perkins; remained in this connection eight years, and in 1878 was the choice of the people for the office of County Clerk. He was re-elected to this office in 1882, and is now serving his second term with universal acceptance. Mr. Wells was married in this county June 1, 1881, to Miss Sallie M. Mimms, daughter of William T. Mimms of Todd County. Mrs. Wells is a native of Todd County and was born November 1, 1855. Their only child, Mary P. Wells, was born April 20, 1882. Both Mr. and Mrs. Wells are honored members of the church—he of the Christian and she of the Methodist Episcopal Church.

HARRY F. WILLOUGHBY, lawyer, Attorney for Todd County, was born in 1852, in Montgomery County, Tenn. His parents were Frank and Mariah (Hackney) Willoughby, who removed to Todd County, while Harry F. was a small boy. His father was a member of the Baptist Church, by occupation a farmer, and died in this county in 1861. His widow was subsequently married to Mr. W. T. Kennedy, who died in 1877. She is still living and now a resident of the town of Elkton. Harry F. was educated in Todd County, read law in the office of S. W. Kennedy, and was admitted to practice in 1874. From that time until 1876, he was the editor and proprietor of the Elkton *Witness*; later, in connection with Maj. Bristow, he conducted the Elkton *Register*, but sold his interest in this paper to his partner in 1879.   He was elected to the office of County Attorney in 1882, and was serving the county with credit to himself at the time of his death in 1844.   He was a member of the I. O. O. F. and of the A. F. & A. M.

TRENTON DISTRICT.

LYCURGUS H. ARNOLD, Postmaster of Trenton, was born December 29, 1831, in Todd County, Ky., where he grew to manhood and still resides. His father, William P. Arnold, is a native of Louisa County, Va., where he was born in 1806; removed with his parents to Christian County, Ky., in 1812, and thence to Todd County about 1830, where he still resides, an honored and worthy citizen. He is the son of Aaron Arnold, a Virginian. Subject's mother, Amadiah, daughter of William Pettus, of Todd County, is still living. Her children are: Subject, Lucy J., Louisa A. and William A., who died at Camp Chase. Subject was married, in 1856, to Miss Sue, daughter of Capt. George H. Taylor, of Hickman County, Ky. She was born in 1838, and died in 1863, without children. After attending the common schools Mr. Arnold was for three years a student in the academy at Clarksville, Tenn., where he procured a good education. He was, by profession, a farmer, until fifteen years ago, and has, for the last nine years, served the community as Magistrate and Postmaster. He is an honored member of the I. O. O. F., and is, in politics, a Democrat.

WILLIAM H. BARKSDALE, Trenton, was born August 22, 1861, in Todd County, Ky., and has always had his home at his present residence. His father, William O. Barksdale, was born in 1818, in Virginia, and removed to Todd County, Ky., with his parents when quite young, where he died in 1870. He was the son of Hudson O., an old Virginian. Subject's mother, Josephine, daughter of William Talley, was born in 1839, in Todd County, Ky., and is still living. To her husband and herself, were born: Fannie M., Annie (Woodson) and William H., who was married May 15, 1883, to Miss Fannie F., daughter of James W. and Mary (Moore) Taylor, of Todd County, and to them has been born one son—Harry Taylor. Mr. Barksdale is a farmer, owning forty acres of good land, which he cultivates in the crops common to this country, and has his homestead in neat and fine condition.

THOMAS BEAZLEY, Trenton, Ky., is a native of Christian County, Ky., where he was born June 20, 1839, and in early childhood removed to Todd County, where he has since resided. He is the son of James Beazley, who was born in Virginia in 1782; served as a soldier in the war of 1812, and died in 1841. His wife, Elizabeth, daughter of Thomas McDugal, was born in Virginia in 1801, and died in 1867. To them were born, Mary J. (Talley), Elizabeth, Margaret (Campbell), John and subject, who was married May 7, 1878, to Miss Georgia A., daughter of James F. and Mary C. (Chiles) Tutt, of Todd County, and to this union was born one child—James Thomas—March 17, 1879. Mr. Beazley is a farmer, owning 413 acres of good and valuable land in a high state of cultivation. He is a giant in stature, standing fully six feet in height, with an avoirdupois of 417, and gaining, making him the largest man in Todd County, if not the heaviest in Kentucky. Mr Beazley is jolly, social, intelligent and hospitable, and quite active for one of his great weight.

ALEXANDER T. BYARS, Sr., is a native of and has always resided in Todd County, Ky., and was born May 5, 1816. He is the son of John S. Byars, who was born in Louisa County, Va., removed to Todd County, Ky., about 1810, where he died about 1826, and Martha, daughter of Stephen and Mildred (Bagby) Terry, of this county. Unto John S. and Martha Byars were born Stephen, James, Mary A. (Petty), Alexander T. and Sarah M. (Grant). Mr. Alexander Byars was married April 6, 1843, to Miss Harriet, daughter of John and Nancy (Taliaferro) Ederington, of Todd County, Ky., who was born in 1823 and died in 1853. To them were born Sarah E. (Harrel), Francis M. Lee, and Newton R. Mr. Byars was next married September 6, 1854, to Miss Sarah H. Ederington, a sister of his former wife, and from this union sprang Harriet (deceased), Samuel (deceased) Nannie, Alexander T., Jr., John E., and George H. Mr. Byars is engaged in the vocation of farming, possessing 350 acres of valuable and productive land, in a high state of cultivation, and in good condition. He has been successful in his affairs, and is one of the prosperous men of the community. In religion he is a Methodist, and in politics was formerly identified with the Old Line Whig party, but is now conservative.

THE CHESNUT FAMILY. Among the prominent families who

early immigrated to Todd County in the pioneer days, may justly be mentioned the one appearing at the head of this brief sketch. Near the beginning of the present century the widow Chesnut removed from North Carolina to Todd County, Ky., and settled on the Elk Fork of Red River. With her came her sons, Samuel, James, John and Alexander. They were zealous members of the old Seceder Church. Of these sons, Samuel, born in North Carolina, 1793, was a valiant soldier in the war of 1812, and died in 1866. His son, William A. Chesnut, was born October 4, 1819, in Princeton, Ky.; removed to Todd County with his parents in 1828, where he married Margaret M., daughter of David N. and Lydia (McElwain) Russell, of this county, where he died January 30, 1879. Mrs. Margaret M. Chestnut was born September 24, 1822, and is still living. Their children are: Lydia A. (deceased), Samuel D., James W. and Martha J. (Burge). Samuel David Chesnut was born August 2, 1857, at the place of his present residence, in Todd County, Ky., where he has all his life retained his residence. He was favored with a fine classical education, and is still an intelligent student of standard works, and the current literature of the day. He is actively engaged in farming and stock-raising, superintending the family homestead of 540 acres of valuable land, which he successfully cultivates. He is a member of the Masonic Fraternity, and also of Cumberland Presbyterian Church. James W. Chesnut, Trenton, is a native of Todd County, where he was born August 20, 1862, and where he has all his life resided. He is the son of William A. and Margaret (Russell) Chesnut. He early obtained a good education, and in the midst of active duties finds time to devote to reading. In 1881, he commenced merchandising in Trenton (firm style Chesnut & Russell) at which he has been fairly successful. He is extensively engaged in the implement trade, and the firm handle a fair proportion of the produce shipped from Trenton. In religion he is a Cumberland Presbyterian, and in politics a Democrat.

RICHARD C. CHRISTIAN, Trenton, was born in Trenton, Ky., October 28, 1847, and removed with his parents to Ballard County, Ky., where he remained six years, after which he returned to Todd County, in 1865, where he has since resided. He is the son of Abner C. Christian, who was born near Knoxville, Tenn., about 1814, and is still living. Subject's mother, Virginia (Falkner), died 1878. To her and husband were born the following children, viz.: Richard C., William A., David M., and Robert H. In early youth, Richard C. procured a common business education. He was married, June 4, 1882, to Miss Laura M., daughter of William B. and Laura A. (Hill) Gary, of Christian County, Ky., and to them has been born one child—Richard Gary—March 28, 1883. Mr. Christian is engaged in the business of farming, having 103 acres of good farming land, which he is successfully cultivating. He is a member of the Baptist Church, and is identified with the Democratic party.

WILLIAM B. COCKE, Trenton, is a native of Hanover County, Va., where he was born August 29, 1824, and resided until 1867, when he removed to Todd County, Ky., his present place of residence. His father, William N. Cocke, was born in Hanover County, Va., where he died in 1826, at the age of twenty-four years. He was the son of Benjamin, also a native of Hanover County, where he died in 1822, having been a soldier in the war of 1812. Subject's mother, Eliza S., daughter of Reuben and Mary (Duke) Nuckals, of Louisa County, Va., was born in 1802, and died in 1882. To her and William N. were born William B., as above, and Mary E. Mr. Cocke received a good education and is a man of extensive reading and more than ordinary intelligence. He was married October 10, 1844, to Miss Catherine M., daughter of Thomas and Ann O. (Holladay) Duke, of Louisa County, Va., and this union has been blessed with William H. (who died in the army), Ann E. (White), Herbert H., Edgar L. and Ida O. (widow of S. T. Moore). Mr. Cocke is engaged in farming, owning seventy acres of first-class land, in a fine state of cultivation, and in good condition. He is a Baptist and is identified with the Democratic party. Samuel T. Moore, son of John Moore, of Todd County, Ky., was born May 4, 1844, and died June 21, 1880. On November 16, 1876, he was married to Miss Ida O., daughter of W. B. Cocke, of Todd County. He died possessed of 244 acres of very valuable farming land. Their children are Katie A. and Mattie H. (See Mr. A. N. Moore's sketch.)

CHARLES B. CRUTCHFIELD is a native of Spottsylvania Co., Va., where he was born December 27, 1841. His grandfather's wife was Elizabeth L., daughter of Gen. Garrett Minor, of Virginia. In 1861 he enlisted in Company E, Ninth Virginia Cavalry, in which he served until the end of the war. His father, Stapleton, was born in Spott-sylvania County, in 1808, and died there in 1859. He was the son of Maj. Stapleton Crutchfield, Sr., a soldier in the war of 1812. Subject's mother, Sarah A., daughter of Maj. William Alsop, of Spottsylvania County, Va., was born in 1812, and died in 1850. She was a niece of Gen. Joseph Rogers, and her grandfather served in the war of 1812. To her and husband were born Corbin, subject, Sallie W. (Gatewood), Robert and Barton. Subject was married October 17, 1871, to Miss Lucy T., daughter of Col. Elijah G. and Sidney L. (Morrison) Sebree, of Trenton, Ky., and this union has been favored with three children : Ada S., Sidney B. and Edgar M. Mr. Crutchfield is engaged in farming, having 315 acres of first-class land well improved, and in fine culture. He is a member of the Masonic fraternity ; also of the Christian Church, and is identified with the Democratic party.

THOMAS P. DANCE, Trenton, was born October 15, 1822, in Simpson County, Ky., where he grew to manhood. He removed to Logan County in 1850, and to Todd County, his present place of residence, in 1882. His father, Peter Dance, born in 1792 in Chesterfield County, Va., settled in Kentucky in 1816. He was a soldier in the war of 1812, and died in 1856. He was the son of Edward Dance, of Virginia, who died about 1800. Subject's mother, Lucy Boiseau, of Prince Edward County, Va., and later of Simpson County, Ky., was born in 1790, and died in 1851. Her father, John, was a Revolutionist. To her and husband were born: John E., Robert C., subject, James W., Daniel B., Martha P. (Satterfield), Benjamin P. and William O. Subject was favored with a good English education. He was married in 1849 to Miss Flowers, of Logan County, Ky. He is a farmer, and owner of 237 acres of good land in a fine state of cultivation. For twenty years he has been an Elder in the Cumberland Presbyterian Church. He was formerly an Old Line Whig.

DR. JOSEPH S. DICKINSON, Trenton, is a native of Louisa County, Va., where he was born, January 1, 1827, and in 1831 removed to Todd County, Ky., where he grew to manhood, and has since resided. His father, Roscoe C. Dickinson, was born in Louisa County, Va., in 1802, and died here in 1863. He was the son of Capt. Cole Dickinson, a gallant soldier in the war of Independence, who died in 1844, aged seventy years.   Roscoe C.'s wife was Emily, daughter of Jesse and Mary (Boxley) Harris, of Louisa County, Va., and to them were born : Jesse C., subject, John R., Mary E. (Day), James R., William S., Spiller H. and Louisa V. (Reeves).   Dr. Joseph S. was married October 24, 1854, to Miss Martha G., daughter of Edmund Ware, of Todd County, Ky. She was born in 1836, and died in 1876.   To them were born : Howard R., Marietta (Bacon), Annie W. and William Joseph.   The Doctor was next married, October 15, 1878, to Mrs. Fannie M. Carroll, daughter of James Perkins, of Todd County, and to them was born one child—Philip G. Dr. Dickinson commenced the study of medicine in 1847 with Dr. Runyan, of Trenton, Ky., and graduated in 1849 in the medical department of the University of Louisville, after which he was for ten years a partner of his preceptor.   In 1851–52 he attended lectures at Jefferson Medical College, at Philadelphia.   Dr. Dickinson has been successful in his practice, remaining at Trenton.   He owns 700 acres of valuable land in good condition.   He is a Granger, a member of the Baptist Church, and a Democrat.   His portrait appears on another page.

MRS. LUCY A. FOX was born in Christian County, Ky., April 11, 1824, and removed to Todd County in 1838, where she still retains her residence.   She is the honored daughter of James Clark, who was born in 1791, reared at Frankfort, Ky., and served his country as a gallant soldier in the war of 1812, and died in 1877.   He was the son of Matthew Clark, a native of Virginia, who died in Kentucky about 1830. Subject's mother, Susan S., daughter of Col. Beverly Stubblefield (of Revolutionary fame) and his wife Mary (Shelton), was born in Virginia, 1797, and died in Kentucky in 1854.   Their children are : Mary E. (Cabaniss), Susan J., Matthew B., James M., Lucy A., Eliza S. (Gary), Emma V., William, Joseph A., Frances M. (Garnett), Alexander C., Richard S., Martha L. (Gary) and Susan J. (Shanklin).   Subject was married July 19, 1852, to Dr. Newton Fox, of Todd County, Ky. He was a native of Danville, in this State, and died in Todd County in 1855, at the age of fifty-two years.   As a result of this union two daughters were born, viz. :   Susan S. (Byars) and Lucy N. (Byars).   Mrs. Fox is the owner of 150 acres of very productive land.   She is a Baptist, and is remarkable for her extensive knowledge of standard works and current literature.

GEORGE E. GARTH was born December 4, 1839, at the old Garth homestead, in Todd County, Ky., where he grew to manhood. His father, William Anderson Garth, was a native of Albemarle County, Va., where he was born in 1796. He removed to Todd County, Ky., in 1810, where he died in 1843. He was the son of Elijah Garth, of Virginia, who was born in Albemarle County in 1773, and died here in 1816. By his fearless activity he rescued many lives at the burning of the theater in Richmond, Va. His father, Thomas Garth, was of Scotch descent. Subject's mother, Elizabeth B., daughter of George and Mary (Baker) Saffarans, of Gallatin, Tenn., was born in 1809, married in 1829, and is still living. To her and husband were born: Webb C., Mary S. (Bell), Julia T. (Fort), Martha T. (Todd), subject, Elizabeth V. (Ware) and William A., who died at San Antonio, Tex. Subject was favored with a good collegiate education, and is a man of extensive reading. He was married April 15, 1862, to Miss Louisa E., daughter of Edmund and Louisa (Anderson) Ware, of Todd County, and this union has been blessed with five children, viz: Nora L., Ella W., William E., George E., Jr., and Bessie. Mr. Garth is a farmer, and has 236 acres of very valuable and productive land, well improved, and in a fair state of cultivation. His attention is largely directed to Jersey cattle, Southdown sheep and Berkshire hogs. Mr. G. is a Granger and a Democrat.

DR. ROBERT R. GRADY was born September 28, 1842, in Todd County, Ky., where he still resides. His father, James T. Grady, was born in Todd County, and is still living here; he is the son of Jesse Grady, of Virginia, who came to Kentucky in an early day and died here. Dr. Grady's mother, Nancy C. (Pendleton), whose parents came from Virginia, was born in this county and is still living. To her and her husband were born Nannie C. (Webb), Mary E. (married to Smith, afterward to Nelson), Sarah F. (Moore), subject, and Lucy P. (Tinder). The Doctor procured a good education in youth, and in 1862 commenced the study of medicine with Dr. Whitaker, of Clarksville, Tenn., and after attending three courses of lectures at Jefferson Medical College, Philadelphia, graduated in 1865, and has been successfully engaged in the practice of his profession in Todd County since that time. Dr. Grady was married May 11, 1870, to Miss Mollie, daughter of Nofflett and Sarah A. (Marshall) Webb, of Todd County. She was born December

29, 1850. To them have been born Robert B., Nannie V. and Will H. Subject is a farmer having 300 acres of valuable land in a good state of cultivation, on which wheat and stock have received his most careful attention. He is also extensively engaged as a trading man. In the commencement of his business career, Dr. Grady started at the bottom round of the financial ladder, and by industry and perseverance has amassed a handsome estate. He is a member of the Christian Church and a Democrat.

MARCUS M. GRAVES was born in Christian County, Ky., July 2, 1850. He removed to Todd County in 1871, where he at present resides. His father, Robert N. Graves, a native of Todd County, was born in 1824, and is still living; he is the son of Joseph P., who was born in Virginia, and died in 1856, about sixty-five years of age. Marcus M.'s mother, Maria L. (Bowles), was born in 1826, and died in 1867. To herself and husband were born Ossian A., William N., Marcus M., Franklin P., Mary L. (Gresham), Ellen V. (Buie), Joseph M., James H. and Robert T. September 2, 1875, Marcus M. was united in marriage with Miss Virginia A., daughter of Wiley and Penicia (Wood) Brumfield, of Christian County, and to them were born Maggie V., Eugene, Claudia, and one unnamed. Mr. Graves is engaged in the profession of farming; owns 300 acres of good land, well improved and in fine condition. Besides the bounteous products of his well managed farm, he is also a successful dealer in live stock. In 1882, he prepared a series of fine fish ponds, graded and walled with stone, and fed by living springs. Into these fine ponds Mr. Graves is successfully introducing German carp, and trout. Mr. G. is a member of the Baptist Church, and a Democrat.

DR. GEORGE A. HARREL, Trenton, was born October 24, 1841, in Todd County, Ky., where he was reared and entered service as Lieutenant of Cavalry in the late war, where he remained eighteen months. His father, William C. Harrel, was a native of Nelson County, Ky., where he was born in 1812; removed to Todd County, 1820, and in 1872 migrated to Missouri, where he is still living; he is the son of Isaac, of Nelson County; Isaac was the son of Moses Harrel. Subject's mother, Caroline C., daughter of Alexander and Mary (Frazer) McElwain, of this county, was born in 1819, and died in 1865. Their children are: Subject, James T., Augusta T., William I., Ephraim P., John M., Lee T.

and Mary Bell. Subject was favored with a good education, having spent four years as a student in Bethel College. In 1859, he commenced the study of medicine with Dr. S. H. Sullivan, of Trenton; read one year with Dr. J. S. Miller, of Keysburg, attended lectures at the University of Pennsylvania, and graduated at Long Island College Hospital, Brooklyn, N. Y., in 1864. He commenced the practice of his profession in Trenton, Ky., where he has met with great success, and at present resides. December 13, 1865, Dr. Harrel was married to Miss S. Ellen, daughter of Alex T. and Harriet (Ederington) Byars, of Todd County, Ky., and to them have been born five children viz. : George W. (deceased), Sandy B., Ellen (deceased), Sallie M. and William C. Dr. Harrel is the owner of a good farm, which he rents to tenants. He is a member of the Masonic fraternity, a Baptist and a Democrat.

MELVILLE C. HUNTER, Trenton, Ky., is a native of Robinson County, Tenn., where he was born July 9, 1838, and removed to Todd County, Ky., in 1848, and has since retained his residence here. He is the son of Matthew and Elizabeth (Moody) Hunter ; the former died in 1848, and the latter in 1849, in Montgomery County, Tenn. Their offspring are : Melville C., as above, Virginia (Carnall), Medora (Gossitt) and Benjamin F. Hunter. October 23, 1861, Mr. Melville C. Hunter was married to Miss Izetta, daughter of Thomas and Fannie (Stout) McQuary, of Todd County, Ky., and to them have been born : William W., Frank and James S. Mr. Hunter by vocation is a farmer, owning ninety-seven acres of good and valuable land, in fine condition, which he is successfully cultivating in the staple crops of the country. In religion he is a Methodist.

JAMES C. McELWAIN was born May 14, 1821, near Russellville, Ky.; removed with his parents in childhood to Todd County, where he was reared and still resides. He is the son of Alexander, a native of the city of Cork, Ireland, where he was born in 1780, and emigrated with his widowed mother to Maryland, in 1790, thence to Logan County, Ky., about 1800 (whither his mother and family followed him), and purchased 1,000 acres of land south of Shakertown, where the mother died. Alexander married Mary W. Frazier, of Logan County, Ky., and to them were born : Frances (Parrish), Eliza J. (Young), Mary (Young), John W., Caroline (Harrel), James C., and Alexander B. James C. was married in 1841 to Miss Mary, daughter of Gabriel L. Yancy, of Todd County, and this union was blessed with : Clementine (Chiles), Maria L. (Bronaugh), James W., Mary W. (Hord) and Edward L. After the death of his wife in 1861, subject married, in 1862, Miss Elizabeth A., daughter of George O. Thompson, of Hopkinsville, Ky., and from this union sprang : Ellen G., George A., Gertrude and Carrie. Mr. McElwain is engaged in the business of farming, owning 225 acres of very fine land, which he is successfully cultivating in wheat, corn and tobacco. He is a Cumberland Presbyterian, a Granger, formerly an Old Line Whig, but now a Democrat.

ALEXANDER McELWAIN is a native of Robinson County, Tenn., where he was born October 28, 1845, and removed with his parents to his present location in Todd County, Ky., in 1849, where he still retains his residence. His father, John W., born in 1816, and died in 1853, was the son of Alexander McElwain, of Ireland. John W.'s wife was Martha D., daughter of Samuel Barclay, of Warren County, Ky., and to them were born : Thomas W., Mary J. (Foster), Alexander, Martha A. (Reeves), Virginia L. (married Sullivan and afterward Pollard), Samuel B., and Irene J. (wife of Dr. Morrison). Alexander is a farmer by profession, and owns 209 acres of good land in a fine state of cultivation, on which he raises wheat, corn and tobacco.

ALEXANDER O. McLEOD, farmer, was born December 17, 1848, in Spottsylvania County, Va., where he grew to manhood, and removed to Todd County, Ky., in 1867, his present place of residence. His father, Richard A., of Virginia, died there in 1853. He was the son of Richard A., Sr., a Revolutionary soldier. Subject's mother, Maria L., daughter of John T. Day, of Virginia, died 1853. To her and husband were born : Subject, Mary L. (Smith), James E. and Marion L. Subject received a good English education. He was married, June 13, 1880, to Miss Hattie E., daughter of Dr. W. C. and Mary S. (Farley), Russell, of Todd County, and from this union sprang two children : William O., February 20, 1882, and Russell E., September 16, 1883. Subject is a farmer, having 125 acres of fine land, in a good state of cultivation. In politics he is a Democrat.

DOUGLAS MERIWETHER was born August 25, 1842, in Carroll County, Miss., and in 1858 removed to Ballard County, Ky., where he remained until 1861, when he enlisted in Company C, Seventh Kentucky Mounted Infantry, and continued in the service until the end of the war. His father, Robert E. Meriwether, was a native of Todd County, and died in Ballard County, Ky., 1860, aged about fifty years. He was the son of Douglas, Sr., who was born in Albemarle County, Va., and died in Carroll County, Miss. Douglas, Sr., was the son of Nicholas Meriwether, also a native of Albermarle County, Va. Robert E.'s wife was Susan H., daughter of Maj. Thomas S. and Margaret N. (Meriwether) Terrell, of Ballard County, Ky., and their union was blessed with offspring, as follows: Thomas J., subject, Robert E., Margaret N. (Davis), Mary E. (Bacon), and Mayo C. Subject's educational advantages were good, having been educated at select schools. On the 8th of October, 1867, he was married to Miss Carrie C., daughter of Rev. John D. and Nannie M. (Meriwether) Furguson, of Todd County, Ky., who was born December 16, 1848, and to them have been born: Robert E., January 1, 1870; Lucy E., January 23, 1871; Nannie M., August 21, 1872, and Margaret D., June 29, 1881. Mr. Meriwether is a farmer by profession, having 320 acres of valuable and productive land, in an excellent state of cultivation. He is a member of the Knights of Honor, and his wife is a worthy member of the Reformer's Church.

ANDREW NEWTON MOORE. The worthy subject of this sketch was born June 2, 1840, on the family homestead, where he now resides, in Todd County, Ky. His father, John Moore, was born in 1799, in Augusta County, Va.; after the death of his wife, removed to Tennessee, remained there one year, and then came to Todd County, Ky., about 1808, where he died in 1882. He was the son of David Moore, Jr., a Virginian, who purchased this tract of land in 1804, and died here in 1826, at the age of sixty-two years. David, Jr.'s wife was Jennie McClung. David, Jr., was the son of David, Sr., whose wife was Miss Evans. David, Sr.'s, father was Andrew Moore, who went from Scotland to Ireland, and thence to America. His wife was Miss Baxter. Subject's mother, Narcissa, daughter of Ransom, and Sarah (Foster) Tinsley, died in 1876, at the age of sixty-seven years. Her union with John Moore was blessed with the following-named children: Sarah J. (Chiles), David T., Andrew N., William D., Samuel T. and Mattie V. Mr. Andrew N. Moore obtained a good education, at select schools, and at

Bethel College; is a man of extensive reading in standard books, and current literature. He was married March 24, 1864, to Miss Sallie F., daughter of James and Nancy (Pendleton) Grady, of Todd County, Ky., and from this union sprang : M. Jennie, born August 29, 1866 (deceased) ; William N., August 10, 1868; Nannie G., July 18, 1870 (deceased) ; Lucy May, January 21, 1872, and Johnnie, June 4, 1874 (deceased). Mr. Moore is by vocation a farmer, owning about 600 acres of valuable and productive land in a high state of cultivation, and in fine condition. On the place are numerous living springs, and each plat of ground is arranged with such forethought and skill that stock may have access to pure water, from any one field, during the pasturing season. Spring Creek also passes through the place, which greatly enhances its value. Mr. Moore is living for his children, and takes a commendable interest in their education and advancement. He is a member of the Grange ; also of the Baptist Church, and is identified with the Democratic party.

JAMES R. PENDLETON, Trenton, was born in Todd County, Ky., November 20, 1850, and has always retained his residence here. His father, Harvey B. Pendleton, was born in 1811 and died about 1854 ; he was the son of John Pendleton. Subject's mother, Louisa M., daughter of George and Betsey Carnall, of Todd County, was born in 1831. To her and her husband, Harvey B., were born : Martha A. (deceased), James R. and Cenara (deceased). James R. in youth procured a good English education, and is a reader of good books and papers. He was married, November 10, 1874, to Miss Sarah V., daughter of Nofflet and Sallie A. (Marshall) Webb, of Todd County, Ky., and to them were born : Marcellus E., August 5, 1875 ; Louisa E., October 7, 1876 ; Sallie A., June 8, 1878; Nancy C., November 10, 1879, and James E., January 27, 1882. Mr. Pendleton is a farmer owning 245 acres of first-class land in a fine state of cultivation and in good condition. He is a member of the I. O. O. F. also of the Christian Church, and is a Democrat.

HON. CRITTENDEN REEVES was born in this county December 28, 1842. In 1849, he moved with his brothers to Missouri ; remained there until 1856, and then returned to Todd County. Of his father, an obituary notice says : " Benjamin H. Reeves, the eldest son of Brewer and Martha Reeves, was born in Augusta County, Va., March 21, 1787, and moved with his parents to Christian County, Ky., about the commencement of the present century, and settled on the West Fork of Red River. Shortly after their arrival in Kentucky his father died, leaving his widow and infant children in comparatively a wilderness, surrounded by the red men of the forest. His mother, a lady of uncommon energy, firmness, and fine powers of mind, richly stored with the truths of the Gospel, in the absence of anything like good schools, laid the foundation for his future elevation in life by her industry, and, with his assistance, they managed to support the younger members of the family. To them he was both a parent and an elder brother; his heart seemed to be entwined around them during life. By his own generous worth and energy of character he soon acquired the esteem and confidence of his countrymen. On the declaration of war by the United States against Great Britain in 1812, he took up arms in defense of his country's rights, and was, on the fourth day of July in that year, elected Captain of the first company of volunteers from Christian County, and in a short time joined the army in the then Territory, now State, of Indiana, stationed at Vincennes; was shortly after promoted to the rank of Major; commanded an escort to the relief of Zachary Taylor, the present President of the United States. In November, 1812, he returned to Kentucky, having been, at the August election previous, elected a member of the Legislature of Kentucky from Christian, and took his seat as a member of that body on the first Monday in December thereafter, and continued a member of that body, with the exception of one or two years, until 1818, when he moved to the then Territory of Missouri. In 1821 he was elected a Delegate from the county of Howard to assist in framing a Constitution for that State, and was, a few years thereafter, elected Lieutenant-Governor of Missouri. In 1826 he was appointed by the Government of the United States a Commissioner to survey and mark out a road from Missouri to the Spanish provinces in a direction to Santa Fe. In the recent Indian wars on the frontiers of Missouri, he again took up arms in defense of his country. In 1836 he returned from Missouri, and settled in Todd County, Ky. The partiality of his countrymen soon called him to represent them in Legislature in several successive years. He filled many civil and military offices in Missouri and Kentucky. In private life his virtues shone most conspicuous —a dutiful child, a kind husband, a fond parent, a devoted friend. Warm-hearted, generous, and devoted in his sentiments, he had many personal and devoted friends.   About the first of January last his health began to decline rapidly, and on Monday, the 16th day of April, 1849, at his residence in Todd County, having, as his friends fondly hope, made his peace with God, with a smile on his countenance, and without a struggle or a groan, fell asleep in Jesus, universally lamented by his family, relations and friends." Brewer's sons were: Benjamin H., Willis L., Ottaway, and Archibald.   Subject's mother was Virginia T. (Garth) Reeves, who died in 1850.   Col. Benjamin's children are: William L., Jennette (Leonard), Mary (Wilson), Benjamin, Missouri (Ainslie), Eugenia (Griffin) and our subject, who procured a good education at the common schools in the county and at the Central College of Missouri.   At the commencement of the late war, he enlisted in Company I, First Kentucky Cavalry, in which he remained two years.   December 16, 1863, he was married to Miss Louisa V., daughter of Squire Roscoe C. and Emily (Harris) Dickinson, of Todd County, who died June 16, 1874.   To them were born: Elijah S., Eugenia A., Benjamin H. and John C.   Subject was next married October 14,. 1875, to Miss Martha, daughter of John W. and Martha D. (Barclay) McElwain, of Todd County, Ky., and this union has been blessed with: Robert D., Luke P. B., Martha V. and Belle C.   In 1879, Mr. Reeves was chosen a member of the Legislature of his State ; and his public career, while in the discharge of his duties, was endorsed by his constituents in his return to the same honorable position in 1881.   He is a prominent and high-toned gentleman, and certainly has a bright future before him.   He is by profession a farmer, owning 187 acres of valuable and productive land, which he is successfully engaged in cultivating, in the profitable staples of this country.   He is a Granger, and also an active member of the Democratic party.

COL. E. G. SEBREE was born in what is now Trenton District, Todd Co., Ky., in 1817, and is a son of Fendal J. and Martha C. (Garth) Sebree, natives of Albemarle County, Va., and of English and French descent.   Prior to the war of 1812, the father was a resident of Richmond, Va.   He subsequently took part in that conflict, being stationed for some time at Norfolk.   Some time in 1813 he came West.   He first went to St. Louis, where he was offered one-half of the present site of the city for a mere nominal sum.   Not liking the looks of the place, he came to what is now Todd County, and settled two miles south of the precinct villxge of Trenton. There he turned his attention to farming, and at one time owned several hundred acres. His death occurred in 1835. Our subject was the eldest of a large family of children, of whom but two are now living: F. J. and E. G. The latter remained at home until about fourteen, and then came to Trenton, where he clerked in the store of his uncle, Granville Garth. There he remained for five years, and then began merchandising for himself, at Trenton. In this business he remained for about seven years. He next turned his attention to farming. He first purchased the nucleus of his present farm at $11.50 per acre. He owned at one time about 1,700 acres, a part of which has since been divided among his children. For many years he was an active speculator in cotton, and he has also been engaged to a considerable extent in developing the rich coal mines in Hopkins County. Col. Sebree was married to Miss Morrison, a daughter of Archibald and Lucy (Fox) Morrison. The parents were early settlers in northern Kentucky, the father being a soldier in the war of 1812. The result of this union was six children, viz.: Fendal, Lucy, Cora, Mattie, Georgie and E. G., Jr., who is now a prominent young attorney at Hopkinsville. Col. Sebree has avoided as much as possible political notoriety, the only office that he ever held being that of Representative to the Lower House of the Kentucky Legislature for the two sessions from 1853 to 1857. During the war he was a prominent Union man, but since that time he has avoided politics as much as possible. It was mainly through the efforts of Col. Sebree that the Evansville, Henderson & Nashville Railroad was built. In 1853 he and other gentlemen living along the line of the proposed road conceived the idea of building it. They obtained a charter under the name of the Henderson & Nashville Railroad Company, and commenced operations. The contemplated road was to run from Henderson to a point on the Kentucky and Tennessee State line, to connect with the Edgefield & Kentucky Railroad, making a line from Henderson to Nashville. In 1854 Col. Sebree, then President of the Henderson & Nashville Railroad Company, went to London, England, for the purpose of negotiating the bonds of the Railroad Company. Not being able to make satisfactory arrangements concerning them, he returned home and continued work on the road, nearly all of it that was graded before the late war having been done under his personal supervision. The company's resources finally utterly failed, and they ceased operations in 1857, owing Col. Sebree a large amount of money, in payment of which they gave him mortgage bonds on the road. In 1867 suit was brought by Sebree et al. to foreclose the mortgage, and upon its sale, under decree, Col. Sebree became the purchaser, and organized another company for the purpose of completing the road—a charter having been granted by the Kentucky Legislature on the 27th day of January, 1867, to Sebree and others, creating the Evansville, Henderson & Nashville Railroad Company—under which company the road was finally completed. The road is now owned by the Louisville & Nashville Railroad Company, being probably the best piece of property they have. Col. Sebree's biography would be incomplete without this short sketch of the Evansville, Henderson & Nashville Railroad; for with this road his fortunes were bound up for many years—from 1853 to 1878—when he sold to the Louisville & Nashville Railroad Company a controlling interest in the bond of the Evansville, Henderson & Nashville Railroad Company, which gave that company the control of the road. And it was very largely due to his faith in the enterprise and to his energy and exertion that the work was finally pushed to completion, opening up as it does to the markets of the world one of the finest mineral and agricultural regions in the world. He has been rewarded for his energy and enterprise by the value the road gives to the vast coal property owned by the St. Bernard Coal Company, of which Col. Sebree is and has been since its organization, the President. Some two years ago, Col. Sebree was stricken with paralysis, and has since been almost entirely disabled from active life. At present his valuable farm is cultivated by his children. Mrs. Sebree is a member of the Christian Church. Col. Sebree's portrait appears in this volume.

JAMES B. TALLEY, farmer, was born June 18, 1846, in Todd County, Ky., where he has always resided. His father, Dr. Zachariah Talley, was a native of Sumner County, Tenn., where he was born in 1817, and grew to manhood, after which he removed to Todd County, Ky., where he died in 1849. He was the son of Zachariah, Sr., a Virginian. Subject's mother was Mary J., daughter of James Beazley, of Todd County. To her and husband were born two sons : James B., and Zachariah, Jr. James B. was married October 30, 1867, to Miss Nannie C., daughter of C. N. Webb, of this county, and to them have been born: Zachariah B.,

Annie B., Ada V., Cordie N., Bettie D. and Mary J.   Mr. Talley is a farmer by profession, owning 250 acres of good land in a fine state of cultivation.   He is a member of Mt. Zion Baptist Church, and in politics affiliates with the Democratic party.

MRS. SALLIE E. TAYLOR was born in Todd County, Ky., October 29, 1845, where she still resides.   Her father, Reuben O. Manion, was born in this county in 1823, where he is still living.   He is the son of James Manion, a native of South Carolina, a Revolutionary soldier, who lived until about 1849.   Subject's mother, Eliza R., daughter of John and Rebecca (Reed) Pendleton, of Todd County, was born October 19, 1822.   The union of herself and husband was blessed with nine children, among whom were three pairs of twins, each single birth alternating with the dual.   Of these children, Mary C. (Taylor), subject, Nancy J. (Bryan), and James A., are living, and John A. (deceased).   Mrs. Taylor was favored with a good English education, and on December 18, 1861, was married to Capt. Benjamin R. Taylor, of Todd County.   He was born June 4, 1837, and died October 26, 1879.   From this union sprang nine children—Maud, Lorena (deceased), Robert L., Mary I. (deceased), Wiley R., James A., Wallace (deceased), John M. and Nettie (deceased). Mrs. Taylor is engaged in farming, having 600 acres of fine land.   In religion she is connected with the Baptist Church.

JOHN W. TUTT, merchant and farmer, was born November 23, 1846, in Todd County, Ky., where he has resided all his life.   His father, James F. Tutt, was born in 1814, in Woodford County, this State, and is still living.   He is the son of James L., born 1777, and he the son of Lewis, an Englishman, who was the grandfather of Gov. John M. Palmer, of Illinois.   Subject's mother is Mary (Fletcher) Chiles.   Her children are: Arthur C., William J., John W. (subject), Georgia A. (Beazley) and Samuel L.   John W. obtained a classical education.   He was married, in 1872, to Miss Mary D., daughter of John M. and Martha Jackson, of Montgomery County, Tenn., and to them have been born Alpheus B., M. Ruth, A. Pearl, George I. and Wallace J.   In 1870, Mr. Tutt commenced the business of general merchandising, at which he has been successful, now owning four establishments.   He is also the owner of 125 acres of splendid land, in fine condition.

DR. JAMES H. WAKEFIELD is a native of Rockport, Ind.,

where he was born August 14, 1821. At the age of twelve years he removed with his parents to Spencer County, Ky., where he grew to manhood. His father, James Wakefield, was born 1790, in Nelson County, Ky.; removed to Indiana in 1818; thence to Todd County, Ky., in 1848, where he died in 1856. He was the son of John, of Pennsylvania, who previous to 1775 immigrated to Kentucky, where he died in about 1815. Subject's mother, Elizabeth, daughter of James Heady, of Nelson County, Ky., was born in 1788, and died in 1827. To subject's father were born : John, Elizabeth (McRocklin), James H., Indiana (married first to Brown then to Jiles), Louisiana (Wakefield), Benjamin H. L., Hilliard B., Zerilda, Eliza, William H. and Joseph B. Subject in 1841 commenced the study of medicine with Dr. James J. Heady, of Spencer County, Ky., and graduated at the Louisville Medical University in 1845; practiced ten years at Merom, Ind.; thence at Daysville, Todd Co., Ky., fifteen years, and retired from practice in 1867, when he settled at his present residence, and engaged in agricultural pursuits. Dr. Wakefield has been thrice married, first in 1849, to Miss Sarah Wills, of Merom Ind., to whom were born James and William. His second marriage, in 1862, was to Miss Octavia C. Mann, of Todd County, Ky., to whom were born Elizabeth and John; his third marriage, in 1874, was to Miss Mary F. Burrus, of Todd County, whose children are : Charles B., Morrison H., Robert W., Matthew and Ova C. Dr. Wakefield is owner of 400 acres of valuable land, in a fine state of cultivation. In politics, he was formerly an Old Line Whig, but now affiliates with the Democratic party.

EUGENE O. WATTS was born in Montgomery County, Tenn., November 11, 1848, and removed with his parents to Todd County, Ky., in infancy, where he has continued to reside. He is the son of Charles G. Watts, who was born in Todd County in 1818, where he died in 1879, and Caroline E., daughter of Dabney and Agnes (Walton) Smith, his wife, who was born in Virginia. Their children are : Alice A., Eudora A. (Sladyen), Eugene O., Thomas D., Charles H., George W., Frank W., Walter L. and Carrie E. Eugene O. was married in 1871 to Miss Emma H. Redmon, of Trenton, Ky., and from this union sprang : Harry W., born October 8, 1872; Rulie R., April 30, 1876. Mrs. Watts died May 16, 1877, and Mr. Watts was next married, December 20, 1883, to Miss Lucy W., daughter of David and Mary (Rollow) Dickerson, of

Montgomery County, Tenn., who was born February 13, 1855. Subject's grandfather, Thomas Watts, was long a Baptist minister, who died about 1860. Mr. Watts (our subject) procured a good English education. He is a farmer by profession, having 151 acres of fine land in a good state of cultivation. He is a member of Mount Zion Baptist Church, and is a Democrat.

GEORGE W. WATTS, farmer, was born November 19, 1855, in Todd County, Ky., where he grew to manhood, and is still residing. He is the son of Charles G. and Caroline E. (Smith) Watts, of this county. In youth George W. procured a fair business education, and is a reader of books and current news. On January 24, 1883, he was married to Miss Mary E., daughter of David and Mary (Rollow) Dickerson, of an old Virginia family, now residing in Montgomery County, Tenn. Mr. Watts is a neat and tasty farmer, engaged in the successful cultivation of corn, wheat and tobacco. In religion he is a Baptist, and is identified with the Democratic party.

CHARLES WILLIAM WARE is a native of Christian County, Ky., and was born November 16, 1826. In 1827 he removed with his parents to Todd County, where he grew to manhood and has since that time had his residence; he is the son of Edmund Ware, who was born in Franklin County, Ky., in 1799, and removed to Christian County about 1820; he was married in 1824, to Miss Louisa V., daughter of Nicholas M. and Sarah T. (Bullock) Anderson, of Todd County, and from this union sprang: Sarah J. (Runyon), Charles William, Mary A. (Edmunds), Jasper A., Susan B. (Runyon), Martha G. (Dickinson), Nicholas M., and Louisa E. (Garth). Charles W. Ware was united in marriage October 9, 1861, to Miss Elizabeth V., daughter of William A. and Elizabeth B. (Saffarans) Garth, of Todd County, Ky., and this union was blessed with five children, all living, viz.: William M., born July 23, 1862; Charlie B. (Walton), June 22, 1864; Lizzie V., August 14, 1867; Edmund, February 24, 1870, and Charles Walter, March 7, 1875. Mr. Ware was reared to the mercantile business, but for the last twenty-five years has pursued the vocation of a farmer, in which he has been very successful, owning at present 800 acres of very valuable and productive land, well improved; his residence, which is near the Trenton depot, is doubtless one of the very best in Todd County. In religion

C22

Mr. Ware is a Baptist, and in politics was formerly an Old Line Whig, but at present acts with the Democratic party; he has been often urged by the people of his county to represent them in the Legislature, but never consented to offer his services. On another page will be found Mr. Ware's portrait.

HARDIN J. WOOD. To chronicle a complete sketch of the Wood family, including their acts and enterprises, their wholesome influence on the development of Todd and Christian Counties, would be a task too great, however pleasing, to undertake in the preparation of this local history. No proper history ever can be written without mention of this important family; leaving the details of their record to be written in letters of gold in the memories of those whose good fortune it has been to know them better than the writer. In the history of Christian County it will be seen that Bartholomew Wood, in 1796, settled at the present site of Hopkinsville, where he spent his life, and of whom frequent mention is made in the history of that city. His son, Bartholomew T. Wood, was born in North Carolina, and at the time of the emigration of the family to Christian County, then just being organized, was a mere lad. His after-life was inseparably interwoven with the progress of the new county, in the history of which his portrait is preserved, and where he died in 1866. His wife was Nancy Saffarans, a native of Rockingham County, Va. She died at Hopkinsville, Ky., only a few days subsequent to the death of her husband. They reared a family of nine children, as follows: Daniel B. S. Wood, Patsey T., Hardin J., George W., Elizabeth (Taylor), Catherine (Gwynn), Cynthia (Smith), Dr. Benjamin S. and Susan V. Wood. Hardin J. Wood, whose name introduces this sketch, was born in Hopkinsville, Ky., August 6, 1821. He was there reared to manhood, and from there removed to Todd County in 1850, at which time he settled the farm on which he now lives. His early education was such as could be obtained by attending the pioneer schools common to his boyhood. He was married in Todd County, November 1, 1848, to Miss Georgiana Cross, daughter of George and Virginia Cross (*nee* Garth). To these parents were born eight children, viz.: George Cross, Louis Garth, Eugene, John Hardin, Willie, Nannie, Georgia Virginia, and an infant who died unnamed. Mr. Wood has devoted his life to the pursuits of the farm, and now owns a tract of 1,700 acres of valuable land in the most desirable portion of Todd and Christian Counties. For years he has been one of the most extensive farmers in southern Kentucky, having in a single year produced 75,000 pounds of tobacco. Of the upright life of Mr. Wood we will not speak in detail; suffice it to say he has never appeared as a witness in court, never sued or suffered himself to be sued, and now in his declining life he remains in the quiet seclusion of his comfortable home, awaiting the summons that will call him from the scenes of his long, useful life. The management of his extensive interests is largely entrusted to the care of his honored sons.

JOHN H. WOOD, the son of Hardin J. Wood, was born in Todd County, Ky., May 26, 1855, where he still has his residence. He was married, October 21, 1874, to Miss Lillie A., daughter of Dabney O. and Mary E. (Dickinson) Day, of this county, from which union sprang one child—Dasie—born September 8, 1877. Mrs. Lillie A. Wood died January 2, 1881. After good advantages at the select schools of the country, subject was a student at Franklin College for a period of four years. He transacted his father's business until married, when he engaged in farming, having 258½ acres of very productive land, in a high state of cultivation. He was also engaged in the livery business until recently, when he closed that out, and is employed as a commercial tourist for the States of Tennessee, Kentucky and Mississippi. Mr. Wood is an affable and gentlemanly man, of genial, social qualities, and with bright prospects before him.

ROBERT D. YOUNG was born November 5, 1845, in Logan County, Ky., where he grew to manhood. He removed to Todd County in 1870, where he has since resided. His father, Robert H. Young, was born near Petersburg, Va., and died in 1874, aged sixty-one years. He was the son of John Young, a native of Virginia, who removed to Kentucky about 1832, where he died. Robert H.'s wife (subject's mother) was Mary, daughter of Alexander McElwain, of Todd County. To her and husband were born: Charles T., William K., Alexander F., Robert D. and John W. On November 29, 1871, Robert D. was married to Miss Sarah M., daughter of James and Fannie C. (Thornhill) Deeds, of Todd County, born 1851 and died 1876, and to them was born one son—James B. Mr. Young next married March 15, 1877, Miss Nellie E., daughter of John R. and Amanda (Burge) Muir, of Todd County, and from this union sprang: Flora A., Mary A. and Robert O. In 1882 Mr. Young was elected Magistrate of Trenton District, which position he fills with honor. He is a farmer by profession, having 350 acres of good and productive land, in a high state of cultivation. His residence was recently consumed by fire, and he is now engaged in constructing one that will be an ornament to the neighborhood.

ALLENSVILLE PRECINCT.

R. D. BELLAMY was born in Lexington, Fayette Co., Ky., on December 14, 1818, and is a son of John and Sarah (Johnson) Bellamy. The father was a native of Dinwiddie County, Va., and came to the State in 1810. In 1812 he was drafted into the war, but procuring a substitute he was excused. While a resident of that county he turned his attention to the carpenter's trade. In 1819 he came to Todd County and turned his attention to farming. Soon after his arrival here he built a distillery near Daysville. This he ran for some time; he afterward put up a distillery on Elk Fork, in this district, and purchased the mill which had been erected by Mr. Stephen Ray. Both of these industries he managed for many years, and at one time he was one of the wealthiest men of the county. He was a Magistrate in his district for a number of years, and at the time of the adoption of the new Constitution he was next to the senior Magistrate of the county. He was a member of the Christian Church, and of the Masonic fraternity. His death occurred in April, 1860; that of the mother in 1831. Our subject is the fifth of ten children, of whom four are now living: John, in Girard, Macoupin Co., Ill.; Eliza, wife of J. H. Terry; Margaret, wife of Hiram Wallace, and Robert D. The old field schools of the county furnished the latter his education; he remained at home until fifteen, and then went to Port Royal, Tenn., where he learned the carpenter's trade. He remained there eight years, and then came to Old Allensville. He only remained here one year, and then went to Keysburg, Logan County. Here he followed his trade for twelve years. In 1866 he came to Allensville and opened a furniture store and cabinet shop, and is still engaged in the business; he now carries a stock of about $1,000. Mr. Bellamy was married the first time in Port Royal, Tenn., in 1839, to Miss Sarah A. Northington, a daughter of John and Mary (Norflett) Northington, natives of the Carolinas. This lady was born in Port Royal, and was the mother of four children, three of whom are living, viz.: John T., in Montgomery County; Mary, wife of William N. Gaines, of Robertson County, Tenn., and Minerva, wife of Archer Bobbitt, of Port Royal. Mrs. Bellamy died in 1852, and in 1855 Mr. Bellamy was married in Keysburg, Logan County, to Mrs. Susan Wood (*nee* Howard), a daughter of David and Susan (Halsell) Howard, natives of Jessamine County. This lady was born in Logan County, and is the mother of one child, now deceased. Mr. and Mrs. Bellamy are members of the Baptist Church. He is a member of Keysburg Lodge, I. O. O. F., and was one of the charter members of the Old Allensville Lodge. He is now serving as Trustee of the village.

R. H. COLEMAN was born in Dinwiddie County, Va., on July 24, 1840, and is a son of Edmund N. and Eliza (Watkins) Coleman. The parents were both natives of Virginia, the father being born there on September 29, 1797; the mother on October 17, 1798; the former was of Irish descent, the mother of Welsh. When subject was about eighteen months old the parents came to Logan County, Ky. They lived there only one year, and then came to this county; here they settled on the farm now owned by subject, and here the father died on April 28, 1867, the mother on January 27, 1877. Both were members of the Methodist Church. Subject was the youngest of a family of seven children, of whom two are living: Mary A., wife of John W. Clark, of Logan County, and Robert H. The latter's education was received in the schools of the county. He began to learn the carpenter's trade, but did not keep it up very long; he commenced for himself when twenty-one. He now owns about 240 acres, with about 200 acres in cultivation. Mr. Coleman was married in this county on February 18, 1873, to Miss Sallie E. Chesnut, a daughter of John and Ruth (Vance) Chesnut. The father was a native of South Carolina. The mother was born near Mecklenburg, S. C. Both were early settlers in this county. Mrs. Coleman was born here on February 6, 1851. Three children have blessed this union, viz.: Lella, Robert N. and Nora. Mr. Coleman is a member of the Methodist Church, and Mrs. Coleman of the Cumberland Presbyterian denomination. Mr. Coleman has also been identified with the Masonic, Grange, and Knights of Honor fraternities.

W. S. GILL was born in this county on July 9, 1838, and is a son of Coleman and Mary L. (Watkins) Gill. The father was born in Fauquier County, Va., in 1806, and came to Todd County in 1810 with his parents, who settled about one mile south of the Lasley Mill in this district, and there the latter died. The father, upon reaching manhood, turned his attention to farming, and settled near the mill; here he lived for upward of twenty years. He then moved to the south part of the precinct; here he lived until his death, which occurred on January 22, 1880. He was in his life-time a member of the Christian Church. The mother died on November 10, 1860. Subject is the third of eight children, three of whom are now living: W. W., in Logan County; Mrs. Lizzie Allensworth, of Haydensville Precinct, and W. S. The education of the latter was received chiefly in the schools of the county. He commenced life for himself at twenty-two, and then settled east of Allensville on a farm of 150 acres; he came to his present place in 1876; he now owns 300 acres of land, of which 275 are in cultivation; he also pays some attention to stock-raising. Mr. Gill was married in this district on March 8, 1860, to Miss Sallie Hughes, a daughter of E. W. Hughes, Allensville. Mrs. Gill was born in this county on October 15, 1841, and is the mother of eight children, of whom six are now living: Waltus H., now a lawyer in Palestine, Tex.; Lelia, wife of J. B. Small, Jr.; Hugh, Earnest, Ned and Emmett. Mr. Gill is a member of the Christian Church, and has been a member of the Good Templar and Grange fraternities; he has served as School Trustee for a number of years. Mrs. Gill is a member of the Methodist Church, and is a graduate of the Clarksville Female Academy.

G. H. GILL (deceased) was born in this county on February 2, 1841, and is a son of Coleman and Mary (Watkins) Gill. The parents were natives of Virginia, and came to this county when children. Subject was the fourth of a family of eight children, of whom three are now living. His education was received in this and Montgomery County (Tenn.). When about twenty-one he enlisted in Capt. McLaine's Company, under Gen. Morgan, and remained in the service three years. Returning to this county, he resided on the home farm for a number of years. In 1880 he came to the farm now occupied by his widow, and at the time of his death owned 350 acres. In 1877 he purchased an interest in Graham's Mill, and ran it in connection with Thomas Graham until the fall of 1880, when the latter sold out his interest. Mr. Gill then continued its operation. Mrs. Gill now has it in charge. It is a water-power mill, and is valued at $6,000. Subject served as Magistrate of the county, and was a consistent member of the Christian Church, as is also his wife. He was married on April 19, 1866, to Miss Douie Mallory, a daughter of Benjamin and Mary (Williams) Mallory. The father was a native of Virginia, the mother of North Carolina. They came to Robertson County, Tenn., where they resided. The father died in 1850, the mother in 1863. Mr. G. H. Gill died on March 3, 1882, leaving a family of six children—five sons and one daughter—to mourn his loss. Mrs. Gill is at present carrying on the home farm.

CHARLES W. HADDOX was born in Logan County, Ky., on November 5, 1842, and was a son of Joseph and Mary (Williams) Haddox. The parents were natives of Virginia, and came to Logan County in an early day, where they lived and died. Subject was the fifth of eight children, of whom three are now living: Amelia W., wife of William Drain, of Clarksville; Mary L., wife of J. T. Donalson, and Claude E. The schools of Keysburg furnished his education. He remained at home until seventeen, and then went into the war; he first went out in Col. Hutchingson's Brigade; he remained there one year, and then enlisted under Gen. Morgan. He was afterward captured and sent to Camp Douglas, and subsequently transferred to Camp Chase; he was kept in prison about eighteen months, and then, returning, re-entered the army, remaining out until the close of the war. After the war he began merchandising in Keysburg, where he remained until 1866; he then came to Todd County, where he turned his attention to farming; he first had 200 acres, and afterward increased it 500 acres. This farm is now carried on by his widow, Mrs. Haddox. In 1869 he purchased Frazier & Winston's grocery in Allensville, and ran it by himself a short time. He then took in J. T. Donalson as a partner. After two years he sold out, but re-engaged in business at the end of six months at the same place. He took in his brother, C. E. Haddox, as a partner, and remained in business until 1882; he was one of the leading merchants of this point during the time he was engaged here; he was also a large produce buyer, and was probably one of the most extensive stock-dealers in southern Kentucky. He was married on November 20, 1866, in this county, to Miss Sallie B. Wims, a daughter of P. A. and S. A. (Mimms) Wims. The father was born near Richmond, Va., and came to this county in an early day, where he resided until his death in 1879. The mother was born in this county, and died here in 1880. Mrs. Haddox was born in this county on March 3, 1849, and to her have been born three children, one of whom, Charles Augusta, is still living. Mr. Haddox died here on August 27, 1882. In his life he was a consistent member of the Methodist Church, as is also his widow, who still survives him.

B. D. JOHNSON was born on the same farm on which he now resides, on November 18, 1832, and is a son of Samuel and Margaret (Hudson) Johnson. The father was a native of Maryland, being born there on November 27, 1786. When a mere youth his father moved to Fayette County, where the latter died. Subject's father came to this county in 1815, where he settled on an adjoining farm. Here he procured a Government patent for 400 acres, but only resided there two years; returning to Jessamine County he married Miss Hudson on October 2, 1816, who was born in that county on May 21, 1797. Soon after his marriage he returned to this county, and settled on the farm now owned by subject. He finally owned some 1,200 acres, which he afterward divided among his children. He died on December 12, 1861; the mother on July 30, 1837. Subject is the youngest of seven children, of whom three are living: J. H., J. W. and B. D. The latter's education was received in the common schools of the county. He commenced to have charge of the home place at eighteen, and ran it until his father's death; he then inherited 275 acres, and of this he now has about 200 acres in cultivation. Mr. Johnson was married in the Hadensville District in January, 1863, to Miss Helen Hollins, who was born in Hadensville District, February, 1838; she is a daughter of Richard and Susan (Higgason) Hollins. They were natives of Louisa County, Va., and came to this county in 1837, settling in the Hadensville District. There the father died in 1869; the mother in 1844. This union has resulted in two children—Ida and Richard. Mr. and Mrs. Johnson are members of the Christian Church.

N. B. RILEY was born in Logan County, Ky., September 14, 1841, and is a son of John and Mary (Murphy) Riley. The parents were natives of South Carolina, and came to Cumberland County in an early day. In 1841 they moved to Logan County; there the father died in

1882, the mother in 1857. Our subject was the youngest of eight children; his education was received in the common schools of the county; he remained at home until twenty-six, and then, commencing life for himself, settled down on the home farm. In 1872 he came to Todd County and settled on his present farm, where he now owns about 600 acres, of which there are about 500 acres in cultivation. He is also paying some attention to stock-raising. In March, 1883, he became a partner with Mr. C. E. Haddox in Allensville. The firm now carry a stock of about $8,000 worth of groceries, hardware and agricultural implements. They are also commission merchants, handling about 50,000 bushels of grain per year. Mr. Riley was married in 1867 to Miss Isabella Page, a daughter of Wilson Page, of Logan County. This union has resulted in one daughter and four sons. September 6, 1861, subject enlisted in the Eighth Kentucky Regiment, C. S. A. He went out as Lieutenant, and in September, 1862, was promoted to the rank of Captain. He was captured at the battle of Fort Donelson, sent to Johnson's Island, and was detained there six months. He was then exchanged, and re-entered the service. He was honorably discharged in April, 1864. He was elected Magistrate in 1882, and is still holding that office. He is a member of the Christian Church.

JOHN W. RILEY. This gentleman, who is a son of James Riley and Mary A. (Rose) Riley, was born in Logan County, Ky., June 18, 1855. He was reared on his father's farm in his native county, where his parents are still living; was educated in the Browder Institute, and is now devoting himself to the pursuits of agriculture with marked success. He came to Todd County in 1878, and the following year purchased of John L. Atkins the farm on which he now lives; his farm, one of the best stock farms in the county, consists of 254 acres of improved land, situated on the Allensville and Elkton road, midway between those towns. Mr. Riley is one of those aggressive, public-spirited young farmers who has only to be known to be appreciated. He is not only giving attention to general farming, but is doing much toward the improvement of the stock of his county. In 1875, in Logan County, Mr. Riley was married to Miss Eddie A. Rutherford, daughter of Ham and Permelia Rutherford, (*nee* Adams). Mrs. R. was born in Logan County, November 22, 1855. Her parents are now residents of Logan County. The marriage of Mr.

Riley has resulted in the birth of two children : Norma, born August 30, 1876 ; Napoleon Riley, born February 22, 1881. Both Mr. and Mrs. Riley are members of the Allensville Christian Church. In politics Mr. R. is a Democrat, and is the Collector of Tax for the Allensville & Elkton Turnpike Company.

DR. B. M. TRABUE was born at Columbia, Adair Co., Ky., June 3, 1827, and is a son of William and Elizabeth (McDowell) Trabue. Our subject's grandparents made their escape from France, and coming to this country settled on Staten Island. They lived there some years, and then with the other early pioneers came to this State. The grandfather was captured by the Indians, but afterward escaped, and lived here until a good old age. The father was a mechanic, but did not follow his trade very much. He paid most of his attention to farming and milling. Our subject was the fifth of six children, of whom four are living. His schooling was obtained in the colleges at Frankfort and Lexington, Ky. In 1846 he commenced the study of medicine with Dr. Winston, of Columbia. Remained under his preceptor three years, and in 1848 and 1849 he attended lectures at the Transylvania University at Lexington, Ky.; returning to Columbia he followed his professional calling there until 1853. He then came to Allensville, and is now the oldest resident physician in the precinct, having a fair share of the practice of the community. Dr. Trabue was married in 1853 to Miss Fannie Sale, a daughter of Dr. L. P. Sale, formerly a resident of Logan County. Mrs. Trabue is a native of this county, and the mother of nine children, of whom eight are living— three sons and five daughters. Dr. Trabue is a member of the Allensville Baptist Church, and of Allensville Lodge, No. 182, A. F. & A. M.

DR. I. N. WALTON was born in Henry County, Tenn., August 19, 1827, and is a son of Simeon and Mary (Henry) Walton. Mr. Simeon Walton was a native of Louisa County, Va., having been born there in 1789, but his parents were of Welsh descent. He came to Robertson County, Tenn., when two years old, with his parents, where the latter died. Simeon grew to manhood in that county, married Miss Henry, who was a native of that county. In 1811 he came to Henry County, Tenn., where he lived until his death, which occurred in 1865. While a resident of that county he served as a Magistrate. He was a member of the Christian Church. His wife died in 1852. Subject was the seventh of ten children, of whom seven are now living, viz.: Mrs. Martha Crosk, in Bell County, Tex.; Nelson, in Bell County, Tex.; Frank B., in Fort Worth, Tex.; George W., in Bell County, Tex.; Isaac N., our subject; L. N., in Henry County, Tenn.; and Mrs. Louisa V. Williams, in Shelby County, Tenn. Subject's education was obtained at McLemoresville College, Carroll Co., Tenn. He read medicine with his uncle, Dr. T. J. Walton, in Robertson County, Tenn., for three years, and in 1852 and 1853 attended lectures at Louisville. Returning to Robertson County he began the practice of his profession in that county with his uncle. Here he remained until 1855, and then came to Keysburg, Logan County. At this point he remained three years. In 1857 he came to this county and settled on his present farm. Here he practiced his profession until 1868. He then moved to Nashville, where he remained four years. Returning to this county he turned his attention to agricultural pursuits, owning at present about 1,600 acres, of which 1,100 acres are in cultivation. Dr. Walton was married on November 2, 1856, in Logan County, to Miss Olive C. Watkins, a daughter of William and Susan (Cheatham) Watkins. The father was a native of Logan County, his people being natives of North Carolina. He is still living, and is at present devoting his attention to financiering. The mother died in 1881. Mrs. Walton was born in Logan County on Febuary 1, 1832, and is the mother of two children, one of whom—Frank B.—is living. He is married and is living at home. Mr. and Mrs. Walton are members of the Baptist Church. Mr. Walton is a member of Western Star Lodge, No. 9, A. F. & A. M., of Springfield, Tenn.

JOSIAH WILSON was born in Washington County, Ky., on March 11, 1837, and is a son of John H. and Harriet (Pettit) Wilson. The parents were also natives of Washington County, and there they lived and died. The father was a soldier in the war of 1812, and was in the battle of New Orleans. Our subject was the tenth of eleven children, of whom three are now living, viz.: Mrs. Catherine Brook, of East Liverpool, Ohio; Anthony, in Washington County, Ky., and Josiah (our subject). The field schools of his native county furnished the latter's education. He commenced life for himself when twenty-one on a farm in that county. He remained there until 1864, when he came to this county and settled on his present farm. Here he now owns 165 acres, all of which are in cultivation. He also follows stock-trading to some extent, handling about seventy-five head per year. He was married in this county on February 18, 1864, to Miss Sallie A. Terry, a daughter of James H. and Eliza (Bellamy) Terry; the father was a native of Virginia, the mother of Todd County. Mrs. Wilson was born in this county in 1845, and is the mother of one child—Earnest. Mr. Wilson is a member of the Baptist Church; Mrs. Wilson of the Christian. He is a member of Olmstead Lodge, K. of H., and has been identified with the Masonic fraternity.

BIVINSVILLE PRECINCT.

JOHN BROWN BIVIN was born December 2, 1828, in Muhlenburg County, Ky. He is a son of Henry and Elizabeth (Jenkins) Bivin. The father was a native of Maryland, and died in 1876, aged seventy-four. The mother was born in Virginia, and is now living with her son-in-law in this county. When about one year old, J. B. came with his parents to Todd County, Ky., and was reared on his father's farm, where he remained until the age of twenty-one. He lived on a rented farm; four years later he bought a farm of 100 acres, where he lived eighteen years. He then traded it for his present one, consisting of eighty-four acres; he owns in all 384 acres. December 13, 1849, he married Sallie A. Latham, of this county. She died in 1879, aged forty-nine years, leaving four children—Mary E., Gracie A., George H. and Martha J. His second marriage was in 1882, to Mrs. Carneal, of this county; Bertie is their child. By a former marriage, Mrs. Bivin has four children, viz.: Virginia A., Mattie, Rosa and Charles. Both parents are members of the Baptist Church.

WILLIAM O. BUCKLEY, carpenter and millwright, was born July 21, 1844, in Warren County, Ky. His parents are J. H. and Levina (Johnston) Buckley, both natives of Kentucky. The father is a carpenter, still living, in Logan County, at the age of sixty-seven years. The mother died in 1863, at the age of forty-six years. The mother was, and the father is a devoted member of the Christian Church. These parents have had seven children, five of whom are now living. Our subject began for himself at the age of sixteen years. He served about three years in the Confederate Army. He was very fortunate in receiving no wounds, and had remarkably good health. His discharge dates May 11, 1865. He was then at Meridian, Miss. He had no moneyed assistance in starting for himself, but now has accumulated a nice home of thirty-five acres, where his residence is located, in Bivinsville. He is a good workman and does all kinds of carpentering, and has been quite successful, considering his start. He was married November 14, 1867, to Miss Cloantha Gibson, of this county. These parents have one child—Mattie Lou. Both parents and child are members of the Christian Church. As a skilled workman he has few equals in the county.

WILLIAM E. BUIE was born in Missouri, May 14, 1847; his parents are John and Susan (Redphern) Buie. The father is a native of Tennessee, his age about sixty years, and now living in Logan County; the mother was a native of the same State; her death occurred in 1882, aged sixty. Our subject began for himself in 1866; he started with limited means; his business was working a shingle machine, with which he worked for wages eight years, when he moved to where he now lives; he has improved this farm and residence, and now has one of the nicest homes in the northern part of the county; his buildings have been placed here at a cost of more than $2,000; he owns 300 acres of good land in this body, besides farms aggregating in all 883 acres elsewhere, all of which are paid for. Mr. Buie employs from twelve to twenty-five hands on his farms, engaged at farming and logging. He has received about $10,000 from the sale of logs the past year. The principal quantity of tan-bark supplied for two tanneries has been furnished by him and his brother; he has also furnished ties in a very large railroad contract. Mr. Buie has been more successful in business than any other man in this part of the county. He was married in November, 1872, to Miss Delila E., daughter of Alex M. and Elizabeth (Whitlow) McPherson, of this county Their children are: John W., Georgie L., Lizzie Z. and Susan C. Mrs. B. is a member of the Baptist Church.

BENJAMIN F. CARNEAL was born in Todd County, November 16, 1855; his parents are Joseph S. and Lucinda A. (Shemwell) Carneal, both natives of Kentucky. The father was a farmer, and served nine months in the Twenty-fifth Kentucky Regiment, United States Army, during the late war; he had the measles while in the army, and never recovered; his death was caused from that disease; his death occurred June 11, 1883; he was a member of the Baptist Church. The mother is still living at the age of sixty-eight, and makes her home with her son Benjamin. She is a member of the Baptist Church. Of their four children only two survive. Benjamin has always lived on this farm and has come into possession of it; it is a home-like residence, with about eighty-five acres of land, situated about a mile from Clifty Postoffice. He was married October 12, 1882, to Miss Mary Groves, daughter of James and Jane Groves, of Todd County. This union is blessed by the birth of one child—Eldred. Both parents are members of the Baptist Church.

ENOCH J. CATHCART was born April 25, 1849, in Giles County, Tenn.; his parents are Allen J. and Eliza J. (Head) Cathcart, both natives of Tennessee. The father was a blacksmith and wagon-maker; his death occurred about the year 1851; he was a member of the Cumberland Presbyterian Church. The mother died in November, 1875, aged forty-nine; she was also a member of the Cumberland Presbyterian Church. These parents had seven children, five of whom are now living. Enoch J. began quite early in life for himself. Farming has chiefly been his business; he settled near Kirkmansville; he sold out there in 1883, and came to his present location—Bivinsville—and opened out a store and was appointed Postmaster; he keeps a full stock of general merchandise such as is usually kept in a country store. By his courteous manner, obliging disposition and fair dealing he has built himself up a large and increasing trade. He was a member of the Methodist Episcopal Church South for nine years, and formerly acted in an official capacity in the church of his choice; he is now a member of the Masonic fraternity.

WADE M. CLACK was born November 13, 1826, in Simpson County, Ky. The parents were Sterling and Elizabeth (Jones) Clack. The father was a farmer, born in Tennessee; he died in 1868, at the age of sixty-five. The mother died in 1854, aged fifty-five. She was a member of the Baptist Church. Wade M., on starting for himself, worked as a hand for several years. In 1858 he bought a farm of forty acres; he then bought and sold three times before coming to his present location in 1874. He has improved his farm, which contains 140 acres. He was first married in 1855 to Rachel Beasley, of Sumner County, Tenn. These parents have nine children, viz.: Mary E. (the wife of William Dixon), Martha L. (deceased), Martha J. (the wife of D. Blake), Sarah M., Eliza E., Charley, Lucy A., George M. and Sterling M. (deceased). Mr. Clack's second marriage was in 1869, to Hettie Wells. She died in 1871. She was a member of the Baptist Church.

JOHN H. HELTSLEY was born October 18, 1838, in Todd County, Ky.; his parents are Michael and Dorothea (Sears) Heltsley, both natives of Kentucky. The father is engaged in farming and now living in this county; his age is nearly seventy years. The mother died in the fall of 1863, aged about fifty. John H. began for himself at the age of twenty-two years; he commenced by farming on the farm where he now resides, which then contained 112 acres; he held the farm sixteen years, then sold and moved to Arkansas. After remaining there one year he returned and bought the same farm; he now owns 448 acres, about 180 acres of which are improved; he handles live stock, buying and selling more extensively than any other person, except one, in this part of the county; he has at present sixty-four sheep, nine horses and mules, besides other stock. He was married January 29, 1860, to Margaret L. Crawford, of Todd County; her death occurred in 1864, aged twenty-four, leaving one son four years of age—since deceased. His second marriage was to Miss Nancy E. Roe, of Todd County, December 22, 1864. These parents have two children: James M. and Seymour W. Mr. Heltsley has been engaged in selling goods in Bivinsville for more than six years; he did a large and flourishing business for the size of the place; he disposed of his stock in April, 1884. Both Mr. and Mrs. Heltsley are consistent members of the Christian Church. Mr. William Roe was born in Virginia about the year 1818. When about twelve years old he moved to Robertson County, Tenn. There served five years at the tanner's trade, and there remained until his marriage with Miss Margaret Bell about the year 1833. Mr. and Mrs. Roe were the parents of twelve children. Soon after his marriage Mr. Roe came to Todd County, Ky., and here pursued his trade, dressing skins and farming until about 1875, when he removed to Missouri, where he died the same year, his wife having died several years previously in Todd County, Ky.

SAMUEL HINTON was born December 20, 1843, in Simpson County, Ky.; his parents were Jesse and Sarah (Mayes) Hinton, both of whom were natives of Kentucky. The father died October 29, 1879, at the age of fifty-two; the mother is still living with her son Wesley in this county. Samuel Hinton came to this county in 1856, and settled in this district, where he has since resided; he was married May 10, 1863, to Elizabeth Bivin, a native of this county. Eight children were born of this marriage: Sarah E., William I., Atlas H., L. Thomas, Flora L., Rodolphus (deceased), Noah J. and Nettie B. Both parents are members of the Baptist Church. Mrs. Bivin Hinton is a daughter of Henry and Elizabeth Bivin. The father died December 11, 1876, aged seventy-three years; Mrs. Bivin is living at the age of eighty years. They had ten children—five sons and five daughters. Of these children, four sons and four daughters still survive.

DAVID W. JESSUP was born February 21, 1836, in Logan County, Ky.; his parents were Acey W. and Sarah (Johnston) Jessup. The father was a farmer; his death occurred in 1866, aged sixty; the mother died in November, 1857, aged forty. They were both reared in Logan County, and had seven children, four now living. David W. began life for himself at the age of twenty-one; he rented a farm for several years, and in 1874 he came to his present location; he owns 110 acres of land, about thirty-five acres of which are well improved; this has been done by Mr. Jessup. He has been holding the office of Magistrate the past seven years; his continuous re-election evinces the high esteem in which he is held by his fellow-citizens. He was married January 15, 1858, to Miss Elizabeth E., daughter of William M. and Hannah B. (Jones) Lyon, both of Tennessee, coming therefrom in 1849. The father's death occurred in January, 1875; he was well and favorably known in this county; he held the office of Magistrate for twelve years, up to the time of his death The mother is still living in this county, aged sixty-eight. Mr. and Mrs. Jessup have six children, viz.: Mary E. (is the wife of Thomas M. Sisney), Benjamin F., George T., John H., Sallie B. and Seth H. Both parents are members of the Baptist Church.

GEORGE LEAR was born in 1820, in Todd County. His father and mother were George and Nancy (Shuffle) Lear. The father died about the year 1854, aged sixty. The mother died in 1864, aged about fifty-five. George began for himself at the age of twenty-five. He rented from his father for several years before buying. He came to this farm in 1860. He first bought 212 acres good land, and has been buying and selling land since. He was in the United States Army about four months, and, while in the service he was taken with the measles and became disabled, and was discharged in consequence, and has been on the sick list ever since. He was married in 1856 to Miss Julia A. Stevenson, of this county. These parents have five children—three daughters and two sons. Mr. Lear is one of the respected and responsible old settlers of this county. Mary E. was married August 9, 1877, to Jesse Joines, of Illinois. These parents have three children—one daughter and two sons. Four months after the birth of the youngest child, Joines left for Illinois, seemingly without cause, and it is reported he has married another woman. The children of Mrs. Joines are: Noah S., George H. and Dora A. The children of Mr. and Mrs. Lear are: Mary E., Eliza Lavina J., Martha A., John Wesley, George Thomas.

SAMUEL McGEHEE was born in 1826, in Louisa County, Va.; he, with his two brothers John and Thomas, alone remains of a family of nine children born to Dillard and Elizabeth (Tally) McGehee. The father was a soldier in the war of 1812 ; he afterward engaged in farming, and died July 18, 1853, at the age of sixty-three years. The mother died July 9, 1874, between sixty and seventy years of age. Samuel began at the age of twenty-two for himself, without pecuniary assistance, and by his energetic industry has amassed a fine competency. He is a farmer, and owns some 700 acres of land in Bivinsville District. He was married in 1848 to Miss Jane Driskill, daughter of Joseph and Susan Driskill, natives of Kentucky and of Virginia respectively. The children of Mr. and Mrs. McGehee are : William D., John C. H., Benjamin H. (deceased), Oscar I., Elizabeth, James H., Susan, infant (unnamed, deceased), Samuel F., Josephetta, Thomas P. and Rosa E. William Dillard died in 1870, aged twenty-two years ; John C. married Martha Shelton ; Oscar I. married Mary Wells; Elizabeth is the wife of Marion Poe ; Susan is the wife of John Woollard. Mr. McGeehee is a member of the Christian Church and his wife of the Baptist Church. Gabriel Shelton was born April 18, 1825, in Todd County, Ky. His parents were Abraham M. and Jane (Latham) Shelton. The father was born in Pittsylvania County, Va., and the mother in Kentucky. The father was a farmer, and died March 4, 1874. The mother died September 29, 1852. Gabriel began life at the age of twenty-two, with a three-year-old colt as his sole capital. He has now 135 acres of land, about fifty acres of which are improved. He was married March 25, 1847, to Letticia Poe, of this county. Of this union nine children were born, of whom one died in infancy.

WILLIAM C. McGEHEE, merchant and farmer, was born November 9, 1844, in Todd County; his parents were John and Julia A. (Pendleton) McGehee, natives of Virginia. The father is living in this county, and engaged in farming; the mother died June, 1879. Our subject began for himself on the farm at the age of twenty-one; he worked two years on his mother-in-law's farm, and attended land of his own also; he lived at Bivinsville one year, and came to his present location in 1869; he owns 156 acres of land where he now resides; he keeps a store of dry goods and groceries, where he does a good business for a country store; he enlisted in the Union Army in 1863, and served about seventeen months; he took part in the battles of Saltworks and Slaughterville, besides many dangerous skirmishes; he was much impaired in health while in the service, owing to exposure. He was married to Lizzie E., daughter of Thomas and Philadelphia (Young) Taylor. They were married in 1866. These parents have five children, viz.: Charles W., Dora, Lucien A., Horace and Nannie L. Both parents are members of the Baptist Church.

JOHN J. POGUE was born June 18, 1851, in Logan County, Ky.; he is a son of James R. and Sarah (Johnson) Pogue. The father was born in Sumner County, Tenn., and is now living on his farm in Logan County. The mother was born in Logan County; she died December 2, 1882, aged sixty-two. Our subject was raised on his father's farm, and in 1881 he commenced to learn the blacksmith's trade, which he has since followed. August 15, 1882, he came to his present locality, where he has since carried on this business. Mr. Pogue is a minister of the Missionary Baptist Church, having been engaged in preaching since October, 1883; he is a representative man of this district, and at present is Chairman of School District No. 27; he was also Postmaster at this point in 1883. Mr. Pogue was married May 12, 1875, to Lurena J. Sharp, of Logan County. She died September 23, 1878, aged thirty-one, leaving one son—John W. His second marriage occurred September 6, 1881, to Sarah B. Latham, of this county; this marriage was blessed with one son—Vernal C.

HENRY R. RUDD was born July 15, 1842, in Todd County; he is a son of Richard and Lavina (Francis) Rudd, who are natives of Kentucky, and now living in this precinct. Henry R. enlisted in 1861, in Company F, Twenty-fifth United States Kentucky Infantry. This regiment was afterward consolidated with the Seventeenth Infantry; he was then transferred to Company D. After serving eighteen months he was discharged on account of sickness caused by exposure and from the effects of which he has suffered more or less since, which is gradually impairing his health, and leaves him in poor hope of ever being himself again. On returning home he engaged in farming, which he has since continued; in 1874 he came to his present farm, where he is now completing a residence which cost about $300. Mr. Rudd was married August 13, 1863, to Nancy Jane Wells, of Kentucky; she died in 1873, leaving three sons. His next marriage was in 1874 to Elizabeth Heltsley, of this county. This marriage is blessed with one son. They are members of the Missionary Baptist Church.

JOHN STEPHENS. Among the most intelligent and best read men in the precinct may be mentioned the worthy old gentleman whose name heads this sketch. He was born August 18, 1827, in Simpson County, Ky; his parents were Wallace and Mary (Beasley) Stephens, both natives of Virginia. The father was a farmer and died in 1852, aged eighty-seven years; the mother died in 1846, aged sixty-two years. Both parents were active and life-long members of the Baptist Church. John began for himself at the age of twenty-three years; he settled first on a farm in Simpson County; this farm consisted of 126 acres; he lived there twenty-six years; in 1874 he came to his present location, where he has seventy-five acres. He was married, April 28, 1849, to Martha Mayes, daughter of Thomas and Sarah (Bridges) Mayes, both deceased. They were members of the Baptist Church. Mrs. Stephens was born August 16, 1826, in east Tennessee. To Mr. and Mrs. Stephens were born seven children—Mary Elizabeth, Martha L., James T., Jemima E., and three that died in early childhood. Mary E. is the wife of J. Settle; George W., Mary J., John H., Alice and Leslie are their children. Martha L. is the wife of Joseph Garret; Florence, John H. and Rosa E. are their children. Mr. and Mrs. Stephens are members of the Baptist Church.

WILLIAM W. STINSON was born April 23, 1832, in Rutherford County, Tenn.; his parents were Archibald and Elizabeth (Smothers) Stinson. The father was a native of Kentucky, the mother of Tennessee. The father was a blacksmith, and died in 1865, aged seventy years; he was a minister in the Baptist Church for more than thirty years. The mother is still living with her grand-daughter in Logan County at the advanced age of eighty-two years. She is a member of the Baptist Church. William W. was married, December 10, 1851, to Miss Margaret E. Vanderveer, a native of Scott County, Ky. These parents have had seven children, viz.: Joseph P., Sarah J. (deceased), John W. (deceased), Margaret A., Mary A., Robert A. and Richard B. Joseph P. married Anna Turner. Margaret A. married J. W. Whitson. Mary A. married James Moore. After marriage Mr. W. and wife moved to his present locality. It was then his father-in-law's land; he has since purchased the same. This home and surroundings are the type of neatness, comfort and happiness. His present farm contains sixty acres, and is well improved. His wife's parents were Peter S. and Sallie (Barrett) Vanderveer. The former was a native of Pennsylvania, the latter of Ohio. Both parents were life-long and devoted members of the Baptist Church. Mr. Stinson was elected Magistrate to fill the vacancy occasioned by the retirement of Squire Mayes. In June last he was regularly elected to fill the office.

TOWN OF GUTHRIE.

R. N. ADAMS was born October 7, 1842, in Todd County ; he is a son of W. D. and Frances (Grady) Adams. The father was born in Virginia in 1805 ; he died in March, 1876 ; the mother died in 1850. In about 1827 these parents came to Todd County and engaged in farming. Our subject was raised on this farm. He enlisted in 1862 in Company A in Woodward's Cavalry, and served about five months, when he returned home and continued farming. He now owns the homestead with 200 acres ; also 600 acres where he now resides, and 116 acres two miles east of this point ; he owns a house and lot at Morris Station and two town lots in Trenton. In April, 1881, he opened his present store, and carries a general stock of about $4,000. Mr. Adams was married in December, 1865, to Miss Mattie J. Grady, of this county, by whom he had three children—two now living. He is a member of the Masonic fraternity.

W. W. COLEMAN was born November 17, 1821, in Mecklenburg County, Va. He is a son of James B. and Sarah (Williams) Coleman. The father was born June 10, 1796, in the same county and State; he died December 10, 1883, in his eighty-eighth year, in Houston County, Tenn. The mother was born in Amelia County, Va. ; she died in 1879, aged seventy-nine, in Montgomery County, Tenn. Our subject was raised on his father's farm ; about 1843 he came to Montgomery County, Tenn., where he remained till 1850, when he moved to Alabama and was engaged in merchandising till 1867. He then removed to Christian County Ky., and sold goods at Garretsville two and a half years. In May, 1870, he came to Guthrie and was engaged in merchandising two years, after which he came to his farm, and with the exception of two years in selling goods, he has been engaged in agricultural pursuits since. Mr. Coleman was married in 1858 to Mrs. Williams, of Alabama. This union was blessed with one son—James Percy—now a resident of Arkansas, and a teacher at the Southern Collegiate Institute, Franklin County, where he has been the past four years. Second marriage to Mrs. Mildred F. Carneal, a native of Todd County; she has one daughter—Frances Howard—now Mrs. Hackney, also living on the farm.

P. O. DUFFY was born September 10, 1837, in Hartsville, Tenn. He is a son of Francis and Permelia (Parker) Duffy. In 1845 he came with his parents to Todd County and was raised on his father's farm, where he remained until the age of sixteen years. He then secured employment as clerk in the store of Taylor & Duffy, and remained with this firm about one year, after which his father opened a store and he began then to clerk for him. They carried on the business until the death of his father, which occurred May 2, 1858. The business then was closed out. In 1869 he engaged in merchandising and continued until the spring of 1884. In 1879 he was elected Magistrate and still holds the office. He owns a steam saw-mill and operates two steam threshing machines and is engaged in farming. He was married in 1857 to Miss Mary E., daughter of Burnley D. Smith, one of the oldest settlers in the county. They have three sons and five daughters. Mr. Duffy is a member of the Knights of Honor and treasurer of the same organization. He is an old and respected citizen of the county, well and favorably known.

M. HALL, firm of Levy & Hall, dry goods, is a native of Bohemia. In 1845 he came to Grant County, Wis.; was there employed in the dry goods business, where he remained two or three years; he then removed to Randolph County, Ill.; continued in the same business there about three years, after which he went to Louisville, Ky.; there he remained but a short time, and after various other changes came to Hadensville in 1853, and for the past thirty years has been a resident of this locality. He is the oldest business man in Guthrie, and with the exception of an absence of about eight months, he has been in business in Guthrie the past fifteen years. The present firm was established in 1884. Mr. Hall was married, in 1854, to Miss B. J. Halscel, of Montgomery County, Tenn. This lady died October 27, 1883, aged fifty, leaving two children— one son and one daughter.

COLEMAN JORDAN was born November 21, 1812, in Halifax County, Va. In 1829 he came to the neighborhood of Bowling Green, Ky.; soon after removed to Todd County, where he has since resided, and for many years engaged at the carpenter trade, also farming. He was married, in 1846, to Lucy H. Terry. She was born in 1826 in Tennessee. Eight children have been born to this union : Elizabeth, Granville C. A., Tabithe, Maria, Coleman E., Robert, Dixie and Lucy J. His three sons are carrying on the carpenter trade—Granville C. A., Coleman E. and Robert.

MISS SARAH F. KING was born August 23, 1825, in Orange County, Va.; she is a daughter of H. R. and Mary Ann (Peacher) King, both born in the same county and State. The father died in 1838, aged thirty-four; the mother died in 1863, aged fifty-six. When young she came with her parents to within two miles of Clarksville, Tenn.; there lived till 1850 ; she then moved to Todd County, and has since resided with the Meriwether family, first on the Meriville farm, and now on the Fairfield farm. Her brother, John W., entered the Confederate Army in 1861 as First Lieutenant, Company L, Fourteenth Tennessee Infantry ; he was wounded at the battle of Fredericksburg, and from the effects of which died December 25, 1862.

JO LINEBAUGH was born January 12, 1823, in Logan County, Ky.; he is the son of Thomas and Ann (Owings) Linebaugh. The father was a native of Pennsylvania ; he died in 1854, aged seventy. The mother was born in Maryland ; she died in 1868, aged seventy-three. Our subject was raised on his father's farm ; he continued to follow farming until 1877, when he came to Guthrie and opened a drug store, which, after running a few years, he sold out and engaged in the grocery and liquor business, which he still continues. Mr. Linebaugh was married in 1847 to Miss M. J. Reasons, of Montgomery County, Tenn. One son has blessed this union. Mr. Linebaugh is a member of the Board of Trustees ; he owns a farm in Montgomery County of 300 acres, well improved.

DR. W. D. MERIWETHER was born April 21, 1854, in Arkansas; he is a son of Dr. James H. and Lucy (McClure) Meriwether. The father was born in Todd County in 1812, and is now living with his son on this farm. The mother was born in Clarksville, Tenn., in 1830, now deceased. At the close of the war our subject came to what is known as the Meriville farm, originally consisting of 900 acres, which has since been increased to 1,300 acres. The extensive improvements of this farm, which are probably the best in the precinct, were placed there principally by his uncles, Dr. Charles Meriwether and W. D. Meriwether, Sr. They cost several thousand dollars. This property was willed him by his uncle, who named it the "Meriville farm." In 1874 and 1875 our subject attended the University of Virginia, and graduated at the University of Pennsylvania in the class of 1876; he, after graduation, practiced at Jefferson County, Ala., one year, then came to where he now resides and practiced about a year, since which time he has been engaged in superintending his farm. His marriage occurred January 10, 1883, to Miss May Barker, of Arkansas, but raised in Tennessee.

THOMAS S. MIMMS was born April 1, 1839, in Todd County; he is a son of William T. and Parthenia A. Kimbrough, daughter of Capt. Thomas B. Kimbrough, who was one of the earliest settlers of this county. The father was born March 23, 1815, in Christian, now Todd County; he died April 18, 1861. The mother was born December 28, 1817, also in this county. This lady died April 3, 1881. Our subject was married September 16, 1862, to Bell L. Taliaferro, of this county, by whom he has four children—one son and three daughters. They are members of the Methodist Episcopal Church South.

T. P. NORRIS, of the firm of Norris & Tate, dealers in dry goods, notions, etc., was born December 11, 1844, in Montgomery County, Tenn., he is a son of William J. and Polly (Adams) Norris, both natives of the same State and county. The father was born February 24, 1818, and is now living in Ballard County, Ky. The mother died in 1868, aged forty-six years. Our subject was reared in Ballard County, Ky. In 1873 he came to Guthrie, and with his brother, Morgan C., opened a general store. This they continued four years, when the brother died, and they closed out the business. In 1880 the present firm was established. They have been doing an increasing business, their sales now amounting to $8,000 or $10,000 a year. He was appointed Postmaster in March, 1881, and still holds the office; he has been a member of the Town Board, and while a member was Clerk of that body. Mr. Norris was married in 1882 to Miss Luella, daughter of A. M. Covington, of Clarksville, Tenn.

JOSEPH R. PERKINS was born April 21, 1815, in Russell County, Ky. The parents were Richard and Nancy (Graves) Perkins. The father was born in North Carolina; he died June 4, 1847, aged fifty-eight. The mother was born in Virginia; she died March 14, 1848, aged sixty. Our subject came to Elkton in 1834, where he sold goods till 1840, when he came to this farm, where he has since lived. This farm consists of about 600 acres, and is improved with buildings which cost over $12,000. His brother, Judge Ben T. Perkins, a resident of Elkton, has held public offices ever since coming to this county. Mr. Perkins was married in 1837 to Miss M. P. Gray. She was born in Todd County, October 19, 1819. This lady died January 13, 1875, leaving seven children—four sons and three daughters. He is a member of the Christian Church.

J. L. PHILLIPS, agent of the Louisville & Nashville Railroad, was born May 7, 1841, in Mercer County, Ky.; he is a son of John and Rowena (Parker) Phillips, both natives of Pennsylvania. At the age of sixteen our subject engaged in teaching school, and continued at that until the age of twenty-four; he then secured employment with the St. Louis & South-Eastern Railroad, remaining with them about two years. He was employed by the Louisville & Nashville Railroad in 1860, and has been engaged with this company ever since. The past five years he has held his present position, discharging his duties with honor to himself and good satisfaction to the company. He was married in 1857 to Calpumia Powell, a native of Davidson County, Tenn. Three children have blessed this union. Their names are Powell, Willard and Bettie. Powell is in the employ of the same railroad company with his father.

S. PLATOWSKY was born February 14, 1847, in Bohemia. In 1869 he came to St. Louis, where he remained about six months, after which he removed to Tennessee, where he remained till 1871; he then came to Guthrie, and carried on the photographing business one year. In 1872 he opened a store, with a stock of about $50. By strict atten- tion to business his trade has rapidly increased, and he now carries a stock of about $12,000. He also owns this store and residence, valued at about $3,000. This is the oldest business house in Guthrie. He was married December 27, 1871, to Miss L. C. Halscel. She was born in Todd County. This union has been blessed with four children—three daughters and one son.

JOHN McL. ROACH was born June 16, 1843, in Todd County; he is the fourth child of a family of seven born to John and Pamelia Ann (McLean) Roach. The father was born August 13, 1807, and in 1812 came with his father, Gabriel Roach, to this farm. In about 1840 the father bought out the remaining heirs of the estate, and engaged in farming with marked success till the time of his death, which occurred January 22, 1872, leaving his three children in comfortable circumstances. John inherited 140 acres, and bought out his brother's interest; he now owns about 500 acres, and it is one of the finest farms in the county. His residence, which is a very comfortable one, is situated on a gradual elevation, with a commanding view of several miles in every direction; shade and ornamental trees in profusion adorn this home. Mr. Roach also owns property in Guthrie. His mother was the daughter of Rev. Ephraim McLean, of the Cumberland Presbyterian Church, who was the first ordained preacher of that church at Old McAdoo, Tenn. She died March 20, 1870, aged fifty-nine. Mr. Roach was married December 5, 1867, to Miss Sallie Bell, daughter of J. W. Bell, and grand-daughter of the late Rev. Caleb Bell, of this county; he is a member of the Cumberland Presbyterian Church, Masonic fraternity and K. of H. Mrs. Roach is a life-long member of the Methodist Episcopal Church South.

W. H. SALMON was born September 14, 1844, in Todd County. He is a son of Capt. William and E. P. (Cobb) Salmon, parents both born in Virginia; they came to Todd County in about 1829. The father died in 1847. Our subject was raised on his mother's farm. She died in February, 1880, leaving three children: America A., John and William H., who was married April 20, 1882, to Miss Sallie Bell, of Arkansas. One son gladdens their home—David B. This farm consists of about 220 acres of land, well improved.

HON. D. B. SMITH was born January 8, 1827, in Todd County, Ky.; he is a son of Spotswood Smith and Martha A. (Terry). The father was born December 14, 1800, in Louisa County, Va.; he came to Kentucky in 1816, and two years later settled in what is now Todd County, and at present living with his son. Our subject in September, 1844, went to Hadensville, and worked two years for his board in the store of Stephen and John Terry. The third year he secured a position with Ed Payne at a salary of $300 and board, a year; at the expiration of this time he was obliged to give up his situation on account of ill health, although he was offered a salary of $600 should he remain; he then bought the office of Sheriff from William M. Terry, which he held two years; he again bought the same office from Dr. Fox; this he held until the adoption of the new Constitution; he then engaged in farming, which occupation he has pursued ever since with good success; he first bought a farm of sixty acres, which he afterward sold, and then bought 500 acres in Logan County, where he lived ten years; he then bought a farm of 200 acres near Clarksville, Tenn. After holding this two years he traded it for the farm he now owns, where he resides. This farm contains 620 acres. He now owns in all about 1,500 acres. His brick residence was completed in 1867, at a cost of $15,000. Mr. Smith began life a poor boy. By his own energy, honesty and integrity he has become one of the most valuable citizens of the county; he represented Todd County in the Legislature in 1876 and 1877; he was married November 13, 1850, to Olivia D. Tyler, a native of Todd County. His family consists of four daughters, having lost his only two sons and his eldest daughter. See the portrait of Mr. Smith elsewhere.

SAMUEL W. TALIAFERRO is a resident of Guthrie Precinct, and lives upon the farm where he was born April 15, 1843. He is the fifth child of a family of six, born to Samuel W. and Sallie (Moore) Taliaferro. The father was born in Albemarle County, Va., July 19, 1798. In youth he came to Greene County, Ky., a few years later he came to Todd County and settled on this farm, where his widow now resides; he died October 11, 1879. On coming here he worked at the brick-laying trade, and at the end of a few years had earned sufficient means to buy 150 acres of land, which has since been increased to about 500 acres; he applied himself diligently to agricultural pursuits, and as a result was enabled to leave his surviving children each a handsome legacy; he was rigidly honest and exacting, both as to paying and collecting honest debts. An incident may be related which goes to show his honesty. In 1819 he borrowed from a young man a pair of saddle-bags and an umbrella in Kentucky, to take on his trip to Virginia. On his return to Kentucky the young man was gone, and could not be found; after a lapse of over fifty years, he accidentally heard that this friend was living in Hart County, Ky.; these articles being worth about $8, Mr. Taliaferro computed the interest for this length of time with the principal, and deputized a Methodist preacher to call on this man and pay him for these articles with interest; he at first refused but was finally persuaded to accept pay.

Though naturally indisposed to give, he had become by the grace of God, one of the largest, most regular and reliable contributors to the enterprises of the church (Methodist Episcopal Church South), with which he was connected. He was married June 24, 1829, to Sallie (McClung) Moore; she was born in August, 1804, in Virginia; her parents were David Moore and Jennie McClung; they came to what is now Todd County in 1807, and settled near Trenton on Spring Creek; this family consisted of ten children: Polley, Jennie, Nancy, Isabella, Andrew, David, Patsey, John, Betsey and Sallie; the latter is the only surviving member of this family and mother of six children: David, for the past thirty years a resident of Warren County, Ill.; Isabella, Samuel W., Frank, Leroy and Sallie Mac. Leroy died July 18, 1859, aged twenty-four; Samuel W. was married in 1870 to Alice Millen of Todd County; she died June 11, 1880, leaving two children: Samuel W. and Jennie Mac. S. W. owns the farm known as the Squire Terry Place, which consists of 450 acres, and also has charge of his mother's farm. About six years ago he engaged in breeding Jersey cattle and Poland China pigs; his herd of cattle is valued now at about $10,000. See portrait of S. W. Taliaferro, Sr., on another page.

W. F. TATE, of the firm of Norris & Tate, dry goods, notions, etc., was born December 8, 1823, in Todd County, Ky. He is a son of Francis and Martha (McGehee) Tate, both natives of Louisa County, Va. The father was born in 1795, and died in August, 1842. The mother was born in 1797, and died January, 1878. They came to what is now Todd County in 1819, and engaged in farming. Our subject was raised on the farm, where he remained until the fall of 1860, when he moved to Robertson County, Tenn., and there engaged seventeen years in the milling business. After this he moved to Guthrie, where he has since resided. In 1880 he began the mercantile business in the above firm. He was married June, 1857, to Martha H. Goggin, a native of Todd County, Ky.

THOMAS H. WHITE was born in Northumberland County, Pa., July 12, 1852; he is a son of James and Isabella (Frymire) White, also natives of Pennsylvania. Our subject was raised in his native State, there took up the printer's trade, which he followed three years. In 1871 he came to Mason, Tenn., and was employed by the Louisville & Nashville Railroad two years, after which he moved to Covington, Tenn., and was

Agent for the C. &. O. R. R. March 25, 1880, he secured a position as Express Messenger for the Southern Express Company, in which capacity he was employed till February 21, 1881, when he was appointed Agent of the Southern and Adams Express Companies at this point; this position he has since honorably filled. Mr. White was married September 1, 1874, to Miss Jennie Levegood, of Jersey Shore, Penn., by whom he has two children—Howard and Harry. He is a member of Covington (Tenn.) Lodge, No. 150, F. & A. M., K. of H. of Covington (Tenn.), No. 1434, and Ancient Order U. W., No. 58.

DR. R. V. WILLIAMS was born April 1, 1850, in Robertson County, Tenn. He is the son of Rev. R. Williams of the Baptist Church, who was born in 1811, and died May, 1877, in Todd County; his mother was Jane (Fuqua) Williams, who was born in 1812 in Virginia and is at present living with her son, Dr. Williams. In 1870 our subject took up the study of medicine under the preceptorship of Dr. C. A. Elliott, studying four years. He attended the Medical Department of the Louisville University, graduating in the class of 1874. He then located at Woodville, Ballard Co., Ky. He there engaged in the practice of his chosen profession until 1877, when he came to Guthrie, where he has since resided and followed his calling. He was married in November, 1882, to Miss Mary, daughter of the late Rev. Charles M. Day, of Todd County. The latter died in 1879, at the age of seventy-one years.

HADENSVILLE PRECINCT.

F. L. ANDERSON was born November 5, 1856, in Todd County. He is a son of F. A. and Mary (Magill) Anderson. The former died September 12, 1884; the mother is living in Allensville. They were natives of Kentucky. Our subject now owns and occupies this farm, consisting of about 200 acres and known as the old Andrews farm. Mr. Anderson was married December 18, 1879, to Miss Lucy, daughter of Edward Anderson of Paducah, Ky.; they are devoted members of the Methodist Episcopal Church South.

DR. JAMES R. GRADY (deceased) was born in Virginia in 1809, and came to Kentucky when a boy; he had studied medicine and received a certificate at Charlottesville, Va., and graduated at Lexington, Ky., where he received his diploma, following which he practiced his profession about fifteen years, then followed farming until his death in 1870. He was thrice married: first, to a Mrs. Warfield; secondly, to Miss Eliza Allensworth, who became the mother of two children: Nannie R. and Inez I.; thirdly, in 1861, to Miss Martha F. Johnson, daughter of R. G. Johnson, of Virginia. To this last marriage were born: Luly B., Nora E., Edward and James. The two boys died in infancy; Luly is the wife of W. M. Ware, who now has the management of the Grady farm; he is a native of Trenton Precinct, and is the son of C. W. Ware.

R. T. HOLLINS was born December 4, 1832, in Louisa County, Va.; he is the fifth son of a family of seven children born to Richard and Susan (Higgason) Hollins, of the same county and State. The father was born in 1790; he died in 1880, aged eighty-eight. The mother was born in 1801, and died in 1844, aged forty-three years. In 1837 the family came to Todd County, and settled on a farm where Hadensville is now situated. Mr. Hollins donated land to the railroad for depot purposes, etc., and laid out the town. Our subject was raised on his father's farm, and at the age of twenty-one assumed general charge of the business, which he successfully continued till his father's death; he now owns 100 acres of the land formerly owned by his father. In

1875 he bought out P. O. Duffy, with a stock of goods of about $3,000; he at once increased this stock, and has since been engaged in merchandising, carrying a stock of from $6,000 to $8,000. On the completion of the railroad he was appointed agent at this point; he was also the first Postmaster here. Mr. Hollins was married in 1863 to Miss Margaret T., daughter of S. F. Mitchell, of Montgomery County, Tenn. Four children bless this union—three sons and one daughter. They are members of the Christian Church.

R. CLARENCE HOLLINS was born September 22, 1851, in Todd County, Ky.; he was raised in Montgomery County, Tenn.; he is the eldest of five children born to S. P. and P. F. (Knott) Hollins. The parents were born in Virginia. The father was born September 5, 1822. The mother was born in 1832. They are now living on their farm in Montgomery County, Tenn.; there the subject of our sketch was raised and remained until his marriage, which event occurred November 20, 1879, to Victoria Cole, a native of Mount Pleasant, Va. This union is blessed with two sons. Soon after their marriage they moved to Hadensville, where he is now engaged in farming. On a farm of seventy-five acres adjoining this village he lives. He is also a breeder of thoroughbred Poland-China pigs and black Cochin chickens. These chickens are of a superior breed, and are sold for not less than $5 a pair. Mr. Hollins is a member of the School Board, and Agent for the Louisville & Nashville Railroad and Adams Express Company.

VERTNER R. JOHNSON was born July 11, 1861, in Todd County; he is a son of J. H. and G. A. (Wims) Johnson. The parents were both born in this county. The mother was born on this farm; they are now residents of Allensville Precinct. Subject was raised on his father's farm, where he remained till his marriage, which event occurred March 13, 1881, to Miss Nannie B. Pennington. She was born in Louisiana. This union has been blessed with two children—one son and one daughter. After marriage Mr. Johnson came to this farm, which he owns, consisting of 316 acres, and known as the old Andrews farm.

N. E. KAY was born August 19, 1814, in Culpeper County, Va.; he is a son of Gabriel and Fannie (Wagner) Kay, parents both born in the same county and State. When an infant our subject was brought to Todd County with his parents; about two years later his father died; he was brought up on his mother's farm, and at the age of eighteen he went to Nashville, where he secured a position in a wholesale grocery store; remained there ten years; he then went to Arkansas, where he was engaged in merchandising two years, after which he returned to Todd County and was married to Miss Elizabeth Allensworth. She was born in Todd County; she died in 1873, aged fifty-six. Mr. Kay's farm consists of about 800 acres, which is largely improved, and where he has since resided.

W. L. KIMBROUGH was born September 18, 1824, in Todd County; he is a son of T. Winston and Susan (Graves) Kimbrough. The parents were born in Albemarle County, Va. The father came to Christian, now Todd, County in 1797; he first purchased a small quantity of land, and at the time of his death, which occurred in 1868, he had increased this to over 2,000 acres, largely improved. The mother died in 1844, aged forty-six. Our subject at the age of twenty-two commenced farming on land given him by his father; this business he has since followed. In 1850 he engaged in merchandising in Allensville; this business he continued three years. In 1866 he opened a dry goods store at Hadensville; continued this business twelve years, since which time he has been engaged exclusively in agricultural pursuits. His residence was completed in 1860, and is one of the finest in the precinct—cost about $17,000. He also owns about 1,900 acres of land here, well improved, besides considerable property in Texas and Virginia. Mr. Kimbrough commenced life a comparatively poor man; he is now in affluent circumstances, all of which he has acquired by strict attention and a thorough management of business. He was married in 1852 to Miss P. B. Terry, of Logan County, Ky.; this lady died in 1880, leaving four children—two sons and two daughters. Mr. K. has held the office of Magistrate ten years; he is also a member of the Masonic fraternity.

DR. DANIEL R. MERRITT (deceased) was born January 17, 1800, in Williamson County, Tenn. In about 1823 he came to Todd County and practiced medicine and engaged in farming, in both of which he was eminently successful. He erected a very fine brick residence on this farm, costing from $8,000 to $10,000, and owned at the time of his death about 600 acres of land. He died in July, 1883. The Doctor was first married in 1825 to Mrs. Fort, of Robinson County, Tenn. She died in

1829, leaving two children—William and Ann Eliza. By his second marriage he had two sons: Washington, a farmer, who died about six years ago, and Dr. R. Merritt, now practicing near Mayfield, Ky. Third marriage in 1836 to Penelope Hannum, a native of Russellville, Ky.; this union has been blessed with six children: Henry C., now practicing law at Clarksville; Fisher H., now of Montgomery, Ala., engaged in forwarding and commission and planting; Rosa, now the widow of Charles Young; Montgomery, now an attorney of Henderson, Ky.; Philander L., now living at the homestead and having supervision of this farm; and Charlotte H., now wife of William Hannum, of Marysville, east Tenn.

THOMAS U. SMITH is a resident of Hadensville Precinct, and was born on this farm, February 21, 1858. He is the eldest of two children born to R. L. and Lucy A. (Young) Smith. The father was born on this farm in July, 1822. The grandfather, Jesse Smith, of Virginia, traded property in the city of Richmond for a farm near Russellville; that farm he soon after sold and bought this farm, then consisting of 300 acres, which has since been increased to about 700 acres. The father of our subject now lives on his farm near Nashville, Tenn. The mother was born in Robertson County, Tenn. She died August 9, 1882, aged forty-five. Mr. Smith was married April 28, 1880, to Miss Willie, daughter of Winston Henry, of Christian County. Mr. Smith and his brother Eugene attended Warren College at Bowling Green four years, after which they attended the Vanderbilt College at Nashville two years. Eugene graduated from the Literary Department in 1880, and from the Law Department in the class of 1881, since which time he has been practicing law in Nashville.

JOHN F. SNADON is a resident of Hadensville Precinct, and lives upon the farm where he was born October 22, 1826. His parents, George and Sallie (Cross) Snadon were natives of Rockingham County, Va.; came to Todd County in 1822, and settled upon the farm where John F. Snadon now resides. The property originally consisted of some 900 acres, but has since been reduced to 570 acres by the sale of a part of its area. Here Mr. Snadon lives as a gentleman farmer, employing some four to eight hands. The Snadon mansion is a typical Southern home of culture and refinement. A dwelling combining the elegance of modern luxury with the grace of enlightened culture and surrounded by abundant evidences of tasteful expenditure, affords an unstinted hospitality which is the pride of the neighborhood. February, 1864, Mr. Snadon married Miss Sue F., daughter of William and Fannie Weatherford, the father, a widower, now living on his farm at Port Royal, Tenn. Mrs. Snadon was born in North Carolina, but was reared from childhood in Tennessee. She received a liberal education, being graduated by the Greenville Female Collegiate Institute. Two brothers, William G. and Cæsar, are eminent attorneys at Memphis. A sister is the wife of Dr. J. T. Darden, of Montgomery County, Tenn. Another sister is the wife of John W. Jones, a farmer in the same county. Mr. and Mrs. Snadon are the parents of two sons: Frank, attending the Emory and Henry College in Washington County, Va. ; George, married, and living with his parents. Mr. and Mrs. Snadon are active, devoted members of the Methodist Episcopal Church South.

Biographical Index.

BIOGRAPHICAL INDEX.

BIOGRAPHICAL INDEX.